The
Greatest
Climbing Stories
Ever Told

The
Greatest
Climbing Stories
Ever Told

Incredible Tales of Risk and Adventure

EDITED AND WITH AN INTRODUCTION BY
BILL GUTMAN

THE LYONS PRESS
Guilford, Connecticut
An imprint of The Globe Pequot Press

The Lyons Press is an imprint of The Globe Pequot Press.

10 9 8 7 6 5 4 3 2 1

Printed in the United States of America

ISBN 1-58574-614-2

Library of Congress Cataloging-in-Publication Data is available on file.

Contents

Introduction

I do not climb mountains! Why, then, would I undertake the assignment of gathering together some of the most amazing and courageous stories of people who look to the skies and decide to climb there? Just before being contacted about this project, I had completed a book about men and women who participate in high-risk, adventure sports. In doing my research I interviewed a number of mountain climbers and was absolutely fascinated by their courage, their resolve, their love of the mountains, and their ability to continue climbing despite losing friends and, in some cases, almost losing their own lives. Those interviews, coupled with subsequent research, answered some questions and left me with others. Thus I welcomed the opportunity to read and research dozens of additional stories about mountain climbing adventures.

There is really no rationale for someone to try to climb a 29,000 foot mountain in the Himalayas or even a 3,000-foot vertical rockface where there are barely enough cracks to place your hands or get a foothold. Yet climbers do it all the time. Perhaps the classic answer to the question *why?* was given by Englishman George Mallory, who decided he wanted to climb Mt. Everest, the world's highest mountain, in the early 1920s. Asked that inevitable three-letter question, Mallory simply answered, "Because it's there."

In reality, that curt answer may explain mountain climbing as well as anything else. Men and women of adventurous spirit have always looked for new challenges and, as a result, have been drawn to places where their very survival can often be a struggle. If someone asked for volunteers to board the first spaceship to Mars, there would probably be no trouble filling the seats. So there are always going to be people who will look up at the peak of a huge mountain, a peak that is literally up among the clouds, and decide they want to walk there. It's true that mountain climbing is considered a sport, but it's also perhaps the only sport where there is an often used credo that states unequivocally: *You fall; you die.*

Climbing, obviously, is not for the faint of heart. Those who decide to climb the world's highest mountains always refer to going into the *death zone*, which is considered to be in the very thin air above 25,000 feet. In point of fact, anything over 18,000 feet is automatically dangerous. University of Washington high-altitude physiologist Robert Shoene explained why, saying in part, "Very few people can stay indefinitely at altitudes above 18,000 feet and thrive," Schoene said. "There just isn't enough oxygen to feed the body."

Or to put it even more clearly and in the words of one veteran climber, "If someone flew you to the top of Everest and dropped you off, you would die pretty quickly."

Thus climbers have to acclimate, go higher and higher very slowly so their bodies can adjust to the thinning air. At the highest altitudes, many use supplemental oxygen, but some still take the challenge of climbing without. Falling victim to oxygen deprivation, or *hypoxia*, is just one pitfall climbers must endure. Just plain falling is another, and so is the x-factor of the weather, which can produce deadly storms and equally deadly avalanches. Some of the world's most skilled and careful climbers have falling victim to an avalanche, a huge wall of rushing of snow coming down on them with unabashed fury . . .

In addition, reaching the top of a major mountain is often just half the battle. Getting back down is the other. Many a harrowing mountain experience, or *epic*, as the climbers call it, has occurred on the descent, coming back from reaching, or attempting to reach, the summit. These are just some of the realities of mountain climbing, some of the potential dangers that lurk every time a climber, or team of climbers, decides to go up high. And this is also what makes their stories so compelling.

It isn't difficult finding great adventure stories from the mountains. The trick was to find just the right ones to include in this collection. It wouldn't be very hard to fill a book with epic adventures from the world's two highest mountains—Everest and K2. Everest has been a symbol for the ultimate climbing adventure since the mysterious disappearance of Englishmen George Mallory and Sandy Irvine in 1924. K2 is considered by many the harshest of all mountains, with the potential for the most devastating weather. Both mountains are well represented here simply because no collection of climbing adventure stories would be complete without them.

Perhaps a succinct and very accurate description of what it's like to tackle a mountain like Everest came from Sharon Wood, a Canadian climber who was the first North American woman to reach its summit. Even before she embarked on her journey as part of an 11-member climbing team, Wood knew the climbers were taking on a daunting task.

"You know from the get-go that the odds of you personally getting to the summit are pretty low," she said. "We started with eleven good climbers, all pretty strong and with a lot of individual experience. Yet it's still a crap shoot. In the end what determines who goes [for the summit] is who happens to be in the right place at the right time and who's left. Of the eleven climbers, there were four of us who were still strong enough to try and who weren't completely depleted. Two of us made it."

The stories in this collection date back to 1871 and include a number of tales from the early years of the 20th century, epics that involve both men and women. Yes, there were women climbing mountains back then. Also included is the Everest expedition of 1999 that attempted to clear up one of the great mountaineering mysteries of all time, whether Mallory and Irvine had actually made it to the summit of Everest before disappearing in 1924. The discovery of George Mallory's body, still preserved on the frigid upper reaches of the mountain after more than 50 years, proved they had come close. But did they actually make it? That question remains unanswered.

In addition, you will read about a number of epic adventures from the great peaks, including Everest and K2, Annapurna and Denali, which is another name for Mt. McKinley in Alaska, the highest mountain on the North American continent. But there are also stories from so-called lesser mountains, such as Washington's Mt. Ranier, which is only 14,000-some feet high, yet can produce weather conditions similar to Everest. This tale is about three California women who wanted to climb a mountain, chose Ranier, and were caught in a deadly avalanche.

To give a more complete picture of the gamut of emotions experienced by all climbers who continue to go into the mountains, there is story of a woman climber who writes about losing many friends to the mountains, yet continues to see the positive things climbers find when they choose to go back again and again in the face of losing friends and eventually perhaps their own lives.

In addition, there is a fascinating portrait of Alex Lowe, whose consummate climbing skills led him to be called "the Michael Jordan of climbing," referring to the basketball player who is widely acknowledged as the best ever. Lowe's love of climbing and his exuberance for the sport were unparalleled. He had a wife and children, and always took the greatest of care when accepting another climbing challenge. Yet he, too, fell victim to the x-factor, succumbing to an avalanche in 1999 when he was attempting to first climb, then make the first ski descent of the 26,291-foot Mt. Shishapangma in China.

Despite the dangers and often physical stresses of the sport, there is a story by climber Abby Watkins that touts some of the advantages women have in climbing and why she feels the fair sex is well-suited to the sport. Climbers always want to welcome new members to the club, to encourage more people to look up and climb on high.

The Greatest Climbing Stories Ever Told will not always be an easy read. You will travel into the death zone with these climbers and share their sometimes tragic and sometime triumphant experiences, as well as feel their suffering as they battle some of the most difficult weather conditions on the planet. Despite the ever-present danger, most climbers continue to challenge the world's greatest mountains in what is arguably the ultimate man-versus-nature adventure.

The
Greatest
Climbing Stories
Ever Told

We Could Not Give Up

This tale shows just how early women were climbing mountains. American Marguerite "Meta" Brevoort was a pioneer climber in the 19th century. Brevoort brought her 14-year-old nephew to the Swiss Alps in the mid-1860s with the hope that the mountain air would improve the boy's health, which it did. Soon she decided she wanted to be the first woman to climb the 14,690-foot Matterhorn. Her first attempt in 1869 failed, and when she finally made it two years later she soon learned that another woman, Lucy Walker from England, had done it first. Brevoort would later become the first woman to make winter ascents of the Wetterhorn and the Jungfrau, also in the Alps, feats which are now considered the beginning of serious winter mountaineering by women. This account is about another 1871 climb, of the 12,903-foot Bietschhorn in the Alps, which show that even the women of long ago had an adventurous spirit that could not be diminished.

Five years ago, as we stood on the summit of the Nesthorn, we had gazed both admiringly and longingly at the Bietschhorn, whose magnificent outline and exquisitely-beautiful details form one of the most prominent features of that perfect view. At once we expressed a wish to attempt it, and were not a little disappointed at Almer's most discouraging reply that it was too *schwer* [difficult] for us. Though only too right, as we have since found out, he did not stick long to his opinion; so that for several years we had put down the Bietschhorn on our list of summer projects without ever having actually attacked it. Nor when we left Zermatt on the morning of the 18th of September 1871, did there appear to be much hope of our then accomplishing it. The weather seemed to have fairly gone to pieces. Dark and lowering from

1

the first, we had not reached Randa before the rain began to come down in a gradually-increasing deliberate way, which gave no hope of mending for that day at least. So, as we jolted along in our rattling little conveyance, seeking for as much shelter as we could get from a huge red cotton umbrella, borrowed for us by the driver from some chalet on the road, we began recasting our plans to suit altered circumstances. . . .

I cannot say that we felt very despondent at the prospect of rest and ease which this change of plans implied, for we had been working very hard indeed for the past fortnight. Almer was equally inclined to view matters cheerfully, as he would now be able to visit a great cattlefair at Meyringen, where he hoped to have an opportunity of buying "the last sweet thing" in the way of cows and pigs—a prospect seemingly as charming to him as a day's shopping in Paris would be to most ladies. "And the Bietschhorn will be for next year;" and it seemed to float away dreamily with all the other "unvisited Yarrows" of our experience. At St. Nicolas we had to give up our little carriage, and being burdened with a tent and more baggage than the two Almers could conveniently carry, we took as porter to Visp the youngest of the three brothers Knubel, Peter Joseph by name, with whom we had only parted a day or two before. But as we journeyed on the weather began to show most decided symptoms of improvement. The rain ceased, the low hanging mist, which had hitherto enveloped the whole valley, as with a veil, gradually dispersed, the clouds broke away, and the sun shining out in the most brilliant mood imaginable, soon lent life, colour, and cheerfulness to the whole landscape. This was irresistible. We all agreed that it would be trifling with Fortune to slight such manifest tokens of her favour; and giving up all thoughts of inglorious ease and fat cattle, the Bietschhorn again became our motive and hope.

Next morning was beautiful, and as we gazed upwards at our peak, which just showed its summit above the darkly-wooded hills which wall in the valley, we longed to be off at once; but one of our party being a slow walker, and the days already very short, we knew it would be impossible to reach the top at any decent hour unless we started from some higher point than the inn. The first day's walk would necessarily be a short one, as we could go no farther than the base of the mountain, and there pass the night in a tent, setting off early the next morning.

As there was no use in leaving Reid before noon, we amused ourselves with looking over the "livre des voyageurs," and in trying to make out, as well as we could with an imperfect knowledge of German, the account given in the Swiss "Jahrbuch" for 1869–70 by M. de Fellenberg of his ascent of our mountain.

Whether it was that we did not arrive at the true meaning of the text, or that we were in a very reckless and absurd frame of mind, I know not; but there were parts of the narrative which made us shout with laughter, although I think they were intended to excite very different feelings in the reader. From it we gathered that at one time the luckless narrator and his companions were obliged to descend an arête literally à *califourchon* [by straddling]. Instead of compassionating their most uncomfortable position, a spirit of madness seized us, and we laughed till we were tired as we imagined them. But "rira bien qui rira le dernier" [who laughs last, laughs best] proved a true proverb in our case, for the time came when we fully realized what the difficulties of that same ridge were, and when they no longer affected our risible faculties. Meanwhile, unconscious of our approaching doom, we laughed, feeling quite positive that *we* should never ascend or descend in that fashion.

Our host looked as if he had once seen a ghost, and had never quite recovered from his fright. He really was so devoted to our comfort that we felt quite grateful to him, until he informed us that he made no money at all by his inn, and kept it from purely philanthropic motives. After that, we considered him as only following a strong natural vocation for hospitality—in fact, a sort of lay monk of the order of St. Bernard on a mission in the wilderness of the Lötschthal. He appeared to think that we must feel hungry every half-hour, and was constantly coming in to propose some new kind of refreshment, as well as to report progress concerning the provisions being got ready below; and thus let us into the secret of the "wildness," if one may so call it, of his larder. It was the result of the hunting propensities of a very profitable lodger he was entertaining for the summer, who spent all his time in the woods shooting, accompanied by a curious dumb dog, whose acquaintance we also made. This dog could not bark, and wore a bell that his master might know his whereabouts. As our dog Tschingel, who was with us, came originally from the Lötschthal, and very much resembled our new friend (except in his dumbness), we tried to persuade him to fraternize with one who was probably some near connection; but Tschingel indignantly repudiated the theory, and showed the most worldly-wise contempt for his poor relation, not suffering him to enter the dining-room. We were also much interested, and indulged in sundry speculations as to the origin and history of a very ancient pike and part of a suit of armour, both of a gigantic size, which our host told us had been found in a neighbouring village, while clearing away the ruins of some cottages which had been burnt down. A dagger, found at the same time, and of equally wonderful proportions, he had given, he said, to M. de Fellenberg.

At noon we set off—a funny-looking party. Christian and Ulrich Almer carried the ropes and provisions, Knubel the tent, Siegen some blankets, a Ried porter a *hotte* [container] full of nondescript articles for the cuisine; and, lastly, an Oberlander, who had asked Almer to employ him, was loaded with a huge bundle of straw, which made him look like a walking haystack, and which was intended for those who were to sleep outside the tent. Nothing could be more beautiful in its way than was our walk to the camping-place. After crossing the little stream in front of the inn, and going through some meadows, we entered the most solemn old pine-woods. The brilliant sunshine which streamed here and there through their somber branches dispelled all gloom, but could not banish the feeling of quietness and mystery peculiar to them. We were sorry to leave their shade for steep, stony grass-slopes. The men here began to gather firewood as they strolled along. We climbed slowly, looking back continually at the various new peaks now showing themselves on the opposite side of the valley. Among these the Breithorn was conspicuous, and the broad, level summit of the Petersgrat became plainer every moment. Siegen and the Ried porter, who was his servant, soon showed symptoms of fatigue, and were continually suggesting that it was time to set up the tent, as, if we went too far, it might be inconvenient to get water. Almer lent a deaf ear for a long while to all their remarks, until we had got on to the lower end of the great rocky mass which divides the Nest and Birch glaciers, and culminates in a point marked 3,320 on the Federal map. Here he proposed that we should halt, whilst he pushed on alone to reconnoiter. Away he went, climbing up some very steep rocks in his usual rapid manner, and was soon out of sight. This seemed a favourable opportunity for examining Siegen with more attention than we could give him whilst walking. And he really was worth inspection, somewhat resembling one of Salvator Rosa's brigands, but still more the conventional stage representation of Mephistopheles. His dark eyes, heavy eyebrows, long black hair, and still longer moustaches, with that peculiar twist in them remarkable in those of the chief personage in "Faust," were most picturesquely set off by a slouched hat, ornamented with a long trailing bunch of cock's feathers. It was impossible not to attempt a sketch of him, and to this he lent himself very complacently, recounting the while various details of M. de Fellenberg's ascent, and dwelling especially on the really amazing quantity of wine he had helped to consume on that occasion. We were much edified, when, as he pulled out his handkerchief, two or three sets of beads came out with it, which, he laughingly said, were none too many for the Bietschhorn.

In about an hour Almer returned, having found exactly the place for our camp; and, much to Siegen's regret, we all set off to reach it, and arrived there at 4 P.M., the whole ascent from Reid, with numerous halts, having only occupied 3½ hours. The two porters were sent back somewhat later. Our position was a commanding one. Looking back towards Reid (which we could not actually see), the Nest glacier was on our left, far below us, the rocks on which we were standing rising very precipitously above it. On our right were wild savage cliffs, which rose higher and higher behind us, until, far above, we could see the sharp summit of our peak looking down upon them. It seemed almost to beckon us on to attempt it, as it shone out gloriously in the light of the setting sun, the rays of which made the snowy range on the opposite side of the valley glow with new beauty. In the midst of this splendid scene, and after a much-enjoyed supper, we retired to rest, full of hope for the morrow, though somewhat chilled by the cold September night air.

The night proved sharp and frosty, and we did not start the next morning till after 5:30 A.M., when the sun had gained a little strength. The party consisted of a lady, myself, the two Almers, Knubel, and Siegen. It was thought best to leave Tschingel, our faithful dog, behind in the tent, *not* because of any supposed incapacity on his part, as he [according to Cicely Williams, Tschingel was actually female] was perhaps the most accomplished mountaineer of the party, but because Almer feared that he would throw down stones from above upon us, as he always chooses his own route on the ascent and insists upon leading.

We began at once to climb the steep rocks immediately behind our camp, and at 6:50 A.M. got on to the Nest glacier, near a large cave or hole formed by the rocks overhanging the glacier at their point of junction, on the side of the rocky mass mentioned above. With this cave, which we scarcely noticed at the time, we afterwards became rather intimately acquainted. Mounting the glacier gradually, meeting with a few crevasses, we soon reached the center of the semicircle plainly visible on the map, and at the very foot of the mountain, which we now saw for the first time from tip to toe, being even able to distinguish one of the stone men on the summit.

It may not be out of place here to give a slight sketch of the peak of the Bietschhorn. It is formed by the union of three principal arêtes, running roughly towards the north, south, and west. The summit is a long and extremely shattered ridge, out of which rise three rocky towers, nearly equal in height. The southern arête falls away precipitously towards the valley of the Rhone, but the two others are more practicable. Mr. Leslie Stephen, when he made the first ascent of the mountain, in 1859, seems to have followed the northern arête on his ascent and descent. When the mountain was climbed for the second time, in 1867, by M. de Fellenberg, the ascent was effected, I believe, by the western, and the descent by the northern arête. Several attempts to ascend the peak failed, and ours was the next successful ascent. As will be seen, we exactly reversed M. de Fellenberg's route.

It was after 7:30 A.M. when we halted for breakfast in the center of the semicircle mentioned above, after which repast we parted with Siegen, who showed no unwillingness to return to the tent, Knubel having petitioned to be allowed to go to the top, and Almer thinking that as Ulrich was also with us we could very well dispense with Mephistopheles. Turning to the left, our party of five marched over the glacier to the base of the northern arête, which we began slowly to ascend. The rocks were very rotten, and fell down at the slightest touch, so that we had to be very cautious in our movements. We gained the crest of the arête, after a good deal of trouble, at 10:30 A.M., and followed it henceforth, with slight deviations, to the summit. It very soon turned into a very sharp snowridge, which had a threatening corniche overhanging the Jägi-firn of the Federal map. The weather up to this time had been perfect, and whenever we could afford the time, we had been only too glad to pause and gaze at the magnificent prospect which began to unfold itself before us. But now a change came over the fair scene. A strong icy wind began to whistle about our ears, and rising clouds to surround us. The ridge along which we were cautiously stepping was already quite difficult enough, without this most unpleasant companion, and now became utterly impracticable. Abandoning it, therefore, for a while, we crept along the projecting rocks just below it, over-hanging the Nest glacier, until it became somewhat wider, and we were able once more to return to it. But the snow here turned into ice, and many a weary step had to be cut before the first stone man was reached at 12:30 P.M. The wind was still howling and nipping our noses, ears, and fingers pitilessly; but, although there was now no hope of a view, we *could* not give up our summit. It was with difficulty that we made our way along the shattered ridge, trying, whenever we could, to keep below it. At length we reached the top at 1:10 P.M., the ascent having occupied 7½ hrs., including all halts. We could see nothing beyond the rocks immediately around us, as we were enveloped in clouds, which the wind drove about tumultuously. But, although we regretted the magnificent prospect from the top, we were struck with the grandeur of what we could see—jagged rocks, splintered into every conceivable shape, piled up or strewn out in fantas-tic confusion. The drifting clouds also enabled us occasionally to form some idea of the startling precipices on all sides.

After a very slender and hurried repast, we turned to descent at 1:30 P.M., leaving our names in a bottle, carefully placed in the cairn. It was shortly after that a startling sight greeted us. The sun was glaring through the clouds, like a smouldering ball of fire. Suddenly we perceived a rainbow around us, and in the space between it and the sun our shadows were distinctly projected. I was almost unearthly to see these figures of gigantic proportions moving as we moved.

We had not got back to the first stone man, and the clouds were becoming more broken every moment, so that there was a chance of our being seen in the valley. We therefore tied an old red handkerchief, which our host at Reid had asked us to use as a flag, to a stick, which was planted in the cairn, and was in a few minutes distinctly seen at Reid and at Kippel. We had no time to spare, and I rather believe the unexpressed wish of each of us was to get safely down again.

According to our original plan, we were to have descended direct to Raron, between Turtmann and Visp in the Rhone valley, at the opening of the Bietsch Thal—a route which some of us still think would have been the best to adopt. Siegen, however, had so opposed it, that Almer had given it up before starting. We then determined to return the same way by which we had ascended. That way, however, had proved so dangerous towards the top, that Almer, with his usual prudence, altered our course. The upper part of the western arête being impracticable, he therefore led us down the great rock couloir, which opens out near the first cairn, and is well shown on the Federal map, being the space between the western arête and a spur of the southern. It was very steep, and the rocks, as everywhere else on this mountain, were of the most treacherous and unstable description, with no fixed principles to speak of. Almer meant, after descending this couloir for some distance, to mount to the right, in order to gain the crest of the arête, and to descend by the northern face to the Nest glacier—an excellent plan, had it not proved impracticable, owing to the many little ridges which shot out from the main ridge, and had every one to be crossed to gain the crest at a practicable point. At first we were very cheerful about it, expecting every one of these contradictory obstacles to be the last, but no sooner had we surmounted one than another cropped up before our disappointed eyes, and we began to lose patience. It would have been bearable, of course, however fatiguing, had we had any time to spare, but the light was fast fading, and, hurry as much as we could, we felt that night was approaching without any sign of a deliverance. So here we were, *we* who had felt so confident that we should never follow M. de Fellenberg's route, descending the very way he went up! And such rocks as they were! In the morning there had been some pretence at cohesion, owing to the night's frost, but now they had only too completely recovered their independence. They rolled down if one did but look at them. One immense fragment suddenly broke loose from a ledge which we had just descended, and falling on the rope between Almer, who was leading, and his immediate follower, dragged them both off their feet. They went rolling over and over, pulling down Ulrich, who came next, so that the three executed several prodigious somersaults before they were stopped by the last two of the party. The rope was found to be almost cut through where the boulder had struck it. A second occurrence of the kind, only a little less alarming, followed soon after; and what with Almer's continual "Geben sie acht," "Dieses ist nicht fest," "Dieses ist ganz locker" [take care—these aren't solid], and the continual rattling of stones about us, we became quite bewildered, and began at times to fancy that the whole mountain was coming down about our ears like a card-house. The twilight was fading away when we crossed the last little ridge, and at length set foot on the arête at its extreme western end. The moon had risen, but our old enemy, the wind, which had never ceased to blow, drove the clouds over her face, only allowing us occasional faint glimmers of light as we stumbled along, with many a fall on the cruel hard rocks, which, touch them ever so lightly with foot or hand, set off at once with an avalanche of smaller stones in their wake. At length, bruised, weary, and sleepy, we reached the snow-field forming the summit-level of the Bietsch joch at 8:20 P.M., after a most painful descent of 6¼ hrs., the like of which we had never experienced, and hope never to experience again. The wind had now completely buried the moon in a bank of clouds, and the only light we had was that of a faintly-twinkling star or two. This mattered little so long as we were on the snow, through which we plunged rapidly, keeping to the right, until in 25 minutes we arrived at the exact spot where we had breakfasted in the morning. We knew this, because we here found a precious little barrel of wine, left buried in the snow, the recovery of which we had been for some time anticipating, as we had had nothing to drink since quitting the summit.

After this our difficulties began again. The glacier which still lay between us and the rocky mass, on the lower part of which stood our tent (our tent!), which had become to us the very embodiment of home comforts and safety, had been traversed without much difficulty in the morning, but to descend it in almost total darkness was a very different thing.

We groped along after Almer, who guided himself in a wonderful manner, occasionally even recovering for a few minutes our morning's track by feeling with his hands for the steps cut in the ice, literally going à tâtons [feeling his way]! Whenever we came to a crevasse, Ulrich sat down, and held his father by the rope, that he might creep over to find a safe way, and then direct us how to follow him. It was of course impossible, even with his consummate skill, to make rapid progress, and indeed we could not tell that we were not going backward instead of forward. We lost all hope of getting off the glacier for the night, but it was so bitterly cold that Almer would not allow us to make any halt, fearing lest we should freeze. A pleasant prospect this, of creeping almost on all fours about a glacier, with the wind whistling around us in the most derisivie manner! Now and then the men would speak to one another, and in the midst of the incomprehensible patois gibberish which they always adopt on trying occasions, we could hear the word "loch," and remembered a cave at the edge of the glacier which we had passed in the morning. It seemed so utterly improbable that we should ever find it again, that we gave no thought to the subject. What, then, was our delight when Almer exclaimed (this time in comprehensible German) that he felt sure that we were near that cave. Untying himself, he went off to reconnoiter, and joyfully called out to us to follow his track, as he had found it. It showed how closely he must, on the whole, have kept to the straight road, that in spite of occasional wanderings, we actually came out a the *very* place where we had taken to the ice in the morning. It was entirely due to his marvelous skill and sagacity that we did not spend the night on the ice. It was not a few minutes past 11 P.M. as we found out by striking one of a few precious matches which we had brought. Our tent was not very far off, but we were too thoroughly tired out to think of any more scrambling down the rocks which lay between us and it. So we thankfully descended one by one into the cave, which was large enough to contain us all, though not the most comfortable of places. However, we were only too glad of the shelter which it afforded us from the cold wind which howled outside, and too delighted to be off the ice and able to sit down to complain of anything. We had no more provisions, not having expected to be out so long, so that the satisfaction of eating was denied to us. We still had a very little wine, but that little was in a spiteful cask, out of which it was very difficult for an unpractised person to drink, and pouring it out into a leather cup in the dark was altogether too wasteful a process. Matches were now and then struck to find out the time. In spite of cold, hunger, and discomfort, we would drop off to sleep for a few minutes; but whenever a dead silence showed this to be the case, Almer would jump up and begin yodeling in the most aggravating manner, or else he would circulate the hateful little cask, addressing us in the liveliest manner, and thus to our disgust effectively rousing us from our slumbers, which the cold rendered very dangerous.

Before daylight the wind ceased and snow began to fall. We were not able to leave the hospitable hole till nearly 5 A.M., after a stay of 6 hrs. We then followed our previous day's route down the rocks, amid the falling snow, and regained the tent at 6:30 A.M. Siegen came to greet us with a bottle of champagne, provided by our philanthropic host, for which we heartily blessed him. The thoughtful man had sent up two porters to the tent, to find out what had become of us; and seeing us afar, they lit a great fire, the very sight of which was cheering on that wintry-looking morning. Tschingel, who had threatened to devour poor Siegen when he first tried to enter the tent on his return the day before, and was only pacified by the most abject advances from him, gave us an uproarious welcome. The kettle soon boiled, and we had some hot tea and coffee, after which we took a good rest in the tent, and descended to Reid in rain later on in the day. Our host received us with the choicest hospitality in his power—a dish of brains for dinner.

Thus ended and adventure which was not far from having a serious end, since, in all probability, had we spent the night on the ice, this paper would never have been written.

Of Advantage to My Sex

ANNIE SMITH PECK
CLIMBS THE NORTH PEAK OF HUASCARÁN, 1908

Annie Peck, an American writer and lecturer, also became fascinated by the Alps after looking up at the Matterhorn in the late 19th century. She knew right then and there she wouldn't be happy until she climbed it, something she achieved in 1895. Two years later she went to Mexico and climbed the 18,700 foot Orizaba, now called Citlaltepec. That climb earned her the world's altitude record for women, though it was broken a short time later. After failing to climb Bolivia's mysterious Mount Sorata, Peck then set her sights on a mountain in Peru, Huascaran which, in a time when the heights of mountains weren't always accurately measured, was rumored to be very high. In 1908, at the age of 48, Peck scaled the north summit of the mountain, said to be 21,800 feet high. This is her account of that dangerous climb, completed in darkness and high winds, as well as the difficult descent that followed.

In fairly good season we encamped that night on the plain at the top of the saddle, in two days from the snow line, a feat which I had previously hoped with Swiss guides to be able to accomplish. The exceptionally cold day, the coldest I had experienced in my six efforts on this mountain, was followed by a high wind at night—an unpleasant contrast to our previous experience here, when all three nights had been almost windless. In the early morning, I thought it wiser to postpone our final effort till the fierce wind should abate; we should also be in better condition following a rest from two long and hard days' labour. Had I expected to make the attempt on this day I should have insisted upon an earlier start. Both guides, however, though not anxious to set out early, were in favour of going, asserting that we might find less wind higher up, if not that we could turn back. On the contrary, unless the wind died down altogether, it was more likely to be worse above, and it was against my better judgment that I yielded to their wishes.

At the late hour, for such a climb, of eight o'clock, we set forth, myself and the two guides only, as with the two Swiss the Indians [sic] would not add to the safety of the party, probably the reverse. For the cold ascent, I was wearing every stitch of clothing that I had brought:—three suits of light weight woolen underwear, two pairs of tights, canvas knickerbockers, two flannel waists, a little cardigan jacket, two sweaters, and four pairs of woolen stockings; but as most of the clothing was porous it was inadequate to keep out the wind, for which I had relied upon the eskimo [sic] suit now at the bottom of a crevasse. I had not really needed it before, nor worn it except at night. Now when I wanted it badly, it was gone. I am often asked if my progress is not impeded by the weight of so much clothing, to which I answer, No. All of the articles were light, and garments which cling closely to the body are not burdensome. I never noticed the weight at all. A skirt, on the contrary, however short and light, anything depending from the waist or shoulders, is some hindrance to movement and of noticeable weight. I had not an ounce of strength to spare for superfluities, neither do I consider that an abbreviated skirt would add to the gracefulness of my appearance, or if it did, that this, upon the mountain, would be of the slightest consequence: while in rock climbing the shortest skirt may be an added source of danger.

A woollen face and head mask, which I had purchased in La Paz, provided with a good nose piece as well as eye-holes, mouth-slit, and a rather superfluous painted moustache, protected my head, face, and neck from the wind. An extra one, which I had brought along, a rather better article except that it left the nose exposed, I offered to Gabriel, Rudolf having brought a hood of his own. Somewhat to my surprise, as the guides had seemed always to despise the cold and to regard my warnings as superfluous, this offer was accepted with alacrity. My hands were covered with a pair of vicuña mittens made for me in La Paz with two thicknesses of fur, one turned outside and one in. For these, until the day before, I had had no use; they now kept even my cold hands comfortable. In fact, as the sun rose higher, they became too warm and were exchanged for two pairs of wool mittens, one of which, however, did not cover the fingers. The fur mittens, being too large to go into my pocket or leather bag, were handed over to Rudolf, who was next to me, to be put into his rück-sack.

I had repeatedly warned the men of the great danger of freezing above, not so much from the actual cold as from the rarity of the air, telling them how

Pelissier (one of Conway's guides), with two pairs of stockings, had had his feet frozen on Aconcagua so that they turned black, and he barely escaped losing them; how Zurbriggan, Maquignaz, and others had been frost-bitten on Aconcagua and Sorata. In spite of this, they hardly seemed to realize the necessity of so much care. They stated that their shoes would admit of but one pair of their heavy woolen stockings and seemed quite unconcerned as to the possibilities of freezing.

The men carried food and tea for luncheon (the latter I had sat up to make the night before, after the rest had gone to bed), the hypsometer to take observations, and my camera. The mercurial barometer I had left in Yungay, from misgivings that I might have to carry it if it was brought along. As there was no extra clothing of mine to transport, since I had put it all on, I ventured to ask if one of the guides could carry up the warm poncho, fearing that I might need it when we paused for luncheon or on the summit. It was rather heavy and a considerable burden at that altitude, but Gabriel said he could take it; to the fact of my extreme, apparently superfluous caution, and of Gabriel's willingness and strength, I certainly owe the possession and soundness of all my limbs, as I also owe Gabriel my life. The canteen of alcohol, which was used to light the fire of our kerosene stove, and from which also a small draught night and morning was given to the Indians, was carried some distance from the tent lest the temptation to drink this in our long absence should prove too much for them. When the can was deposited in the snow, with which it was half covered to make sure that it would not blow away, I inquired, "Are you sure you can find this on our return?" Both men replied that they certainly could.

Considering the altitude our progress seemed rapid. On the slope above the camp no steps were needed, but when, after an hour or less, we turned to the left, making a long traverse among great crevasses, walls, and appalling downward slopes, it was necessary that steps should be cut all of the time. The snow was in a worse condition than before. It had been hard enough then (though softer in the middle of the day), but not so smooth. Now the severe cold had made it harder still, while the high wind had blown from the exposed slopes all of the lighter particles, leaving a surface smooth as glass, such as Gabriel said he had never seen in Switzerland except in small patches.

Coming out at length upon a ridge where we were more exposed to the wind I felt the need of my vicuña mittens which had seemed too warm below. I delayed asking for a while, hoping to come to a better standing place; but as none appeared, calling a halt I approached Rudolf, who continually held the rope for me, while Gabriel was cutting the steps, so that the delays necessary on the previous ascent were avoided. Rudolf, taking the mittens from his rück-sack with some black woven sleeves I had earlier worn on my forearms, tucked the former under one arm saying, "Which will you have first?" I had it on the end of my tongue to exclaim, "Look out you don't lose my mittens!" But like most men, the guides were rather impatient of what they considered unnecessary advice or suggestions from a woman, even an employer; so, thinking, he surely will be careful of my mittens, I refrained and said, "Give me the armlets!" A second later Rudolf cried, "I have lost one of your mittens!" I did not see it go, it slipped out at the back, but anything dropped on that smooth slope, even without the high wind, might as well have gone over a precipice.

I was angry and alarmed at his inexcusable carelessness, but it was useless to talk. I could do that after we got down, though under subsequent circumstances I never did. I hastily put my two brown woolen mittens and one red mitt on my left hand, the vicuña fur on my right which generally held the ice axe and was therefore more exposed. Onward and upward for hours we pressed, when at length we paused for luncheon being too cold and tired to eat the meat which had frozen in the rück-sack, and the almost equally hard bread; though we ate Peter's chocolate and raisins, of which we had taken an occasional nibble, each from his own pocket, all along the way. (I had found a few raisins in one of the stores and bought all they had.) The tea, too, was partially frozen in Rudolf's canteen. About two o'clock, [Rudolf] Taugwalder declared himself unable to proceed. I was for leaving him there and going on with Gabriel, but the latter urged him onward, suggesting that by leaving his rück-sack, he might be able to continue with us. This, after a short rest, he did, finding that we were going on anyway. Gabriel now carried the camera and hypsometer, in addition to the poncho, besides cutting the steps.

The latter part of the climb was especially steep. All, suffering from cold and fatigue, required frequent brief halts, though we sat down but twice on the way up and not at all at the top. At last we were approaching our goal. Rounding the apparent summit we found a broad way of the slightest grade leading gently to the northern end of the ridge, though from below, the highest point had appeared to be at the south. On the ridge, the wind was stronger than ever, and I suddenly realized that my left hand was insensible and freezing. Twitching off my mittens, I found that the hand was nearly black. Rubbing it vigorously with snow, I soon had it aching badly, which signified its restoration; but it would surely freeze again (it was not three o'clock) in the colder hours of the late afternoon and night. My over-caution in having the poncho brought up now proved my salvation. This heavy shawl or blanket, with a slit in the middle, slipped over my head, kept me fairly warm to the end, protecting my hand somewhat, as well as my whole body. At the same time, it was awkward to wear, reaching nearly to my knees, and was the cause of my slipping and almost of my death on the way down. But for the loss of my fur mitten I should not have been compelled to wear it except, as intended, on the summit.

A little farther on, Gabriel suggested our halting for the observations, as the wind might be worse at the extremity of the ridge. The slope, however, was so slight that there probably was no difference. Rudolf now untied and disappeared. I was so busy over the hypsometer that I did not notice where he went, realizing only that he was not there. While, careful not to expose too much of my left hand, I shielded the hypsometer from the wind as well as I was able with the poncho, Gabriel struck match after match in vain. Once he lighted the candle, but immediately it went out. After striking twenty matches, Gabriel said, "It is useless; we must give it up." With Rudolf's assistance in holding the poncho we might have done better. But it was past three. That dread descent was before us. Sadly I packed away the instrument, believing it better to return alive, if possible, than to risk further delay. It was a great disappointment not to make the expected contribution to science; perhaps to have broken the world's record, without being able to prove it; but to return alive seemed still more desirable, even though in ignorance of the exact height to which we had attained.

Rudolf now appeared and informed me that *he* had been on to the summit, instead of remaining to assist with the hypsometer. I *was* enraged. I had told them, long before, that, as it was my expedition, I should like, as is customary, to be the first one to place my foot at the top, even though I reached it through their instrumentality. It would not lessen their honour and I was paying the bills. I had related how a few feet below the top of Mt. St. Elias, Maquignaz had stepped back and said to the Duke of Abruzzi, "Monsier, a vous la gloire!" And Rudolf, who with little grit had on the first attempt turned back at 16,000 feet, compelling me to make this weary climb over again, who this time had not done half so much work as Gabriel, who had wished to give up an hour below the summit, instead of remaining here with us to render assistance with the observations, had coolly walked on to the highest point! I had not *dreamed* of such an act. The disappointment may have been trivial. Of course it made no real difference to the honour to which I was entitled, but of a certain personal satisfaction, long looked forward to, I had been robbed. Once more I resolved, if we ever got down again, to give that man a piece of my mind, a large one: but after all I never did, for then he had troubles enough of his own, and words would not change the fact. Now, without a word, I went on.

Though the grade was slight, I was obliged to pause several times in the fierce wind, once leaning my head on my ice axe for a few seconds before I could continue to the goal. Gabriel stopped a short distance from the end, advising me not to go too near the edge, which I had no inclination to do, passing but a few feet beyond him. I should like to have looked down into the Llanganuco Gorge, whence I had looked up at the cliff and the thick overhanging cornice, such as impended above the east and west cliffs also. We had, therefore, kept in the center of the broad ridge, at least 40 feet wide, it may have been more: it seemed wider than an ordinary city street. Had it been earlier in the day, being particularly fond of precipices, and this would have been the biggest I had ever looked down, I should have ventured near the north edge with Gabriel holding the rope; but now I did not care to hazard delay from the possibility of breaking through the cornice.

My first thought on reaching the goal was, "I am here at last, after all these years; but shall we ever get down again?" I said nothing except, "Give me the camera," and as rapidly as possible took views towards the four quarters of the heavens, one including Gabriel. The click of the camera did not sound just right, and fearing that I was getting no pictures at all, I did not bother to have Gabriel try to take a photograph of me. This I afterwards regretted, as I should like to have preserved such a picture for my own pleasure. But in later days I was thankful indeed that in spite of high wind and blowing snow the other pictures did come out fairly; for it is pictures from the summit that tell the tale, and not the picture of some one standing on a bit of rock or snow which may be anywhere.

There was no pleasure here, hardly a feeling of triumph, in view of my disappointment over the observations, and my dread of the long and terrible descent. If ever I were safely down, there would be plenty of time to rejoice. It was half past three, and soon would be dark. Seven hours coming up! Would it take us as long to return? Steep rocks and icy slopes are far more dangerous to descend, and especially perilous after dark; with those small steps, the prospect was indeed terrifying; so without a moment's rest we began our retreat. The summit ridge, at least a quarter of a mile in length, was quickly traversed, at that altitude a slight change in grade making as much difference as in bicycling.

Gabriel had led nearly all the way up, cutting most, if not all, of the steps. Rudolf had been second, in order to hold the rope for me, avoiding all possible delay. Going down I was roped in the middle, the more usual position for the amateur, Rudolf at first taking the lead and Gabriel occupying the more responsible place in the rear; for in descending, the rear is the post of honour, as that of leader in the ascent; since the strongest of a party must be above, holding the rope in case of a slip on the part of the amateur in front. A guide, of course, is never expected to slip and a good one practically never does. If the rear guard goes, as a rule all are lost.

The guides' shoes being well studded with nails they had not cared to wear the climbing irons, to which they were unaccustomed, and which by impeding the circulation would have made their feet colder. My shoes were more poorly provided, as it was impossible to procure in New York such nails as are employed in the Alps. I had intended to wear the crampons which would have made them unnecessary, but on Gabriel's advice had left them below, lest my feet should be frozen, as the one previously touched by the frost would have greater liability.

At the end of the ridge difficulties began. A smooth slope of 60 degrees is never pleasant. From the beginning of the descent I greatly feared the outcome, but we had to go down and the faster we could go, yet carefully, the better. Presently I saw something black fly away: one of Rudolf's mittens. One might suppose that after losing mine he would have been the more careful of his own. When I inquired afterwards how he came to lose it, he said he laid it down on that icy slope to fasten his shoe. Of course the wind blew it away. Later I learned that after dark he lost the second mitten. This he said was in trying to change from one hand to the other. He thought he had hold of it, but his hand being numb, he could not feel it, and this went also. If he had spoken we should have halted, so that he could make sure. His carelessness seems incredible and inexcusable, and brought disastrous consequences to himself and nearly to us all, almost costing our lives. Probably I should not have slipped, had I not been obliged on account of the loss of my fur mittens to wear the poncho which occasionally prevented my seeing the steps. Certainly Rudolf himself would not have slipped any more than Gabriel, if his hands had not been frozen and himself chilled through, so that one foot froze also; thus his footing was insecure and his grip on his ice axe less firm. It seems almost a miracle that he slipped only once and that we at last got down alive. His carelessness may perhaps be explained by the fact of his being so much affected by the altitude that it rendered him stupid, as below he had seemed as thoughtful and as careful as Gabriel. The latter, however, I had regarded as a trifle the more intelligent, as he was evidently the stronger.

On this steep slope, I deeply regretted the absence of my climbing irons, for the steps were small indeed. On the Jungfrau those made by my guide Baumann were very large, requiring from ten to twenty blows: but this would never do on the much longer slope of Huascarán. Two or three hacks for each were all that Gabriel could give, so they were not half as large as his shoes, little more than toe-holes. He did well enough going up but not on the way down. While zigzagging I missed a step, sat down and slid a few feet, but Gabriel above was holding the rope tight and I easily regained my footing.

Some time after dark it seemed advisable for Gabriel to take the lead (such matters of course I left to them), perhaps because he was more familiar with the way or could see better on the long sloping traverse across the wide face of the mountain in the midst of caverns, crevasses, and those dreadful slopes and precipices; yet as a slide anywhere would have been fatal, one place was just as bad as another, except as some parts were steeper. Gabriel estimated the incline as from 40 degrees to 60 degrees through the greater part of the distance. I had brought with me a clinometer, but never had time and strength to use it. I had been on measured slopes of 42 degrees and 53 degrees on my first mountain, and judging from these, had never afterwards over-estimated any that had been capable of verification. My opinion here coincides with Gabriel's. If anyone should not accept it, the matter is of little consequence as compared with the altitude, which unfortunately I had been obliged to leave unmeasured. But that could be determined at a later date. Whatever it might be, the *fact* of my ascent would stand.

My recollection of the descent is as of a horrible nightmare, though such I never experienced. The little moon seemed always at my back, casting a shadow over the place where I must step. The poncho would sway in the wind, and, with my motion as I was in the act of stepping, would sometimes conceal the spot where my foot should be placed. Although my eye for distance is good, my foot once missed the step, slipping then on the smooth slope so that I fell, as usual in a sitting posture, crying out at the same time to warn the guides. I expected nothing serious, but to my horror, I did not remain where I was. Still sitting I began to slide down that glassy, ghastly incline. As we were all nearly in the same line, I slid at least fifteen feet before coming to a halt, when checked by the rope. Now to get back! The guides called to me to get up, but being all in a heap, with the rope tight around my waist, I was unable to move. The guides therefore came together just above and hauled me up the slope. Thankful again to be in the line of the steps, though now more alarmed than ever, I went onward, resolved to be more careful. But again I slipped, and again slid far below. While from the beginning of the descent, I had greatly feared the out-come, after these slips my terror increased. Several times I declared that we should never get down alive. I begged Gabriel to stop for the night and make a cave in the snow, but, saying this was impossible, he continued without a pause. The snow indeed was too hard, yet in some cavern or crevasse I thought we could find shelter from the wind. Gabriel afterwards asserted that if we had stopped we should all have frozen to death.

Again and again I slipped, five or six times altogether, but always Gabriel held his ground firmly. Always, too, I clung to my ice axe; so to his shout, "Have you your axe?" I could respond in the affirmative, and sometimes with it could help myself back again. Once when I had slipped, I was astonished to see Rudolf dart by me, wondering how he could help me by running far below. Afterwards I learned, that with my pull he, too, had slipped and Gabriel's strong arm alone saved us all from destruction. Had he given way, after sliding some distance we should all have dropped off thousands of feet below. When he saw Rudolf go, Gabriel thought for a moment that we were all lost; but his axe was well placed with the rope around it, and although two fingers were caught between the rope and the ice axe, knowing it was life or death he stood firm until Rudolf recovered himself. Otherwise, Gabriel said afterwards, he never despaired but thought only of going on. Rudolf, however, to my great astonishment, for I had supposed I was the only one who was frightened, confessed later that he never expected to get down alive.

The cold and fatigue, the darkness and shadow, the poncho blowing before me, the absence of climbing irons, the small steps, the steep glassy slopes, presented an extraordinary combination of difficulties. It seemed that the way would never end. I tried to comfort myself with the reflection that accidents do not run in our family, that nothing serious, more than broken ribs or knee-pan—these not in climbing—ever *had* happened to me; but also I was aware that people do not generally die but once. I said to myself, for the first time in my life, I *must* keep cool and do my best, and so I did; but after several of those horrible slides—Well, there was nothing to do but to plod along.

At last, at last—! Before I was aware that we had emerged from among those terrible abysses to the slope above the tent, Gabriel said "Now we are safe; and if you like you can slide." What a tremendous relief I sat down happily, Gabriel walking ahead and guiding me with the rope. At first it was fun, then I went too fast, bobbing here and there, bumping, floundering, finally turning around, sliding on my back, and giving my head a hard whack before I came to a halt. However, we were nearly down and walked on to the tent where we arrived a half past ten, thankful for rest and shelter. There was nothing to drink, we were too tired to eat or sleep, but glad indeed to sit down in safety, too fatigued at first even to lie down. Poor Rudolf! His hands were badly frozen, his fingers black, the left hand worse than the right. He was rubbing them weakly with snow, first one, then the other. I told him he should rub them harder to get up circulation; I felt I ought to myself, but somehow sat there and did not. . .

I was greatly grieved to learn afterwards in Lima that it was finally necessary to amputate most of [Rudolf] Taugwalder's left hand, a finger of his right, and half of one foot. He was unable to travel until December, when the men rode down to Samanco and sailed to Callao, where they took the steamer for Panama and New York, returning in January to their homes in Zermatt. The well-known surgeon, Dr. William Tod Helmuth, kindly examined Rudolf in New York City, and I was glad to hear him say that undoubtedly he had received suitable attention and that the operations, especially the very difficult one on his foot, had been excellently performed.

Concerning the altitude of Mt. Huascarán, in regard to which there has been a rather one-sided controversy, a few words must be said. That I ever asserted the height of the mountain to be 24,000 feet is a deliberate misstatement, to which my articles published in *Harper's Magazine* for January, 1909, and in the *Bulletin* of the American Geographical Society for June of the same year bear witness. . . .

Solely in the interest of science, it is said, an expedition of three French engineers was sent from Paris to Peru to secure the altitude of this one mountain. Apparently the work was done with an extreme care which presupposes accurate measurement; yet $13,000 seems a large sum to spend for the triangulation of a single mountain which it cost but $3,000 to climb. With $1,000 more for my expedition, I should have been able with assistant to triangulate the peak myself. With $12,000 additional I could have triangulated and climbed many mountains and accomplished other valuable exploration. The figures given as the result of this triangulation are 21,812 feet for the north peak and 22,187 for the south. Though it would thus appear that Huascarán is not so lofty as I had hoped, my ten long years of effort had culminated in the conquest of a mountain at least 1,500 feet higher than Mt. McKinley, and 2,500 feet higher than any man residing in the United States had climbed. With this I must be content until opportunity is offered to investigate some other possibilities in regard to the Apex of America.

Ghosts of Everest

ERIC SIMONSON, JOCHEN HEMMLEB,
AND LARRY JOHNSON

Eric Simonson, Jochen Hemmleb, and Larry Johnson write about their 1999 search to unravel the mystery of George Mallory and Sandy Irvine, lost on Mount Everest in 1924. Mallory and Irvine were trying to become the first to reach the summit of the world's tallest mountain 29 years before it was finally climbed successfully. Starting from their final camp at 27,000 feet the two climbers began their ascent. They were last seen on June 8, 1924, at 12:50 P.M. climbing toward the summit. Though the two were never seen again, there was always speculation that they might have reached the summit, only to disappear on the descent. This amazing story doesn't quite solve the mystery after 75 years, but the discovery the climbing team made will become a permanent part of Everest's history.

It was the expedition that couldn't possibly succeed. A group of veteran mountaineers, headed by renowned American expedition leader Eric Simonson and guided by the research of a young German amateur historian named Jochen Hemmleb, would seek to answer exploration's most confounding mystery: What happened to George Leigh Mallory and Andrew Comyn "Sandy" Irvine, who disappeared on the mountain during their assault on the summit, on June 8, 1924?

That the 1999 Mallory and Irvine Research Expedition overshot even its own wild ambitions is by now common knowledge. The news that it had found Mallory's remains at nearly 27,000 feet on the windswept scree of Everest's inhospitable North Face startled the world this spring.

But what has not been known, because the details have not been released until now, is what the expedition discovered about Mallory and Irvine's final day. It is a story that began on May 1, as American mountaineers Dave Hahn, Jake Norton, Andy Politz, and Tap Richards crossed a vertiginous snow terrace on the North Face toward fellow expedition member Conrad Anker. At Anker's feet, frozen in a 75-year-old self-arrest, was a body whose torso was alabaster white, almost perfectly preserved. They had been searching for less than two hours. Jake Norton began scratching out a memorial stone: "Andrew Irvine: 1902–1924."

"This isn't him," Politz suddenly said.

The team looked at the body. They looked at Politz as if he were crazy.

"Oh, I think so," Anker said.

"I don't know what made me say it," Politz said later. "Here was this very old body, perfectly preserved, with very old clothing and the hobnailed boots. I knew it had to be Sandy Irvine; Irvine was who we were looking for, and that's who it had to be."

To find anything at all was unthinkable on Everest's white expanse. The area they were searching was above 26,000 feet—a wide snow terrace the size of 12 wildly tilted football fields, its 30-degree slope ending in a 7,000-foot drop to the Central Rongbuk Glacier below.

Yet here was the corpse, lying fully extended, face down, and pointing uphill. The head and upper torso were frozen into the rubble that had accumulated over the decades. The arms, powerfully muscular still, extended above the head to strong hands that gripped the mountainside, flexed fingertips dug deep into the gravel. The legs extended downhill, one broken, the other gently crossed over it.

"We weren't just looking at a body," says Hahn. "We were looking at an era, one we'd only known through books. The natural-fiber clothes, the fur-lined leather helmet, the kind of rope that was around him were all so eloquent. As we stood there, this mute but strangely peaceful body was giving us answers to questions that everyone had been asking for three-quarters of a century: the fact that a rope had been involved, that there was no oxygen apparatus."

The hobnailed boots, of course, was the giveaway. No climber had died at this altitude between 1924 and 1938, and hobnailed boots had given way to crampons by the eve of World War II. And if anyone had fallen, surely it would have been the inexperienced Irvine. But when Richards began gently separating the ragged clothing—several layers of cotton and silk underwear, a flannel shirt, woolen pullover and trousers, a canvaslike outer garment—he turned over a piece of shirt collar and revealed a fragment of laundry label: G. Leigh-Ma . . .

The climbers looked at one another dumbly. Finally someone said out loud what everyone else was thinking: "Why would Irvine be wearing Mallory's shirt?" But then they found another tag: G. Mallory. Then a third.

"Maybe it was the altitude and the fact that we'd all put aside our oxygen gear," says Hahn, "but it took a while for reality to sink in. Finally it hit us. We were in the presence of George Mallory himself."

"Now I realized why I had said it wasn't Irvine," Politz recalls. "It was the position of the body. The body we were looking for—a body long assumed to be Andrew Irvine—had been seen in 1975 by a Chinese climber, Wang Hong-bao, during a short walk from his Camp VI tent at 26,980 feet. He described the body as gape-mouthed, its cheek pecked by goraks. But this body was face down. What's more, it was too far from the Chinese camp. No one in his right mind would have gone for a short walk where we found this body. I just sat down. My knees literally got weak. My jaw dropped. Next to me, Dave was going, 'Oh, my God, it's George. Oh, my God.'"

Until then, this is what had been known about Mallory and Irvine's last few days: Just after dawn on the morning of June 6, 1924, the two mountaineers crawled out of their canvas tent on the North Col, a wind-savaged, 23,180-foot saddle of rock, ice, and snow between the hulking mass of Everest itself and its lesser northern peak, Changtse. It had been more than two months since they had walked out of Darjeeling, India, toward Tibet, and more than a month since they had established their base camp at the terminal moraine of the Rongbuk Glacier. Twice that month they had tried to push higher on the mountain—once as far as Camp III, at the base of the North Col; once to Camp IV, on the Col itself—and twice miserable weather and mishaps had driven them back down. Finally, in the first few days of June, the team succeeded in establishing two higher camps—Camp V, at 25,300 feet and Camp VI, at 27,000 feet—but two attempts to reach Everest's 29,028-foot summit had failed. They were running out of supplies, the porters were exhausted, and the summer monsoons would arrive any day.

As Mallory and Irvine struggled into their heavy oxygen apparatus, expedition geologist Noel Odell snapped their picture. Irvine, only 22 years old, stood calmly with his hands in his pockets as he watched Mallory fuss with his oxygen mask. A few minutes later, at 8:40 A.M., the pair set off with eight Tibetan porters up the North Ridge toward Camp V. The next morning, with four porters, they pushed higher, to Camp VI, only some 2,000 feet below the summit. The porters descended, carrying with them two notes from Mallory scribbled in pencil on torn-out pages from a small notebook. One was addressed to expedition cinematographer John Noel: "It won't be too early to start looking for us either crossing the rock band under the pyramid or going up skyline at 8.0 P.M." (Mallory obviously meant 8 A.M.) The other note was addressed to Odell, with a gentlemanly apology for leaving Camp IV a mess and a request to bring up a forgotten compass. "Perfect weather for the job!" he added.

The next morning, June 8, Mallory and Irvine faced a series of daunting hurdles on their way to the summit: a crumbly strip of steep limestone slabs now known as the Yellow Band, a nearly vertical 100-foot wall of harder rock that came to be called the First Step, a dicey and exposed ridge walk, and then another 100-foot Second Step, far more difficult than the first. Above the Second Step, a broad, gently rising plateau led to an easier Third Step and then the snow-covered summit pyramid itself.

Later that morning, Noel Odell left for Camp VI, carrying the forgotten compass. The geologist had become exceptionally well acclimatized to Everest's thin air, and he climbed without supplemental oxygen, looking for fossils along the way. At 12:50 P.M. he looked up and saw something unforgettable. "There was a sudden clearing of the atmosphere," he would later write, "and the entire summit ridge and final peak of Everest were unveiled. My eyes became fixed on one tiny black spot silhouetted on a small snow-crest beneath a rock-step in the ridge; the black spot moved. Another black spot became apparent and moved up the snow to join the other on the crest. The first then approached the great rock-step and shortly emerged at the top; the second did likewise. Then the whole fascinating vision vanished, enveloped in cloud once more. There was but one explanation. It was Mallory and his companion moving, as I could see even at that great distance, with considerable alacrity. . . . The place on the ridge referred to is the prominent rock-step at a very short distance from the base of the final pyramid."

Concluding that his colleagues were perhaps three hours from the summit, Odell climbed up to Camp VI, hoping that the others would make it back by nightfall. As a snow squall blew up, he ducked into the tiny two-man tent, finding it strewn with clothing, the climbers' sleeping bags, and spare parts of oxygen apparatus.

Concerned that the camp might be difficult to find in the swirling snow, Odell scrambled another 200 feet up the mountain, whistling and yodeling to guide Mallory and Irvine back. But it was still too early, he realized, for the climbers to come back. At 4:30 P.M., leaving the compass and some food, Odell descended to Camp IV to wait.

But Mallory and Irvine never returned.

Their disappearance would fuel decades of speculation. Did Odell see them, as he originally claimed, above the Second Step, or were they stalled at the much lower First Step, as he later conceded they might have been? Did they reach the summit? If so, did they, singly or roped together, make one false step on the descent? Or were they, exhausted and out of oxygen, forced to spend a fatal night exposed on the roof of the world?

In the years since, two significant clues have emerged. The first was an ice ax, discovered on the Northeast Ridge at 27,760 feet during a 1933 British expedition, and later identified as Irvine's by three parallel nicks etched on its handle. The second was Wang Hongbao's discovery of a body near the 1975 Chinese Camp VI. But despite endless parsing of Odell's account and repeated calculations of climbing rates, departure times, and oxygen use, the world knew little more about Mallory and Irvine's fate than it did in 1924.

Enter Jochen Hemmleb, a tall, stoop-shouldered geology student at Johann Wolfgang Goethe University in Frankfurt, Germany. In 1997, Hemmleb was living in a one-room flat, camping on the floor in a sleeping bag because his bed—as well as nearly every other horizontal surface in the apartment—lay blanketed in piles of old photographs, maps, and books about Everest. A climber and restless world traveler, Hemmleb had spent every spare penny since he was 16 amassing one of the largest and most meticulously analyzed private collections of Everest documents in the world. In the process, he had become obsessed by the fate of Mallory and Irvine. In 1997, after years of poring over the same historical accounts, he decided to strip away the accumulated layers of myth and speculation and to tackle the mystery as a scientific problem.

The ice ax, Hemmleb decided, was a red herring. To him the challenge was straightforward: Locate the site of the 1975 Chinese Camp VI and search an area that could be covered in the 20-minute round-trip that Wang had reported. Unfortunately, the Chinese had released little documentation of the 1975 climb. But by comparing geological background features in photographs of the Chinese Camp VI with those of other expeditions' Camp VI, lining them up on aerial photographs of the ridge, and taking a series of back bearings, Hemmleb deduced that the camp sat on an ill-defined rib of rock bisecting the snow terrace—a site far off today's beaten path to the summit.

Forget the ice ax, Hemmleb concluded. Find the camp and you'd find Irvine.

Hemmleb began publishing his findings on the Web site Everest News. On June 2, 1998, he received an e-mail message from another Everest buff, a 51-year-old American climber and publishing executive named Larry Johnson. Within a week, Hemmleb and Johnson were discussing the possibility of joining a commercial expedition to Everest's North Face and then striking out to look for Irvine themselves. Thumbing through brochures, Johnson noticed a trip run by Eric Simonson's Seattle-based International Mountain Guides—not a summit climb, but one that took clients to 26,250 feet. Johnson contacted him immediately. Simonson—a 43-year-old veteran guide who since age 18 had led some 70 expeditions, seven of them to Everest—told them that their only chance of success was a dedicated search, and the three began planning a formal Mallory and Irvine Research Expedition.

The 1924 British Everest Expedition was bankrolled with £8,000 put up by John Noel, a veteran of the 1922 British Everest Expedition, who planned to film the attempt. Simonson's team cobbled together $300,000 in sponsorship money to get its project off the ground. The 1999 team was swaddled in polypropylene and Gore-Tex. The many layers of technical wear in 1924 included, as expedition leader Edward Felix Norton wrote, "a very light pyjama suit of Messrs Burberry's 'Shackleton' windproof gaberdine" and "a pair of soft elastic Kashmir putties." The 1999 expedition recruited some of America's finest climbers: 37-year-old Dave Hahn, a senior guide on Mount Rainier who'd summited Everest via the North Face in 1994; 36-year-old Conrad Anker, a superb technical rock climber; 39-year-old guide Andy Politz, another Everest veteran; and 25-year-old guides Tap Richards and Jake Norton, who had each summited one of Everest's Tibetan neighbors, 26,748-foot Cho Oyu. In addition to Norton, Noel, and Odell, the 1924 team included surgeon and alpinist Howard Somervell and Geoffrey Bruce, who had made it to 27,500 feet in 1922. And of course Mallory, the finest mountaineer of his day, and Irvine, a second-year Oxford engineering student. The 1999 expedition took computers, digital cameras, and satellite telephones. Mallory and Irvine climbed toward the summit with at least one camera, a collapsible Kodak Vest Pocket model lent to Mallory by Somervell. Before the 1999 expedition left for Everest, Kodak technicians had said that the film, if intact, could probably be developed.

It was this camera that the Mallory and Irvine Research Expedition hoped to find. After recovering from the initial shock of discovering Mallory's body, the climbers hesitantly began trying to free it from the frozen rock. It was like chipping concrete with a knife, but the exhaustingly slow pace afforded plenty of time to study Mallory carefully. The tibia and fibula of his right leg were broken above the top of his boot, and his right elbow was either broken or dislocated. Cuts, abrasions, and bruises ran along his right side, and the climbing rope in which he was tangled had compressed his rib cage. The rope had passed twice around his waist, and the frayed trailing ends were wrapped around his leg and upper body. Goraks had pecked at the body, eating away his legs, buttocks, and abdominal cavity.

Finally lifting up Mallory's right shoulder, Norton reached underneath to find a pouch around Mallory's neck. Inside was something hard and metallic—but not the camera. It was a metal tin of bouillon cubes, "Brand & Co. Savoury Meat Lozenges." With the tin was a brass altimeter missing both its face and hands, and an envelope, perfectly preserved, the ink script of the letter inside crisp and clear. Other items emerged from various pockets: a monogrammed handkerchief carefully wrapped around another group of letters; a fingerless glove; a pocketknife with an antler handle; a box of matches, still usable; scraps of paper with penciled gear checklists; and, deep in one pocket, a pair of undamaged sun goggles. There was also a set of adjustable webbing straps attached to metal spring clips, the kind used to hold an oxygen mask to a helmet.

After taking samples of each layer of clothing and a small skin sample for DNA analysis, the team covered the body with a protective layer of stones. Then Politz read Psalm 103 aloud in a brief ceremony, and the men gathered their gear. "It seems an odd thing to say," said Norton later, "but I don't think any of us wanted to leave him. We were very comfortable being with George. He was so impressive to be with, even in death."

The next morning the climbers descended from Camp V, walked straight into the research expedition's main tent, zipped the flaps closed, and began pulling artifacts out of their packs to show Simonson. (The team had maintained virtual radio silence; Hemmleb, who had remained below at base camp, was still unaware of what they had found.)

"The first thing we gave Eric was the envelope and letter addressed to Mr. George Leigh Mallory," says Norton, "and he just looked up and smiled a very big smile."

On July 11, six weeks after the expedition had returned from Tibet, Hemmleb and archaeologist Rick Reanier sat in a basement room in the Washington State Historical Society Research Center in Tacoma, where the Mallory artifacts had been temporarily archived. Some clues—like Mallory's wristwatch, recovered in a second foray to the body—had proved to be dead ends: Had the watch been stopped by an impact, its balance shaft would have been broken, freezing forever the time of the fall. But when the machinery was examined, the watch was found to be in working order. During this second search, the climbers had also found the likely cause of Mallory's death: a severe head injury.

Picking through the letters and notes, however, Hemmleb and Reanier now made a startling discovery. On the outside of an envelope containing a letter from a mysterious "Stella"—most likely a British journalist—were two columns of numbers: 100, 110, 110, 110, and 110; and opposite, No. 33, No. 35, No. 10, No. 9, and No. 15. Hemmleb and Reanier looked at each other and almost simultaneously realized what the numbers meant. The second column was a list of numbered oxygen cylinders, the first the bottle pressure of each. It was a pressure test list of five of the spare oxygen cylinders Mallory and Irvine had taken for the summit climb. (A sixth cylinder, Hemmleb believes, was probably omitted because it still contained a full charge of 120 atmospheres.)

While still on the mountain, the members of the team had searched for an ancient-looking oxygen bottle that Simonson had noticed wedged under a boulder during a 1991 summit climb. Miraculously, Richards found the old bottle high on the Northeast Ridge, just below the First Step. Hemmleb recognized it immediately by its distinctive shape and dimensions as a 1924 cylinder. On the bottle, in faded paint, was the number 9—a clear match with one of the cylinders listed on the envelope.

A few days after the discovery of the pressure list, Hemmleb and Reanier were back in the museum basement, studying the crumpled bits of paper that had been stuffed in Mallory's pockets—notes that had been largely ignored at the time they were found. They gradually realized that the bits of paper were actually detailed provision lists for the final push to the summit. In Mallory's distinctive handwriting, the lists inventoried food, fuel, supplies, and *six* spare oxygen bottles. Another note, from fellow expedition member Geoffrey Bruce, confirmed that Bruce had sent up more oxygen for Mallory from Camp III.

Hemmleb was stunned. No one had ever known before the details of Mallory and Irvine's preparations for the summit climb. Now the stage was set anew. In addition to the cylinders they had in their packs the morning they left Camp IV, there were six others on the provisions inventory. People had simply assumed Mallory and Irvine set out for the summit with two cylinders each. The principal reason that students of the mystery believed they could not have reached the summit is that two cylinders would not have gotten them there. But they clearly had the option to use at least three each. That fact alone had the potential for rewriting the entire story of their final day.

Going back to the historical record, Hemmleb reread Edward Norton's account of the last days of the 1924 expedition. As Norton lay in his tent suffering from snowblindness following his own unsuccessful summit bid, Mallory sat with him and laid out his plan: "He was determined to make one more attempt, this time with oxygen," Norton had written. "He had been down to Camp III with Bruce and collected sufficient porters to enable the attempt to be staged." But how many cylinders had they used to get to Camp VI? How many would have been left for the final summit push?

Hemmleb read further and came upon a remark that suddenly seemed to provide an answer: "Mallory and Irvine decided to use practically no oxygen up to Camp VI," Norton had noted. "Camp VI having been established with tents and bedding by Somervell and me, nearly every available porter could now be used for carrying oxygen cylinders."

Mallory is often characterized as hopelessly forgetful and occasionally impetuous. On June 6, 1924, as he and Irvine headed up the mountain toward Camp V, he was neither. He had planned the ascent in detail. He knew, for example, that Norton and Somervell had left most of their gear behind at Camp VI, and he had planned accordingly. He had plenty of food. (In addition to the oxygen, the note from Bruce listed provisions that he had also sent up from Camp III the day before Mallory and Irvine departed.) There was also a stove at Camp VI, with the rest of Norton and Somervell's gear. All Mallory needed to take with him was fuel, which the notes on his body indicate is exactly what he did.

It is curious that, over the years, no one has wondered why Mallory and Irvine needed eight porters to accompany them to Camp V when their supplies could have fit easily into one, or perhaps two, backpacks. We now know the reason: They were carrying oxygen cylinders.

In the famous photograph taken as Mallory and Irvine were about to leave Camp IV, Irvine was carrying two cylinders but Mallory apparently only one, lending credence to the reports that he was serious about using very little oxygen until they really needed it. Once they had reached Camp VI, Mallory sent the last four porters back down with a note for Odell reporting that they had climbed "to here on 90 atmospheres for the 2 days." Thus they had used only three-quarters of a bottle each to reach Camp VI from Camp IV. Commentators have suggested that this slow climb rate with oxygen was proof that they were in no fit state for a summit attempt. But they were moving slowly precisely because they were climbing without the benefit of oxygen for at least part of the time.

The critical question is, how many full or nearly full oxygen cylinders did Mallory and Irvine have at their disposal on summit day? The absolute minimum appears to be seven: From Camp IV, Mallory carried one, Irvine two, the porters six; they wouldn't have needed first eight and then four porters if they had had fewer cylinders. They had used the better part of two on the way up, so seven were left. (Even if they had used one during the night, they still would have been left with six.)

When Odell arrived at Camp VI, he noted that there were oxygen cylinders inside the tiny tent but didn't say how many. There were at least two—the empties that Mallory and Irvine had used on their two-day ascent. The day before, Mallory had written to Odell that they'd probably push to the summit on two cylinders each, indicating that they had a choice of more. Also, none of the 1924 expedition members believed oxygen was of any value whatsoever on the descent, so there would have been no reason to leave spares behind in reserve.

In his note to John Noel, Mallory had told him to look for them "crossing the rock band under the pyramid or going up skyline at 8.0." Odell and others interpreted "crossing the rock band" as surmounting the Second Step, high on the Northeast Ridge. At 12:50 P.M., when Odell saw them doing what he thought was just that, he concluded that they were nearly five hours behind schedule.

In fact, nothing in the note suggests that Mallory intended to reach the Second Step by 8 A.M. What it does demonstrate is that he was still uncertain whether they would climb through the Yellow Band, as Norton and Somervell had done, or go directly up the ridge, his preferred route. In the end he chose the latter, and the two were "going up skyline" only 45 minutes to an hour later than estimated. We know this because of "No. 9," the spent 1924 oxygen bottle that Richards retrieved from the Northeast Ridge. Mallory's envelope notes show that No. 9 had 110 atmospheres of pressure. At a full flow rate of 2.2 liters per minute the bottle would have lasted three hours and 40 minutes. If we accept that Mallory and Irvine started near sunrise as Mallory had planned, oxygen cylinder No. 9 would have gotten him (or Irvine) some distance along the crest of the ridge before running out between 8:45 and 9:15.

Cylinder No. 9 also tells us that Mallory and Irvine were climbing strongly that morning. It was discovered 850 feet above Camp VI. Dividing that distance by the time the bottle lasted yields a perfectly respectable climbing rate of 230 feet per hour, roughly the same rate that the 1999 research expedition climbers took to cover the same distance. Moreover, Mallory and Irvine climbed before the era of fixing ropes and would have moved more quickly than modern-day mountaineers, though they would have spent somewhat more time sniffing out the best route.

Finally, cylinder No. 9 was found only 620 feet away from the base of the First Step. If Mallory or Irvine discarded No. 9 and switched to a fresh cylinder sometime between 8:45 and 9:15 A.M., they would certainly not have been at the First Step when Odell saw them at 12:50 P.M. Barring some lengthy, inexplicable delay, they would have been much higher. We can only conclude that Odell was right the first time: He saw Mallory and Irvine at the Second Step, or very possibly higher. Indeed, nothing in his topographical description fits any feature of the First Step.

Andy Politz, who made a point of climbing to the spot where Odell had stood 75 years earlier, remains convinced that what Odell described can only be interpreted as the Third Step. But if bottle No. 9 was discarded below the First Step, at about 9 A.M., it would have been extremely difficult for them to have made it as far as the Third Step by 12:50.

If the First Step is impossible and the Third Step seems unlikely, the only alternative is the Second Step. Its hundred-foot limestone band is climbed in three stages: a traverse to the right to a short rock climb, a steep scramble up a very small snow patch, and finally an ascent of the relatively short vertical headwall near the top. What Odell could have seen was the two climbers coming up that small snow patch and then scaling the headwall at the top "with alacrity."

The 1975 Chinese expedition installed a rickety aluminum ladder on the highly exposed vertical wall, and since then everyone summiting Everest from the north side has relied on the ladder to surmount the last pitch of the Second Step. Only one other team, a 1960 Chinese expedition, had summited without the benefit of a ladder. The 1999 Mallory and Irvine Research Expedition sent Anker, its best technical climber, to find out if Mallory could have, too.

Several hours before dawn on May 17—more than two weeks after the expedition discovered Mallory's body—Anker, accompanied by three team members and two Sherpas, left Camp VI to attempt a free climb of the headwall. By the time they reached the Second Step, four of the climbers had turned back, leaving only Anker and Hahn, who led the first two pitches. Then, as Hahn looked on, Anker scanned the headwall for ascent routes. Two were immediately apparent. To the right of the ladder, in the sun, was a right-slanting crack that looked like the preferred route, but after only a few feet he abandoned it. "The rock was really loose and rotten, with bad fall potential," Anker later said. He immediately turned his attention to the second route, an off-width crack (one that is too wide for a fist and too narrow for a body) that lay in permanent shadow just to the left of the ladder.

Before Hahn could provide him a belay, Anker was near the top of the crack. He had jammed his elbow and shoulder into the crack in an arm lock, inserted a foot and leg into it below, and hoisted himself up. Now he needed to move right, around an overhang. There was a perfectly positioned narrow ledge to make this move possible, but one of the ladder rungs was in the way. He reached to the right, got a firm handhold on the rock face, and pulled across, placing his foot on the rung that blocked the ledge. A few moments later he was at the top of the Second Step. "I was able to knee-bar to the top," he said, "and got a size three Friend [a spring-loaded cam device] at the top of it and then got a hand jam into the crack. I got the Friend in, and then I had to step out." Anker did not end up using the protection he placed, and his brief reliance on the ladder would have been unnecessary had it not been in the way. Anker rated the climb 5.8, adding that at such a high altitude, without oxygen, it felt like 5.10.

By radio, Simonson asked the big question: "Could Mallory have scaled the headwall?" Anker replied that he thought Mallory could have negotiated it—albeit with difficulty. (He has since declared that it's unlikely.) As for Hahn, "There is no question in my mind that an accomplished climber could have climbed that headwall with no aids, and we know Mallory was an accomplished climber. But what I wonder about is the combination of factors. Could they have done it all? In 1924, when the route was unknown? I don't know."

What modern adventurers tend to forget is that early mountaineers had to rely on considerably more grit to pioneer high-altitude exploration in the first place. Look at them, we say; they were so ill-equipped, their oxygen apparatus so primitive, their clothing so appallingly inadequate. But ultimately success on Everest has less to do with either technical skill or modern equipment than with sheer brute strength, guts, and, not incidentally, good weather. And a close reading of the formal expedition reports from that period reveals that these men climbed with remarkable speed, skill, and ease despite often dreadful conditions. They pioneered routes, established camps at sites still used today, and equaled or beat today's climbing rates, often without supplemental oxygen. Mallory, of course, was the best of them all; by all accounts he climbed both with the agility of a cat and with an incredible eye for route-spotting.

Whether they were on the Second Step or the Third Step when Odell saw them, it is clear that Mallory and Irvine had made excellent progress. At this point, there were three pressing issues that they had to deal with on their way to the top: weather, oxygen, and time. Despite the brief squall that hit Odell at Camp VI, it was not storming on Everest that day, and that night was clear and calm. As for oxygen and time, if cylinder No. 9 was emptied between 8:45 and 9:15 A.M., the next cylinder at full flow would have been depleted sometime between 12:45 and 1:15 that afternoon, the very time Odell saw them moving so quickly. There are only three explanations for their speed: They were unbelievably strong despite having run out of oxygen; they had been climbing at less than full flow and so had not yet run out of oxygen; or they had each switched to a third, fresh oxygen cylinder.

If the climbers had carried only two cylinders each, they would now be faced with a terrible dilemma—either abandon the summit and descend immediately to safety, or continue climbing without supplemental oxygen. If they continued, they almost certainly couldn't have reached the summit until around 7 P.M. Even if they turned around immediately, they would not have had enough time in the remaining hour and a half of dusk to descend the summit pyramid, much less the Second Step. Having left all their lighting gear at Camp VI, the two climbers would have had to rely on starlight to see anything. The moon, only a sliver on this night, set shortly after 11 P.M. Simonson and other Everest veterans agree that it is impossible to climb down the Second Step in the dark.

But Mallory's body was found below the Yellow Band, north of the First

Step, not the Second. So he must have come down the step in daylight or dusk. If Mallory and Irvine had turned back immediately when their second cylinder of oxygen ran out, they would have been back at Camp VI sometime later that afternoon, while it was still daylight. Yet if Mallory was descending in broad daylight when he fell, why were his sun goggles in his pocket, when he had seen Norton, his own expedition leader, struck snowblind just two days before? Either the altitude had rendered Mallory both clumsy and stupid, or he and Irvine did not turn back when their second bottles ran out. If so, they must have each had a third cylinder.

Driven on by the realization that the summit was at last within their reach, though no doubt climbing more slowly than they had earlier in the day, Mallory and Irvine could have reached the summit by 5 P.M., just finishing their third oxygen cylinders. By this scenario, and only this scenario, would they have had time to descend through the Second and First Steps with sufficient daylight and have ended up in the Yellow Band in darkness.

Without a definitive snapshot from the famous Kodak Vest Pocket camera, of course, we will still never know if they reached the summit. Yet there is one especially tantalizing, if indirect, clue that they may well have made it. Mallory intended to place a photograph of his wife, Ruth, on the top of Everest. But no photograph of Ruth Mallory was found on his body. Where is her picture, if not at the summit?

Whether they made it or not, somewhere in the gathering darkness Mallory and Irvine fell. They did not fall far, nor did they fall from the dangerous Northeast Ridge, as did half a dozen climbers who perished in recent decades. (In the course of their search, the 1999 team encountered their twisted, frozen corpses scattered in the great catch-basin of the snow terrace.)

We know this because Mallory has told us himself, by the position of his body and the nature of his injuries. He fell to his death from a spot well down the face of the Yellow Band, heartbreakingly close to Camp VI and safety; his injuries are not severe enough for there to be any other explanation. And he did not fall alone. His body was found tangled in a rope that had been snapped, indicating that at the critical moment he had been roped to his partner. That Irvine fell too and was injured, though probably not as profoundly as Mallory, is suggested by the fact that the body found by Wang Hongbao—clearly it must have been Irvine's—was only a ten- or 15-minute walk from the 1975 Camp VI.

This is what seems to have happened: It is late in the day, and the two mountaineers have climbed higher on Mount Everest than anyone before them, much higher. Now, exhausted, dehydrated, and oxygenless, they grope down through the Yellow Band in the dark, with neither moonlight nor lantern nor torch to light the way.

Suddenly, a misstep: Mallory loses his footing and, in seconds, is rocketing down the face past Irvine's position. Or perhaps Irvine slips and pulls Mallory after him. The extra coils of rope in Mallory's hand unravel, and then, after what seems like an eternity but is only a matter of seconds, there is a sharp jerk. The rope catches on an outcropping, Mallory smashes into the cliff face with his right side and dislocates his right elbow, the rope digs into his left side and the jolt breaks ribs. For a millisecond, he thinks he is saved. But the moment ends in a heartbeat as the shock-loaded rope snaps and he continues falling. Almost immediately, he lands on one foot in a section of steep slope. The tibia and fibula of his right leg snap just above the top of his boot.

But he does not stop. His momentum is too great. He is sliding into the vastness of the great North Face, plummeting toward the final drop-off to the Central Rongbuk Glacier thousands of feet below. He is in terrible pain, but he is not dead, and he has not given up. He swings his down-racing body around and digs his fingers into the frozen scree, scrabbles at each passing rock. But he is sliding so fast and the ground is so rough that it rips off his gloves. It is as if he is being dragged behind a runaway locomotive and he is trying to brake the speeding engine by the sheer strength of his fingers. Just at the point that he thinks he may be slowing, however, he hits a tilted slab, flies up, and when gravity takes over again, hits the slope hard, his forehead smashing into a viciously sharp shard of rock. He slides off another ledge and finally stops.

Mallory's fingers still claw the slope. He is face down in the scree. He is losing consciousness. In his last act—it may not even be conscious—he crosses his good leg over the broken one protectively. With merciful swiftness, his agony, his life, ends.

Irvine, also injured but alive, perhaps calls his name. After a while Irvine begins to drag himself eastward toward Camp VI, roughly 400 yards away. But at some point, exhaustion and pain stop him. In the desperate cold of 27,000 feet, Andrew Irvine yields to the mountain.

Camp Six: An Account of the 1933 Everest Expedition

This is yet another Everest story occurring back in 1933 when a British expedition attempted what earlier expeditions had failed to do—climb the world's highest mountain. Written by F. S. Smythe who, along with Eric Shipton, left Camp Six on June 1, for the expedition's second summit try, only to have to turn back some 1000 feet from the summit. As Smythe would write, "The last 1,000 feet of Everest are not for mere flesh and blood. Whoever reaches the summit, if he does it without artificial aid, will have to rise godlike above his own frailties and his tremendous environment. Only through a Power within him and without him will he overcome a deadly fatigue and win through to success."

The sky was clear at daybreak. We had resolved overnight to leave at 5, but a rising wind and intense cold made this impossible. Cold we could have faced, but the addition of wind is too much for mere flesh and blood on Everest.

Matters appeared hopeless until an hour later when the wind suddenly fell to a complete calm. And it did not return. We listened expectantly for the hateful rush and tug of it, but the calm persisted.

Breakfast eaten, we extricated ourselves foot by foot from our sleeping-bags and with much labour and panting pulled on our windproof suits.

Our boots might have been carved out of stone, and they glistened and sparkled inside with the frozen moisture from our feet. I made a vain attempt to soften mine over a candle, but it was useless, and somehow or other I thrust my feet into them, pausing at intervals to beat my bare hands together, or stuff them into my pockets.

We donned every stitch of clothing we possessed. I wore a Shetland vest, a thick flannel shirt, a heavy camel-hair sweater, six light Shetland pullovers, two pairs of long Shetland pants, a pair of flannel trousers, and over all a silk-lined "Grenfell" windproof suit. A Shetland balaclava and another helmet of "Grenfell" cloth protected my head, and my feet were encased in four pairs of Shetland socks and stockings. Gloves are always a problem on Everest, and the ideal glove that is warm yet flexible and will adhere to rocks has still to be designed; in this instance, a pair of woolen fingerless gloves inside a pair of South African lambskin gloves, also fingerless, kept my hands moderately warm.

A slap of Kendal mint cake apiece sufficed for food. It was a mistake not to provide ourselves with more food, but our repugnance for it had been still further intensified during our enforced stay at Camp 6. Apart from this we carried a length of light climbing line, whilst my little "Etui" camera accompanied me as usual.★

At 7 we emerged from the tent and laced the flaps behind us. It was sadly obvious that Eric was far below his usual form. He had eaten less than I since we had arrived at the Camp, and now he complained of stomach pains, and asked me to go slowly—a request I might have made myself had he been fitter.

A shallow snow-filled gully took us diagonally upwards and across the yellow band for the best part of 100 feet. There was no difficulty, but every minute or two we had to halt and lean on our ice axes gasping for breath.

The gully petered out into a great expanse of slabs. Again there was no difficulty; advance was merely a matter of careful balance and choice of the easiest route; yet the angle as a whole on the yellow band is such that a slip would probably end in a fatal slide, especially as the climber would have little strength left to stop himself. Fortunately, our broad, lightly nailed boots gripped the sandstone well. The snow of yesterday's blizzard had been blown from many of the slabs, but here and there where it had accumulated on the shelving ledges we had to tread circumspectly.

Though we left the camp an hour and a half later than Wyn and Waggers had done, the cold was still intense and there was little warmth in the sun which was just peeping over the north-east ridge.

The first and most lasting impression of the climber on Everest will always be the bleak and inhospitable nature of the great mountain. On the yellow band no projecting crags, ridges or buttresses stimulate the interest or the imagination; there is nothing level and the climber must tread a series of outward-shelving ledges where the rope is useless to him. Never have I seen a more utterly desolate mountainside. And above, still a weary way above, was the sum-

---

★This, complete with one film pack, weighs one and a quarter pounds. It takes 3½ inch by 2½ inch photographs.

mit pyramid set squarely at the end of this vast rocky roof; a last tremendous challenge to our failing strength.

Traversing, and ascending slightly, we made for the foot of the first step which, from the moment we emerged from the initial gully, appeared close at hand. Its shape reminded me in some curious way of the summit of a Lake District hill which I had climbed one dewy Spring morning before breakfast to "work up an appetite." It had taken me an hour to scale 2,300 feet of turfy bracken-clad fellside, and now with eleven hours of daylight in hand I was doubtful whether we had the time or strength to climb and descend 1,600 feet. Yet, I was going better than I had expected. Exercise was loosening my cramped and stiffened limbs, and for the first time since arriving at Camp 6 I was conscious of warm blood flowing vigorously in my veins. But, unhappily, this was not the case with Eric. He was going steadily, but very slowly, and it was more than ever plain that there was something wrong with him.

Not far from the first step we crossed an almost level platform covered in small screes, a possible site for a future camp, then traversed almost horizontally. We were immediately below the step when I heard an exclamation behind me. Turning, I saw that Eric had stopped and was leaning heavily on his ice axe. Next moment he sank down into a sitting position.

Many times during the march across Tibet we had discussed what to do in the event of one man of a party of two being unable to continue, and we had agreed that unless he was exhausted and unable to return alone safely his companion should carry on alone, in which decision he would be supported by the expedition and its leader. It was an expedition maxim that no man must go on till he reached a point of complete exhaustion, and Eric was far too good a mountaineer to do this. The saving grace in high-altitude climbing is that there is a point at which a man cannot continue to ascend but can still descend relatively easily and quite safely. This is Nature's automatic safety check.*

---

*I am convinced that this automatic check rules out the possibility of a man collapsing suddenly near the summit of Everest. Such a disturbing possibility has been mentioned as the result of tests carried out by the R.A.F. in a decompression chamber. These tests revealed that at a pressure equivalent to a height of 28,000–30,000 feet many men faint suddenly and without warning. Such tests, however, are artificial inasmuch as they make no allowance for acclimatization, and I do not believe they have any real bearing on the Everest problem. I cannot for an instant believe that under natural conditions nature acts in so arbitrary a fashion. Her processes lead slowly and unmistakably to a logical conclusion. It is only artificial conditions that she resents. Perhaps this is one of the deep-seated reasons why many Everest climbers abhor oxygen apparatus. There is something artificial, unnatural and therefore dangerous in its use on Everest. The argument that it is necessary in high flying, mines, etc., etc., cannot hold water inasmuch as such conditions are unnatural, men not being endowed with the capabilities of birds or moles, which do not, incidentally, require oxygen apparatus to sustain them.

I asked Eric whether he felt fit enough to return to camp safely. He replied unhesitatingly, "Yes," and added that he would follow slowly. This last, though I did not know it at the time, was inspired by generosity. He had no intention of proceeding further and merely said that he would to encourage me and relieve me from all anxiety as to his safety. It was another example of that good comradeship which will one day take men to the summit of Everest.

Leaving him seated on a rock I continued. I looked back after a minute or so, but he had as yet made no move.

There was never any doubt as to the best route. The crest of the north-east ridge, leading to the foot of the second step, was sharp, jagged and obviously difficult. As for the second step, now almost directly above me it *looked* utterly impregnable, and I can only compare it to the sharp bow of a battle cruiser. Norton's route alone seemed to offer any chance of success, and it follows the yellow band beneath a sheer wall to the head of the great couloir.

At first there was no difficulty and a series of sloping ledges at the top of the yellow band took me round a corner and out of sight of Eric. Then came a patch of snow perhaps 30 yards wide. There was no avoiding it except by a descent of nearly 100 feet, but fortunately the snow was not the evil floury stuff I had expected, but had been well compacted by the wind; indeed, such hard snow that step-cutting was necessary.

Step-cutting at nearly 28,000 feet is a fatiguing operation, and the axe seemed unconscionably heavy and unready to do its work. In the Alps one powerful stroke with the adze would have fashioned a step, but sudden spurts of exertion are to be avoided at 28,000 feet, and I preferred the alternative of several light, short strokes. I must have looked like an old hen grubbing for worms, but even so I had to cease work and puff hard after making each step.

High altitudes promote indecision. Projecting through the snow was a rock and at first sight it seemed a good foot-hold. Then I thought it was too sloping and that I had better cut to one side of it. But I had no sooner changed my mind when I decided that perhaps after all it could be used as a foot-hold and would save me a step or two. I must have spent a minute or two turning this ridiculous little point over in my mind before doing what was the obvious thing—avoiding it. It is curious how small problems encountered during a great undertaking can assume an importance out of all proportion to their true worth.

When I had crossed the snow I again glanced back, but there was no sign of Eric following me, and I continued on my solitary way.

Contrary to accepted mountaineering practice, I found that the easiest as well as the safest method of traversing the slabs was to keep the ice axe in the outside hand as there were always little cracks and crannies it put it in. It was a third leg to me and an invaluable companion throughout the whole of the day.

Beyond the snow patch the slabs were covered here and there with loose, powdery snow. This had to be kicked or scraped away before I dared stand on the outward-sloping ledges. Progress was slow, though steady, and as I advanced and saw the final pyramid appear above the band of rocks beneath which I was traversing, there came to me for the first time that day a thrill of excitement and hope. I was going well now, better than when I had parted from Eric, and for a moment there seemed a chance of success.

The bed of the great couloir was hidden, but a subsidiary couloir and buttress separating it from the great couloir were full in view. Both were sheltered from the wind and as a result were still heavily plastered with the snow of yesterday's blizzard. My hopes were dashed as I gazed at the buttress. It was considerably steeper than the rocks I was traversing, and snow filled every crack and was piled deeply on every sloping ledge. Was it climable in such a condition? In the Alps perhaps, but not at 28,000 feet by a man nearing the limit of his strength. And the subsidiary couloir? Even supposing the traverse of the buttress proved practicable, what kind of snow should I find in this narrow cleft? Most likely unstable powder affording no certain footing and impeding every movement. True, it might be possible to avoid it by climbing the rocks at one side, but these, in their turn, were mostly snow-covered.

Instinctively I looked for an alternative. Could I climb directly upwards to a point above the second step and attack the final pyramid without having to continue this long, wearisome and unprofitable traverse? The wall rose above me like a sea cliff, in places it overhung, and every hold, every wrinkle and crack held its quota of snow. There was no visible break in it until the buttress where there was a gap, possibly the point reached by Norton in 1924 which might prove a feasible alternative to the subsidiary couloir. At all events direct ascent was impossible. One thing alone gave me hope: once the subsidiary couloir had been climbed and the rock band passed there seemed every reason to suppose that the principal difficulties were behind. I could see the face of the final pyramid and it did not look difficult. There was a scree slope at the base of it and high a slope of light-coloured boulders. Energy alone would be required to surmount it. Of course, it may hold its surprises, for Everest will remain a stubborn opponent to the last; but I feel confident that once the rock band is below, the change from difficult and dangerous climbing to safe and easy climbing will inspire the climber to outlast fatigue and altitude over the remaining 600 feet to the summit.

The angle of the yellow band steepened gradually as I approached the great couloir. In general direction the ledges were parallel with the band, but they were not always continuous, and once or twice I had to retrace my steps for a yard or two and seek an alternative route. But the climbing was never difficult—it required only unfailing attention to the planting of each foot on the sloping ledges, especially when these were masked by loose snow.

Presently the bed of the great couloir became visible. It was shallow enough not to necessitate any steep descent into it, and was filled with snow, perhaps 30 to 40 feet wide, which ended beneath the rock band. Several hundred feet lower was a pitch of unknown height, beneath which the couloir widened out into a small hanging glacier, then fell steeply towards the Rongbuk glacier, a total height from my position of about 8,000 feet.

It was a savage place. Beyond was the steep and snowy buttress separating me from the subsidiary couloir, and hemming me in above was the unrelenting band of rock, and higher still the final pyramid, a weary distance away, cutting aloofly into the blue.

I approached the couloir along a ledge which bent round a steep little corner. This ledge was comfortably wide until it came to the corner, then it narrowed until it was only a few inches broad. As far as the corner it was easy going, but to turn the corner I had to edge along, my face to the mountain, in a crab-like fashion. The rocks above projected awkwardly, but it was not a place that would have caused a second's hesitation on an Alpine climb. One step only was needed to take me round the corner. This step I funked. The balance was too critical. With arms spread-eagled above me I sought for steadying handholds. They were not essential; balance alone should have sufficed, but I felt I could not manage without them. I could find none; every wrinkle in the rocks sloped outwards. For a few moments I stood thus like a man crucified, while my heart bumped quickly and my lungs laboured for oxygen, and there flashed through my mind the possibility of a backward topple into the couloir—an interminable slide into belated oblivion.

I retired a few yards, and apostrophised myself as a fool. I knew that the traverse was possible, and if Eric had been there I should not have hesitated. Being alone made all the difference.

I tried again, and once more found myself in the spread-eagle position but without the courage to take the one step that would have placed me in safety round the corner.

The only alternative was a ledge about 20 feet below. I was loath to lose even 20 feet of height, but there was nothing for it but to descend.

The slabs separating me from the ledge were reasonably rough, and though there were no very definite holds there were wrinkle and folds. For the rest friction should serve. Facing outwards and sitting down I lowered myself gingerly off the ledge on the palms of my hands. The friction was even better than I had hoped for, and the seat of my trousers almost sufficed by itself to maintain me in position without the additional support of the palms of my hands. There was no awkward corner in the lower ledge; it was wide and honest, and though it sloped outwards and supported a bank of snow three or four feet deep, it brought me without difficulty to the snowy bed of the couloir.

Wyn and Waggers had found the same loose, disagreeable snow in the couloir as had Norton in 1924, but I suspect that they traversed the upper ledge and so crossed higher than I. The snow at my level, as a tentative forward dig with the ice axe revealed, had been hardened by the wind and step-cutting was again necessary.

One step, then a pause to gasp, while the snow at my feet and the rocks beyond swam uncertainly before me. Then another step and another bout of gasping. The snow was very hard and the angle of the great couloir at this point fully 50°. About a dozen steps—I was across at last.

Next, how to traverse the buttress? I must climb almost straight up it for about fifty feet before continuing more or less horizontally towards the subsidiary couloir.

The rocks were steep and snow had accumulated on them untouched as yet by the wind. How had the wind swept the snow in the couloir hard and left the slabs at this side unaffected?

When these slabs are snow-free they are probably not much more difficult than the slabs to the east of the great couloir. There are numerous ledges, and though the general angle is appreciably steeper, there is no necessity for anything but balance climbing, and I confidently believe no insuperable obstacle will prevent the climber from reaching the subsidiary couloir. But now snow had accumulated deeply on the shelving ledges and it was the worst kind of snow, soft like flour, loose like granulated sugar and incapable of holding the feet in position. As I probed it with my axe, I knew at once that the game was up. So far the climbing had been more dangerous than difficult; now it was both difficult and dangerous, a fatal combination on Everest. The only thing I could do was to go as far as possible, always keeping one eye on the weather and the other on the strength I should need to retreat safely.

The weather at all events was fair. In the shelter of the buttress and the wall beyond the subsidiary couloir there was not a breath of wind and the sun shone powerfully—too powerfully, for it seemed to sap my strength and my resolution. I was a prisoner, struggling vainly to escape from a vast hollow enclosed by dungeon-like walls. Wherever I looked hostile rocks frowned down on my impotent strugglings, and the wall above seemed almost to overhang me with its dark strata set one upon the other, an embodiment of static, but pitiless, force. The final pyramid was hidden; if only I were on it, away from this dismal place with its unrelenting slabs. The climber who wins across the slabs to the final pyramid must conquer a sickness of spirit as well as a weariness of body.

With both arms at breast-high level I began shoveling the snow away before me; it streamed down the couloir behind me with a soft swishing noise. Several minutes elapsed before a sloping ledge was disclosed, then I heaved myself up, until first one knee, and then the other, were on it. In this position, like a supplicant before a priest, I had to remain while my lungs, intolerably accelerated by the effort, heaved for oxygen. Then with another effort I stood cautiously upright.

More snow had to be cleared before I could tread a smaller ledge on the slab above; then, to my relief, came a step unattended by this prodigious effort of clearing away snow. But relief is short-lived on Everest and the ledge that followed was covered several feet deep in snow beveled into a steep bank, yet without the slightest cohesion.

Presently I had to stop, as apart from the need to rest overstressed heart and lungs, immersing my arms in the snow brought such numbness to my hands, gloved though they were, that I feared I might let slip my ice axe.

So slow and exhausting was the work of clearing the snow that I began to rely on feel alone. That is to say, when I could I trusted my foot to find holds beneath the snow rather than clear the snow away from the slabs until I could see the holds. I realized full well the danger of this, and whenever possible used my ice-axe pick as an extra support by jamming it into cracks. This last precaution undoubtedly saved me from catastrophe. There was one steeply shelving slab deeply covered with soft snow into which I sank to the knees, but my first exploring foot discovered a knob beneath it. This seemed quite firm and, reaching up with my axe, I wedged the pick of it half an inch or so into a thin crack. Then, cautiously, I raised my other foot on to the knob, at the same time transferring my entire weight to my front foot. My rear foot was joining my front foot when the knob, without any warning, suddenly broke away. For an instant, both feet slid outwards, and my weight came on the ice axe; next moment I had recovered my footing and discovered another hold. It happened so quickly that my sluggish brain had no time to register a thrill of fear; I had acted purely instinctively and the incident was over almost before I knew it had occurred. I did not even feel scared afterwards as I was climbing now in a curiously detached, impersonal frame of mind. It was almost as though one part of me stood aside and watched the other struggle on. Lack of oxygen and fatigue are responsible for this dulling of the mental faculties, but principally lack of oxygen. It is a dangerous state of mind and comparable to the mental reactions of a drunken man in charge of a car. He may believe that his judgment is unimpaired, even that he can drive more skillfully than usual; in point of fact, as statistics and the police court news reveal, he is much more prone to an accident in this condition.

Just before crossing the great couloir I had looked at my watch; it was 10 A.M. Now I looked again. An hour had passed, and I had made about fifty feet of height, not more. At least 300 feet of difficult rocks, all deeply snow-covered, remained to be climbed, before easier ground on the final pyramid was reached. Perhaps I could do another hour or two's work, but what was the use of it? I should only exhaust myself completely and not have the strength left to return.

I shovelled away the floury snow until I had made a space on which I could stand, though I did not dare to sit.

I was high up on the buttress separating the great couloir form the subsidiary couloir. Above me was the band of rock beneath which I had been, and was still, traversing. It looked impregnable except where I was breached by the subsidiary couloir, and the place already mentioned a few yards to the east of this couloir. For the rest, it is Everest's greatest defence, and stretches unbroken across the north face of the mountain. The striated limestone rocks composing it actually overhang in places, and the section above the great couloir reminded me of the well-known pitch in the Central Gully, in Lliwedd, in North Wales.

It is possible, indeed probable, that weariness and altitude distorted my judgment, but there are two things I believe to be true. Firstly, that Norton's route is practicable, and that when the "tiles," as he calls the slabs, are free of snow, they can be traversed without excessive difficulty to the subsidiary couloir, and this can be climbed on to the face of the final pyramid. Secondly, that it is not a practicable route when snow covers the slabs. But there is no doubt that even in the best conditions this part of the climb will tax a climber's powers to the uttermost. The unrelenting exposure of the slabs, dependence on the friction of boot nails for hours on end, added to the physical and mental weariness and lethargy due to altitude, will require something more than strength and skill if they are to be countered successfully. The summit was just in view over the rock band. It was only 1,000 feet above me, but an aeon of weariness separated me from it. Bastion on bastion and slab on slab, the rocks were piled in tremendous confusion, their light-yellow edges ghostlike against the deep-blue sky. From the crest a white plume of mist flowed silently away, like unending volcanic steam, but where I stood there was not a breath of wind and the sun blazed into the hollow with an intense fierceness, yet without warming the cold air. Clouds were gathering, but they were thousands of feet below me. Between them, I could see the Rongbuk glacier, a pure white in its uppermost portion, then rugged and uneven where it was resolved into a multitude of séracs and, lower still, a gigantic muddle of moraines as though all the navvies in the world had been furiously excavating to no logical purpose. Beyond it, the Rongbuk valley stretched northwards towards the golden hills of Tibet, and I could make out the Rongbuk monastery, a minute cluster of minute buildings, yet distinct in every detail through the brilliantly clear atmosphere. With this one exception, I remember no details. My position was too high, my view too vast, my brain too fatigued to register detail. There was nothing visible to challenge my elevation. The earth was so far beneath, it seemed impossible I could ever regain it. The human brain must needs be divinely inspired to comprehend such a vista, and mine was tied to a body fatigued by exertion and slowed down in all its vital processes by lack of oxygen. Somervell's description of the scene is simplest and best: "A god's view."

More by instinct than anything else, I pulled my camera out of my pocket. The photograph I took is pitifully inadequate.

I cannot enlarge on the bitterness of defeat. Those who have failed on Everest are unanimous in one thing: the relief of not having to go on outweighs all other considerations. The last 1,000 feet of Everest are not for mere flesh and blood. Whoever reaches the summit, if he does it without artificial aid, will have to rise godlike above his own frailties and his tremendous environment. Only through a Power within him and without him will he overcome deadly fatigue and win through to success.

Descending even difficult ground at high altitudes is almost as easy as descending at an Apline level, and within a few minutes I regained the great couloir. Recrossing it, I halted on the broad, comfortable ledge to take a photograph. It is curious that I did not remember taking this photograph or the one from my highest point until the film was developed, so I think my action at the time was more automatic than reasoned, as before starting on the expedition I told myself many times that I must take photographs whenever possible. This lends colour to a theory I have long held, that in climbing at great altitudes, when mind and body are in the grip of an insidious lethargy, it is on the subconscious, rather than the conscious, that the climber must rely to push him forwards. Therefore, it is essential that the will to reach the summit of Everest be strengthened by a prior determination to get there. Perhaps it is not too much to say that Everest will be climbed in England.

After taking this photograph it occurred to me that I ought to eat something. I was not in the least hungry, indeed the thought of food was utterly repugnant, especially as my mouth was almost dry, and my tongue leather-like, but in duty bound I pulled a slab of mint cake from my pocket.

And now I must relate the curious incident described in "Everest 1933."

After leaving Eric a strange feeling possessed me that I was accompanied by another. I have already mentioned a feeling of detachment in which it seemed as though I stood aside and watched myself. Once before, during a fall in the Dolomites, I had the same feeling, and it is not an uncommon experience with mountaineers who have a long fall. It may be that the feeling that I was accompanied was due to this, which, in its turn, was due to lack of oxygen and the mental and physical stress of climbing alone at a great altitude. I do not offer this as an explanation, but merely as a suggestion.

This "presence" was strong and friendly. In its company I could not feel lonely, neither could I come to any harm. It was always there to sustain me on my solitary climb up the snow-covered slabs. Now, as I halted and extracted some mint cake from my pocket, it was so near and so strong that instinctively I divided the mint into two halves and turned round with one half in my hand to offer it to my "companion."

It was apparent when I recrossed the couloir that I would do better to return across the yellow band by a lower route. The angle of the band west of the first step is very slightly concave, and on such slabs a degree or two in angle makes all the difference. The western end of the band terminates below in a great cut-off, a sheer precipice which carries the eye in a single bound to the Rongbuk glacier. My return route lay a few yards above and parallel to the edge of this precipice. There was no difficulty whatsoever. Care alone was needed, especially when crossing some patches of snow which, unlike those on the upper part of the band, were treacherously soft and unstable.

Very soon I found myself below the point where I had parted from Eric, but on looking up, could see no sign of him. I now had to make the choice between climbing up at least 100 feet and joining the ascending route or of traversing directly to the camp. To ascend again at this stage was utterly distasteful. I was too tired, and my legs were leaden; they would descend easily enough to traverse horizontally, but I doubt whether I could have dragged them uphill unless hard pressed. A temptation I had to resist firmly was to slant off down the yellow band by Norton and Somervell's route. This was a far easier line than the long, wearisome traverse across a series of shelving ledges to Camp 6. In two or three hours I could have reached Camp 5, even continued on down to the comfort of the arctic tent at Camp 4. Unfortunately, Eric was waiting for me at Camp 6, and if I did not turn up he would naturally assume an accident.

The climbing was simple enough at first, but presently became more difficult. Instead of the easy slabs, which had led us upwards from the camp to the foot of the first step, I found myself on a series of narrow outward-sloping ledges separated by abrupt little walls. These ledges were never continuous for long, and it was necessary when one petered out to descend to another. However, I could still afford to lose height without descending below the level of Camp 6.

This route took me across the band some distance below the place where Wyn and Waggers found the ice axe, but I did not see any further traces of Mallory and Irvine. I remember glancing down at a wide, gently sloping expanse of snow, screes and broken rocks below the band and thinking that if the ice axe indeed marked the point where they slipped, it was possible that their bodies might have come to rest there.

Some of the ledges were wider than others, and I paused to rest at intervals. It was during one of these halts that I was startled to observe an extraordinary phenomenon.

Chancing to look over the north-east shoulder, now directly in front of me, I saw two dark objects in the sky. In shape they resembled kite balloons, and my first reaction was to wonder what on earth kite balloons could be doing near Everest, a certain proof that lack of oxygen had impaired my mental faculties; but a moment later I recognized this as an absurd thought. At the same time I was very puzzled. The objects were black and silhouetted sharply against the sky, or possibly a background of cloud; my memory is not clear on this point. They were bulbous in shape, and one possessed what looked like squat, under-developed wings, whist the other had a beak-like protuberance like the spout of a tea kettle. But what was most weird about them was that they distinctly pulsated with an in-and-out motion as though they possessed some horrible quality of life. One interesting point is that these pulsations were much slower than my own heart-beats; of this I am certain, and I mention it in view of a suggestion put forward afterwards that it was an optical illusion and that the apparent pulsations synchronized with my pulse-rate.

After my first reaction of "kite balloons" my brain seemed to function normally, and so interested was I that, believing them to be fantasies of my imagination, I deliberately put myself through a series of mental tests. First of all I looked away. The objects did not follow my vision, but when my gaze returned to the north-east shoulder they were still hovering there. I looked away again, and by way of a more exacting mental test identified by name a number of peaks, valleys and glaciers. I found no difficulty in Chö-oyu, Gaychung Kang, Pumori and the Rongbuk glacier, but when I again looked back the objects were in precisely the same position.

.

Nothing was to be gained by further examination and, tired as I was with the apparently endless succession of slabs, I decided to carry on to Camp 6. I was just starting off when a mist, forming suddenly, began to drift across the north-east shoulder. Gradually the objects disappeared behind it. Soon they were vague shadows, then, as the mist thickened, they disappeared altogether. The mist only lasted a few seconds, then melted away. I expected to see the objects again, but they were no longer there; they had disappeared as mysteriously as they came.

Was it an optical illusion or a mirage? It may be of interest to state that my height was about 27,600 feet, and that the objects were a few degrees above the north-east ridge about half-way between the position of the 1924 Camp 6 and the crest of the north-east shoulder. This gives their height as about 27,200 feet, and a line connecting me with them would have ended, not in a background of sky, but of clouds and mountains. It is possible, therefore, that imagination magnified some strange effect of mist, mountain and shadow, yet whatever they were, it was a strange and altogether uncanny experience.

The first light mist was a forerunner of other mists which quickly gathered and drifted across the mountainside, concealing familiar landmarks. It might not be easy to find Camp 6 among the wilderness of slabs in a mist, and I began to feel anxious, especially as I could not see the tent. Fortunately, however, two prominent towers on the northeast ridge, which I knew were directly above the camp, showed now and then.

In places the sandstone slabs were intersected horizontally by slippery belts of quartzite. The first intimation I had as to how slippery they were was when I lowered myself down a steep little wall on to an outward-sloping quartzite ledge. It was far more slippery than the sandstone ledges, and I did not dare trust my bootnails upon it. There was no alternative but to climb up to a sandstone ledge, and this ascent, though it cannot have been more than 20 feet, made me realize how tired I was.

Presently the two rock towers were almost immediately above me and I halted and looked round expectancy for the camp. It was still not visible. Was I above it or below it? Had my route-finding been at fault? All about me was a vast labyrinth of outward-dipping slabs. Now and then a puff of icy mist would float out of space and pass djinn-like put the mountainside to the crest of the north-east ridge where it shredded out and rushed away to join in the ceaselessly moving vapour that boiled upwards and outwards from the south-east precipice.

A few more steps. There was something familiar now about the rocks. Suddenly I came to a shallow, gently sloping gully filled with snow. There were footmarks in the snow; it was the gully immediately above the camp. Next instant I saw the little tent snugly bedded in a corner; small wonder I had not seen it before. What a relief! I let out a hoarse croak of joy and quickly scrambled down to it.

Eric was there. It scarcely needed a word on my part to tell him of my failure; he had seen enough to gauge the conditions. He had descended without difficulty and his stomach was much better. We both talked in whispers, for my mouth and throat had been dried up by the cold air. A hot drink was the first thing; I had not known how thirsty I was, for the intense desiccation of high altitudes takes the body a stage beyond the mere sensation of thirst. And the warmth of it; there was life in that drink.

We discussed plans. Now that we had failed our one desire was for comfort, and there was no comfort at Camp 6. Eric was well rested and strong enough to descend to Camp 5; I, on the other hand, felt very tired; that hour of climbing beyond the great couloir had taken it out of me more than many hours of ordinary climbing. We agreed, therefore, that Eric should descend whilst I remained at Camp 6 and descended next morning. It was not a good arrangement; men should not separate on Everest, but another miserable night wedged together in that little tent was not to be borne.

An hour later, at about 1:30 P.M. Eric left. The weather was fast deteriorating; mists had formed above and below and a rising wind was beginning to raise the powdery snow from the face of the mountain. For a few minutes I watched him methodically traversing the sloping shelf, following Jack Longland's descending route; then a corner hid him from sight and I lay back in my sleeping-bag for a much-needed rest.

For the next hour I lay semi-comatose from fatigue; I may even have slept. Then I became suddenly conscious of the tent shuddering violently in a high wind. The rest had refreshed me greatly and my brain was beginning to reassert itself over my tired body. I unlaced the tent flaps and looked outside. A blizzard was blowing; nothing was to be seen but a few yards of slabs over which the snow-laden gusts rushed and twisted. Rapidly the wind increased. I could feel the little tent rising and straining against the guy ropes, and in between the thudding and cracking of its sorely stressed cloth hear salvoes of driven snow spattering viciously against it.

Eric? I was very anxious. He must be having a horrible descent. He would do it all right; he was not one to associate with mountaineering accidents; his calm, detached confidence was a passport to safety in itself. Still, I could not rid myself of anxiety or of a succession of futile yet worrying pictures that flashed through my mind: snow and wind; wind, relentless, battering, snow-filled wind; wind as cold as death; and a lonely, toiling, ice-encrusted figure.

Toward sundown the wind fell appreciably and the clouds blew clear of Everest. Again I looked outside. Every other peak was concealed beneath a roof of clouds stretching in every direction. At that level a tempestuous wind was blowing and now and then a mass seethed upwards as though violently impelled from below and shriveled into nothingness. The sky above was blue-green, never have I seen a colder colour, and the declining sun was entirely without warmth. Now and then little twisting devils of winddriven snow scurried past: small wonder that the Tibetan believes in a cold hell; here were its very flames licking across the slabs of Chamalung.

There was little fuel left and half of it went to cook my supper. It was 6 P.M. when I had finished. I exulted in my comfort. There were now two lots of sleeping-bags to keep me warm and I was soon snug with enough below me to defeat the sharpest stone. It did not occur to me that I was spending a night higher than any other human being; I was purely animal in my desire for warmth and comfort. Neither did I feel in the least lonely; in this respect it seemed as natural to spend a night alone in a tent at 27,400 feet as in a hotel at sea-level.

I remember nothing more until the following morning. Something heavy was pressing on me when I awoke, and I was astonished to find a snowdrift covering the lower half of my body, reaching almost to the ridge of the tent. How had it got there? Then I remembered a small hole which Eric and I had accidentally burnt in the side of the tent during our cooking operations. It was only an inch or so in diameter, yet large enough for the powdery snow to pour ceaselessly through all night like sand through an hour glass, gathering in a drift which filled nearly a quarter of the tent. There must have been a more than usually severe blizzard.*

I looked at my watch: 7 A.M.; I had slept the clock round for the first time since leaving the Base Camp, if not for the first time during the whole expedition. And I was greatly refreshed; as long as I lay without moving I felt almost as though I were at sea-level; my heart was beating slowly, steadily and rhythmically, and my brain was more active than it had been since leaving Camp 4. Perhaps I might be able to settle once and for all the vexed question of the second step before descending to Camp 4. With this idea in my mind I heaved myself up into a sitting position and began energetically to push away the snow. Instantly the familiar panting supervened, and at the same moment I was aware of the intense cold, the greatest cold I remember during the expedition. Within a few seconds sensation had left my hands and I had to push them into the sleeping-bag and put them between my thighs.

---

*The weather both at Camps 5 and 4 was very violent that night.

The sun had not reached the tent, possibly it was behind clouds, and it was useless to think of doing anything until it arrived. It struck the tent a few minutes later, and putting on my gloves I rummaged among the snow for fuel and provisions; it was some time before I found a tin, the last tin, of solid methylated and could prepare a cupful of café-au-lait. I loathed the sight of food, but I managed to force some down. Then I looked outside. One glance was sufficient: even if I had the strength or inclination (and the latter was now at low ebb) for a reconnaissance, the appearance of the weather, to say nothing of the lack of fuel, made an immediate descent imperative. High grey clouds were stealing out of the west and overhead a formless murk was gathering in which the sun was struggling with fast diminishing power, whilst the freshly fallen snow had a dull, lifeless look. Another blizzard was brewing.

The K2 Mystery

DAVID ROBERTS

Climber and writer David Roberts goes back in time to chronicle a 1939 expedition on K2, the world's second highest mountain located in Kashmir. The expedition was led by German-born Fritz Wiessner, considered by many the greatest climber of his time and who hoped to be the first to reach the summit of this angry mountain. Neither Wiessner nor any of his climbing companions reached the summit, though it's thought that Wiessner turned back a mere 750 feet from the summit. It was a feat that should have been hailed, but tragedy awaited them on the descent when four members of their party died. The deaths greatly tarnished Wiessner's reputation and when Roberts wrote this story in 1984 he was trying to find out what really happened.

I t was July 19, 1939. At nine o'clock that morning, Fritz Wiessner and Sherpa Pasang Lama had left Camp IX at 26,000 feet on K2, the second-highest mountain in the world. All day long they had moved upward on slopes of snow, ice, and rock that had never before been climbed. Neither man used oxygen.

Throughout the day, Wiessner had stayed in the lead. At age thirty-nine, he was in the best shape of his life. And at that moment in history, there was no better mountaineer anywhere in the world.

Some of the climbing had been extraordinarily difficult, considering the altitude. With his crampons, ice axe, and handful of pitons, Wiessner had mastered, in succession, a couloir of black ice, a short overhand of iced-up rock, and two rope lengths of broken rock covered with a treacherous skin of ice called verglas. The air was still, however, and Wiessner had been able to take off his gloves and do the hardest moves bare-handed.

Now he made a short traverse to the left, then climbed twenty-five feet up a very demanding wall of rock. At the top of this section, he hammered in two pitons for security. With growing elation, he surveyed the terrain above. The wall continued for another twenty-five feet that, while difficult, lay back at a lower angle than the rock he had just climbed. He knew he could get up this obstacle without much trouble. Above the rock, there was an apparently easy snow slope leading to the summit. It was late afternoon. The two men had reached an altitude of more than 27,500 feet. At the very most, the top of K2 stood only 750 feet higher.

In that moment, Fritz Wiessner stood on the threshold of a deed that, had he accomplished it, might today be regarded as the single most outstanding triumph in the long history of mountaineering. By 1939, none of the highest peaks in the world had been climbed. Only the year before, the seventh major expedition to Everest had been defeated some 2000 feet below the summit, and a strong American effort on K2 had turned back at 26,000 feet. Many experts had begun to doubt that the highest mountains would ever be conquered without oxygen. There are fourteen peaks in the Himalaya that exceed 8000 meters in height. Success on an "eight-thousander" was to become the four-minute mile of climbing. Not until 1950, with the French on Annapurna, was the feat accomplished. Everest was not to be climbed until 1953; K2, not until the year after.

But that July day in 1939, Wiessner and Pasang Lama had K2 in their grasp. It would mean coming down in the night, but the weather was holding splendidly, and the moon would be out, and the two men were in superb condition. Wiessner had no qualms about descending the easy ridge from the summit during the night, if necessary.

He began to move up the last twenty-five feet of the wall. There was a tug at his waist as the rope came tight. Turning to look at his partner, Wiessner saw Pasang smile almost apologetically. As a Buddhist Lama, Pasang believed that angry spirits lurked about the summit at night. "No sahib, tomorrow," said the Sherpa.

When he saw that his companion's resolve could not be shaken, Wiessner thought for a moment about unroping and going for the summit alone. In 1939, however, the ethics of climbing prevented a leader from leaving his partner. But there were twelve days' worth of food and fuel at Camp IX, and the good weather looked as though it would stay forever. He gave in and agreed to descend. The next day would surely bring success.

Never again would Wiessner reach such a height on K2. Instead of claiming a great triumph, he would find himself embroiled for the rest of his life in one of the bitterest controversies in mountaineering history. For reasons that remain unclear today, the camps that had been so carefully supplied as the team moved up the mountain had been systematically stripped—the sleeping bags were removed and much of the food thrown out in the snow. As an indirect result of this catastrophe, four members of the 1939 expedition perished on K2. Wiessner returned to the United States not to be laurelled for his heroic attempt on the great mountain, but to be plunged into the unjust opprobrium of his peers.

Fritz Wiessner turned 84 this February. He still rock climbs regularly at a creditable standard. His long career has been crowned with achievement, both in and out of the mountains, and with deep happiness. Toward other climbers, Wiessner has always maintained a generous and magnanimous stance. For several generations of mountaineers all over the world, he has become a hero.

But K2 remains the great disappointment of his life, and when he talks about it his voice shakes with the sense of betrayal that has lingered in his memory of that expedition for the last forty-five years.

Part I: The Mountain And The Climber

K2 stands at the head of the Baltoro Glacier in the Karakoram of Pakistan, some 900 miles northwest of Everest. Seen from a distance, it is a striking, pyramidal peak, more beautiful than Everest, just as it is the harder ascent. The mountain was first attempted in 1902 by a small party that included the redoubtable Oscar Eckenstein, and again in 1909 by an Italian team led by the brilliant explorer Luigi Amedeo, Duke of the Abruzzi. Both parties had to turn back a little above 21,000 feet, nowhere near the 28,250-foot summit; but for such an early era, both expeditions were remarkable efforts.

The mountain was not attempted again until 1938, when a small but strong American party of four made a late but bold assault on the Abruzzi Ridge, the line first tried by the Italians. Paul Petzoldt, a cowboy from Wyoming, and Charles Houston, a Harvard-educated medical student, pushed up to 26,000 feet before having to quit. This expedition, too, had been an exceptional feat. Wiessner's attempt would be next.

His credentials were superb; born in Dresden in 1900, he had done his first climbs as a teenager in the Elbsteingebirge, the cluster of intimidating sandstone pinnacles near the banks of the river Elbe. In the second decade of this century, probably the hardest pure rock climbs in the world were done on these towers by Wiessner and his cronies, a fact not broadly recognized until the 1960s, thanks to the subsequent isolation of East Germany from the mainstream of climbing culture.

After World War I Wiessner moved on to the Alps, where he made some of the finest first ascents of the 1920s. Two of his most memorable were the southeast wall of the Fleischbank, which a German commentator later called "the great problem of its time," and the oft-attempted north wall of the Furchetta. In 1932 Wiessner went on his first Himalayan expedition, a pioneering effort on Nanga Parbat, where he reached 23,000 feet.

By 1929 Wiessner had emigrated to the United States, where he ran a very successful chemical business. He began climbing with American friends, in effect teaching them what European alpinism was all about. As Wiessner's latter-day friend Richard Goldstone puts it, "He probably went down a little bit in standard from what he had done in Germany when he came to the U.S. But he was so far ahead of the people here, they didn't understand what he was doing."

One of Wiessner's finest American accomplishments was the first ascent of Devils Tower in Wyoming in 1937, on which he led all the hard pitches. (Goldstone: "Fritz took along his standard three pitons. He basically soloed it.") Another was the first ascent of Mount Waddington in British Columbia's Coast Range, certainly the hardest climb yet completed in North America.

It was Wiessner, in 1937, who first won official permission for an American expedition to K2, but business commitments prevented his going to Pakistan the next summer. Charles Houston took over the leadership of the 1938 expedition, while Wiessner retained permission for 1939, should Houston's party not reach the summit.

As he began planning for the 1939 expedition, Wiessner was disappointed that none of the four veterans from the previous year's attempt could go again. By spring he had recruited two other first-rank mountaineers, one of whom had led the second ascent of Mount McKinley. Only four weeks before the team's departure, however, both had to back out.

The remaining party was so weak that Wiessner pondered postponing the attempt for another year. But the American Alpine Club urged him to persevere, and so the team sailed for Europe in late spring. Two of the members, Chappell Cranmer and George Sheldon, were twenty-one-year-old Dartmouth students. Eaton Cromwell had made many climbs in the Alps and Canada, but none of great difficulty; he was now forty-two years old. Dudley Wolfe, at forty-four, was a strong skier and alpinist but had little technical experience. After the team had embarked, an AAC mentor persuaded twenty-eight-year-old Jack Durrance, a Teton guide and one of the country's best climbers, to join the expedition. To Wiessner's great surprise, Durrance showed up in Genoa with an explanatory letter from the well-meaning AAC executive.

"I was a little worried then," says Wiessner today. "I knew Jack as a great sportsman, and I knew he was strong. He had done some climbing in Munich when he lived there, and he had good climbs in the Tetons. But I also knew he was very competitive, which might cause troubles. Actually, at that time I liked Durrance, and hoped he could do well."

Wiessner lives in retirement on an idyllic country estate in Stowe, Vermont. He is a short man, perhaps five feet five. He looks extremely fit, and the barrel chest and strong arms of his best days are still in evidence. His bald pate and great-browed forehead dominate his expressive face: as he talks, strong wrinkles delineate his forehead, and his eyebrows arch with meaning. He speaks in a clear, emphatic voice, still heavy with a German accent. His manners and bearing breathe old-world civility; his smile could conquer a drawing room. But he is equally captivating when he conjures up the troubles of the past. And the troubles in 1939 began when Wiessner and Durrance met.

"After we had reached base camp," Wiessner says, "and were on our first trip up the glacier, I wanted to check a little bit on safety and roping. We had two ropes. Soon Jack's rope started to put up speed, trying to go faster than the others. Cromwell and Wolfe said to me, 'What's up? Do we have to do this running?' When we got back to base camp, I gave a long talk. I said, 'Look, fellows, I can tell you right now, we will never climb this mountain if there's competition between the members. Get it out of your head. We have to work really hard and work together.' Jack didn't say anything, but seemed to agree."

Nevertheless, during the first five weeks above base camp the expedition went much as planned. The 1939 party had the advantage of knowing where the 1938 camps had been placed and, in some of them, benefited from rock platforms that had been built the previous year. Slowly a logistical ladder of supplies was constructed up the mountain. The Sherpas were tremendously useful in stocking the camps. Each camp was equipped with three sleeping bags, air mattresses, stoves, and gasoline. "I believed," says Wiessner, "that if you climb a mountain like this, you want to be sure, if something goes wrong or somebody gets ill, you can hold out for at least two weeks in any camp. If a man had to come down in very bad weather, he ought to be able to just fall into a tent, and everything would be there."

But in other respects, Wiessner insisted on a spartan, lightweight style. Oxygen was standard on Everest, but Wiessner refused even to bring it to base camp on K2. "My ideal has always been free climbing," he explains. "I hated mechanical means. I didn't even want walkie-talkies on the mountain."

Even as the chain of supplies was being built up, some of the climbers were having trouble. Because of his late inclusion in the party, Durrance had to wait for his high-altitude boots, specially made in Munich, to arrive. Cranmer almost immediately came down with a serious illness, probably pulmonary or cerebral edema. At base camp, Durrance, who was a medical student, nursed him back to health. According to Wiessner, Cromwell had the idea that being up high for very long was unhealthy, and soon he too wanted to go down. Wiessner suspects that these worries, continually expressed, made Durrance apprehensive. Sheldon got chilblains on his toes and went no higher than Camp IV. Among the sahibs, only Dudley Wolfe kept up fully with the high-altitude work of Wiessner and the best Sherpas.

Once Durrance's boots had arrived, he started eagerly up the route with Wiessner and Wolfe. Carrying loads to Camp VI, however, he began to move very slowly. On July 12, after five days of storm, Wiessner, Wolfe, and Durrance, with seven Sherpas, prepared to ferry supplies from VI to VII. Says Wiessner, "A very short distance above VI, Jack told me, 'Fritz, something is wrong with me. I am ill. Maybe I am not well-enough adjusted to the altitude. I will go back to VI and come up tomorrow and or the next day.'" Durrance turned around and descended to Camp VI.

Wiessner, Wolfe, and three Sherpas stayed at VII. The others returned with Durrance to VI, planning to bring more supplies the next day. But on July 14, instead of coming up with loads, Durrance retreated down the mountain. Even more unfortunately, from Wiessner's perspective, Durrance took two Sherpas with him, including the most experienced, Pasang Kikuli, who had been ear-marked for a summit attempt but was suffering from frostbite. Wiessner's purist refusal to use walkie-talkie radios meant that he now had no way of communicating with Durrance, who did not stop until he was all the way down to Camp II.

The advance guard pushed on and established Camp VIII at 25,300 feet. From there, Wiessner sent two Sherpas down to VII to meet up with the anticipated contingent of Durrance and several Sherpas. Left at VIII were Wolfe, Pasang Lama, and Wiessner. After two days of storm, this trio set out upward again, but immediately got bogged down in extremely deep, loose snow. Wiessner literally had to swim through the drifts. Wolfe, the heaviest of the three, exhausted himself trying to flounder up a trough Wiessner had plowed in the drifts. He decided to return to camp and make another attempt the next day with the others. (Loose, new-fallen snow often compacts after a day of sun.)

Wiessner and Pasang Lama pushed on and established Camp IX. For security, they built a rock wall completely around the tent. The next day, July 19, they made their first attempt on the summit. It ended when Pasang, afraid of the coming night, refused to let out any more rope. "No, sahib, tomorrow!" he pleaded, and Wiessner gave in.

On the way down, as Pasang rappelled over a cliff, the rope got entangled in the crampons on the back of his pack—he was carrying both men's pairs. With a furious effort, the Sherpa got the rope loose, but the crampons came loose too. Wiessner watched with a sinking heart as they bounced away into the void. The descent grew more difficult, and only at 2:30 A.M. did the men regain Camp IX. To Wiessner's consternation, no one had arrived from below.

Nevertheless, the camp was well stocked and the weather continued to be perfect. Wiessner had decided on an easier alternative for the second attempt. It was a route up a gully that he had planned originally, but had given up when avalanches from an immense ice cliff near the summit had roared over it. On July 18, on their climb up to Camp IX, Wiessner and Pasang Lama had crossed the one-hundred-foot-wide track of such an avalanche, and this had led Wiessner to choose the more difficult rock-and-ice route of the first attempt. In the middle of that attempt, however, he had had a good view of the alternative route, and could see that no more avalanches were likely to come down for some time, and so the gully route was now safe.

The men rested the whole next day. I was so warm in the thin air that Wiessner sunbathed naked! At 6 A.M. on July 21—three hours earlier than their previous attempt—the two men left Camp IX to go for the summit. The alternative route lay over hard snow that had turned, in the sun, to ice. The loss of the crampons came home with a vengeance. In the crucial gully, as Wiessner later wrote, "With crampons, we could have practically run up it, but as it was we would have had to cut 300 or 400 steps. At these heights that would have taken more than a day." Once again the two men descended to Camp IX.

Wiessner was still quite confident of making the summit, however. The team members coming up in support would undoubtedly have crampons, as well as more provisions. Thinking his teammates were probably ensconced at Camp VIII, Wiessner decided to go down on July 22 to pick up Wolfe, more food and gas, and the all-important crampons. Pasang carried his sleeping bag down, but Wiessner, certain he would return, left his in the tent at Camp IX.

Without crampons, the descent was tricky, especially since the Tricouni nails (which climbers used on the soles of their boots in the days before Vibrams) had been worn dull on both men's footgear. "Pasang was behind me," recalls Wiessner. "I should have had him in front, but then I would have had to explain to him how to cut steps. I had just got my axe ready to make a few scrapes, when suddenly he fell off. I noticed immediately, because he made a funny little noise. I put myself in position, dug in as much as possible, and held him on the rope. If I hadn't been in good shape, hadn't climbed all those 4000-meter peaks in the Alps, I wouldn't have had the technique to hold him." Wiessner makes such a belay sound routine, but it was a difficult feat.

At VIII, Wiessner had expected to find Durrance and the other Sherpas with their precious loads. Instead, Dudley Wolfe was there alone. He was overjoyed to see Wiessner, but furious that no one had come up from below. He had run out of matches two days before and had been able to drink only a little meltwater that had run off a ground cloth.

By now Wiessner was utterly perplexed by the absence of reinforcement from below. At Camp VII, however, he knew the bulk of the reserve food had already been cached. With a quick trip down to VII for supplies, the three men could still probably climb K2 without any help from below. Wiessner could use Wolfe's pair of crampons to lead the ice.

So on July 23 the trio started down to VII. Wolfe, not the most graceful of climbers even on his good days, was tied in to the middle of the rope. Pasang Lama was ten or fifteen feet in front, Wiessner the same distance in the rear. Once again the snow got icy, and Wiessner had to go first to cut steps. As he leaned over in a precarious position, Wolfe accidentally stepped on the rope. The jolt pulled Wiessner off.

"I immediately called back, 'Check me! Check me!' " Wiessner remembers. "Nothing happened. Then the rope came tight to Dudley, and he was pulled off. The rope tightened to Pasang behind, and he too came off. We were all three sliding down, and I got going very fast and somersaulted.

"I had no fear. All I was thinking was, how stupid this has to happen like this. Here we are, we can still do the mountain, and we have to lose out in this silly way and get killed forever. I didn't think about family, and of course I was never a believer in Dear old God.

"But getting pulled around by the somersault and being first on the rope, it gave me a little time. I still had my ice axe—I always keep a sling around my wrist—and just in that moment the snow got a little softer. I had my axe ready and worked very had with it. With my left hand I got hold of the rope, and eventually I got a stance, kicked in quickly, and leaned against the axe. Then bang! A fantastic pull came. I was holding it well, but it tore me down. But at that time I was a fantastically strong man—if I had a third of it today I would be very happy. I stood there and I wanted to stop that thing. I must have done everything right, and the luck was there too."

Wiessner's belay has become the stuff of legend. Very few men in all of mountaineering history have performed the like: having already been pulled off a slope, to recover, gain a stance, and, with only the pick of an ice axe for purchase, to stop the otherwise fatal falls of three men roped together.

The men made their way on down to Camp VII at 24,700 feet. There they received an incomprehensible shock. Not only was there no one in camp: The tents had been left with the doors open. One was full of snow, the other half-collapsed. The provisions that had been so carefully carried up nine days before lay wantonly strewn about in the snow. Most of the food was missing, as were all the sleeping bags.

Utterly dismayed and confounded, the three men cleaned out one tent and repitched it. It was too late to go farther down. With one sleeping bag and no air mattresses, they huddled through a bitterly cold night. In the morning the weather was raw and windy. Wolfe decided to stay with the one bag at Camp VII while Wiessner and Pasang went down to VI. Despite all their setbacks, the trio was still of a mind to push upward. Surely there would be sleeping bags and food still at VI, and there ought to be at least six Sherpas there as well.

On July 23 the two men headed down. At VI they found only a dump of two unpitched tents and some provisions: again the sleeping bags and air mattresses were gone. Grimly Wiessner and Pasang continued the descent. Camp V, IV, III . . . still no sleeping bags. At nightfall, the men reached Camp II, supposedly the best-provisioned camp on the mountain. No sleeping bags! Utterly worn out, Wiessner and Pasang took down one tent and wrapped themselves up in it while they tried to sleep in the other. Their fingers and toes froze, and they got no sleep.

By the time the two men reached the level glacier the next day, they were dragging themselves along, often falling. Wiessner recalls the effort: "We were so exhausted. We would go 100 or 200 meters, then sit down a little. Suddenly we look, and there comes a party up the glacier. It was Cromwell with some Sherpas. My throat had gotten very sore, and I could hardly speak, but I was mad enough. I asked him, 'What is the idea?' "

"He told me they had given us up for dead. He was just out looking to see if he could find any sign of anything on the glacier. I said, "This is really an outrage. Wolfe will sue you for your neglect.' We went on to base camp. The cook and the liaison officer came out and embraced me and took me to my tent. Pasang Kikuli and all the Sherpas came and embraced me. But Durrance didn't come for about half an hour.

"When he did, I said immediately, "What happened to our supplies? Who took all the sleeping bags down? And why were they taken down?' Durrance said, 'Well, the Sherpas . . . ' It was blamed on the Sherpas."

It is a measure of Wiessner's intense commitment to K2 that even after such a colossal setback, he still had hopes of making another attempt on the summit. All that was needed to rebuild the logistical ladder, he reasoned, was to get the sleeping bags back into the camps and to bolster the food supplies above. Also, Dudley Wolfe was waiting alone at Camp VII. On July 26, Durrance and three Sherpas set out, hoping to climb all the way up to VII. Wiessner planned to follow in two days, after recuperating from his ordeal.

Durrance, however, could go only as far as Camp IV before altitude sickness forced him down again on the third day. He left two Sherpas at IV, with instructions to go up to VII and explain matters to Wolfe. Meanwhile, Wiessner had not recovered from his debilitating descent, and Pasang Lama was in even worse shape. When Durrance reappeared, Wiessner realized that at last all hope of climbing K2 had to be abandoned. It remained only to bring Wolfe down.

Despite his exhausted state, Wiessner wanted to try to climb up to VII himself, but Pasang Kikuli dissuaded him, saying he himself would go up to get Wolfe and bring him down. Instead, on July 29, Kikuli and another Sherpa went all the way from base camp to VI—a gain of 6800 feet—in a single day. This feat of fortitude remains virtually unmatched in Himalayan history. On the way, Kikuli picked up the two Sherpas who had been left by Durrance at Camp IV.

The next day, this rescue team of four found Wolfe in a bad state. He had lost, it seemed, the will to live. Again he had run out of matches, and he had lain apathetically in his bag without eating. He had gown so lethargic, in fact, that he had not left the tent to defecate. The Sherpas tried to rouse him, but he declared that he needed another day of rest before he could make the descent. Without sleeping bags, the Sherpas could not stay at VII, so they went down to VI, determined to try to prod Wolfe into descending the next day. A storm intervened, and it was not until the day after, July 31, that Pasang Kikuli, Pinsoo, and Kita started out again to climb up to VII. They left Tsering alone in VI with orders to have tea ready.

At base camp, little could be known of the doings high on the mountain. Through binoculars Durrance had seen three figures cross the snow just below Camp VII. Finally, on August 2, a terrified Tsering returned to base alone. On July 31 he had brewed tea and waited. No one had come the rest of the day, nor all of the next day. After that, he could wait no longer.

Wiessner made one more attempt to go up the route. He left on August 3, with two Sherpas, and it took him two days to "drag" himself, in his own phrase, to Camp II. On August 5 a full-scale storm broke, dumping twelve inches of snow and ending any further hopes of rescue. On August 7 the expedition turned its back on K2.

The fate of Dudley Wolfe, Pasang Kikli, Pinsoo, and Kitar has never been determined. It may be that the Sherpas reached Wolfe, and all four men perished in an avalanche or in a roped fall like the one Wiessner had barely managed to stop. No trace of any of the four has ever been found.

Part II: Aftermath

During Wiessner's absence in the middle of July, the mood at base camp had worsened. Sheldon, Cranmer, and Cromwell wanted nothing more than to head for home. In the end Cranmer and Cromwell left early, leaving Wiessner and Durrance to bring up the rear as the expedition left the Baltoro Glacier for good.

"We were together every day," says Wiessner. "Durrance looked after me as if I were a baby. He made pancakes for me. And every day we talked. I just couldn't comprehend what had happened on the mountain. 'I don't understand it, Jack,' I told him, 'why those sleeping bags were taken out after all our agreements.' He kept answering, 'It was a matter of those Sherpas.'

"I kept asking him. Finally, he stood there and shouted, 'Ah, Fritz! Stop it! Stop it! We have talked about it long enough.'"

Once the men reached civilization, they parted. World War II had broken out. Wiessner traveled from Karachi to Port Said, then took a liner back to the United States. Durrance traveled in the other direction, across the Pacific. The two men would not set eyes on each other again until thirty-nine years had passed.

Upon his return, Wiessner went into a hospital in New York City. His many nights out on K2 had caused severe arthritic problems in his knees. He was bedridden for six weeks. Durrance came to New York City, stayed in a hotel, and sent some belongings to Wiessner in the hospital. He never paid a visit.

In his bed, Wiessner brooded about the stripped camps. He had talked not only to Durrance but to the Sherpas. They tended to blame Tendrup, one of their younger men. Gradually Wiessner deduced that, after he had parted with Durrance on July 14, something like the following chain of events must have unfolded.

Durrance had immediately descended to Camp II, taking with him Pasang Kikuli and another Sherpa. This left two Sherpas at Camp VI, who were soon joined by the two sent down by Wiessner. Kikuli had appointed Tendrup the leader of this group of four. Their orders were to carry loads to Camps VII and VIII in support of the summit effort.

Tendrup, however, came down with Kitar from a ferry to Camp VII, claiming that he was sure the three men in the lead had been killed in an avalanche and urging all the Sherpas to descend at once. The other two Sherpas refused to go along with the story and stayed put in Camp VI. Tendrup and Kitar descended to IV, where they ran into Pasang Kikuli, who angrily ordered them back up the mountain. So the pair made another foray up to VII. There they yelled up toward VIII, but got no answer. The silence added credibility to Tendrup's avalanche story, and the four Sherpas broke open Camp VII, scattering the supplies on the snow—exactly why remains problematic—before heading down the mountain with the sleeping bags from VI and VII. At base camp, the other Sherpas called Tendrup a devil who wanted to wreck the expedition. Wiessner concluded, however, that Tendrup was not so much malevolent as lazy—that he had invented the avalanche story to get out of carrying loads. Even so, this explained only the missing bags at VI and VII. Why had the lower camps also been stripped? Wiessner puzzled over this point for days. Then, he says, among his personal papers from the expedition, he came across a note he had earlier overlooked. It had been left for him by Durrance at Camp II on July 19. According to Wiessner, the note congratulated him and Wolfe for making the summit, then explained that the day before (July 18, on the eve of Wiessner and Pasang Lama's first summit attempt) he had ordered the bags from the higher camp and from Camps IV and II—thirteen bags in all—taken down to base, in anticipation of the expedition's departure and to save valuable equipment. The implication was that Durrance assumed Wiessner, Wolfe, and Pasang Lama would be bringing their own bags down all the way from Camp IX. When Wiessner had found this note at Camp II, he had been too exhausted and emotionally overwrought to make sense of it. Now, in the hospital, it supplied the missing piece to the puzzle.

Wiessner says today, "As I told others, I had no ill feelings against Durrance, but I thought a man should be honest. If only he had come to me and said, 'I'm sorry, Fritz, I made a mistake. I meant the best. I wanted to save the sleeping bags,' I would have accepted this without hard feelings." But Durrance never communicated with Wiessner.

According to Wiessner, he deposited the all-important note in the files of the American Alpine Club. When he later tried to locate it, it was gone. Assuming Wiessner's interpretation is correct, what could have possessed Durrance to pull out support so flagrantly behind the summit trio? The defeatist mood of base camp must have contributed to a shared impatience to go home. Moreover, the sleeping bags were the most valuable gear on the expedition. If indeed Wiessner, Wolfe, and Pasang Lama had made the summit and descended without mishap, they would probably have brought their own sleeping bags with them, obviating the need for the bags in the intermediate camps. Sitting at base camp day after day with no news from above is a vexing business: the mind all too easily begins to invent theories about the maneuvers out of sight above. More than one Himalayan leader has felt the urge to pull out and go home while the advance guard was still high on the mountain. But another suggestion with respect to K2 is that everyone at base camp had given Wiessner's party up for dead and the survivors were retrieving the equipment. Cromwell had virtually admitted this when he had found Wiessner and Pasang Lama staggering across the glacier.

What was done was done. The loss of four men on K2 was a deep tragedy, but Wiessner's extraordinary feat in reaching 27,500 feet without oxygen, with no strong teammates except the Sherpas, ought to have been widely hailed for its excellence. Instead, one of the sorriest chapters in American climbing politics was about to unfold.

The American Alpine Club launched an investigation of the expedition, headed by some of the most distinguished men in American mountaineering. Ostensibly, their purpose was to "point the way towards a greater control of the risks undertaken in climbing great mountains." But the investigation report made some patronizing conclusions. It claimed that the expedition's "human administration seems to have been weak"; that there was "no clear understanding" of plans between Durrance and Wiessner when they parted; that it was an "error in judgment" to leave Sherpas alone in the middle camps; and that an ill climber (presumably Wolfe, who was not in fact ill) should not have been left alone to make his own decisions. The brunt of all these criticisms fell on Wiessner. Correspondingly, the committee gave Durrance's actions an implicit but total whitewash. The club sent a letter to members summarizing the report and ended by congratulating itself for the investigation, with its "valuable contribution" in the way of guidance "if Himalayan expeditions are undertaken again."

There were two significant calls of dissent. One came from Al Lindley, the strong mountaineer who had had to back out of K2 shortly before the party left for Pakistan. Lindley argued cogently that Wiessner was being dealt a serious injustice by the report, for the simple reason that "the action of the Sherpas and Durrance in evacuating these camps was so much the major cause of the accident that the others are insignificant" the other came from Robert Underhill, who as much as any American had brought the techniques of the Alps to this country. Underhill's long rebuttal came to this eloquent conclusion:

> What impresses me most is the fact that throughout all the bad weather, the killing labour and the grievous disappointments, [Wiessner] still kept up his fighting spirit. Except Wolfe, the rest of the party were excusable enough, finished and thru—quite downed by the circumstances; toward the end they wanted only to get out and go home. Wiessner, with Wolfe behind him, was the only one who still wanted to climb the mountain. Far be it from me to blame the others; I know well that if I had been there myself I should have come to feel exactly the same way, and probably much sooner. But this leads me to appreciate Wiessner the more. He had the guts—and there is no single thing finer in a climber, or in a man.

These wise appeals, however, fell on deaf ears. In November 1941, Wiessner resigned from the American Alpine Club.

To understand the harshness of the American reaction, one must reflect on the climate of the 1930s. The British, who had invented alpinism a century before, were becoming increasingly conservative as climbers. The best routes in the Alps were being done by Germans, Austrians, and Italians. As political tensions between Britain and Germany escalated in the 1930s, British rock climbers began to derogate their German counterparts as suicidal risk-takers. There was no more dangerous prewar climbing arena than the north face of the Eiger, where the best alpinists in Europe competed for the first ascent, at the cost of a number of lives. When four Germans succeeded in 1938, Hitler awarded them medals. These likable young men were thoroughly apolitical; nevertheless, a sour-grapes reaction dismissed them and their brethren as Nazi fanatics, throwing their lives away on *Nordwände* for the glory of *Führer* and *Vaterland.*

In this nasty debate, American climbers, who were technically decades behind the Europeans, tended to sympathize with the British. Fritz Wiessner, though the had come to America in 1929, long before Hitler had risen to power, was a German; he was a far better climber than anyone in this country; and he seemed willing to take greater risks than American climbers. The AAC reaction to K2, then, amounted to institutional conservatism tinged with chauvinistic passions of the onset of the war.

The drama reached its nadir a few months after Wiessner was released from the hospital. "One day my secretary in my New York office told me that two men from the FBI had come by," Wiessner recalls. "I went down to the FBI office and met two very nice young chaps—they were both Yale graduates We sat down and talked. They wanted to know my whole history, and they had the funniest questions. Such as, 'You go skiing often in Stowe in the winter, do you not? That's very near Canada, isn't it? Can you get easily over the border?' I said, 'Yes. It's quite a distance to walk, but I am in Canada very often anyway because I have a business in Toronto.' And they laughed.

"I wasn't very keen on Roosevelt then. And so they said, 'You don't like the president? You made some remarks about him.' I said, 'Well, I wasn't the only one. There are very many people who feel that way!' They laughed again.

"They asked about some of my friends. We sat there half an hour, then we just talked pleasantly. On the way out I said, 'Now look, fellows, I was pretty open to you. I have my definite suspicions. Would you tell me the names of the men who put you up to this? They said, 'Naturally we can't do that.' So I said, 'Let me ask this question: Was it some climbers from the AAC?' They nodded. They said, 'Don't worry about it. You know who we had here yesterday? We had Ezio Pinza, the famous opera singer. It was the same thing, a little jealousy from his competitors. They complained that he was a Mussolini follower.'"

Wiessner can joke about the episode today, but it must have been a chilling encounter.

The 1939 K2 expedition began to recede into the past. In 1956, in the journal *Appalachia,* Wiessner published a brief, restrained narrative of the climb from his point of view. The editor invited any readers with dissenting versions to speak up. None did.

Sadly, the expedition itself settled into a somewhat ambiguous place in climbing history. At its worst, the second-guessing British analysis prevailed; thus a book like Kenneth Mason's *Abode of Snow,* summarizing an utterly garbled version of the events on K2, could sermonize, "It is difficult to record in temperate language the folly of this enterprise."

Wiessner for the most part put the controversy behind him. In 1945 he married Muriel Schoonmaker, an American woman, with whom he has climbed and traveled extensively for almost forty years. Their daughter, Polly, is a research anthropologist; their son, Andrew, an advisor to Representative John Seiberling.

Most climbers tail off drastically after the age of forty or quit altogether. Wiessner has climbed steadily now for seventy years. In the United States he pioneered routes on local cliffs all over the country. As Richard Goldstone says, "There are these crags in the woods that people come upon and think they've discovered. Then they find a rusty old piton high on some route. Fritz was there in the 1940s."

Well into his seventies, Wiessner could still lead 5.9 climbs comfortably. Even today, at the age of eighty-four—hobbled by the arthritis that has plagued his joints since 1939, the survivor of a heart attack on a climb in France in 1969—Wiessner can second some 5.9s, and he regularly goes to the Shawangunks of New York State and solos both up and down easy routes that he "put in" forty years ago. There is no other example in mountaineering history of a climber keeping up such standards at that age.

In 1966 a number of AAC members, led by Bill Putnam, Andy Kauffman, and Lawrence Coveney, persuaded Wiessner to rejoin the club. In an act that went some way toward expiating the wrong that had been done him years before, the club soon afterward made him an honorary member for life.

In December 1978, the annual AAC banquet meeting was held in Estes Park, Colorado. The previous summer, four Americans had finally reached the top of K2. The slide shows to be presented at the meeting were accordingly focused on K2, and Jack Durrance, who lives nearby in Denver, was invited to talk. Wiessner got word of this development and flew back from a meeting in Europe in order to be present. This writer, who was present, vividly remembers the events that ensued.

All day in Estes Park the rumors flew that the long-delayed confrontation was about to take place. Durrance was finally going to tell "his side" of the story. Meanwhile, a veteran of the 1953 K2 expedition managed to talk Wiessner and Durrance into saying hello to each other. It was the first time they had met since parting in India in 1939. The meeting was curt in the extreme.

A number of AAC old-timers took Durrance aside. They managed to talk him out of making any inflammatory remarks. Their belief was that whatever dirty laundry remained from 1939, this meeting to celebrate American success on K2 was not the place or time to air it. Durrance gave in. His slide show carried the expedition up to base camp, then closed abruptly with a photo of himself in "retirement" in a cabin near the Tetons.

Later, at the banquet, Wiessner was given a special toast in recognition of his years of service to mountaineering. The crowd's reaction was deeply emotional. And the whole assemblage rose to its feet, applauding wildly—except for Durrance, who remained seated, his face fixed in a scowl.

In the course of researching this article, I asked Jack Durrance for his version of the events. Though he has never publicly told his side of the story, Durrance consented to an interview, during which that version emerged. On later reflection, however, Durrance decided against allowing his remarks to be published.

For more than forty years, the 1939 K2 expedition has lain under a cloud of criticism and rumor. Yet younger climbers the world over have come to an appreciation of it that is relatively free of the biases that animated the 1930s. And their response has been one of almost unilateral reverence and awe.

Wiessner was far ahead of his time. His refusal to rely either on oxygen or radio, criticized as cranky in his day, has come to seem an uncompromisingly high-minded example of "clean climbing." The logistical organization of the assault was utterly brilliant. Good weather helped the expedition get as high as it got, but the solid buildup of camps with tents, food, and gas amounted to the kind of textbook execution no other expedition had yet pulled off in the Himalaya.

The most astounding facet of this accomplishment is that Wiessner performed it with only one able-bodied American teammate and a group of dedicated Sherpas. The other four sahibs were of only marginal help low on the mountain. Equally astonishing is the fact that Wiessner led every bit of the route himself. On contemporary expeditions to Everest, the route had been put in only by the laborious leapfrogging of separate teams. On K2 in 1939, one man "in the shape of my life" broke every step of virgin ground himself.

Then, at his highest point, he was ready to climb through the night to reach the summit—a feat that had never been attempted in the Himalaya. There were only, at most, 750 feet to go; as subsequent parties found, those last 750 feet were mostly easy walking on a snow ridge. It is possible that even Wiessner might have lacked the strength to cover that last bit, but it seems more likely that he would have made it.

Forty-five years from his decision late that afternoon of July 19, Wiessner wonders whether he made a mistake. He considers what he might do, given another chance, at the moment when Pasang Lama balked and held the rope tight. "If I were in wonderful condition like I was then," he says, "if the place where my man stood was safe, if the weather was good, if I had a night coming on like that one, with the moon and the calm air, if I could see what was ahead as I did then . . . then I probably would unrope and go on alone." Wiessner pauses, his thoughts wrapped in the past. "But I can get pretty weak, if I feel that my man will suffer. He was so afraid, and I liked the fellow. He was a comrade to me, and he had done so well."

from Annapurna

MAURICE HERZOG

This excerpt, from Maurice Herzog's book of the same name, chronicles a 1950 French Expedition in which several members reached the summit of the 26,504 foot mountain in Nepal. They were the first to reach the summit of a mountain higher than 8,000 meters and it should have been a time of joy. But like so many expeditions into the death zone the euphoria of reaching the summit was immediately tempered when someone asked, "Well, what about going down?" The descent became a nightmare, as a ferocious storm blew across the mountain and changed joy to a question of survival. As Herzog wrote in part, "The night was absolute hell. Frightful onslaughts of wind batter us incessantly, while the never-ceasing snow piled up on the tents." This is yet another tale of how the mountains can reduce even the bravest of men.

On the third of June, 1950, the first light of dawn found us still clinging to the tent poles at Camp V. Gradually the wind abated, and with daylight, died away altogether. I made desperate attempts to push back the soft, icy stuff which stifled me, but every movement became an act of heroism. My mental powers were numbed: thinking was an effort and we did not exchange a single word.

What a repellent place it was! To everyone who reached it, Camp V became one of the worst memories of their lives. We had only one thought—to get away. We should have waited for the first rays of the sun, but at half-past five we felt we couldn't stick it any longer.

"Let's go, Biscante," I muttered. "Can't stay here a minute longer."

"Yes, let's go," repeated Lachenal.

Which of us would have the energy to make tea? Although our minds worked slowly we were quite able to envisage all the movements that would be necessary—and neither of us could face up to it. It couldn't be helped—we would just have to go without. It was quite hard enough work to get ourselves and our boots out of our sleeping-bags—and the boots were frozen stiff so that we got them on only with the greatest difficulty. Every movement made us terribly breathless. We felt as if we were being stifled. Our gaiters were stiff as a board, but I succeeded in lacing mine up; Lachenal couldn't manage his.

"No need for the rope, eh, Biscante?"

"No need," replied Lachenal laconically.

That was two pounds saved. I pushed a tube of condensed milk, some nougat and a pair of socks into my sack; one never knew, the socks might come in useful—they might even do as Balaclavas. For the time being I stuffed them with first-aid equipment. The camera was loaded with a black and white film; I had a color film in reserve. I pulled the movie-camera out from the bottom of my sleeping-bag, wound it up and tried letting it run without film. There was a little click, then it stopped and jammed.

"Bad luck after bringing it so far," said Lachenal.

In spite of our photographer Ichac's precautions taken to lubricate it with special grease, the intense cold, even inside the sleeping-bag, had frozen it. I left it at the camp rather sadly: I had looked forward to taking it to the top. I had used it up to 24,600 feet.

We went outside and put on our crampons, which we kept on all day. We wore as many clothes as possible; our sacks were very light. At six o'clock we started off. It was brilliantly fine, but also very cold. Our super-lightweight crampons bit deep into the steep slopes of ice and hard snow up which lay the first stage of our climb.

Later the slope became slightly less steep and more uniform. Sometimes the hard crust bore our weight, but at others we broke through and sank into soft powder snow which made progress exhausting. We took turns in making the track and often stopped without any word having passed between us. Each of us lived in a closed and private world of his own. I was suspicious of my mental processes; my mind was working very slowly and I was perfectly aware of the low state of my intelligence. It was easiest just to stick to one thought at a time—safest, too. The cold was penetrating; for all our special eiderdown clothing we felt as if we'd nothing on. Whenever we halted, we stamped our feet hard. Lachenal went as far as to take off one boot which was a bit tight; he was in terror of frostbite.

"I don't want to be like Lambert," he said. Raymond Lambert, a Geneva guide, had to have all his toes amputated after an eventful climb during which he got his feet frostbitten. While Lachenal rubbed himself hard, I looked at the summits all around us; already we over-topped them all except the distant Dhaulagiri. The complicated structure of these mountains, with which our many laborious explorations had made us familiar, was now spread out plainly at our feet.

The going was incredibly exhausting, and every step was a struggle of mind over matter. We came out into the sunlight, and by way of marking the occasion made yet another halt. Lachenal continued to complain of his feet. "I can't feel anything. I think I'm beginning to get frostbite." And once again he undid his boot.

I began to be seriously worried. I realized very well the risk we were running; I knew from experience how insidiously and quickly frostbite can set in if one is not extremely careful. Nor was Lachenal under any illusions. "We're in danger of having frozen feet. Do you think it's worth it?"

This was most disturbing. It was my responsibility as leader to think of the others. There was no doubt about frostbite being a very real danger. Did Annapurna justify such risks? That was the question I asked myself; it continued to worry me.

Lachenal had laced his boots up again and once more we continued to force our way through the exhausting snow. The whole of the Sickle glacier was now in view, bathed in light. We still had a long way to go to cross it, and then there was that rock band—would we find a gap in it?

My feet, like Lachenal's, were very cold and I continued to wriggle my toes, even when we were moving. I could not feel them, but that was nothing new in the mountains, and if I kept on moving them it would keep the circulation going.

Lachenal appeared to me as a sort of specter—he was alone in his world, I in mine. But—and this was odd enough—any effort was slightly *less* exhausting than lower down. Perhaps it was hope lending us wings. Even through dark glasses the snow was blinding—the sun beating straight down on the ice. We looked down upon precipitous ridges which dropped away into space, and upon tiny glaciers far, far below. Familiar peaks soared arrow-like into the sky. Suddenly Lachenal grabbed me.

"If I go back, what will you do?"

A whole sequence of pictures flashed through my head: the days of marching in sweltering heat, the hard pitches we had overcome, the tremendous efforts we had all made to lay siege to the mountain, the daily heroism of all my friends in establishing the camps. Now we were nearing our goal. In an hour or two, perhaps, victory would be ours. Must we give up? Impossible! My whole being revolted against the idea. I had made up my mind, irrevocably. Today we were consecrating an ideal, and no sacrifice was too great. I heard my voice clearly:

"I should go on by myself."

I would go alone. If he wished to go down it was not for me to stop him. He must make his own choice freely.

"Then I'll follow you."

The die was cast. I was no longer anxious. Nothing could stop us now from getting to the top. The psychological atmosphere changed with these few words, and we went forward now as brothers.

I felt as though I were plunging into something new and quite abnormal. I had the strangest and most vivid impressions, such as I had never before known in the mountains. There was something unnatural in the way I saw Lachenal and everything around us. I smile to myself at the paltriness of our efforts, for I could stand apart and watch myself making these efforts. But all sense of exertion was gone, as though there were no longer any gravity. This diaphanous landscape, this quintessence of purity—these were not the mountains I knew: they were the mountains of my dreams.

The snow, sprinkled over every rock and gleaming in the sun, was of a radiant beauty that touched me to the heart. I had never seen such complete transparency, and I was living in a world of crystal. Sounds were indistinct, the atmosphere like cotton wool.

An astonishing happiness welled up in me, but I could not define it. Everything was so new, so utterly unprecedented. It was not in the least like anything I had known in the Alps, where one feels buoyed up by the presence of others—by people of whom one is vaguely aware, or even by the dwellings one can see in the far distance.

This was quite different. An enormous gulf was between me and the world. This was a different universe—withered, desert, lifeless; a fantastic universe where the presence of man was not foreseen, perhaps not desired. We were braving an interdict, overstepping a boundary, and yet we had no fear as we continued upward. I thought of the famous ladder of St. Theresa of Avila. Something clutched at my heart.

Did Lachenal share these feelings? The summit ridge drew nearer, and we reached the foot of the ultimate rock band. The slope was very steep and the snow interspersed with rocks.

"Couloir!"

A finger pointed. The whispered word from one to another indicated the key to the rocks—the last line of defense.

"What luck!"

The couloir up the rocks though steep was feasible.

The sky was a deep sapphire blue. With a great effort we edged over to the right, avoiding the rocks; we preferred to keep to the snow on account of our crampons and it was not long before we set foot in the couloir. It was fairly steep, and we had a minute's hesitation. Should we have enough strength left to overcome this final obstacle?

Fortunately the snow was hard, and by kicking steps we were able to manage, thanks to our crampons. A false move would have been fatal. There was no need to make handholds—our axes, driven in as far as possible, served us for an anchor.

Lachenal went splendidly. What a wonderful contrast to the early days! It was a hard struggle here, but we kept going. Lifting our eyes occasionally from the slope, we saw the couloir opening out onto . . . well, we didn't quite know, probably a ridge. But where was the top—left or right? Stopping at every step, leaning on our axes we tried to recover our breath and to calm down our racing hearts, which were thumping as though they would burst. We knew we were there now—that nothing could stop us. No need to exchange looks—each of us would have read the same determination in the other's eyes. A slight detour to the left, a few more steps—the summit ridge came gradually nearer—a few rocks to avoid. We dragged ourselves up. Could we possibly be there?

Yes!

A fierce and savage wind tore at us.

We were on top of Annapurna! 8,075 meters, 26,493 feet.

Our hearts overflowed with an unspeakable happiness.

"If only the others could know. . . ."

If only everyone could know!

The summit was a corniced crest of ice, and the precipices on the far side which plunged vertically down beneath us, were terrifying, unfathomable. There could be few other mountains in the world like this. Clouds floated halfway down, concealing the gentle, fertile valley of Pokhara, 23,000 feet below. Above us there was nothing!

Our mission was accomplished. But at the same time we had accomplished something infinitely greater. How wonderful life would now become! What an inconceivable experience it is to attain one's ideal and, at the very same moment, to fulfill oneself. I was stirred to the depths of my being. Never had I felt happiness like this—so intense and yet so pure. That brown rock, the highest of them all, that ridge of ice—were these the goals of a lifetime? Or were they, rather, the limits of man's pride?

"Well, what about going down?"

Lachenal shook me. What were his feelings? Did he simply think he had finished another climb, as in the Alps? Did he think one could just go down again like that, with nothing more to it?

"One minute, I must take some photographs."

"Hurry up!"

I fumbled feverishly in my sack, pulled out the camera, took out the little French flag which was right at the bottom, and the pennants. Useless gestures, no doubt, but something more than symbols—eloquent tokens of affection and goodwill. I tied the strips of material—stained by sweat and by the food in the sacks—to the shaft of my ice-axe, the only flagstaff at hand. Then I focused my camera on Lachenal.

"Now, will you take me?"

"Hand it over—hurry up!" said Lachenal.

He took several pictures and then handed me back the camera. I loaded a color-film and we repeated the process to be certain of bringing back records to be cherished in the future.

"Are you mad?" asked Lachenal. "We haven't a minute to lose: we must go down at once."

And in fact a glance round showed me that the weather was no longer gloriously fine as it had been in the morning. Lachenal was becoming impatient.

"We must go down!"

He was right. His was the reaction of the mountaineer who knows his own domain. But I just could not accustom myself to the idea that we had won our victory. It seemed inconceivable that we should have trodden those summit snows.

It was impossible to build a cairn; there were no stones; everything was frozen. Lachenal stamped his feet; he felt them freezing. I felt mine freezing too, but paid little attention. The highest mountain to be climbed by man lay under our feet! The names of our predecessors on these heights raced through my mind: Mummery, Mallory and Irvine, Bauer, Welzenbach, Tilman, Shipton. How many of them were dead—how many had found on these mountains what, to them, was the finest end of all?

My joy was touched with humility. It was not just one party that had climbed Annapurna today, but a whole expedition. I thought of all the others in the camps perched on the slopes at our feet, and I knew it was because of their efforts and their sacrifices that we had succeeded. There are times when the most complicated actions are suddenly summed up, distilled, and strike you with illuminating clarity; so it was with this irresistible upward surge which had landed us two here.

Pictures passed through my mind—the Chamonix valley, where I had spent the most marvelous moments of my childhood; Mont Blanc, which so tremendously impressed me! I was a child when I first saw "the Mont Blanc people" coming home, and to me there was a queer look about them; a strange light shone in their eyes.

"Come on, straight down," called Lachenal.

He had already done up his sack and started going down. I took out my pocked aneroid: 8,500 meters. I smiled. I swallowed a little condensed milk and left the tube behind— the only trace of our passage. I did up my sack, put on my gloves and my glasses, seized my ice-axe; one look around and I, too, hurried down the slope. Before disappearing into the couloir I gave one last look at the summit which would henceforth be all our joy and all our consolation.

Lachenal was already far below; he had reached the foot of the couloir. I hurried down in his tracks. I went as fast as I could, but it was dangerous going. At every step one had to take care that the snow did not break away beneath one's weight. Lachenal, going faster than I thought he was capable of, was now on the long traverse. It was my turn to cross the area of mixed rock and snow. At last I reached the foot of the rock band. I had hurried and I was out of breath. I undid my sack. What had I been going to do? I couldn't say.

"My gloves!"

Before I had time to bend over, I saw them slide and roll. They went further and further straight down the slope. I remained where I was, quite stunned. I watched them rolling down slowly, with no appearance of stopping. The movement of those gloves was engraved in my sight as something irredeemable, against which I was powerless. The consequences might be most serious. What was I to do?

"Quickly, down to Camp V."

Rébuffat and Terray would be there. My concern dissolved like magic. I now had a fixed objective again: to reach the camp. Never for a minute did it occur to me to use as gloves the socks which I always carry in reserve for just such a mishap as this.

On I went, trying to catch up with Lachenal. It had been two o'clock when we reached the summit; we had started out at six in the morning, but I had to admit that I had lost all sense of time. I felt as if I were running, whereas in actual fact I was walking normally, perhaps rather slowly, and I had to keep stopping to get my breath. The sky was now covered with clouds, everything had become gray and dirty-looking. An icy wind sprang up, boding no good. We must push on! But where was Lachenal? I spotted him a couple of hundred yards away, looking as if he was never going to stop. And I had thought he was in indifferent form!

The clouds grew thicker and came right down over us; the wind blew stronger, but I did not suffer from the cold. Perhaps the descent had restored my circulation. Should I be able to find the tents in the mist? I watched the rib ending in the beak-like point which overlooked the camp. It was gradually swallowed up by the clouds, but I was able to make out the spearhead rib lower down. If the mist should thicken I would make straight for that rib and follow it down, and in this way I should be bound to come upon the tent.

Lachenal disappeared from time to time, and then the mist was so thick that I lost sight of him altogether. I kept going at the same speed, as fast as my breathing would allow.

The slope was now steeper; a few patches of bare ice followed the smooth stretches of snow. A good sign—I was nearing the camp. How difficult to find one's way in thick mist! I kept the course which I had set by the steepest angle of the slope. The ground was broken; with my crampons I went straight down walls of bare ice. There were some patches ahead—a few more steps. It was the camp all right, but there were two tents!

So Rébuffat and Terray had come up. What a mercy! I should be able to tell them that we had been successful, that we were returning from the top. How thrilled they would be!

I got there, dropping down from above, The platform had been extended, and the two tents were facing each other. I tripped over one of the guy-ropes of the first tent; there was movement inside, they heard me. Rébuffat and Terray put their heads out.

"We've made it. We're back from Annapurna!"

Rébuffat and Terray received the news with great excitement.

"But what about Biscante?" asked Terray anxiously.

"He won't be long. He was just in front of me! What a day—started out at six this morning—didn't stop . . . got up at last."

Words failed me. I had so much to say. The sight of familiar faces dispelled the strange feeling that I had experienced since morning, and I became, once more, just a mountaineer.

Terray, who was speechless with delight, wrung my hands. Then the smile vanished from his face: "Maurice—your hands!" there was an uneasy silence. I had forgotten that I had lost my gloves: my fingers were violet and white and hard as wood. The other two stared at them in dismay—they realized the full seriousness of the injury. But, still blissfully floating on a sea of joy remote from reality, I leaned over towards Terry and said confidentially, "You're in such splendid form, and you've done so marvelously, it's absolutely tragic you didn't come up there with us!"

"What I did was for the Expedition, my dear Maurice, and anyway you've got up, and that's a victory for the whole lot of us."

I nearly burst with happiness. How could I tell him all that his answer meant to me? The rapture I had felt on the summit, which might have seemed a purely personal, egotistical emotion, had been transformed by his words into a complete and perfect joy with no shadow upon it. His answer proved that this victory was not just one man's achievement, a matter for personal pride; no— and Terray was the first to understand this—it was a victory for us all, a victory for mankind itself.

"Hi! Help! Help!"

"Biscante!" exclaimed the others.

Still half intoxicated and remote from reality I had heard nothing. Terray felt a chill at his heart, and his thoughts flew to his partner on so many unforgettable climbs; together they had so often skirted death, and won so many splendid victories. Putting his head out, and seeing Lachenal clinging to the slope 100 yards lower down, he dressed in frantic haste.

Out he went. But the slope was bare now; Lachenal had disappeared. Terray was horribly frightened, and he could only utter unintelligible cries. It was a ghastly moment for him. A violent wind sent the mist tearing by. Under the stress of emotion Terray had not realized how it falsified distances.

"Biscante! Biscante!"

He had spotted him, through a rift in the mist, lying on the slope much lower down than he had thought. Terray set his teeth, and glissaded down like a madman. How would he be able to brake without crampons, on the wind-hardened snow? But Terray was a first-class skier, and with a jump turn he stopped beside Lachenal, who was suffering from concussion after his tremendous fall. In a state of collapse, with no ice-axe, balaclava, or gloves, and only one crampon, he gazed vacantly around him.

"My feet are frost-bitten. Take me down . . . take me down, so that Oudot can see to me."

"It can't be done," said Terray sorrowfully. "Can't you see we're in the middle of a storm. . . . It'll be dark soon."

But Lachenal was obsessed by the fear of amputation. With a gesture of despair he tore the axe out of Terray's hands and tried to force his way down; but soon saw the futility of his action and resolved to climb up to the camp. While Terray cut steps without stopping, Lachenal, ravaged and exhausted as he was, dragged himself along on all fours.

Meanwhile I had gone into Rébuffat's tent. He was appalled at the sign of my hands and, as rather incoherently I told him what we had done, he took a piece of rope and began flicking my fingers. Then he took off my boots with great difficulty for my feet were swollen, and beat my feet and rubbed me. We soon heard Terray giving Lachenal the same treatment in the other tent.

For our comrades it was a tragic moment: Annapurna was conquered, and the first eight-thousander had been climbed. Every one of us had been ready to sacrifice everything for this. Yet, as they looked at our feet and hands, what can Terray and Rébuffat have felt?

Outside the storm howled and the snow was still falling. The mist grew thick and darkness came. As on the previous night we had to cling to the poles to prevent the tents being carried away by the wind. The only two air-mattresses were given to Lachenal and myself while Terray and Rébuffat both sat on ropes, rucksacks, and provisions to keep themselves off the snow. They rubbed, slapped and beat us with a rope. Sometimes the blow fell on the living flesh, and howls arose from both tents. Rébuffat persevered; it was essential to continue painful as it was. Gradually life returned to my feet as well as to my hands, and circulation started again. Lachenal, too, found that feeling was returning.

Now Terray summoned up the energy to prepare some hot drinks. He called to Rébuffat that he would pass him a mug, so two hands stretched out towards each other between the two tents and were instantly covered with snow. The liquid was boiling though scarcely more than 60 degrees centigrade (140 degrees Fahrenheit). I swallowed it greedily and felt infinitely better.

The night was absolutely hell. Frightful onslaughts of wind battered us incessantly, while the never-ceasing snow piled up on the tents.

Now and again I heard voices from next door—it was Terray massaging Lachenal with admirable perseverance, only stopping to ply him with hot drinks. In our tent Rébuffat was quite worn out, but satisfied that warmth was returning to my limbs.

Lying half unconscious I was scarcely aware of the passage of time. There were moments when I was able to see our situation in its true dramatic light, but the rest of the time I was plunged in an inexplicable stupor with no thought for the consequences of our victory.

As the night wore on the snow lay heavier on the tent, and once again I had the frightful feeling of being slowly and silently asphyxiated. I tried, with all the strength of which I was capable, to push off with both forearms the mass that was crushing me. These fearful exertions left me gasping for breath and I fell back into the same exhausted state. It was much worse than the previous night.

"Rébuffat! Gaston! Gaston!"

I recognized Terray's voice.

"Time to be off!"

I heard the sounds without grasping their meaning. Was it light already? I was not in the least surprised that the other two had given up all thought of going to the top, and I did not at all grasp the measure of their sacrifice.

Outside the storm redoubled in violence. The tent shook and the fabric flapped alarmingly. It had usually been fine in the mornings: did this mean the monsoon was upon us? We knew it was not far off—could this be its first onslaught?

"Gaston! Are you ready?" Terray called again.

"One minute," answered Rébuffat. He didn't have an easy job: he had to put my boots on and do everything to get me ready. I let myself be handled like a baby. In the other tent Terray finished dressing Lachenal whose feet were still swollen and would not fit into his boots. So Terray gave him his own, which were bigger. To get Lachenal's onto his own feet he had to make slits in them. As a precaution he put a sleeping-bag and some food into his sack and shouted to us to do the same. Were his words lost in the storm? Or were we too intent on leaving this hellish place to listen to his instructions?

Lachenal and Terray were already outside.

"We're going down!" they shouted.

Then Rébuffat tied me on the rope and we went out. There were only two ice-axes for the four of us, so Rébuffat and Terray took them as a matter of course. For a moment as we left the two tents of Camp V, I felt childishly ashamed at leaving all this good equipment behind.

Already the first rope seemed a long way down below us. We were blinded by the squalls of snow and we could not hear each other a yard away. We had both put on our *cagoules,* for it was very cold. The snow was apt to slide and the rope often came in useful.

Ahead of us the other two were losing no time. Lachenal went first and, safeguarded by Terray, he forced the pace in his anxiety to get down. There were no tracks to show us the way, but it was engraved on all our minds—straight down the slope for 400 yards then transverse to the left for 50 to 200 yards to get to Camp IV. The snow was thinning and the wind less violent. Was it going to clear? We hardly dared to hope so. A wall of seracs brought us up short.

"It's to the left," I said, "I remember perfectly."

Somebody else thought it was to the right. We started going down again. The wind dropped completely, but the snow fell in big flakes. The mist was thick, and, not to lose each other, we walked in line: I was third and I could barely see Lachenal who was first. It was impossible to recognize any of the pitches. We were all experienced enough mountaineers to know that even on familiar ground it is easy to make mistakes in such weather. Distances are deceptive, one cannot tell whether one is going up or down. We kept colliding with hummocks which we had taken for hollows. The mist, the falling snow-flakes, the carpet of snow, all merged into the same whitish tone and confused our vision. The towering outlines of the seracs took on fantastic shapes and seemed to move slowly around us.

Our situation was not desperate, we were certainly not lost. We would have to go lower down; the traverse must begin further on—I remembered the serac which served as a milestone. The snow stuck to our *cagoules,* and turned us into white phantoms noiselessly flitting against a background equally white. We began to sink in dreadfully, and there is nothing worse for bodies already on the edge of exhaustion.

Were we too high or too low? No one could tell. Perhaps we had better try slanting over to the left! The snow was in a dangerous condition, but we did not seem to realize it. We were forced to admit that we were not on the right route, so we retraced our steps and climbed up above the serac which overhung us. No doubt, we decided, we should be on the right level now. With Rébuffat leading, we went back over the way which had cost us such an effort. I followed him jerkily, saying nothing, and determined to go onto the end. If Rébuffat had fallen I could never have held him.

We went doggedly on from one serac to another. Each time we thought we had recognized the right route, and each time there was fresh disappointment. If only the mist would lift, if only the snow would stop for a second! Only Terray and Rébuffat were capable of breaking the trail and they relieved each other at regular intervals, without a word and without a second's hesitation.

I admired this determination of Rébuffat for which he is so justly famed. He did not intend to die! With the strength of desperation and at the price of super-human effort he forged ahead. The slowness of his progress would have dismayed even the most obstinate climber, but he would not give up, and in the end the mountain yielded in face of his perseverance.

Terray, when his turn came, charged madly ahead. He was like a force of nature: at all costs he would break down these prison walls that penned us in. His physical strength was exceptional, his will power no less remarkable. Lachenal gave him considerable trouble. Perhaps he was not quite in his right mind. He said it was no use going on; we must dig a hole in the snow and wait for fine weather. He swore at Terray and called him a madman. Nobody but Terray would have been capable of dealing with him—he just tugged sharply on the rope and Lachenal was forced to follow.

We were well and truly lost.

The weather did not seem likely to improve. A minute ago we had still had idea about which way to go—now we had none. This way or that. . . . We went on at random to allow for the chance of a miracle which appeared increasingly unlikely. The instinct of self-preservation in the two fit members of the party alternated with a hopelessness which made them completely irresponsible. Each in turn did the maddest things: Terray traversed the steep and avalanchy slopes with one crampon badly adjusted. He and Rébuffat performed incredible feats of balance without the least slip.

Camp IV was certainly on the left, on the edge of the Sickle. On that point we were all agreed. But it was very hard to find. The wall of ice that gave it such magnificent protection was now ironical, for it hid the tents from us. In mist like this we should have to be right on top of them before we spotted them.

Perhaps if we called, someone would hear us? Lachenal gave the signal, but snow absorbs sound and his shout seemed to carry only a few yards. All four of us called together: "One . . . two . . . three . . . Help!"

We got the impression that our united shout carried a long way, so we began again: "One . . . two . . . three . . . Help!" Not a sound in reply!

Now and again Terray took of his boots and rubbed his feet; the sight of our frost-bitten limbs had made him aware of the danger and he had the strength of mind to do something about it. Like Lachenal, he was haunted by the idea of amputation. For me, it was too late: my feet and hands already affected from yesterday, were beginning to freeze up again.

We had eaten nothing since the day before, and we had been on the go the whole time, but men's resources of energy in the face of death are inexhaustible. When the end seems imminent, there still remain reserves, though it needs tremendous will power to call them up.

Time passed, but we had no idea how long. Night was approaching, and we were terrified, though none of us made any complaint. Rébuffat and I found a way we thought we remembered, but were brought to a halt by the extreme steepness of the slope—the mist turned it into a vertical wall. We were to find next day that at that moment we had been only 30 yards from the camp, and that the wall was the very one that sheltered the tent which would have been our salvation.

"We must find a crevasse."

"We can't stay here all night!"

"A hole—it's the only thing."

"We'll all die in it."

Night had suddenly fallen and it was essential to come to a decision without wasting another minute; if we remained on the slope, we should be dead before morning. We would have to bivouac. What the conditions would be like, we could guess, for we all knew what it meant to bivouac above 23,000 feet.

With his axe, Terray began to dig a hole. Lachenal went over to a snow-filled crevasse a few yards further on, then suddenly let out a yell and disappeared before our eyes. We stood helpless: should we, or rather would Terray and Rébuffat, have enough strength for all the maneuvers with the rope that would be needed to get him out? The crevasse was completely blocked up save for the one little hole which Lachenal had fallen through.

"Lachenal!" called Terray.

A voice, muffled by many thicknesses of ice and snow, came up to us. It was impossible to to make out what it was saying.

"Lachenal!"

Terray jerked the rope violently; this time we could hear.

"I'm here!"

"Anything broken?"

"No! It'll do for the night! Come along."

The shelter was heaven-sent. None of us would have had the strength to dig a hole big enough to protect the lot of us from the wind. Without hesitation Terray let himself drop into the crevasse, and a loud "Come on!" told us he had arrived safely. In my turn I let myself go: it was a regular toboggan-slide. I shot down a sort of twisting tunnel, very steep, and about 30 feet long. I came out at great speed into the opening beyond and was literally hurled to the bottom of the crevasse. We let Rébuffat know he could come by giving a tug on the rope.

The intense cold of this minute grotto shriveled us up, the enclosing walls of ice were damp and the floor a carpet of fresh snow; by huddling together there was just room for the four of us. Icicles hung from the ceiling and we broke some of them off to make more head room and kept little bits to suck— it was a long time since we had had anything to drink.

That was our shelter for the night. At least we should be protected from the wind, and the temperature would remain fairly even, though the damp was extremely unpleasant. We settled ourselves in the dark as best we could. As always in a bivouac we took off our boots; without this precaution the constriction would cause immediate frost-bite. Terray unrolled the sleeping-bag which he had had the foresight to bring, and settled himself in relative comfort. We put on everything warm we had, and to avoid contact with the snow I sat on the movie camera. We huddled close up to each other, in our search for a hypothetical position in which the warmth of our bodies could be combined without loss, but we couldn't keep still for a second.

We did not open our mouths—signs were less of an effort than words. Every man withdrew into himself and took refuge in his own inner world. Terray massaged Lachenal's feet; Rébuffat felt his feet freezing too, but he had sufficient strength to rub them himself. I remained motionless, unseeing. My feet and hands went on freezing, what could be done? I attempted to forget suffering by withdrawing into myself, trying to forget the passing of time, trying not to feel the devouring and numbing cold which insidiously gained upon us.

Terray shared his sleeping-bag with Lachenal, putting his feet and hands inside the precious eiderdown. At the same time he went on rubbing.

Anyhow the frost-bite won't spread further, he was thinking.

None of us could make any movement without upsetting the others, and the positions we had taken up with such care were continually being altered so that we had to start all over again. This kept us busy. Rébuffat persevered with his rubbing and complained of his feet; like Terray he was thinking: We mustn't look beyond tomorrow—afterwards we'll see. But he was not blind to the fact that "afterwards" was one big question-mark.

Terray generously tried to give me part of his sleeping-bag. He had understood the seriousness of my condition, and knew why it was that I said nothing and remained quite passive; he realized that I had abandoned all hope for myself. He massaged me for nearly two hours; his feet, too, might have frozen, but he didn't appear to give the matter thought. I found new courage simply in contemplating his unselfishness; he was doing so much to help me that it would have been ungrateful of me not to go on struggling to live. Though my heart was like a lump of ice itself, I was astonished to feel no pain. Everything material about me seemed to have dropped away. I seemed to be quite clear in my thoughts and yet I floated in a kind of peaceful happiness. There was still a breath of life in me, but it dwindled steadily as the hours went by. Terray's massage no longer had any effect upon me. All was over, I thought. Wasn't this cavern the most beautiful grave I could hope for? Death caused me no grief, no regret—I smiled at the thought.

After hours of torpor a voice mumbled "Daylight!"

This made some impression on the others. I only felt surprised—I had not thought that daylight would penetrate so far down.

"Too early to start," said Rébuffat.

A ghastly light spread through our grotto and we could just vaguely make out the shapes of each other's heads. A queer noise from a long way off came down to us—a sort of prolonged hiss. The noise increased. Suddenly I was buried, blinded, smothered beneath an avalanche of new snow. The icy snow spread over the cavern, finding its way through every gap in our clothing. I ducked my head between my knees and covered myself with both arms. The snow flowed on and on. There was a terrible silence. We were not completely buried but there was snow everywhere. We got up, taking care not to bang our heads against the ceiling of ice and tried to shake ourselves. We were all in our stockinged feet in the snow. The first thing to do was to find our boots.

Rébuffat and Terray began to search, and realized at once that they were blind. Yesterday they had taken off their glasses to lead us down and now they were paying for it. Lachenal was first to lay hands upon a pair of boots. He tried to put them on, but they were Rébuffat's. Rébuffat attempted to climb up the chute down which we had come yesterday, and which the avalanche had followed in its turn.

"Hi, Gaston! What's the weather like?" called up Terray.

"Can't see a thing. It's blowing hard."

We were still groping for our things. Terray found his boots and put them on awkwardly, unable to see what he was doing. Lachenal helped him, but he was all on edge and fearfully impatient, in striking contrast to my immobility. Terray then went up the icy channel, puffing and blowing, and at last reached the outer world. He was met by terrible gusts of wind that cut right through him and lashed his face.

Bad weather, he said to himself, this time it's the end. We're lost . . . we'll never come through.

At the bottom of the crevasse there were still two of us looking for our boots. Lachenal poked fiercely with an ice-axe. I was calmer and tried to proceed more rationally. We extracted crampons and an axe in turn from the snow, but still no boots.

Well—so this cavern was to be our last resting-place! There was very little room—we were bent double and got in each other's way. Lachenal decided to go out without his boots. He called frantically, hauled himself up on the rope, trying to get a hold or to wiggle his way up, digging his toes into the snow walls. Terray from outside pulled as hard as he could. I watched him go; he gathered speed and disappeared.

When he emerged from the opening he saw the sky was clear and blue, and he began to run like a madman, shrieking, "It's fine, it's fine!"

I set to work again to search the cave. The boots had to be found, or Lachenal and I were done for. On all fours, with nothing on my hands or feet I raked the snow, stirring it around this way or that, hoping every second to come upon something hard. I was no longer capable of thinking—I reacted like an animal fighting for its life.

I found one boot! The other was tied to it—a pair! Having ransacked the whole cave I at last found the other pair. But in spite of all my efforts I could not find the movie camera, and gave up in despair. There was no question of putting my boots on—my hands were like lumps of wood and I could hold nothing in my fingers; my feet were very swollen—I should never be able to get boots on them. I twisted the rope around the boots as well as I could and called up the chute:

"Lionel . . . Boots!"

There was no answer, but he must have heard for with a jerk the precious boots shot up. Soon after the rope came down again. My turn, I wound the rope around me. I could not pull it tight so I made a whole series of little knots. Their combined strength, I hoped, would be enough to hold me. I had no strength to shout again; I gave a great tug on the rope, and Terray understood.

At the first step I had to kick a notch in the hard snow for my toes. Further on I expected to be able to get up more easily by wedging myself across the runnel. I wriggled up a few yards like this and then I tried to dig my hands and my feet into the wall. My hands were stiff and hard right up the wrists and my feet had no feeling up to the ankles, the joints were inflexible and this hampered me greatly.

Somehow or other I succeeded in working my way up, while Terray pulled so hard he nearly choked me. I began to see more distinctly and so knew that I must be nearing the opening. Often I fell back, but I clung on and wedged myself in again as best I could. My heart was bursting and I was forced to rest. A fresh wave of energy enabled me to crawl to the top. I pulled myself out by clutching Terray's legs; he was just about all in and I was in the last stages of exhaustion. Terray was close to me and I whispered:

"Lionel . . . I'm dying!"

He supported me and helped me away form the crevasse. Lachenal and Rébuffat were sitting in the snow a few yards away. The instant Lionel let go of me I sank down and dragged myself along on all fours.

The weather was perfect. Quantities of snow had fallen the day before and the mountains were resplendent. Never had I seen them look so beautiful—our last day would be magnificent.

Rébuffat and Terray were completely blind; as he came along with me Terray knocked into things and I had to direct him. Rébuffat, too, could not move a step without guidance. It was terrifying to be blind when there was danger all around. Lachenal's frozen feet affected his nervous system. His behavior was disquieting—he was possessed by the most fantastic ideas.

"I tell you we must go down . . . down there. . . ."

"You've nothing on your feet!"

"Don't worry about that."

"You're off your head. The way's not there . . . it's to the left!"

He was already standing up; he wanted to go straight down to the bottom of the glacier. Terray held him back, made him sit down, and though he couldn't see, helped Lachenal put his boots on.

Behind them I was living in my own private dream. I knew the end was near, but it was the end that all mountaineers wish for—an end in keeping with their ruling passion. I was consciously grateful to the mountains for being so beautiful for me that day, and as awed by their silence as if I had been in church. I was in no pain, and had no worry. My utter calmness was alarming. Terray came staggering towards me, and I told him: "It's all over for me. Go on . . . you have a chance . . . you must take it . . . over to the left . . . that's the way."

I felt better after telling him that. But Terray would have none of it: "We'll help you. If we get away, so will you."

At this moment Lachenal shouted: "Help! Help!"

Obviously he didn't know what he was doing. . . . Or did he? He was the only one of the four of us who could see Camp II down below. Perhaps his calls would be heard. They were shrieks of despair, reminding me tragically of some climbers lost in the Mont Blanc massif whom I had endeavored to save. Now it was our turn. The impression was vivid: we were lost.

I joined in with the others: "One . . . two . . . three . . . Help! One . . . two . . . three . . . Help!" We tried to shout together, but without much success; our voices could not have carried more than ten feet. The noise I made was more of a whisper than a shout. Terray insisted that I should put my boots on, but my hands were dead. Neither Rébuffat nor Terray, who were unable to see, could help much, so I said to Lachenal: "Come and help me to put my boots on."

"Don't be silly, we must go down!"

And off he went once again in the wrong direction, straight down. I was not in the least angry with him; he had been sorely tried by the altitude and by everything he had gone through.

Terray resolutely got out his knife, and with fumbling hands slit the uppers of my boots back and front. Split in two like this I could get them on, but it was not easy and I had to make several attempts. Soon I lost heart—what was the use of it all anyway since I was going to stay where I was? But Terray pulled violently and finally succeeded. He laced up my now gigantic boots, missing half the hooks. I was ready now. But how was I going to walk with my stiff joints?

"To the left, Lionel!"

"You're crazy, Maurice," said Lachenal, "It's to the right, straight down."

Terray did not know what to think of these conflicting views. He had not given up like me, he was going to fight; but what, at the moment, could he do? The three of them discussed which way to go.

I remained sitting in the snow. Gradually my mind lost grip—why should I struggle? I would just let myself drift. I saw pictures of shady slopes, peaceful paths, there was a scent of resin. It was pleasant—I was going to die in my own mountains. My body had no feeling—everything was frozen.

"Aaah . . . aah!"

Was it a groan or a call? I gathered my strength for one cry: "They're coming!" the others had heard me and shouted for joy. What a miraculous apparition! "Schatz . . . it's Schatz!"

Barely 200 yards away Marcel Schatz, waist-deep in snow, was coming slowly towards us like a boat on the surface of the slope. I found this vision of a strong and invincible deliverer inexpressibly moving. I expected everything of him. The shock was violent, and quite shattered me. Death clutched me and I gave myself up.

When I came to again the wish to live returned and I experienced a violent revulsion of feeling. All was not lost! As Schatz came nearer my eyes never left him for a second—20 yards—ten yards—he came straight towards me. Why? Without a word he leaned over me, held me close, hugged me, and his warm breath revived me.

I could not make the slightest movement—I was like marble. My heart was overwhelmed by such tremendous feelings and yet my eyes remained dry.

"It is wonderful—what you have done!"

K2 The Savage Mountain

CHARLES S. HOUSTON M.D. & ROBERT H. BATES

Written by Charles S. Houston, M.D. and Robert H. Bates, this book excerpt also details the power of the world's second highest mountain. Both Americans were part of the 1953 expedition in which both storms and illness kept anyone on the team from reaching the summit. As if often the case, the descent proved more hazardous and harrowing with freezing cold, frostbite, and eventually the death of a climber as the unwanted companions that can drive the spirit from a man. It was Charles Houston who asked the question when morale was at the lowest point, a question almost all mountaineers must ask at one time or another. He turned to a companion and said, "What are we doing here?"

The Highest Men in the World

August 1—Swiss day. We saw the sun again, through racing clouds which said, "Go on, the storm is over. The sky will soon be blue, the sun warm." Leaving Bates and Streather to follow next day, the rest of us broke camp, taking all save two tents and a little food and fuel with us. We started up the long, hard climb to Camp VIII. Schoening and Gilkey were busily packing food from VII to VIII as we struggled up the last stretch of the Black Pyramid, moving very slowly with our packs, for even 35 pounds weighs heavily at that altitude. Five hours later we reached Camp VII. As we passed the now empty ice ledge, we met Schoening and Gilkey returning through the clouds at VIII to guide us up. We strapped crampons on our clumsy Korean boots, added more supplies to our packs, and climbed up on the huge steps carved in the ice by our pioneers. It was a nasty stretch, pure green ice as smooth as a skating rink, with only scattered stones here and there. We were all frankly relieved to reach the snow, where our footing was secure although more difficult.

I thought that day would never end. I was counting steps, my hope being to climb ten steps before stopping, but I found that I had to stop more and more often. Finally, in the deep snow, I unroped and set my own pace, for the men above seemed tireless. Often the clouds hid them from me, but I had their tracks, knee or thigh deep, to follow. About six o'clock, close to exhaustion, I reached Camp VIII, where a tiny tent in this white wilderness would be our home. The rest were equally tired, but we all managed to pitch two more tents, blow up our air mattresses, cook supper, and crawl into bed. It is surprising even now to recall how quickly we recovered. Morale was magnificent. We were within striking distance of the goal. The summit might still be ours.

We spent a sleepless night with the wind beating about us, but next morning the sun shone hot and full and we dragged out our snow-caked sleeping bags and our wet clothes to dry. Gilkey and Schoening felt miserable. They had shared one of the "impermeable" nylon tents, a fabric which does not "breathe." Both men blamed this semi-suffocation for their illness. Both had severe headaches and felt nauseated. Schoening saw double. Neither was able to do much for an hour or two.

Over the radio I made plans with Bates and Streather at Camp VI to meet them at Camp VII around noon. After enjoying the unaccustomed sunlight for an hour or two, we hurried down to the empty ledge at VII to bring back what few loads of food remained there. The wind and clouds were so bad again that we felt certain that our friends would have turned back. We packed up loads and started upward. Through the storm Craig heard a shout. We listened. Sure enough, a hail from far down the pyramid. They were still coming, but far, far below. We held a hurried conference. Without tents it was too cold for us to await them there. Late as they were, it seemed almost impossible that they could reach Camp VIII that day, and neither they nor we had a tent in which to sleep at VII. They must be sent back to Camp VI. Altogether we shouted again and again, "Go back, go back." The wind mocked us. Finally we started to climb again to VIII, certain that our message must have been received.

But some little voice within reminded me of the strong determination of these two men. From the Camp at VIII I gathered up the pile of willow wands, 3-foot wooden dowels painted black at one end. Passing these out to the others in the party, we planted one dowel every 50 feet up the slope as we climbed. This would guide the others if they should come through the snow which had already completely buried our morning track, and would soon hide the tracks we were then making. We arrived at Camp VIII late in the afternoon, thoroughly cold and exhausted. It was growing dark. "They will never come now," said Pete. As he spoke there came a weary shout. It was our friends, exhausted, triumphant, cold, and hungry.

"Yes, we heard your shouts," said Streather. "But we thought you meant *we* are going back." "So we kept on," added Bob. "Thank God for your willow wands. We had no idea where your camp was and couldn't see a thing. Your tracks were completely gone above the ice steps."

While Pete and Art pitched a tent for them, George and I hastily boiled up a pot of tea, only to spill the whole pot as we poured. Our tent floor was flooded, our sleeping bags soaked, but who cared? The party was all together, all well. We had the men, we had the food, we had the will, but would we get the weather? It was a happy evening with high excitement which kept us talking until late.

The night was long and our sleep broken. Battering gusts of wind flapped the fabric of the tent against our heads with malicious force. Snow sifted through tiny holes in the tent and through the ventilators, covering us with powder. Crowded as we were with boots and clothing, food bags, stoves, and pots, there was little room to turn or stretch. Sleep was fitful and broken. The wind screamed about us; snow hissed on the tent walls.

Day broke a sickly gray. No sun penetrated the dense white mist of cloud and tortured snow. Only our watches advanced the hours. Snow piled in drifts about the tents until a sudden change in the wind swept them clear and piled new drifts elsewhere. We were disinherited from the earth, our only horizon the tents. Once or twice during the day a man would move from one tent to another, chat for a while, and then stumble off. But no one could live long in that white hell of wind and driven snow; fine sharp ice crystals penetrated our lungs, smothered and choked us. Only by cupping heavy gloves about his mouth could a man draw a breath. Though it was not terribly cold, perhaps 0°F., the chill of the tearing wind was bitter and we were cold even in all our clothing. There was nothing to do save lie in our sleeping bags, where fortunately we were warm, and wait—and hope—and wait.

Our one contact with the world, the world of people and things (not the world of tents and snow and wind), was the radio. Every morning at seven and every evening at six I took the wonderful little Raytheon walkie-talkie out of my sleeping bag, where I usually kept it to warm the batteries. Anxiously I would wait for the stroke of six.

"Hello, Base Camp. Hello, Base Camp. This is Camp VIII. Can you hear me? Over." And a cheerful voice would answer, "Hello, Charlie, I hear you very well. Give my your news, please. Over."

"Well, Ata, the storm keeps on up here. There is nothing to see, and we can't get out. But we are fighting-fit and ready to go. What is your news? Over."

"Here too we have storm, Charlie. Even at Base a foot of snow fell today. None of the peaks can be seen. The wind is terrific. Over."

"Ata, tell me the weather forecast." And Ata would answer sadly, "Charlie, tonight Radio Pakistan said, "At 24,000 feet the weather will be cloudy with heavy snowfall. Winds will be westerly, blowing 40 to 45 knots, occasionally gusting to hurricane velocity.' I'm sorry, Charlie, but if the forecast is right, you will have more storm tomorrow." I could feel the sorrow and the anxiety in his voice. I knew how he longed to help us, how powerless this energetic and determined man must feel. But his presence at Base Camp, his voice on the radio, gave us new strength.

As we lay in our tents, or visited each other through these stormy days, our thoughts were always on the summit. Endlessly we discussed plans. Over and over again we made out careful lists of the supplies we would carry to Camp IX, supplies for two men for three days. Three days that might give us victory. But three *good* days they must be! Three clear, calm days. On the first day the whole party would move two men to a camp as high as possible on the summit cone, somewhere in the black towers to the east of the ice, perhaps above 27,000 feet. On the second day these two would make their bid for the summit, returning that night to Camp VIII. On that same day a second team would move up to Camp IX to help the first party down if successful, to replace them and make a second try on the third day if they had failed.

"Three days—just three clear days," we said.

August third and fourth were like the first and second. Wind and driven snow. Mist and cloud. Tents flapping against our heads and shoulders. For an hour once or twice in those days we saw a sickly sun, were able to crawl out and stretch our legs in the deep drifts.

Despite the continuing storm, our spirits were so high, our confidence so strong, that we selected the summit teams on August 3. I had anticipated that various factors would eliminate three or four men from a possible summit try, but here were eight climbers, all apparently fit and eager to go higher. The philosophy of our expedition had avoided one-man decisions, and I was reluctant to choose by myself the men who might have the great chance for the crowning effort. We took a secret ballot, therefore, selecting our two best men by vote of all. Each of us thought carefully and long, and when I crawled back from the other tents through the blizzard, I was prouder than ever before of my party. When the ballots were counted, Bell and Craig were to be the first team, Gilkey and Schoening the second. But I asked Ata not to tell their names to the porters when I radioed him that night, for one of our cherished hopes was to preserve the anonymity of the summit pair—if they succeeded. We hoped to report, "Two men reached the top"—no more, no less. We felt that this would doubly underline the team nature of our enterprise. It would emphasize as strongly as we could the interdependence of the climbing party. But this was not to be.

The lulls were rare and brief. During the fourth night the wind gained new force. George Bell and I watched the nylon walls of our tent stretch and pull. Runs appeared in the fabric. We knew that the cloth could not last long.

I wondered aloud, "George, shall we get out of our tents now and make a dash for another?"

"I think we'll last till daylight," was his calm answer. "It will be tough to get into boots and move our gear in the dark."

"Even if we could survive the wind," was my mental note.

So we slept fitfully, and every time I looked up the runs were wider and longer. With dawn came a little lull, then terrific gusts. Our tent was going, and George and I rushed into boots and parkas, and blundered out into the storm as the tent went down, its poles snapped and the fabric torn. Each pulled his sleeping bag from the wreckage and crawled into another tent. A second trip for food was all we could manage in the wind and cold. Streather and Bates pretended to be glad to have me crowd into their tent, a French model with lining which made it very cramped even for two. George piled in on Dee Molenaar and Bob Craig. The storm reached its peak. The day wore on.

Can such an ordeal be remotely conceived as "pleasure" or "sport?" Are we masochists to "enjoy" such a battering, such cold, such wind, lack of food, lack of sleep, lack of water? Emphatically not. Our stay at Camp VIII, ten days of hardship and anxiety, was terribly hard. It brought each of us down to fundamentals. The deepest springs of character were tapped for our survival. The lack of oxygen at great altitudes may dull the mind and weaken the body, but there is an inner strength of spirit, a bigger power which emerges undiminished, even magnified, to bring a man through such an experience. We faced nature's wildest forces with our pitifully feeble tent and clothing as our only weapons, plus our inner determination. Perhaps it is this conquest, conquest of one's self through survival of such an ordeal, that brings a man back to frontiers again and again. It may be a storm at sea, the arctic cold, or the desert heat. It may be a frontier of the spirit or of the mind. By testing himself beyond endurance man learns to know himself. He endures and grows. Each generation passes the limits defined by its elders; the passage of the oceans, the reaching of the poles, flight, the four-minute mile, the theory of relativity, atomic fission. In a small way the conquest of a great peak is such a frontier.

But we did not think much about *why* we had come. Our whole energies were focused on survival, though we still planned to go higher. Not one of us but wished the job were done; not one of us but longed for Base Camp and for home. Apathy grows strong on high peaks, the body becomes feeble, the force to advance declines. Simple jobs—writing a diary, taking photographs, cleaning the cooking pots—loom as major undertakings. It seems too hard, too tiring to do anything but lie still and rest, and yet someone managed to go out for more food bags, and at the same time to supply the other tents. Someone tightened the guy ropes on all tents. When we could melt snow, someone had strength to clean and fill the pots, and someone else took tea to those in the other tents. Bob Bates read aloud to us for hours. Dee Molenaar painted. We all wrote diaries; my own was now over 200 pages long. Weakened, hungry, thirsty though we were, I was able to say truthfully to Ata over the radio on August 6, "We're fine; morale is excellent. George and Tony have slightly frosted toes, and we're all thirsty, but things look pretty good."

Ata's reply, "Radio Pakistan forecasts more wind and snow," was hard.

The sixth of August was an anniversary for me, for on that day in 1934 three of us had made the first ascent of Mount Foraker in Alaska, returning late in the night through a storm much like the present, but at an altitude little more than half our present height. Surely this date must bring good luck. But when we awoke the wind was as bad as ever, and I spent the day writing in my diary a long account of our sensations, our hopes, and our fears.

During the afternoon for the first time we discussed retreat. George Bell had two frostbitten toes which had grown worse even in his sleeping bag, and Bob Craig had ominous spots on his heels. Dee was feeling poorly. Schoening, Streather, and Gilkey seemed to be the strongest, but all of us were weaker than we had been a few days before. We could not sleep much in the noise and pounding which the wind gave; we had little to drink and only cold food to eat. Retreat seemed wise, but perhaps we could recoup at Camp VI and return when the weather cleared for a final summit try.

Was this an irrational hope at this point? Was our judgment so warped by altitude that we really believed that we could go higher? Ata says no. He says, and I am inclined to agree, that we seemed in full possession of our faculties, and that our radio discussions and decisions were sound. We now believe that we were still strong enough to make the attempt, that had the weather cleared on August 7 we could have gone much higher.

We were not to be so tested. On August 7 came the cruelest blow. The day began brighter, the clouds were higher, the wind blew less. We crawled from our tents and stumbled around camp like castaways first reaching shore. As Art

Gilkey crawled out to join us, he collapsed unconscious in the snow. We rushed to him and he smiled feebly. "I'm all right, fellows; it's just my leg, that's all."

We half carried him to his tent and pulled off his clothes. As soon as I examined him, I knew with a sinking heart that real trouble had hit us.

"I've had this Charley horse for a couple of days now," said Art anxiously. "I thought it would be gone by now. It's sure to clear up in another day—isn't it?" the last was added in a voice that carried no assurance. The diagnosis was all too clear. Art had developed thrombophlebitis. Blood clots had formed in the veins of his left calf, cutting off the circulation and jeopardizing his leg. Already the ankle was swollen and an angry red. Reassuring him as best I could, I wrapped both legs snugly in Ace bandages and rejoined Bates and Streather in our tent. One look at my face sobered them as I explained the situation. "What's more," I concluded, "sometimes bits of clot break off and are carried to the lungs. At sea level this embolism is often fatal, and up here—" I shrugged, not having the heart to finish.

"Whatever caused this?" asked Tony. "I never heard of such a thing. Art didn't have any sickness or injury, did he?"

"I can't tell you what caused it. It's a disease which usually hits older people, or surgical patients," I explained. "I have never heard of it in healthy young mountaineers."

Then Bob asked the question we were all thinking, "How soon will he get better, Charlie? What are his chances?"

This was hard to answer. Under ideal circumstances the condition often clears in ten days to three weeks, though it may last longer. Under our conditions of dehydration, cold, and anxiety, it seemed unlikely he would improve. I didn't have the heart to add the latter, but optimistically I predicted ten days, and I explained to them the possibility of a pulmonary embolism. Bob went out to tell the other men. I sat for a few minutes, then crawled to Art's tent. I did the best I could to explain his condition, leaving out the complications, taking as optimistic a note as I could, trying to hide my awful certainty that he would never reach Base Camp alive.

By this catastrophe our whole fortunes had been changed. Before, we had been clinging to our camp, hoping for the clear weather which might bring success. Now we could only hope for weather good enough to try to lower Art down the mountain. I talked with Schoening and Craig, both of whom had done a great deal of mountain rescue work. Both said we could somehow manage to get Art down, but their statements lacked conviction. I did not believe them. I knew, we all knew, that no one could be carried, lowered, or dragged down the Black Pyramid, over the dreadful loose rock to Camp V, down

House's Chimney. My mind's eye flew over the whole route. There was no hope, absolutely none. Art was crippled. He would not recover enough to walk down. We could not carry him down.

But we could try, and we must. The day seemed settled, though cloudy and cold. We packed quickly, taking sleepers, camera, food, and only one tent because Camp VI was adequately stocked. Art Gilkey, in his sleeping bag, was wrapped in the wrecked tent, and a climbing rope secured around him. In the sickly sun we took some pictures of the party. The Third American Karakoram Expedition at its highest point! About ten o'clock, with a last look around, we started off.

Just then we came close to an action which would have been fatal. I have what amounts to an obsession about leaving tidy campsites, and I hated to leave, even here, such a messy camp. So I began to throw over the cliff all of the surplus food and to pull down the tents. Someone stopped me. "Come on," he said. "The snow and wind will take care of all this mess." We started down. At first it took all our strength to pull Art through the powdery snow, waist deep. Soon, as the slope grew steeper, we had to hold back, and hold back hard. Within a few hundred yards, what we should have anticipated became obvious: the whole slope of fresh snow was ready to avalanche. New snow had piled in even deeper on the ice, snow so cold that no consolidation could occur. As we cut down this slope, jarring it, the whole mass, tons upon tons of powder snow, would have plunged down the cliff. We had watched hundreds of these powder-snow avalanches from below. Now we were too close to one. Thanks to Pete Schoening and George Bell, we saw the danger in time and started back.

Our return to camp was terribly difficult. We could neither carry nor drag Art; instead we hauled on the ropes and on his arms as he gave great leaps with his good leg. It must have been harder for him than for us, and we were close to exhaustion when we reached our tents, those tents and that food which I had come so close to casting over the cliff.

Our position, bad enough before this discovery, was now desperate. There seemed to be no real hope that Art would recover enough to climb down or even to help us lower him. We could not ourselves survive much longer under these conditions at this altitude. Already we had lived longer than any other climbers at such a high camp, and the privation and strain had taken its toll. But our escape route was cut off. It would take many days—if no new snow fell— for the slope to consolidate. I could see no hope, no way out of our position.

"Charlie, Pete and I think we can find a route down the rock ridge to the east of the ice slope. You know, on the left as you look up from Camp VII. Remember that rock ridge?" Bob Craig broke in upon my thoughts, trying to sound hopeful. "We want to have a look at it."

"Yes, I remember the ridge," I answered. "It's terribly steep; it's plastered with new snow; but it certainly will be safe from avalanches. It will be easier to lower Art down that than to drag him through the snow, and safer. Go ahead if you feel like it today."

Despite the wind and clouds, now returned in almost full force, Schoening and Craig set out. Some two hours later, while the rest of us settled in our tents, their weary shouts reported success and they straggled back to camp. Despite the wind, they had gone down the rock rim for 400 feet, and through the blown snow and driven mist had looked down and across to the ledge at Camp VII. Their route, though difficult and dangerous, was safe from avalanches. They were convinced that the unknown section between them and Camp VII could be done. At any rate, it was a way down, and it was free from avalanches.

I slept that night the sleep of utter exhaustion. Mind and body were beaten and numb. As I lay in the hazy half-light between sleep and wakening next morning, I was conscious that the wind had slackened. "This may be our chance to get Art down," I thought again and again in the dull repetition of fatigue. For an hour I lay thinking; then the stirring beside me showed that Bates and Streather too were awake, and we started breakfast.

So simple a phrase does not do justice to the complex operation involved. I lay in a narrow hole between Bob and Tony, who had the outside berths. We had changed places each day, for the two men on the outside got colder and wetter, while the middle man slept poorly on the crack between the two air mattresses and was pummeled by his neighbors on two sides instead of one. As middle man it was now my job to make tea. I twisted and crawled and wriggled, dragged a dirty pot from beneath someone's boots, filled it with snow drifted into the tent. Balancing the stove on a pot lid between my two inert companions, I was able to light it after only six matches. The *dekshi* of snow was carefully placed on top after I had wiped dry the bottom of the pot, for drips of excess snow would put out the stove. For nearly an hour I balanced the stove and dekshi till tea was made, protecting it from the flapping tent, which blew out the tiny flame several times. Finally the water boiled. Some water went to another pot for cereal, but most was for tea. Prospects of food aroused my stuporous neighbors, and in a very complex series of maneuvers they sat up and we ate. We had so little to drink the preceding week that this meal tasted delicious and raised our spirits.

"This looks to be a good day—maybe the beginning of good weather," said Tony.

"If it is, then we've got to decide what to do," Bob answered. "Start down with Art or wait another day or two. Do you think his leg will be well enough for him to climb down soon, Charlie?"

Sadly I destroyed this optimistic thought: "I don't think there's a chance of his climbing today or for the next week or so. We must choose between carrying him down in this dubious weather today or waiting until tomorrow in hopes it will be better."

We talked this over among ourselves for a while; then I crawled to the other tents. In each I found cheerful faces.

"Charlie," said Bob Craig, "what about a dash for the summit from here? We could do it easily."

"Or maybe we could move two men up to IX today," chimed in Pete. "I'm game. We might as well do something while we wait for Art's leg to get better."

I looked at them closely to be sure they were in earnest. Here was no foolish, blind bravado, no desperate "summit or die" attitude. Nor was there any idea of retreat without our friend. Their courage was tremendous, their morale superb.

"It seems to me we can do one of three things," I said seriously. "We can sit tight today, hoping tomorrow will be better. Carrying Art will be bad enough, and we shouldn't try it except in reasonably good weather. Or we can start for VII now, even in the clouds, because tomorrow may be bad again. The forecast just now said clouds and wind. Or, and I think this is the best idea, all of you fellows can hurry down to VI today, leaving me to take care of Art. The supplies up here will last the two of us for at least ten days, and you can all come up to help us down, well rested, when the weather is really settled.

The others were reluctant to split the party at this point, and after some discussion we decided to wait another day. Then we would either all go down or, if necessary, Streather, Art, and I would remain at VIII while the others descended.

Art felt and looked better, and his leg hurt less. "I'll be climbing again tomorrow," he said. It was heart-rending to see his courage, to know that his hope could not possibly come true. But I did hope a better day would come for the terrible work ahead of us, a day when we could see, a day without storm.

Meantime the wind decreased somewhat and the sun's heat could almost be felt through the dense cloud which enveloped us like cotton. We staggered around camp in the deep drifts, locating supplies, repitching tents. I made my daily medical rounds, looking at George's toes, which were by now badly frosted, and at Bob Craig's red and painful heels. For a long time I talked with Art, rebandaging his legs. He did seem better, but now the right leg was slightly tender, too. It was clear that he would not climb.

For several days we had talked about moving *up*. We did not want to retreat with bowed heads, beaten, discouraged. We would go down with colors flying.

One last puny gesture of defiance must be made. Schoening and Craig were our fittest climbers now. They put on their warmest clothing, tied on their climbing rope, and set out—upward. For an hour they climbed through the steep new snow, over hummocks and across wide cracks. They could see nothing in the dense clouds but they were going *up*. After two hours they returned, having climbed perhaps 400 feet. They were still far from the summit cone. But their gesture underlined our spirit. We were not beaten.

At six o'clock I called Ata. "Hello, Base Camp, Hello, Base Camp. This is Camp VIII. How do you hear me?"

Cheerful as always, Ata replied, "I hear you very well, Charlie. How is Art? How are you all standing up in this storm?"

"We are very good Ata," I tried to sound sure. "Art seems a little better today, but I don't see any prospect of his being able to climb for a long time." I went on, "What have you to suggest for therapy, Ata?"

"Charlie, that isn't my field," said Ata, an eye specialist. "I can't suggest anything to do for him but what you're already doing. But I do strongly urge that I come up to help you. After all, you have two or three frostbite cases besides Art, and I can share your burden. Over."

My eyes watered as this new sign of this wonderful man's affection for us, his determination to share our ordeal. "Ata," I replied, "you can't possibly get up here in this weather."

"I could try," he broke in.

"And furthermore," I went on, "there isn't anything you can do. We must handle this from here."

I talked over our plans with him and he agreed with our decision: if the next day were not good enough to carry Art down, the others would proceed to VI, leaving me with Art and Tony, who insisted on staying with us.

"Pray for good weather, Ata," I concluded.

"You are fighting now for all your lives," said Ata. "We here in Base Camp have been praying for you for many days."

August 9 was grim and cold. The storm returned in all its fury. Snow screamed against the tent; wind beat upon us in renewed viciousness. Nothing could be done. We could not leave the tents and live.

This was our lowest time. For the first time I thought we might all perish here in this pitiless storm. We would never leave Art; none of us had even thought of it. But we could not move him in storm; indeed, we could not move ourselves in the storm of that day.

Art had begun to cough during the night, a dry, hacking cough. My fears were confirmed as I listened to his chest. At least two clots had been carried to his lungs, for I could hear two congested areas. He looked dreadful; his pulse was pounding at 140 per minute. But his courage never faltered. He had no pain—he said—but he admitted that the cough was a nuisance. I moved in with him that morning and Schoening took my place. Through the stormy afternoon we talked briefly or read. There was little to say. We knew the odds against us, but we had made our plans. Art said nothing of himself. He had never talked about his death, though he was too wise not to see its imminence. He apologized for being a burden upon us. He encouraged us, spoke of another summit attempt—after we got him down.

The embolism to his lungs made retreat even more imperative. He could not live long up here. He would probably not live through the descent, but we must give him all the chance we could. We must do it soon. That evening I called Base Camp. "Ata, Art had a pulmonary embolism. His condition is poor. We *must* get him off the mountain. We are going to start down tomorrow unless the weather is impossible. All of us are weaker, but morale is very high. I will call you tomorrow morning at seven. If possible we'll start soon afterward."

On that note we slept.

The Accident

We all knew that some of us might never get down the mountain alive. Each had long recognized the near impossibility of evacuating an injured man from the upper ledges of K2. We had told one another that "if somebody broke a leg, you could never get him down the mountain," but now that we were faced with Gilkey's helplessness, we realized that we *had* to get him down. We didn't know how, but we knew that we had to do it.

Schoening in particular, and also Bob Craig and Dee Molenaar, had done a lot of mountain rescue work, and the rest of us placed great confidence in their faith that somehow we could get our casualty to Base Camp. Gilkey's high morale and his confidence in us was a great boost to our spirits and we faced the job ahead with strong determination. When on the morning of August 10 Charlie Houston thrust his shoulders through the tunnel entrance of the tent where Schoening, Streather, and I, shoulder rubbing shoulder, had tossed during the long night hours, we spoke almost in unison: "How is he?"

"We've got to take him down," said the doctor. "His other leg has a clot now and he can't last long *here.*"

The wind was hammering the tent fabric so hard that we had to yell at one another. Drifts of fine powder snow were sifting in through a strained seam in the tent vestibule, though we had done our best to keep the shelter airtight, and we could feel the whole tent vibrate as gusts stretched the fabric to the utmost.

"What? Move in this storm?" said someone.

"We've got to," said Houston. "He'll soon be dead if we don't get him down."

Nothing needed saying after that, for we knew what this decision meant. All of us had fought mountain storms before, but we had never seen anything like the duration and violence of this furious wind and snow that was still battering us. We all knew the story of the storm on Nanga Parbat in 1934, when nine members of a German expedition had died of exhaustion while battling the wind and snow. Willy Merkl, Uli Wieland, and Wili Welzenbach had been famous mountaineers, but a storm had exhausted them and killed them one by one. Here on K2 we had not only the storm to fight but the steepest part of the mountain, and we were trying to bring down these precipitous slopes a crippled companion as well!

We all realized that our adventure had now become grim, for the odds against getting Art down were obvious, and our own position was getting more critical all the time. While Houston and Schoening were easing Art out of his tent into the storm, the rest of us began packing light loads to take down. We would need one tent in case of emergency, and we took the Gerry tent, our lightest one. We also might need a stove and pot, and some meat bars, chocolate, or quick-energy food that needed no cooking. Often the effects of altitude so weaken one's determination that doing nothing becomes a positive pleasure, but this was no time for lethargy, and as we moved purposefully out of the tents into the stinging blasts of snow, we knew that we had to move fast, while fingers and toes still had feeling. Little was spoken. Each of us realized that he was beginning the most dangerous day's work of his lifetime.

Gilkey seemed in no pain as we wrapped him in the smashed tent, put his feet in a rucksack, and tied nylon ropes to him in such a way that they cradled him. Four ropes, tied to this cradle, could be held by one man ahead, one man behind, and one on either side. We had already put on all our warm clothing—sweaters, wool jackets, down jackets, and nylon parkas—and stripped our packs to the minimum. As we worked, the disabled man watched the preparations silently. He was an experienced mountaineer and realized what all of us were up against. But he knew also that we would never leave him, and that we would bring him down safely if it were humanly possible. Art's cap was pulled down over his face, which looked drawn and bluish-gray, but he gave a wan smile whenever someone asked, "How is it going?"

"Just fine," he would say. "Just fine." And his mouth would smile. He never showed a moment's fear or the slightest lack of confidence, but he realized of course that he had been stricken by something that was likely to be fatal, that his condition was getting worse, and the he was 9,000 feet above Base Camp in a terrible monsoon storm. The nearest tent, at Camp VI, was 2,000 feet below. He knew that we could not carry him down the tricky route we had come up, and that we must go only where we could lower him. Even in perfect weather with all men in top physical condition, the task might prove impossible—yet Art Gilkey could smile and his smile gave us strength.

While we were adjusting the tow ropes, Schoening and Molenaar strapped on their crampons and disappeared into the storm. They were to find the best route past the dangerous avalanche slope that had blocked us a few days before, and to go over to the Camp VII cache to get a climbing rope that was strung on the ice slope just above. It would be useful in the descent. After their departure Houston called Base Camp on the walkie-talkie and told Ata-Ullah our plans. "It's pretty desperate, Ata," he said grimly, "but we can't wait. We're starting down now. We'll call you at three o'clock."

Each man took his place on a rope tied to Gilkey and for a couple of hundred yards we lunged hard at the tow ropes to pull Art through the knee-deep drifts of powder snow; then gravity took over and we had to hold back just as strongly to keep our helpless 185-pound load from plunging into the abyss. The steep slope we were on disappeared below us into nothingness. Was there a cliff there, a jumping-off place? We strained our eyes peering into the storm, but we could not wait for clearing weather. Instead we had to depend on Schoening and Molenaar, who had gone ahead to scout out the way. As we descended, Craig and Bell pulled the front ropes, one on each side, and Houston directed operations from a point immediately behind Gilkey, while Streather and I anchored the rope higher up. Gradually we worked our way to a rock ridge, climbed down alongside it, and them began to lower Gilkey down a steep snow slope leading to a snow chute and an ice gully below. This route was not the one we would have taken had Gilkey been able to walk, but now we had no choice: we could go only where we could lower our companion, and we had faith that the two men ahead would find a route down. Once we were well started, return to Camp VIII would be impossible for any of us.

The wind and cold seeped insidiously through our layers of warm clothing so that by the end of the third hour none of us had feeling in his toes any longer, and grotesque icicles hung from our eyebrows, beards, and mustaches. Goggles froze over and we continually raised them on our foreheads in order to see how to handle the rope. Moving the sick man was frightfully slow. We had to belay one another as well as Gilkey, and our numb fingers would not move quickly. Somehow, when we got to the steepest pitch, however, someone managed to tie two 120-foot nylon ropes together and we started to lower Gilkey down, down in the only direction the slope would permit. Houston and I, braced on the storm-swept ridge, backs to the wind, could feel the terrible gusts trying to hurl us off the rocks. We could not see where we were lowering Art, but we could hear faint shouts from Schoening and Molenaar, who were out of sight below. As we slowly payed out the coils of rope, thankful that they were of nylon and would not freeze in kinks, Bob Craig unroped from us and climbed down alongside the injured man to direct the descent. Soon he was completely obscured, too, but Streather climbed down to where he could see Craig's arm signals, yet still see us, and so we belayers had communication with Craig and Gilkey and knew whether to lower or to hold the rope. Alternately we anchored and payed out the line until we were nearly frozen, and our arms were strained when Tony Streather, whom we could barely see, turned and shouted, "Hold tight! They're being carried down in an avalanche!"

We held. Our anchorage was good and the rope stretched taut. For a moment snow flurries blotted out everything, and then we could hear a muffled shout from Streather. "They're still there!" The rope had broken loose a wind-slab avalanche of powder snow that had roared down over both men, blotting them from sight. Craig clung to the rope to Gilkey, and held on to it for his life. The pull of the hissing particles must have been terrible, but the avalanche was of unconsolidated snow. The falling powder slithered out of sight and down off the side of the mountain, where it must have kept falling long after we could hear it. When it was gone, Craig still clung to the rope, gray and very chilled. Both men were safe. The grim descent continued.

Schoening and Molenaar, who were not far from Camp VII, soon were able to reach Gilkey, but it seemed like hours to the four of us on the icy rocks of the wind-swept ridge before they shouted up that they had him strongly belayed "on the edge of a cliff," and we could climb down. Stiffly we shifted from our frozen positions, and climbed clumsily down the steep, crumbly rocks to the snow chute above the ice gully. Houston and I were on one rope, Bell and Streather on the other. All were so cold, so near exhaustion, that moving down and over dangerous, snow-covered ice stretched us to the limit. Through the murk of blowing snow we saw Schoening standing in front of a large, rounded rock that had become frozen onto a narrow ledge. His ice ax was thrust deep into the snow above the rock, and the rope with which he held Art Gilkey was looped tightly around the shaft of the ax. The sick man was at the edge of a 20-foot cliff, beneath which we could glimpse the ice gully dropping off steeply into the storm toward the Godwin-Austen Glacier nearly 2 miles below.

Schoening looked like a man from another world. So much frost had formed on our beards that faces were unrecognizable, and we knew that we were fast reaching the breaking point. We could not continue much longer without shelter from the driving storm and food to renew our energy. Some 150 yards below us to the east was the tiny shelf, nicked into the ice slope, where Schoening and Gilkey had spent the night of July 30 during their reconnaissance above camp VI. We had called it Camp VII, or Camp VII cache. None of us had expected anyone to spend another night there, but Bob Craig, whose struggle against the avalanche had so completely exhausted him temporarily that he could hardly tie a crampon strap, had been belayed over to this site to rest and clear some of the avalanche snow that had seeped under his parka. We yelled to him to try to enlarge the ledge. Meanwhile, with Schoening anchoring the rope, we lowered Gilkey slowly over the short rock cliff until he was resting against the 45-degree ice slope. Streather, who was roped to Bell, climbed down to Gilkey. Schoening held Gilkey's rope firmly while Houston belayed me across a delicate pitch of steep, hard ice, and then Houston climbed down to a point opposite the man suspended against the slope. The problem now was not to get Gilkey down, but to swing him across the steep ice slope to the ice shelf at Camp VII. Our plan was to get a firm anchorage and then pendulum him across, but unfortunately the ice near him was too hard for axes to be driven in and the slope was relentlessly steep.

Even during the best weather conditions the maneuver would have been dangerous, and our position at that moment I shall never forget. Schoening was belaying Gilkey, who hung 60 feet below him, suspended against the sharply angled ice. On the same level as Gilkey, and 40 feet across from him, five of us, facing into the stinging, drifting snow, were searching for a place where we could stand and anchor the rope to Gilkey as we pulled him across the ice in the direction of Craig on the ice shelf. With our spiked crampons biting the hard ice, Streather, Houston, Molenaar, and I stood close together. Bell and Streather were roped together, Houston and I were on a rope together—and Molenaar had just "tied in" to a loose rope to Gilkey. He had done this when Craig had unroped and gone over to the ice shelf to rest, and it was Molenaar's precaution that saved us all. For George Bell, who was some 60 feet above us, began to descend a delicate stretch of hard ice in order to help with Gilkey's ropes. At that moment, what we had all been dreading occurred. Something threw Bell off balance and he fell.

I never saw Bell fall, but to my horror I saw Streather being dragged off the slope and making desperate efforts to jam the pick of his ax into the ice and stop. Streather had been standing above the rope from Houston to me. In almost the same instant I saw Houston swept off, and though I turned and lunged at the hard ice with the point of my ax, a terrible jerk ripped me from my hold and threw me backward headfirst down the slope. *This is it!* I thought as I landed heavily on my pack. There was nothing I could do now. We had done our best, but our best wasn't good enough. This was the end. Since nobody was on the rope with Houston and me, there was no one else to hold us, and I knew that nothing could stop us now. On the slope below, no rock jutted on which the rope between us could catch. Only thousands of feet of empty space separated us from the glacier below. It was like falling off a slanting Empire State Building six times as high as the real one.

Thrown violently backward, with the hood of my down jacket jammed over my eyes, I had a feeling of unreality, of detachment. The future was beyond my control. All I knew was that I landed on my pack with great force, bouncing faster and faster, bumping over rocks in great thumps. The next bound I expected to take me over a cliff in a terrible drop that would finish it all, when, by a miracle, I stopped sliding.

I was on my back with my hood over my eyes and my head a yard below my feet. My arms, stretched over my head, were so completely tangled with taut rope that I could not loosen them. I was helpless, and when I tried to move, I realized that I was balanced on the crest of some rocks and that a change of position might throw me off the edge. The rope had apparently snagged on a projection—though how and where I couldn't imagine—but it might not be securely caught. Whether it was firmly held, whether anyone else was alive, I did not know, but I didn't need to wait. Almost immediately I heard a groan coming from nearly on top of me. "Get me loose," I called, and immediately I felt the pressure of a leg braced against my shoulder and the rope was pulled off my arms.

Grabbing a rock, I swung my head around. Dee Molenaar and I were clinging to a rocky outcrop at the side of a steep ice slope, studded with rocks, about 150 to 200 feet below the place where we had been working on the ropes to Gilkey. Blood from Dee's nose trickled across his mustache and beard, and he looked badly shaken. My rope was tight to someone or something above, and I heard a distant yell, "Get your weight off the rope!" Fifty feet higher, through a mist of blowing snow, I could see Tony Streather staggering to his feet, a tangle of ropes still tight about his waist. Below me I heard a cry, "My hands are freezing!" and, looking down, to my amazement I saw George Bell, who seconds before had been 60 feet above me. Now about 60 feet *below*, he was climbing up over the edge of nothingness. He wore neither pack nor glasses and was staggering up over the steep rocks, obviously dazed, with his hands held out grotesquely in front of him. His mittens had been ripped off in the fall, and already the color of his hands had turned an ugly fish-belly white. If his hands were badly frozen, of course, we might never be able to get him down off the mountain.

Turning to Molenaar, I thrust my pack into his arms. Most of the lashing had ripped loose and the walkie-talkie radio, which had been on top, was gone; my sleeping bag was half off, held by a single twist of line. Without sleeping bags we were unlikely to survive the night, no matter how we tried! Molenaar wore no pack, I imagined that his sleeping bag also had been torn off in the fall. Whether or not the tent someone had been carrying had survived the fall, I didn't know. "For God's sake, hold this," I yelled above the wind, placing my load in Molenaar's arms. (For all I knew, mine was the only sleeping bag to survive the fall, and we must not lose it now.) The loose pack was awkward to hold securely while we were standing on such steep rock, but Molenaar grasped it and I unroped and started to climb shakily down to meet Bell. As I climbed down, I wondered about the ropes that had saved us. They were snagged to something up above, but the driving snow kept us from seeing what was holding them. Luckily I had a spare pair of dry, loosely woven Indian mitts in the pouch pocket of my parka, and when I reached Bell, whose face was gray and haggard, I helped him to put them on. Already his fingers were so stiff with cold that he couldn't move them, but balancing on projections of rock on the steep slope, we struggled to save his hands and finally forced the big white mittens past his stiff thumbs and down over his wrists.

Bell's fall had ended with him suspended over the edge of a ledge, below which the slope dropped away precipitously for thousands of feet. The weight of his pack pulled him head down, and he had lost it while trying to get right side up and back over the ledge. While Bell crouched down, working desperately to warm his hands under his parka, I left him, for Molenaar and I had seen a crumpled figure lying below a 30-foot cliff on a narrow shelf that seemed projecting over utter blankness below. It was Houston. Somehow a rope to him was snagged high above us, too. Climbing unsteadily but cautiously, for I was not roped and felt shaken by the fall, I worked my way down the steep rocks and across to the ledge. Houston was unconscious, but his eyes opened as I touched his shoulder. When he staggered to his feet, I felt relief it is impossible to describe.

"Where are we?" he asked. "What are we doing here?"

He was obviously hurt. His eyes did not focus and he appeared to be suffering from a concussion. Again and again I tried to persuade him to climb up the cliff, while Molenaar anchored the rope still attached to him from above. He didn't understand. "Where are we?" he kept saying, for my replies did not convey any meaning to him in his confused state.

The wind and blowing snow were searing our faces. We were all near exhaustion and in danger of crippling frostbite. If we were to survive, we had to get shelter at once, or we would be so numbed by exposure that we could not protect ourselves. What had happened in that Nanga Parbat storm which had taken so many men was a grim reminder. All of us working together did not now have strength enough to pull to carry Houston up the steep rock and snow to the ice ledge, 150 feet above, which we had called Camp VII.

"Charlie," I said with the greatest intensity, looking directly into his eyes, "if you ever want to see Dorcas and Penny again [his wife and daughter], climb up there *right now!*"

Somehow this demand penetrated to his brain, for, with a frightened look and without a word, he turned and, belayed by Molenaar, fairly swarmed up the snowy rocks of the cliff. Instinct and years of climbing helped him now in his confused condition, for he climbed brilliantly up to Molenaar. I followed more slowly because, being fully conscious, I had great respect for this steep rock wall, and with great care I pulled myself up over the snow-covered slabs. When I reached Molenaar, he was looking puzzled and very unhappy as he tried to answer Houston's repeated question, "What are we doing here?"

In the Shadow of Denali
(Alaska's Mt. McKinley)

JONATHAN WATERMAN

Jonathan Waterman has penned this excerpt from his book of the same name, one which is subtitled, **Life and Death on Alaska's Mt. McKinley.** This section is about the life of a guide on McKinley, yet another aspect of mountaineering. Guiding on the mountain began in 1960 and this account concentrates on the legendary Swiss expatriate guide, Ray Genet. It is not an account of a singular expedition, but rather covers the trials and tribulations of the guides and their clients, and how each guide has to do things his way.

Paying for the Summit

Each year a thousand climbers engage Denali. More than three hundred of them are guided, and in years when the weather is kind, more than half these clients reach the summit, steered, towed, cajoled, protected, and insured by an amiable tribe of mountain guides.

Even the earliest climbers on Denali tried to hire guides. In 1903 a Canadian horsepacker warned the American journalist Robert Dunn about his journey to Denali: "You don't want no Swiss guides. They're handy high up on rocks and ice, but lose themselves in the woods. Six weeks across Alasky swamps? They'd die or quit you the first day."

Dunn, Frederick Cook, three roustabouts, and fifteen horses beat through more than three hundred miles of brush and muskeg, "under the curse of mosquitoes and bull-dog flies," without guides. If an experienced climber or guide had accompanied them, they might have reached the summit instead of their ten-thousand-foot high point on the Northwest Buttress.

Before Hudson Stuck, archdeacon of the Yukon, first climbed Denali ten years later, he had hired guides on Mount Rainier and in the Canadian Rockies. Stuck did not go against the fold, and he knew that the continent's highest peak demanded the services of a guide. In 1913, Stuck underwrote all the expenses and gave everything but money to the legendary "Seventy-Mile Kid," Harry Karstens, to scout Denali, break trail, then chop hundreds of steps. Finally, Karstens and Walter Harper led the archdeacon to the top. When Stuck could plod no higher, he promptly fainted.

On America's highest alp, climbers weren't paid to take anyone to the summit until another several hundred climbers and forty-seven years had passed. But in the Canadian Rockies and the European Alps, guiding had always been linked to climbing.

European guiding originated when well-to-do sportsmen, often English, hired local farmers to pack their lunches, haul the ladders, and attend to all of the other mundane details of mountaineering. Guides seldom climbed on their own, but, for a price, mountain peasants were eager to pack loads, scout routes, chop steps, and break trail—tasks considered gauche by their clients.

Before World War II, America had few climbers, and mountains such as Denali were considered utterly remote. In the accessible mountain ranges of the world, guiding was relatively straightforward. But on Denali, it couldn't begin until Washburn and the skiplane "opened up" an easy route in 1951. Walking in sixty miles was not an option for clients.

Guiding began on Denali in 1960. Rainier guides and veteran climbers Lou Whittaker, Jim Whittaker, and Pete Schoening escorted John Day to the summit. Day had convinced the three northwestern mountaineers to climb Denali in a "speed ascent," which took them three days from 10,000 feet. While descending from Denali Pass, someone slipped, fell, and pulled the whole team downward: Day broke his leg, and Schoening—whose famous reactions with an ice ax had saved five men from falling off K2 in 1953—was knocked unconscious.

Fifty people mobilized to evacuate Schoening and Day. The highest airplane landing up to that time had been made at 14,300 feet. Another pilot stripped down his helicopter, including the battery, then plucked off Day, Schoening, and another climber, stricken with altitude illness. Rescue headlines blazoned in newspapers across the country.

Rainier Guide Service later made a few more tentative forays, but most guides lacked the audacity to make such a formidable mountain a business goal.

Traditionally, a guiding career involved a long climbing apprenticeship on many mountains, and in the 1960s American guides were conservative and somewhat in awe of the suffering that even an ordinary ascent of Denali demanded.

So it stood to reason that the first full-time guide on Denali was a European who had never followed American guiding traditions and who had never climbed any significant mountain until he summited on Denali in the winter of 1967. Afterward, the expatriate Swiss Ray Genet and his companions shuffled into the hospital with frostbitten toes. While Dave Johnston and Art Davidson took months to recover, Genet healed his frostbite in three short weeks by marathon dancing in the nightclubs of Anchorage. That summer, he resumed his house painting business, all the while plotting his return to Denali.

By 1968—given Genet's European mountain roots, his entrepreneurial *savoir faire,* and his fame from the first winter climb—Denali became ripe for the picking. In his swashbuckling wisdom, Genet knew that his business would never flourish under the straitlaced image of most American guide companies, so he cultivated his bushy black beard, his outrageous orange climbing suit, and his trademark bandanna wrapped "pirate style" over his forehead. The pirate's credo—"To the summit"—exhorted clients never to settle for anything less; Genet often brayed that clients would summit if he had to drag them there. His bombastic style made him undisputed king of the mountain for more than a decade.

He escorted huge groups, who left an indelible imprint of feces, trash, and overcrowding. He was also fond of saying that he was in the business of selling "ego trips to climbers."

Until he died, the Pirate lived by the sword. In 1972 one client fell and broke a leg. The next year three of his indisposed clients were helicoptered out from 14,300 feet on two different occasions. In 1976 the Pirate jumped out of a helicopter near the summit to save a young woman's life. It was not uncommon for him to shoulder his victims as if they were bundles of firewood. Had he lived to board the 1980s, rattling his ice ax like a saber, Hollywood would surely have courted him for movie rights.

In a time when American climbers disdained sponsorship, Genet's woolly face decorated countless Tang advertisements. Certainly the Pirate reached his own 20,320-foot apogee with much more frequency than the astronauts Tang usually sponsored.

When I first met him, in 1976, the burly *Burgführer* was carrying a sick man down from 17,000 feet. Hours later, the twenty-four-year-old client died of pulmonary edema.

I also watched Genet retrieve a pack that an unguided stranger accidentally dropped from 16,200 feet and fell 1,000 feet; Genet ran down, then selflessly jogged this considerable distance back up the fixed ropes to return the pack to its stunned owner.

Three days later, on July 5, more than eighty people waited to stand atop the urine-stained summit that is no larger than an ordinary bathroom. Then Genet summited.

He would later boast that he went to the top of Denali forty-three times (actually twenty-four); once, on an uncrowded day, he claims that he and a companion became the first to mate on the roof of North America; in 1991 one of his sons, Taras (twelve), became the youngest climber to summit.

On that July 5 day of the crowded Bicentennial year, he only whipped out his radiotelephone to place phone calls to three separate women; first he yelled at the caller already on the party line to hang up. Dozens of remote cabin dwellers and mountaineers heard the pirate's distinctive baritone booming over the airwaves. His opening salutation to these women, "Hi, honey, it's Ray, I'm on the summit of McKinley!" was answered three times with various degrees of incredulity. After praising each woman as his highest object of affection, he signed off: "I love you, baby!"

His client who had died of pulmonary edema preyed heavily on Genet's mind because even hauling the man down on his back had come to naught. That afternoon a helicopter flew into the 14,300-foot basin and picked up the stiffened client, wrapped in an American flag.

I saw Genet two days later. He was cursing out Frances Randall, caretaker of the Kahiltna base camp airstrip. Randall insisted that some frostbitten Mexicans had priority over Genet, who would have to wait his turn for a flight out. The quarrelsome Genet was unrepentant, arguing that it was *his* mountain. Sitting on their packs, the three Mexicans stole glimpses at Genet as if he were Pancho Villa reincarnated. When the long-awaited skiplane finally skidded onto the glacier, he jumped on board alone—even though there was room for the injured climbers. With his usual bluster he commanded the pilot not to spare any horses on the way back to Talkeetna, where his women would be queuing up at the airstrip. The black-toed Mexicans said nothing.

Most women back in Talkeetna reviled him because he'd walk up unannounced and pinch their rear ends. One climber recalled having to jump off the street because Genet would have run him over. When this pedestrian tried to stand up to Genet, he merely pushed him aside and shouted, "Stay out of my way!" Conversely, up on the mountain, after barking out orders to his guides, cooks, and clients all day long, Genet would come crawling into his tent at night and softly ask his tentmate if he would mind fixing Genet some warm milk and honey from the expedition supplies.

Genet really believed it was his mountain. When Gary Bocarde, Michael Covington, Rainier Guide Serivce, and others began arriving with regular clients during the mid-1970s, the Pirate bluffed that the Park Service had given him the only guiding permit for the mountain. Some guides even believed him.

Bocarde once told a reporter, "His attitude [toward clients] was, 'I'll get you up there, no matter what.' That kind of attitude can be dangerous."

Bocarde recently said, "He clearly handled 'em like animals, dragging 'em along with the rope. And if there was a woman in the group, he was always tied into her."

One of Genet's former chief guides, Brian Okonek, said, "It's amazing that he didn't have more accidents and fatalities, given his style; I don't know if it was his dynamic leadership or good luck, but he was *out there*. Genet did know how to get the most out of a person. He didn't do any pretrip screening for people, and he took people who didn't have any right being on the mountain, but he knew when to quit pushing them. Eventually, though, things fell apart because he wasn't real organized; he had too many clients and too few guides. Also, the community equipment was in terrible shape, the first-aid kit was non-existent, and you didn't know how many people were coming until the clients showed up."

In 1979 sled-dog racers Joe Redington and Susan Butcher were hauled to the summit by Genet. Redington, who was otherwise impressed by his guide, conceded to reporter Bill Sherwonit, "I saw him work on some people that never would have made it there. Some of them he kind of abused a little bit."

When asked about the caches and refuse abandoned on the mountain, Genet said, "It used to be called caching and now it's called trashing. It's not a major problem." Nonetheless, Genet spawned a system of caches and trash dumps that environmentally aware climbers found loathsome. From 1971 to 1976, members of the Denali Arctic Environmental Project hauled more than a thousand pounds of refuse down the mountain. Its leader, Gary Grimm, carefully pointed his finger at Genet and blamed much of the trash on commercial guides "who seem to be more interested in profits than in environmental quality."

During his last few years of guiding, the indefatigable Pirate had grown so weary that he hired assistants. Climbers such as Jim Hale (eventually fired by Genet because he turned clients away from the summit in dangerous avalanche conditions) helped the clients up the mountain for ten days. Then Genet flew in, sprinted 7,000 feet up, and towed as many as forty-two clients, cooks, and assistants in one long, undulating summit mambo line. After topping out, Genet sprinted back down without dealing with any clients.

At the end of the guiding season in 1979, Genet told Okonek that guiding was getting old, that he'd had a long, hard summer and he wanted someone to help him. He didn't mention the upcoming Everest trip, but Okonek would never forget Genet's paternal advice: "There's a lot of people out there who can care for you, but mountains are dangerous and unforgiving. You gotta take care of yourself."

A month later Genet impulsively thrashed to the top of Everest after battling a gastrointestinal illness. On the summit he carefully left his last cache: a handwritten note.

While descending with the leader's wife, Hannelore Schmatz, Genet's supplementary oxygen ran out. Sherpa Sungdare insisted that they continue down, but Genet, in typical contentious form, refused. At 27,800 feet, Schmatz and Genet began the highest and longest sleep performed by any man and woman. He was forty-eight years old.

Sungdare ran down to the 26,000-foot South Col. He grabbed an oxygen bottle and hustled back up that very night to try to save his clients—just as Genet would have on Denali. But when Sungdare arrived, neither Genet nor Schmatz needed any more oxygen. Sungdare descended, utterly despondent. (Sungdare would lose nine toes to frostbite, climb Everest four more times, then commit suicide in 1989.)

Michael Covington escorted Genet's hysterical companion, Kathy Sullivan and their son out of the Everest base camp. That winter, two Poles uncovered Genet's last cache on the summit. It read: "For a good time call Pat Rucker 274-8402 Anchorage, Alaska USA."

In 1980 Denali National Park officials finally began controlling guide companies. Seven exclusive permits were issued. Over the years, guides were asked to bring down their trash, defecate into plastic bags, and lead no more than fourteen members at once. For the most part, guides cleaned up their act. Although foreign "bandit" guides continue to plague the seven "conessionaires," the mountain is definitely cleaner and perhaps a bit safer than in the halcyon days of Genet.

Okonek, now one of the concessionaires, says, "Guiding has come a long way since Genet died. Now guides have more training; we know a lot more about altitude, screening clients, and things that were developed over years by trail and error."

The myth of the Pirate still lives. Genet Expeditions was a sought-after service that retained its credo. "To the summit," despite frequent reprimands from the Park Service for unsafe guiding. Finally, in 1992, the Denali National Park superintendent revoked Genet's guiding permit.

In the spring of 1981 I signed on under Michael Covington as a Fantasy Ridge Mountain Guide on Denali. My boss wore an electrified Afro, a euphoric grin, and a Nepalese Z-stone necklace. Michael insisted that he loved guiding; he'd sooner rot, he said, than work nine to five. Two years earlier he had leapfrogged a nine-hundred-foot rope up the Cassin Ridge with several clients climbing the ropes behind him. He claimed he had created a new technique—while Brad Washburn had fine-tuned *expedition style* on the West Buttress Route and Doug Scott had climbed the south face *alpine style,* Michael introduced *capsule style* to Denali.

Despite Michael's noxious "Slim Sherman" cigar smoke, the director of Fantasy Ridge Alpinism became my role model. After hiring me, he provided plane fare and a $700 monthly wage. Even though seasoned Denali guides made twice (now four times) as much, most climbers didn't grouse about free climbing trips. Furthermore, the salary included room and board—a tent plus all the freeze-dried food you could eat.

After climbing the west rib with John Thackray for fun, I arrived back at the base camp. Here I fell into repose and waited for my job, guiding eighteen circuitous glacial miles (three miles by raven wings) to Denali's summit. I assured Michael that reclimbing the mountain with clients would be, in climberspeak, "a real cruise."

While I was sprawling over a half-inch-thick ensolite pad—insulating me from the several-hundred-foot-thick glacier—a Niagaran avalanche flooded the mile-and-a-half-high face of Mount Hunter—two ridges away from Denali. After suppressing the instinctive urge to run, I turned back to my unflinching cribbage opponent, one of scores of nameless mountain guides who slink about Talkeetna's saloons and Denali's glaciers. The avalanche spindrift cloud passed over us like the radioactive fallout from a nuclear bomb; I tried to look as composed as my nearby associate.

Guide mercenaries can be identified by white "raccoon" eye rings where sunglasses have blocked the beginnings of skin cancer elsewhere on their faces. They share a cologne of urine and sweat mixed into their synthetic clothing, chicly labeled Petzl, Berghaus, or Helly Hansen—versus the Columbia, L. L. Bean, and R.E.I. labels sported by their clients. Some of these guides are unassuming and soft-spoken. Most of them curse, chew, spit, smoke, fart, brag, blow harmonicas, sing off key, flaunt their egos, and conduct themselves in a manner that would lead to their excommunication from church, their mortification in public, or their eviction from apartments.

I was not surprised when my fellow guide Steve Gall sauntered out of the skiplane wearing a bandanna pirate-style around his forehead. He was blowing smoke rings from a Slim Sherman wedged between his fingers.

As the seven clients jumped (and fell) out of the skiplane, I began to envision our group dynamics. Even a neophyte Denali guide like myself could sense that there were insurmountable obstacles ahead. Our congenitally uncoordinated Baptist minister, Phil, told us that we didn't have to worry because God would see us safely up the mountain. Phil had been directly appointed by his own Chief Guide in the Sky to climb the mountain so that he could return home and better direct his misguided flock, sinners all, from the Baptist backwaters of southern Georgia. In Denali guide parlance, our minister appeared to be only one of "a school of tuna."

Our biggest catches were the Texans Ernest and Evelyn Chandler, living out the great American Dream by climbing its greatest peak. Ernest was forty pounds overweight with a heart condition, while his pale, slender wife would easily kite away if the wind blew more than fifty miles per hour. In this business, however, the consummate Denali businessman knows that as long as his clients' money is green, anyone can pay for the summit. I made several inquiries about our lame-looking clients, aged nineteen to sixty-three. *Tuna.*

My colleague Steve seemed strangely resigned about his new charges. Moreover, he was so unfazed and dedicated to the mission at large that he must have known something I didn't. Our troubles began only a mile up the Kahiltna Glacier, seventeen miles from the summit. The Chandlers, with the exception of their nineteen-year-old son Walt, could not drag their sleds; Steve took Evelyn's, while I took Ernest's. Another mile farther, Steve lashed Evelyn's pack on top of his. And a hundred yards from camp, Ernest collapsed.

He clutched his chest as his pulse raced like the traffic on Interstate 20. When he calmed down an hour later, he allowed that he would have been fine if he had taken his heart medicine. While slumped in his sleeping bag, he summoned his most authoritative basso and announced that he would be continuing up the mountain in the morning. I agreed with anything he said in order to comfort him, then continued plying him with tea as an excuse to monitor his speedy pulse and erratic breathing. At 7:00 A.M., after quietly radioing Doug Geeting for an evacuation, I bulldozed the protesting Ernest into the skiplane before his wife could interfere. I told Geeting not to bring Ernest back to the mountain under any circumstances, even though he had paid the $1,200 guide fee.

That afternoon, while Steve shuttled loads with the others, I escorted Evelyn back to the landing strip so she could rejoin Ernest in Talkeetna. After I lifted Evelyn aboard the plane, I asked the bush pilot, Don Lee, if he'd given my note to a friend, Chris Kerrebrock, who was attempting the Wickersham Wall on the other side of the mountain. Don's face dropped. "You didn't hear?" he asked.

"No."

Don walked me to the side of the airstrip. "Chris died in a crevasse fall."

I thanked Don for telling me, walked over the hill and out of sight from the climbers at base camp, then screamed as loudly as I could. "Why him?" I yelled, and suddenly climbing Denali seemed so frivolous and self-indulgent that I seriously considered commandeering the next plane to Talkeetna.

Certainly, no climber is immune to the death of a friend. It can happen to anyone at any time, but when it does, the surprise is inconceivable. The sense of loss darkens the dazzling light of the mountain; it sours the sweetest camaraderie; it turns all reverence to disdain. I felt (as the late Lionel Terray had titled his climbing memoirs) that I had become a Conquistador of the Useless.

It would be difficult to resume climbing now, even with a friend, let alone five paying clients who had never been on a big mountain before. "I'm spent," I thought. Escorting charges up the West Buttress Route was going to take everything I had. I convinced myself that since Chris had been a guide, too, he would've stayed with his clients in a similar situation, so I began skiing the five miles back up the glacier.

When I came to the first easily crossed crevasse and stared down into its onyx throat, I was so stricken that I sat down and imagined what it would be like to be wedged in fifty feet down like Chris had been, virtually unhurt after his companion tried every trick in the book to free him. Chris knew he was finished, so he asked Jim Wickwire to relay messages of love to friends and family. Chris thanked Jim for his help, make him promise not to solo up the glacier until help came (so Jim wouldn't also fall in a crevasse), then summoned his courage as he waited for the lying warmth of hypothermia to take him away.

The crevasse beyond my skitips seemed to plunge like an infinite elevator shaft, or it might have been twenty feet deep, but I cursed it until my throat grew hoarse. Then I held my breath. As I glided over the narrow crack, I imagined freefalling into black space—like Theodore Koven, Allen Carpé, Jacques Batkin, Johnny Mallon Waterman, and Chris Kerrebrock had all done on Denali—my heart pounding in arrhythmic terror.

Meanwhile, Steve dealt with our sanctimonious client Phil, who tripped over his snowshoes, dragged like bottom fish on the end of the rope, and spilled a pot of water in the tent. When I finally returned to the eight-thousand-foot camp in a blue funk, I heard a tirade: "Phil," Steve shouted, "you're nothing but a low-life, worm-eating, shit-licking son of a whore!"

There was nothing to do but laugh; I was back in the fray. I had to concentrate on the clients' needs now.

Our Baptist minister did not take kindly to Steve's rebukes. After a few days, following every new assault of profanity, Phil gently chided, "Stevey, I *jus doan* think *y'all* can talk to a human *bean'* this way."

Over the coming weeks, the other clients—Jack, Fran, Bruce, and young Walt—found solace in Steve's latest invectives against Phil. They would titter at every new "maggot" or "dickhead" or "pussyface" as if Steve were lampooning the Ayatollah. It became apparent that Steve was trying to relieve every one of the frustration of Phil. Diurnally, Phil would spin judgmental Bible lessons to anyone within earshot; nocturnally, he would bellow out a cacophony of guttural snoring beside his tentmates.

When forced to share a tent with me one night, he implored, "Jonny, *y'all* really need to spend some time with this Good Book here." He knew that I was mourning Chris; Phil wanted to help. He would lift the Bible and touch my shoulder when he talked, but I let him sermonize unhindered, because a good guide is supposed to listen—despite Phil's drooping, drooling lower lip and basset-hound face. Despite his righteous and windy lectures. And despite his lone, spastic guffawing after jokes that we couldn't understand.

After the first week, Steve and I agreed that we could not take Phil to the summit because he would endanger the team if he "ran out of gas" the way he did while carrying loads. So Steve and I alternated baby-sitting Phil and keeping him on a tight rope.

Statistically speaking, Phil was fairly safe. During the 1980s, of 2,284 clients who attempted the summit, only 1 died; of 5,247 nonguided climbers, 33 died (5 in crevasses). Most Denali guides will concede that every team of clients is stacked with a "walking time bomb" like Phil. Usually "the Phils" retreat or get evacuated after the first few days. The fact that they rarely die, fall in crevasses, break legs, get frostbitten toes, scald fingers, torch hairdos, asphyxiate tentmates, or are strangled by their guides has a lot to do with the incessant vigilance of those guides. Phil, however, was convinced it had more to do with miracles.

While shuttling loads to 14,300 feet, I warned Phil to step over the obvious crevasse; I was particularly concerned about crevasses lately. By this time most of the climbers on the mountain had heard that four rangers took an entire day, chopping ice and rigging pulleys, to remove Chris's corpse from the crevasse.

Phil paused at the edge of a sixteen-inch by two-hundred-foot slot of blue space, squinted his eyes as if to make a calculation, then stepped directly into the hole. In the ten seconds it took me to sprint back to him, he slipped into the slot like a greased pig into a hay shredder, kicking away and widening the crevasse walls as he stretched the rope leading to a teammate and fell to his hips, then up to his chest. When I arrived at the lip, he was undermining his last vestige of support; I grabbed his chest harness and wrestled him back onto the glacier. Phil flopped on the snow with sweat streaming down his face, lips funneling for air, carabiners jangling on his harness. When he finally spoke, he thanked God for his salvation; I was not mentioned.

That night Steve and I pitched our own tent fifty yards away and out of earshot of Phil. The others gave Phil a gag order: All sermons except emergency prayers were forbidden. We had already put knives, matches, stoves, and cooking off-limits to Phil.

Phil had pushed us all to the brink. I had reached that point, inevitable for even the most patient and compassionate of Denali guides (which I was not), when even nine-to-five work seemed inviting. Steve was reconsidering being a roughneck, where he had worked long hours at no small risk to his health on the barren oil fields of Wyoming.

Even Covington, whom we had seen puffing cigar smoke and pitching his tent on the Kahiltna Glacier, would experience burnout. He had been red-eyed and ready to explode because one client, a former narcotics agent, threatened to bust him for smoking a joint. Three years later, after Michael brought clients partway up "the Cassin"—a sought-after ridge that ends on the summit ridge after three miles of undulating granite and ice—he turned to his charges and said, "We're going down." He later confided that he was "fried" and in such a state that he couldn't take responsibility for clients. Ever the gentle businessman, Michael refunded their money, just as he did for Ernest and Evelyn Chandler.

Clearly, burnout is a disease of guides rather than clients. It is not unusual to see the regulars returning to Talkeetna wasted, even if no one died on the mountain. You can find these guides with sunken eyes at the ranger station, nursing beers and blackened digits at the Fairview Inn, stuffing fistfuls of pizza into their mouths at the deli, or aboard the next inbound plane shouting inanities to their clients when asked questions as simple as the time of day.

The reasons for burnout are clear. When push comes to shove on Denali, the conscientious guide, like the captain aboard a sinking ship, will overlook his own needs to attend to those of his charges. Consequently, guides become thin, dehydrated, or frostbitten while they're haranguing their clients to eat, drink, or dress properly. Or they become exhausted because they can't trust anyone else to cook meals, break trail, or grope through a whiteout. And if a rescue breaks somewhere on the mountain, it is the guide who evacuates a stranger all night, then turns around to tow his clients another thousand feet up the mountain.

Furthermore, the caliber of clients on Denali is not equal to that of guided teams on difficult and lesser-known peaks such as Mount Huntington, Mount Foraker, or Mount Hunter. The clients who are drawn to Denali tend to be executives or white-collar workers who equate "biggest with the best."

As Okonek says, "They don't love mountains like guides do; they don't make it part of their life. Nor do they really have the desire to climb; they just want to *have* climbed and then move on to something else."

There are three other well-known climbers, all in their forties, who have cumulatively worked the mountain longer than any other triumvirate of Denali guides. Collectively, these three men (all passing into and out of Talkeetna each summer) have logged nine marriages—due, no doubt, to their sporadic income, the stress of their prolonged absences from home, and their inability to leave the pressures of work up on the mountain.

With a few exceptions, even the most acclaimed Denali guides stop challenging themselves on their personal climbs. Going on a fun mountaineering trip, without clients, is so easy to associate with the burnout work of mountain guiding that many guides stop climbing altogether. Mountain guides share that dilemma of tennis pros, football coaches, and ski instructors, who seldom compete or even play at their former levels of glory because they're too harried making a living from their expertise. The end result is the exclusive separation of these pros from their salary-paying clients.

One renowned Denali climber and former climbing guide, David Roberts, wrote, "guiding was being teacher, dorm mother, drinking buddy, cook, and janitor rolled into one relentless package. You set up an ironic gap between yourself and the students, taunting them with private jokes shared with coleaders. You kidded about 'repairing to the nearest pub' at the first drop of rain, but you began to hope that nobody would show up so you could cancel a trip. You stopped explaining the rules and simply dictated them."

At 17,200 feet, on the eve of our departure for the summit, I told Phil please to shut up. After pulling his ice-cold and rancid bare feet off my stomach, I swore an oath not to ruin my vision of Denali by guiding it ever again.

We left at 6:00 A.M. the prescience of great disaster seemed to hover closer than the lenticular clouds over nearby Mount Foraker. Despite Phil's presence, I prayed for mercy.

Every trip has its saviors. Jack, Fran, Bruce, and Walt had put up with Phil for seventeen days without complaint. Hopefully, Phil would become too weak to ruin our summit day; then Steve or I would take him back down so his long-suffering teammates could reach the summit in peace. But at 19,000 feet, Phil, despite his sluglike pace, could not be persuaded to turn back. And Walk felt too sick to continue.

Steve volunteered to pull Phil and the others to the summit. Before I turned around to escort Walt down, I pulled the emergency Dexedrine out of my first-aid kit and handed it to Steve.

"What's this?" he asked.

"Speed," I replied, "in case Phil runs out of gas."

Three interminable hours later, Steve finished yanking Phil the final ten yards, blessing him with the usual round of heated verbs and graphic nouns. Phil collapsed onto the snow without his traditional reply, and unlike Archdeacon Stuck sixty-eight years earlier, he could not even utter the *Tè Deum*. Steve reveled in the exuberance of Jack, Bruce, and Fran, and they all forgot about Phil as the continent fell beneath their cramponed feet. As Phil lay unconscious, they had much to celebrate, not the least of which being that Jack was sixty-three years old.

When it came time to leave, Phil couldn't move; Steve was shocked. He asked Phil to stand up, but Steve's desperate and gentle prodding bounced off deaf ears. Steve pulled out the Dexedrine with shaking fingers, pried open Phil's lips, and helped him wash it down with a slug of water that was mostly ice cubes. Now Steve lit into him anew, unleashing a litany of original verbiage more brackish than anything he had ever heard on the Wyoming oil fields. As if responding to a dream, Phil rose to this fresh layer of indecency, as if the devil himself were speaking, and forced himself to his feet, morally outraged and croaking, *"Y'all* can't talk to a human *bean'* this way."

Steve figured that if he could just keep Phil moving, the Dexedrine might jolt his adrenal glands into action. During the first hour, Phil toppled a dozen times. Steve let him rest briefly, pumped him to his feet with more verbal heresy, and wondered if Phil would force them to bivouac in thirty-below zero, which could doom them all. The other three lurched down in distressed funks, alternately turning to yell such provocative suggestions as "You're a loser, Phil!" toward their martyr.

A half mile below the summit, at the 19,650-foot Archdeacon's Tower, Steve realized that Phil was still moving, that both the drug and the blasphemic insults had taken effect. The minister became a veritable jukebox of complaints, which offset some of the barrage from his companions and turned his face blue. They arrived back in camp eighteen hours after leaving, and I spent the rest of the morning monitoring Phil. Although everyone else snoozed in blissful exhaustion, Phil was wired for sound. He couldn't shut up.

The next day Steve had bloodshot murder in his eyes. Since it was my turn to deal with Phil, I insisted that Steve take the day off; if Phil didn't somehow kill himself, Steve would gladly do the job. Guiding novices down the most interesting 3,000 feet of the West Buttress Ridge and headwall is never relaxing, but with Phil tottering every step of the way, our passage became one of the most angst-ridden trials since Whymper's ill-fated Matterhorn descent of 1865—when one climber slipped and pulled his ropemates to their deaths.

At 14,300 feet Steve had napped and spent the day kibitzing with other climbers. Since he seemed relaxed again, I offered him the rope with everyone but our minister; the foursome trotted down to the 11,000-foot camp while I chaperoned Phil. Five hundred feet down, I strapped Phil's pack onto my own. At Windy Corner, Phil stepped into the same crevasse from a week earlier.

Phil asked for frequent rest stops. After he caught his breath he issued that patronizing smile and boasted of the glory of his Chief Guide, who had lifted him onto and back down from the summit. In that syrupy drawl Phil schemed of the magnificence of his homecoming. Wiping the drool from his lip, he predicted how all the troubled teenagers in his parish would come to him for advice, *"Ah'll* say that *Ah,* too, have *experu-minted* with drugs." I couldn't forget that Phil had exhausted his tentmates for three weeks with his stentorian snoring and his presumptive preaching. By now I pondered violating the First Commandment.

I had long concluded that getting to the top of Denali was not worth an iota of blackened tissue, let alone giving up one's life. Phil was probably similar to hundreds of other clients who had been dragged to our highest piece of geography. His physical unpreparedness and naïveté about his own survival, let alone the safety of his companions, had spoiled the trip for most of the clients, whom I now appreciated greatly for their efforts. His lack of respect had also defiled the mountain.

Phil's experience seemed an off-kilter joke to the memory of a safe climber such as Chris Kerrebrock, who suffered a cruel, slow, unjust death. If the God of Phil's prayers did exist, Chris would not have been made to wait for three hours to die inside an open ice coffin, looking up at three vertical miles of cocked avalanche slopes.

When Phil demanded his fiftieth rest stop of the day, I took action. "To the base camp" became my credo; I performed just as relentlessly as Genet and Covington and Bocarde and Okonck and Gall had performed in their own long and distinguished guiding careers, but in reverse. In front of thirteen stunned clients from a Rainier Mountaineering group, and forty yards from Steve's tent, I began dragging Phil with the rope, belly down in the snow. Most of the camp watched in silence; Fran and Bruce and Jack and Walt applauded vigorously.

The only voice that could be heard under the otherwise placid sunset clouds was a nasally distinctive but snow-muffled Georgia-twanged judgment. "Jonny, Jonny," Phil whimpered, *"y'all* can't treat a human *bean'* this way!" When I reached the tents, bathed in peach alpenglow, I untied from the minister as if unhooking an inedible bottom fish.

Steve passed me a cup of steaming tea, a smoking cigar, and a smile pregnant with congratulations; he would chaperone another dozen groups up Denali. I never guided the mountain again.

Stories off the Wall

J O H N   R O S K E L L E Y

An outstanding American mountaineer, John Roskelley organized a team to climb the imposing Uli Biaho in Pakistan's Karakoram Range in 1979. Roskelley wanted to climb the East Face, which was vertical and ledgeless, yet had the same kind of crack systems as El Capitan, the most famous of Yosemite's rockfaces. Only Uli Biaho had altitudes up to 20,000 feet with extreme mountain weather and, as Roskelley put it, "zero possibility of rescue." This had to be a real team effort, and that is the focus of Roskelley's story, as he describes what it takes to put a team together and then hold it together through the emotional ups and downs, the moments of courage and fear, all the while knowing that only superb teamwork will allow the climbers to both succeed and survive.

B locky and angular, like a chunk of black marble chipped and molded by Michelangelo, the six-foot-two marine sergeant embodied his corps' credo, "The Few, The Proud, The Marines." Even his United States Marine Corps fatigues, called "baggies" by most recruits, fit him like a Hong Kong suit.

"You!" he commanded, "get your feet down." There was none of this "Please" or "Thank you." And there didn't need to be.

I followed the direction in which his oversized meathook was pointing. There slumped America's premier rock climber, Ron Kauk, lying in his theater seat, legs crossed, feet over the back of the seat before him waiting for the night's movie, *Warriors* to begin.

Kauk, a Cochise look-alike with his shoulder-length, thick brown hair, kept in check with his trademark folded bandana, turned his head in slow motion and squinted at the sergeant with a glint in his dark eyes that said, "Maybe I will, maybe I won't." then, at that same speed, he removed his feet and sat up. From my seat on the aisle, I could hear the sergeant's breath quicken, as if air were a precious commodity. His carotid arterial cords dilated to the width of a climbing rope and threatened to explode as he contemplated action. Then his eyes closed, reptilelike, as he searched his memory for another one so insolent. The sergeant hadn't seen this long-haired creep before. Not around the American Embassy compound, and certainly not in all the days he had been in charge of operating the embassy's movie theater in Islamabad. The sergeant disappeared.

Kauk went back to jostling and kidding two sixteen-year-old embassy-employee daughters sitting next to him, while I caught a full breath. That coal-black marine, with muscles in his face bigger than my biceps, had me on the edge of my seat. The lights dimmed to match my loss of enthusiasm, and *Warriors* began.

The credits were still unraveling unknown actors when Kauk again raised his feet to the back of the seat before him. He hadn't even lowered into a full theater seat slouch when a rock-hard quadriceps bumped my elbow. It was the marine.

"YOUUUU! COM'ERE!" the marine bellowed. "NOWWWW!"

Kauk pointed to himself as if to say, "Little ol' me?" stood up, then crab-legged to the aisle and into the waiting grip of his accuser. Acting as if Kauk were cholera-ridden, Kim Schmitz and I squeezed into our seats and let him pass unobstructed. Despite the ruckus of New York street gangs fighting on screen, boisterously loud music and solid oak lobby doors, the Marine Corps sergeant's earsplitting dressing down of Kauk reached the audience.

"What are you going to do?" Schmitz asked.

It is circumstances such as the one then before me that separate a true expedition leader from your classic load-carrying mountain-climbing grunt. Should I interfere? Negotiate? Order a team attack? After all, I was leader of the American Uli Biaho Expedition, and with that came certain responsibilities.

"Nothing," I replied. "He got his butt into it, let him get his own butt out."

Schmitz grunted an affirmative. He recognized leadership when he heard it. Kauk, with a cowed appearance and, perhaps, temporary hearing loss, eventually retook his seat. His feet stayed glued to the floor.

The 1979 American Uli Biaho team of Kauk, Schmitz, Bill Forrest, and myself, a unit I hoped would mold into perfection by the sum of its four parts, arrived in Islamabad, Pakistan, as distinct individuals. Each of us had at least one thing in common—climbing—but life-styles, work ethics, and a generation gap were question marks in regard to compatibility.

I sought the best climbers for Uli Biaho. Two years earlier, five American alpinists, Dr. Jim Morrissey, Galen Rowell, Dennis Hennek, Schmitz, and myself, had been the first to climb to the summit of Great Trango Tower in the midst of the Karakoram Range. As I turned to belay Morrissey to the sun-baked summit, a sabertooth-shaped peak across the Trango Glacier jolted that spot in my brain reserved for nightmares, or those "challenges" best kept to my dreams.

"Galen, what's that peak across the glacier?" I asked. Rowell, one of America's best mountain photographers and a walking, breathing, mountain encyclopedia, knows the name, height, known attempts, and successful summits of every peak visible on the horizon and beyond.

"Uli Biaho," he replied. "The French attempted a route in 1976, but so far it's unclimbed."

I wasn't interested in avoiding any difficulties or following a path. I wanted the face before me, the East Face—vertical, ledgeless, yet shot with Yosemite-like crack systems. It would be a climb like El Capitan, but at altitudes up to 20,000 feet, with extreme mountain weather, zero possibility of rescue, a 4,000-foot unexplored route, and an insane, 4,000-foot approach through a 100-yard-wide glacial combat zone shot with climber-seeking missiles to Uli Biaho's rock base. Seemed reasonable to me.

Standing on the summit of Great Trango Tower after three days of struggle, Uli Biaho seemed another light-year ahead of my time. But a seed of hope fell on fertile soil—soil thick with experience, rich in desire, and at the right time in my life to foresee a destiny. Uli Biaho would feel my boots.

Uli Biaho demanded a team. T-E-A-M: A group of people organized for a particular purpose. Not a P-A-R-T-Y: A group of people out for fun and games.

Too many American expeditions organize a party and expect to put one together that works, functions, and performs. What drives me to pursue a peak or route may not drive another, equally motivated climber. Not only did I have to find three more compatible individuals to make a team of four, but each had to possess skills that, when added to those of the others, would lead to success.

I first heard of Kim Schmitz from my two-years-to-the-wiser sister, Pat. "Miss Liberal University of Washington," as I referred to her, dated Schmitz's best buddy, Jim Madsen. Schmitz and Madsen, both six-foot-plus, broad shouldered, and muscular, were stunning the California climbing locals in the late

1960s by setting speed records on Yosemite's big walls. Their team ended abruptly in 1969, when Madsen, on a false-alarm rescue, made the first free descent off the top of El Capitan. Another speed record of sorts. Schmitz overcame Madsen's untimely death and went on to set climbing standards in Yosemite Valley for another decade.

Schmitz was difficult to get to know in Yosemite, where he was a guru of sorts, but as Pat's little brother I did receive a nod or two as I endeavored to climb the "classics." In early September 1971, after earning my stripes on the Dihedral Wall on El Capitan and other big walls, I asked him if he wanted to climb the North American Wall.

"Nope," Schmitz declined. "I'm trying to do all my El Cap routes in two bivouacs or less."

His point was made. My Dihedral Wall partner and I had taken six days to succeed. I wasn't quite up to the guru's legacy. It didn't matter. Mead Hargis, another superb climber living in the Valley, and I flashed the climb, considered the hardest rock climb in the world at the time, in a little over two bivouacs. Schmitz no longer just nodded a greeting.

Our first climb together was on Trango Tower in 1977. Schmitz and I teamed up in the streets of Rawalpindi and bonded on the trek along the Braldu River to Trango. His habit of quite introspection was unnerving at times, as if talk was for those who had nothing to say. If I wanted to know how to take a "Schmitzification," one of his tactless attempts to sum up a usually ridiculous situation, I would search his eyes. His large cheekbones and strong Germanic chin could have been chiseled in stone, but Schmitz's turquoise blue eyes were as easy to read as the next weather pattern in the sky. Schmitz wanted Uli Biaho.

As good as Schmitz was on big walls, I still wanted one of the younger Yosemite big-wall rock specialists on the team. There was a gang of them, like the Lost Boys in *Peter Pan,* living and breathing rock climbing all year round in the Valley, pushing vertical limits only the birds thought were possible. Ron Kauk was the best of these free-spirited athletes that only an Olympic gymnastic coach could appreciate.

To perform high-angle gymnastics on rock takes a high strength-to-weight ratio. Kauk, at 150 pounds and five feet nine inches of Jimmy Dean lean, was perfectly proportioned, plus he had the flexibility of a Labrador retriever and the grace and balance of Rudolf Nureyev. But it takes more—a lot more—to be the best. It takes the big D—Desire—and Kauk had that too.

He bouldered for hours each day; worked out in the makeshift Camp VI gym of hanging ropes, tilted boards, and balance chains; and practiced on past horror routes, while attempting and succeeding on next-to-impossible cracks. Given another athletic direction in life, Kauk could have been an Olympic champion in any sport. As it was, he lived with other Camp IV "regulars," hunted for food, bummed a buck or two, and worked part-time when convenient.

Kauk reminded me of me, except that I didn't have the guts when I was a kid to walk away from society's burdens. He did. We're raised to accepted direction from our parents and society based on what's "good for you." But Kauk didn't listen. Why be another generic graduate who regurgitates generic information? He wanted the clean Yosemite air, not L.A. smog; friends who understood the freedom of rock climbing, not social clubs and lettermen sweaters; time to excel, taste adventure, and be himself.

I liked Kauk instantly. To survive year after year in Camp IV takes ingenuity, intelligence, and an easygoing attitude. Kauk had it all, plus a personality that said, "Relax, life's to enjoy, so let's have some fun." There was one enigma. Would he be there on departure day? The granite in Yosemite in June is warm and beckoning, and there's always the chance that a day's stunt work for a movie crew might come along, enough work to let him live for another year in the Valley. Was his commitment there? Schmitz was worried. And, since I didn't know Kauk, except for a brief telephone conversation, that had me worried.

"Kauk doesn't take to responsibility," Schmitz said. "We've got to find someone who will put him on the plane and organize him."

"I'll get on it," I promised, despite the impossible task. "Meanwhile it's your job to keep him pumped up."

I studied the team. It had everything—strength, experience, depth, youth. . . . Wait, there it was. Youth needs balance. I needed someone on the other end of the climbing spectrum. Schmitz and I would be in Nepal climbing Gaurishankar prior to making our way to Pakistan. Our two teammates would have to finish organizing the Uli Biaho Expedition in the States, then meet us in Rawalpindi. To get Kauk to Asia, on time, with expedition money and equipment, I needed someone with all our skills . . . plus maturity. That's a tall order in any sport. But in climbing? No way.

Then Bill Forrest came to mind. *The* Bill Forrest of Forrest Mountaineering, a profitable business. *The* Bill Forrest of the Black Canyon of the Gunnison. *The* Bill Forrest who may have introduced Fred Beckey to mountaineering. He'd been around long enough. Bill Forrest was my answer to pre-trip organization once I left the States, and the key to getting Kauk away from Yosemite, on the plane, and in Pakistan on May 31. Forrest was the only mature climber I knew who was capable, and perhaps willing, enough to go with three yahoos like us. He said yes.

F-O-R-R-E-S-T. That's how I spelled relief. I intended to have most of the expedition financed and organized before leaving with Schmitz for Gaurishankar that spring, but two months of last-minute details had to be taken care of, including getting Kauk onto the plane. Quite, sincere, efficient, and trustworthy, Forrest was the man for the job.

I first met Bill Forrest in 1976, after my ascent of Nanda Devi in India. I was in Denver, riding the fleeting summit of success by describing heroic deeds before audiences, when the opportunity to meet the Colorado climbing legend presented itself. Not only were Forrest's ascents recognized as innovative, but his company, Forrest Mountaineering, was profitable, progressive, and competing with Chouinard's Diamond C.

Forrest's middle name should have been Easy. If I needed help contacting a corporation—he paved the way; if Kauk didn't have the right sleeping bag— Forrest gave him one from his store in Denver; if our funds didn't balance— Forrest anted up out of his own pocket. With his thoughtful disposition, a smile straight out of a Roy Rogers movie, and a quite, down-home laugh, Forrest was as easy to get along with as a meandering brook. With a profitable business like Forrest Mountaineering to his credit, Forrest was obviously sharp enough to have been in a business suit and working on Wall Street. But Forrest is his own man, and is drawn to the climber's game. I was comfortable with Forrest within minutes of meeting him—and that said it all.

Four pieces to the puzzle. Would they fit? One of the great questions in mountaineering is teamwork. What brings one group of individuals together and tears another apart? Leadership? Organization? Compatibility? As we rendezvoused in Islamabad at the home of my friend Andy Koritko, chief security officer at the American Embassy, I couldn't find a flaw. Optimistic perhaps, but never had I felt better about a team.

After Kauk's run-in with the marine, I knew it was time to get the team out of Islamabad. Our life at the Koritkos had been a step into paradise. As head of embassy security, Andy Koritko opened the American Embassy's facilities to us, which meant cold Heinekens in a Moslem country, embassy parties, cheeseburgers, lounge chairs around the pool and pretty bikini-clad teenyboppers who surrounded Kauk and teased him unmercifully. Kauk ignored their innuendos, flirtations, and young girl games, while Schmitz and I, sunbathing nearby, drooled over ourselves, hoping for just a moment of their time for the "old" folks. And Forrest? Well, he just wanted to get started climbing.

After eight days of negotiations with Mr. Naseer-Ullah Awan, Pakistan's head of Mountaineering and Tourism, and representatives of Pakistan International Airways (PIA, or Perhaps It Arrives), the Uli Biaho team was set to fly to Skardu in far northern Baltistan.

"What are you saying?" I asked Kauk.

"I don't like it," he replied. "There's too much rockfall."

Another squadron of rock missiles whined and bashed down the gully. Kauk and I squeezed closer together beneath a bombproof ice wall and waited for a reprieve.

"It's the time of day, Ron," I argued. "We'll start earlier tomorrow to avoid the rock. Give it a chance."

I didn't like the 100-yard-wide, 4,000-foot-high gully either. It flushed all of Uli Biaho's East Face debris onto us like a sewer pipe, but it was our only path to the wall. If I wasn't careful, Kauk would spook and quit.

"Let's cache our loads here, drop to camp, and come back tomorrow," I suggested, with more optimism than I actually felt. "It'll look better in the cool of the morning."

"Not for me," he replied, stuffing his pack with personal gear I thought we would leave.

Schmitz and Forrest were eagerly awaiting our reconnaissance report. I emphasized the great ice-climbing, the protection behind the ice walls, and suggested an early-morning departure to void rockfall. Then Kauk spoke for the first time in hours.

"I'm not going on the route," he said. His eyes darted from the gully to us, then back to the gully. Kauk's admission put him in unfamiliar territory. I didn't speak, fearing we would lose Kauk without giving him some time to think it over

Schmitz did. "And why not?"

"I don't like the rockfall," Kauk replied.

"Why, you big baby," Schmitz said, as if it were a fact, rather than opinion. This started an all-out verbal war, Kauk screaming at Schmitz, while Schmitz, knowing he had Kauk's goat, replied evenly time after time, "You're a big man in the Valley, but you're nothing here," along with a variety of other Schmitzi-fications. Schmitz finally said, "We wouldn't take you anyway."

And with that, Kauk replied, as expected, "Well, I'm going, and to hell with you."

Schmitz looked over at me with a glance that said, "And that's how you handle Ron Kauk, America's rock climbing prima donna."

Forrest and I just shook our heads and continue packing—for four.

The fear within oneself too often creates mountains out of molehills. At the end of the day, Kauk let the little gremlins that feed on the unknown get the best of him again. "It's too dangerous," he said, after a long silent spell listening and watching the gully. "I'm not going."

We let it stand at that. He'd struggled with it all day and, despite Schmitz's attempt to restore Kauk's motivation with the "old boy" method, it was his decision. I knew it had taken a lot of guts to get there.

Forrest, Schmitz, and I climbed to Kauk's and my cache before dawn the next morning. Loaded with upwards of seventy pounds each, we dashed across the gully to the better-protected, higher-walled right side. Skirting large, vertical ice walls and climbing smaller seracs, we made our way to the upper ice field below the face. Intensified by the midmorning heat, rockfall ricocheted through the gully, warning us to avoid the bottleneck and seek safety along the granite walls.

Leaving Forrest to chop out a future bivouac spot, Schmitz and I donned our armor of helmets, slings, hammers, pitons, and sundry climbing gear, to test the wall's resistance. I led a quick 150 feet of ledges and cracks to a pedestal. Like the toe leather of an old shoe, the low-angled, weathered rock at the base of the wall was broken and worn, but as I climbed higher, the granite wall cleansed itself of rubble and decay and aimed for the sky in a single 4,000-foot sweep. Schmitz jumared to my stance, then led another long pitch through blocks and up short cracks.

Burdened under fifty pounds of hardware and gear as I cleaned the pitch, I leaned far to my right to surmount a block and felt a snap in my lower back, then pain.

"Time to head down, Kim," I said, as I reached his belay. "I pulled a muscle in my lower back and it won't be long before I can't walk."

By 1:30 P.M., we were down climbing the low-angled sections of ice in the gully and setting rappels over the seracs, trying to avoid the continual rock and ice fall. While we were beneath a series of twenty-foot-high ice blocks, two gravity-fed, climber-crushing boulders cut loose above Schmitz. He faced them squarely, defiantly, pitched one way, then dodged another as they hurtled by. Without so much as a *"whew,"* or a change in the patented Schmitz muted expression, he turned downslope and continued to descend as though avoiding a close encounter with death was on his daily job sheet.

On June 20, I stayed below on the glacier, cocked sideways, distorted by spasms, and unable to move without stabbing lower-back pain. While I lay in my sleeping bag, Forrest and Schmitz, supported by a recharged, and suddenly enthusiastic, Kauk, carried group gear partway up the gully. The team was now positioned for the final push up the gully—but I was unable to move.

Doubt within one's mind: Can there be a more difficult adversary? I lay quietly absorbing the pain, watching my teammates disappear down the glacier toward base camp for food and rest, sensing an end to my dreams of climbing Uli Biaho.

I'd had back problems since falling through a second-story stairwell and landing squarely on my backside while working construction in 1968. Periodically, the injury would reoccur and I would be immobile for days. But this was a first while on an expedition. With weeks of effort ahead of us—carrying massive loads and contorting in any number of strained positions day and night—could I recuperate quickly enough to continue? Would I be a burden to the team? Should I even take the chance of reinjuring my back and ending the climb for the others?

Two days later, my teammates had not returned. Out of food, irritated with their complacency, and discouraged with my injury, I limped down the glacier toward base camp. As I descended, the pain and discomfort diminished with work, and my spirit, depressed by inaction, returned. Once again, self-inflicted doubt, the disease of discouragement, proved to be more disabling and harder to overcome than physical injury. The four of us were now ready to attempt the face.

"Kim," I said, "I want you and Bill to team up. Ron and I will take the lead the first day, while you guys haul. The next day's yours."

I wanted to climb with Kauk. He was considered the best rock climber in the world. What better way for me, a self-proclaimed mountaineer, to improve my skills than to watch Kauk perform on Uli's untested walls. I was fast on rock, but with his more-recent years in the Valley, Kauk had added to his repertoire small time savers and special techniques that I wanted to add to my climbing "tools." Furthermore, like a young puppy in a kennel with an older dog, Kauk had begun a friendly harassment of the easygoing Forrest, mostly as a time filler during dead periods of the expedition. Regardless of his intent, I didn't want his youthful exuberance to lead to a confrontation on the climb, as hunger and exhaustion fed stressed-out tempers, and the slightest added catalyst might stop the expedition in a rope length. On the other hand, Schmitz and Forrest were well matched, both in climbing and personality, and, most important, they got along.

Kauk and I leapfrogged four leads up two-inch to four-inch cracks the first day. At four o'clock, we descended to help Schmitz and Forrest haul our seven sixty-pound haul bags to our high point, a four-foot-wide ledge big enough for cooking and for two to sleep on. Kauk and I spent the night close by in our aluminum-framed hanging hammocks, called Porta-ledges. By morning, clear skies had given way to thick clouds and light snowfall.

"Oh, shit!" Kauk said, early on the morning of the 25th. "Schmitz, you got kerosene in the pot."

"It's in the water bottles we filled last night, too," Forrest added, sniffing his container.

There was no more ice on the tiny ledge for more water. None of us wanted to drink kerosene-tainted water, so we dumped it out. It would be a dry day until evening, when we could melt ice at our next camp.

As Schmitz and Forrest began leading new pitches, Kauk and I repacked the haul bags, adjusted the weight of each evenly, then began the tedious, back-breaking work of hauling them up the wall. Isolated rock and ice falling from thousands of feet above spit and cracked on the wall around us. Yells from Schmitz and Forrest warned us of the biggest or closest impending missiles.

On the third day, Kauk and I led parallel crack systems, penduluming into alternate cracks to avoid running water. Forrest and Schmitz, having fine-tuned their haul system by trial and error, moved quickly enough to catch me cleaning one of Kauk's long, difficult pitches. At midafternoon, I reached a seventy-degree, forty-foot-high ice field in the shape of a flying bat, the only obvious landmark we had pinpointed earlier on the featureless East Face from the glacier far below. Ice debris and small rocks showered the haul team, as Kauk led one more short, hundred-foot pitch above the ice field. Schmitz's raucous verbal abuse of Kauk's ancestry, and the real danger of cutting loose an executioner block onto Schmitz, brought Kauk back to my belay and our night's bivouac.

Fluid intake is the single most important factor in preventing health problems at high altitudes and while undertaking physically strenuous activity. Our lack of water the previous day almost proved disastrous.

Dehydrated, no one slept peacefully on Bat Ledge at 18,000 feet. Kauk and I hung in our hammocks above our teammates, who were sleeping on narrow ice platforms that had been excavated after hours of labor. Forest, puffy in the face, lethargic, and nauseous, was obviously showing the early signs of high altitude disease.

While Forrest rested and hydrated at the bivouac site the next morning, Schmitz, Kauk, and I led and fixed 450 feet of rope. Schmitz led the crux, an overhanging gully stuffed with loose debris, that had Kauk and me cowering on the open wall, dodging death blocks, and wondering if Uli Biaho—or, for that matter, any peak—was worth the risk. At each belay, our conversation turned to Forrest. It was my responsibility, as leader, to see that everyone returned alive and well. If Forrest didn't improve by the next morning, Uli Biaho would take second place to safely evacuating Forrest to base camp.

I expected to begin evacuating Forrest on the morning of June 28, if there was no indication he had improved during the night. To continue to a higher altitude would sentence him to death if he was suffering from high altitude disease.

"How ya' Feeling, Bill?" I asked, as I started the stove.

Bill opened his tightly drawn sleeping bag hood, then peered out over the Karakoram Range as if seeing it for the first time. "A lot better," he replied. "Nausea's gone and I feel a lot stronger."

He looked better. His edema, a characteristic sign of fluid retention that had all but closed his eyes the day before, was gone. Before me was the Bill Forrest I knew—enthusiastic, energetic, determined.

Decisions are never clear-cut. Just when I think I've got the situation under control and I've made my decision, a gray area appears. In this case, Forrest seemed to have recuperated.

But questions still remained. Would he worsen as we went higher, a typical scenario for high altitude-related diseases? Could a three-man team evacuate an unconscious Forrest from a higher elevation or a more difficult situation? Forrest helped us make the decision. "I'll let you know if I begin to feel worse, but we can't give up now."

"All right," I agreed. "But, Bill, you will have to jumar behind us and without a load. I don't want you working at all."

As the morning sun heated our camp, we packed quickly, then began hauling our bags up the four fixed ropes above us. After days of working together, not a moment was lost to wasted effort, nor an extra calorie spent on needless work.

The obvious crack system and deep open book we had followed up the left side of the East Face for days ended abruptly as our route and the southeast corner met. We continued on a vertical granite desert of discontinuous cracks, elephant-ear flakes, and small roofs.

At the fifth roped pitch above Bat Ledge, Schmitz and Forrest stopped to set up our four hammocks under a four-foot-wide roof. Kauk and I, released from the slow, monotonous drudgery of hauling bags and carrying packs, enjoyed two more long leads of effortless direct aid up round-edged cracks. At the end of the second lead, the summit block, an ugly assortment of icy ramparts, impossible-looking overhangs, and deep chimneys, was visible far above, but in another space and time. The hardest climbing was obviously yet to come.

We stashed the hardware at our high point and descended to the aerie built by Schmitz and Forrest, four brightly colored Porta-ledges stacked in cliff swallow-fashion on the slightly overhanging wall. Our view stretched from Paiyu Peak to the southwest to Masherbrum to the southeast, with the second-highest mountain on earth, K2, dominating the skyline to the northeast. In addition, innumerable other peaks, snakelike glaciers, and unexplored canyons highlighted the panorama and filled our senses.

The wisps of mare's tails that had sped westward throughout the day as we climbed were pursued by peak-eating cumulonimbus clouds, which trapped the day's heat like a billowy comforter. I lay sweating on my hammock and watched as each peak was gobbled up by the approaching storm. By 3:00 A.M., a cold front had arrived and wet snow had begun to fall, blanketing the cool rock and forming puddles of water in the low points of our hammocks.

The windless, mild-mannered storm drifted slowly through the Karakoram throughout the morning. Rather than risk hypothermia while exposed on the wall, we chose to spend the next day resting out of the weather in our bivouac. By midmorning, the four of us had dug out our hammock covers and secured them in place. We now had some protection from snowfall, dripping wall water, small ice and rock debris, and the intensifying wind. Water, a precious and rare commodity on the wall below, trickled down the granite, along our anchors, and onto the hammock webbing, to eventually soak our sleeping bags, clothing, and everything attached to the wall.

I wrote in my diary, on June 29:

I'm sometimes confused as to what I'm doing here, looking out at miles of rock and glacier, walls of ice, [and] peaks of unsurpassed beauty. Sitting on small ledges, or standing in slings, checking anchors and ropes, double checking, trusting my life to three others. Beating my hands in cracks—cold, swollen, bleeding and sore. Deadly rockfall and continuous ice. Where will it end, and for what purpose do I keep at it? Have you ever heard the whir of instant death whisk by on wings of fear? Rocks can speak, but you must always manage to hear them from beginning to end. Never break their sentence. One of the reasons I climb so hard, is so I can get above anything that can fall.

"My sleeping bag!" Schmitz, a putzer first-class, one who seems to move himself and other things continuously without purpose, yelled in frustration.

I peered, orb-eyed, out the slit in my hammock cover, through the snow-storm, and down at Schmitz. Fifty feet below him, hung up on the only ledge for 2,000 feet, a short, narrow step with a rock hook, was his sleeping bag. A teasing breeze swung it back and forth along the wall, threatening to steal it forever form Schmitz. Moving faster than I thought possible, he set up a rappel line and dropped to his bag before the breeze grew to a wind. He stopped his infernal putzing after that.

We climbed higher on June 30, but not by much. Wet clothes, cold temperatures, and thick clouds dampened our enthusiasm and made it difficult to quicken our pace. Kauk and I, haul-bag boys for the day, waited in the insufferable chill, dodging debris set loose by Schmitz and Forrest. The thin, iced cracks proved difficult. Eight hours and three hundred feet higher, they rappelled to our night's hanging bivouac.

Despite another storm approaching from Skardu, Kauk and I hauled gear to Schmitz's high point the following morning. He had led a partial pitch before abandoning the overhanging iced-up crack system and descending to our bivouac. I continued from his last piton, zippering up the hairline crack with knife blades and tied-off ice screws. I was in a devil-take-all mood, the kind of attitude I needed to abandon my fears and charge forward regardless of the outcome.

Kauk exposed the team's melodramatic foolishness as it surfaced, with a macabre sense of humor straight from *The Far Side*. There were no sacred cows. The continual storms, dehydration, our cracked and bleeding hands, granola three times a day, iced-up cracks, sleepless nights, stuck haul bags, Schmitz's putzing, even Forrest's illness, were fodder for laughter. I knew when one of Kauk's poignant jokes had hit Schmitz: his eyes would begin to sparkle, then the lines in his usually somber expression would lighten, until, as hard as he tried not to, a smile cracked upon his lips. For a few hours, Uli Biaho was not so dangerous—death not so close.

Ron led one hundred feet to a bivouac site, a crackless, sloping bulge that looked safer than the prospects above. While Schmitz and Forrest drilled holes for bolt anchors, Ron and I fixed another three hundred feet of rope up an open book and gully system. We were now back on the East Face and six hundred feet below the summit ridge, a razor blade of rock crowned with house-sized ice mushrooms. A light snow fell as we rappelled to the worst hanging bivouac of the trip, cooked and rehydrated, and talked of the end in sight.

We went for the summit on July 2. I awoke at 4:00 A.M., hydrated the crew, then set off two fixed lines at 7:30 A.M. It was my lead from the top of the ropes. We were below a ninety-five-degree wall, forty feet wide, enclosed by vertical side walls. A crack broke the joint of each corner.

I tried the right corner along a rotten and loose flaked chimney. It was too dangerous. I retreated and traversed left along snow, ice, and rock behind a detached flake of granite, then up a body-wide squeeze chimney. Schmitz seconded the pitch, reached my anchors, then aided an easy sixty-foot crack to an overhang. My next lead was easy aid, and I was soon on a good ledge, followed closely by the team.

"Ron," I said, "the ugliness above is *your* bag. It's all yours."

A skin-eating, five-and-a-half-inch crack, deep in the corner we had been following, leaned slightly over us. It was past noon when Kauk moved off the ledge and began engineering a path up the off-width crack with bong pitons stacked back to back, sideways, and any way that would hold his weight. Kauk couldn't seem to find any of his humor on this pitch. He ended it short below another leaning off-width five-inch crack.

Schmitz finished off the five-inch, A3 section, without a word. I jumared and cleaned the pitch to his belay. It was my turn to lead again.

I free-climbed over several chockstones, then aided a perfect one-to-two-inch crack, until it flared to four inches. As soon as the four-inch crack widened, I changed cracks, aiding one that narrowed to three inches and smaller. My pitch had everything. After aiding a one-inch crack in a V-shaped corner, I chimneyed a crack the width of my helmet with no protection to an alcove beneath an ice block clogging the ever widening chimney.

It was 6;00 P.M. Kauk, and then Schmitz, reached my stance. We were a pitch below the ice-mushroomed ridge and a long way from the summit.

"Kim," I said, "we can't spend the night out. Let's fix the three worst pitches, go back down to our bivy, then try again for the top tomorrow."

Schmitz reluctantly agreed. After not summiting on Gaurishankar, he wanted the summit of Uli at any cost and was willing to bivouac without gear to get it. Kauk, on the other hand, was not about to risk his neck beyond his norm for Uli Biaho. In fact, his discomfort had turned to anger. As far as Kauk was concerned, the icy ramparts above, the cold, and our late predicament were all preludes to disaster. I sensed an oncoming rebellion and, accordingly, made the decision to descend. Forrest, a pitch below, was as ready and willing to bivouac as Schmitz, but trusted my judgment. Guided by starlight, we arrived at our bivouac late in the evening.

Thoughts of defeat filled my mind as I tried to sleep. Each of us had to have them. The route had turned from a clean, open wall with perfect cracks to an ugly assortment of gigantic stacked blocks, webbed together with rock-hard gray ice and crowned with immense umbrella-like cornices. The summit, well protected by battlements of rock and ice, was hidden somewhere above these monstrous cornices. Conceivably, some feature on the ridge could stop us short of the summit. It had happened on one peak or another to all of us during our years in the mountains. Not knowing what was above us, we let defeat sneak its way into our thoughts, like the thick, rising mist, until exhaustion kept it at bay.

By 7:00 A.M. we were on the move, jumaring to our high point. As Kauk got into a bombproof belay, I surveyed the ice plug blocking the chimney above me. It was my kind of terrain—a mountaineer's terrain—rock flakes, snow hummocks, icy cracks, and overhangs, known appropriately to mountaineers as mixed alpine shit.

I nailed a flake on the right side of the chimney, then crab-legged left underneath the ice plug. Kauk, directly below me, became a target for all the falling debris displaced by my thrashing as I struggled to gain altitude.

The one-ton ice plug that blocked my way was loose. Using my ice hammer sparingly, I chimneyed between it and the rock wall, finally reaching high enough to chop its left side away enough to crawl on top. Once past the ice plug, I surmounted one more chockstone on the ridge before pussyfooting along a sugar snow ledge to the safety of a rock cavern. Kauk, freezing from the snow that had cascaded down upon him while he was sitting in the morning chill, cleaned the pitch slowly, bringing with him my crampons and camera.

I led off again, surmounting a seventy-five-degree snow bump to steep ice steps on the left side of the ridge. One hundred and forty feet from Ron, I reached a sharp corner above a vertical, sixty-foot-wide chimney and set up my belay. Eighty feet above me on the crest of the knife-edged ridge, and leaning in my direction, was a mushroom of ice that resembled a great blue whale sounding from the deep, with its tail down-ridge and its nose against the summit wall. It must have weighed three hundred tons. There was daylight underneath its belly, and, as much as I hated the thought, that keyhole looked like the quickest route to the top.

Kauk, jumaring the rope, reached my side. He apparently didn't realize the danger of the ice perched above us, so I asked for a belay and began front-pointing up the sixty-degree ice slope. I hadn't gone far, when I swung my single ice hammer into the blue ice and a ten-pound block broke loose, but temporarily stayed put.

"Watch this block, Ron," I warned, as I continued. "It could go anytime."

As if on cue, my rope caught on the block's edge and knocked it loose. I yelled. Ron ducked, but the block, as if seeking human flesh, hit him squarely on the arm.

He cradled the arm, leaned into the rock, and moaned.

"Is it broken, Ron?" I yelled down to him. So close were we climbing to the edge of control, I feared a disaster was now about to unfold.

"That's it," he yelled back, obviously scared and angry. "I'm going down."

I could deal with an attitude problem, but a broken arm was something else altogether. Balanced on steep ice squarely beneath the whalelike ice mushroom, I was not in a position to sit tight and wait for Kauk to make a decision to climb. I gave him a few minutes to regain his composure, then asked him to finish belaying me to the keyhole beneath the ice mushroom. Robotically, he did so, angrily cussing away at his pain and our fragile predicament.

Then Schmitz arrived at Kauk's side. A discussion ensued.

"Whaddaya mean, you're going down," Schmitz asked, in a tone he reserves for lower life. "So you got hit. It's not broken. I was right, you're nothing but a big baby."

And, so it was that Kauk came next, probably to get away form all the Schmitzifications pouring from Kim.

While Schmitz and Kauk yelled at each other below, I had them tie another rope to the first, allowing me to lead through the keyhole and up a seventy-degree ice slope to avoid belaying under the mushroom. Within a few minutes I had traversed back over them and onto the last summit ridge. Once Kauk had reached my side, I led a low-angled snow pitch, the first easy pitch on the climb, to the top of the gully and into the setting sun.

A short walk and an easy slope away was the snowcapped summit. One by one, each of us climbed to its broad top, soaked in the evening's warmth, cried a little, laughed a lot, and, for just a few brief moments, forgot about the cold, thirst, and danger below.

Fifteen minutes on the summit and it was time to go. For the next two and a half days, we rappelled, lowered haul bags and retreated. There were unavoidable incidents, close calls, bad bivouacs, and flared tempers, but as one we reached the bottom and the horizontal world we're used to calling home.

I often ask myself what the key to success was on Uli Biaho. God knows, success like ours doesn't happen every expedition. It was the team.

Putting aside my leadership, our goal, the route, the weather, and the dozens of other elements that make up an expedition, the players are what make or break the game. Schmitz, Forrest, Kauk, and I came together, body and soul, for one brief moment in time—and succeeded. Another time, another place, or a different team member, and Uli Biaho would still be a dream, instead of a memory.

The Other Side of Everest

MATT DICKINSON

Matt Dickenson arrived at Mt. Everest in 1996 to film an expedition by British climbers on the North side of the mountain. Dickenson, Alan Hinkes and three Sherpa guides set out for the summit a short time after the storm that led to the tragedy described in Jonathan Krakauer's *Into Thin Air.* Though the author had limited climbing experience he describes the phenomena known as summit fever that he felt as he neared the top. "In that final hour there was really only one single focus in my entire being; the desire to reach the top of the world had become all consuming. It had extinguished my concern for my fellow climber, blocked my capacity for questioning my own actions, and turned me into little more than a robot . . . placing one foot in front of the other like a pre-programmed machine."

Sunset must have been an incredible sight, but all I saw of it was a glimmer of red light reflected in the metal of an oxygen cylinder outside the tent. I was determined to conserve every single scrap of energy and getting out of the tent to take a still photograph was not a priority no matter how splendid it was.

Our main discussion was about the oxygen. With three members of our own team now definitely out of the equation, there was the possibility that we could take an extra cylinder each for the summit push. The pro was that we would be able to set the cylinders on a higher flow with the obvious advantages that would bring. The con was the weight, and extra six kilogrammes—a very serious consideration given the physical demands of what lay ahead. We talked round the issues and decided we would postpone a decision until we packed to leave in a few hours time. (In fact when it came to it Al decided he would take an extra cylinder and I decided against it.)

By 8 P.M., we were into the third round of melting snow, when footsteps approached from outside. A figure crouched down at the entrance to the tent, red-eyed and desperate. It was the Hungarian climber who, with Reinhard Wlasich, the Austrian, had been attempting the North Face without oxygen.

His first words were in French but when he saw our blank faces he changed to English.

"I need some . . . have you a way to help . . . some oxygen and some gas . . . please." His speech was slurred and barely understandable. He sounded like he was suffering from the onset of high-altitude sickness.

"Take it easy and calm down a bit. Now what's the problem?" Al made some space for him to kneel in the front of the tent.

"My friend is dying. I want you to try and help me rescue him. We're in that tent over there." He pointed out into the night.

"You're talking about Reinhard?"

"Yes. Reinhard. He's dying. If we don't get him down the mountain he'll be dead. You have to help me."

"What about the Norwegian doctor—Morton. Has he seen him?"

"He did. This afternoon."

"And what did he say?"

"He has oedema—on the lungs and cerebral."

"Is he conscious?"

"He's in a coma."

"Well, if he's in a coma he *is* going to die. There's no way anyone can get him off the mountain. Have you got oxygen?"

"It's finished. Can I take a bottle?"

"You can take as much as you need. Have you got a regulator?"

"Yes. But if we go now we can rescue him."

"How?" Al was icy calm.

"I don't know. We can carry him. I have to do something!" The Hungarian was distraught, and beginning to vent his frustration as anger on us.

"There's nothing we can do. No matter how many people we had up here, we still couldn't get him down to five. Think about the rocks, how are you going to lower him down?"

The Hungarian went quiet. In his heart he knew that Al was right. Even if Reinhard had been conscious, a rescue would have been impossible. The fact that he was in a coma was as a death sentence here at 8,300 metres.

"How much longer do you think he will live?"

"I don't know. He's hardly breathing."

Al and I exchanged a glance. The same thought occurred to both of us at the same time: the Hungarian, determined to stay with his fellow climber right to the bitter end, was even now putting his own life in danger.

"Listen. Your friend is definitely going to die. You have to get off the mountain or you'll die too. Do you understand?" Al was speaking forcefully now, driving the news as hard as he could into the Hungarian's confused mind. He went quiet once more as this sank in.

"You'll be dead by tomorrow night if you stay here. So take two oxygen bottles now, get through the night, and come back at first light to take another bottle to get you back down to five. OK?"

The Hungarian nodded slowly.

"You're doing as much as you can by staying with him. But he can't be rescued. If you stay here now you'll be putting other lives in danger. Are you still fit enough to get down tomorrow on your own?"

"Yes." His reply was barely audible.

He picked up the two oxygen bottles and walked off into the night, the very picture of a broken man. I wondered what kind of hell he was returning to: within a few hours Reinhard would be dead by his side.

"You know the strangest thing?" A chilling memory had come back to me.

"What?"

"When you and Barney decided to turn Brian back on the ridge you saw Reinhard and his mate carrying on and said he might die."

"That's true. I could see by the speed they were moving that they were heading for trouble."

Then another memory hit me—a recollection of a discussion I had with Al before leaving for Kathmandu.

"And do you remember the conversation we had when you came round for the meal?" Al had visited us in Hertfordshire a few weeks before the expedition left. "You predicted this would happen. You said we'd get to camp six and find someone in exactly that state. In fact I think you specified it would be an Eastern European."

"Yeah, I do remember."

"Don't you think that's bizarre?"

Al thought for a moment. "Not really. There's so many disorganized teams on Everest these days you're more likely than not to find someone in trouble here."

And with that we resumed the cooking and the subject was closed. But in my mind the extraordinary conversation we had just had with the Hungarian was churning away. Why didn't I feel more compassion for him? Why hadn't we at least offered to go and check on Reinhard just in case he had miraculously recovered?

The truth was that the mountain had dehumanized me and hardened my emotional response. The news about Reinhard's impending death had neither surprised me nor shocked me. Instead it seemed normal. This is camp six—8,300 metres, my mind was telling me, this is where people *do* die if something goes wrong. Reinhard was beyond help. We all were. To be prepared to go this high, we had all willingly made an unwritten pact with the mountain that says "I'm putting myself in a position where I know I can die." Given that level of personal commitment, perhaps it is not surprising that luxuries like pity and compassion are often left behind at base camp along with other unnecessary baggage. If we had brought those emotions with us, perhaps we would be needing them now—for ourselves?

I was beginning to understand what the Death Zone really means.

At 11:20 P.M. Al drifted off into a light sleep, his rhythmic breathing muffled by the oxygen mask. At midnight, summit day would begin.

Even though my body craved it, for me there was no question of sleep. I was like a child lying wide-eyed in bed on Christmas Eve. Expectation ran like an adrenalin shot through my body. I pulled the frozen fabric of the down sleeping bag as tight as I could around my head and lay perfectly still.

Staring into the dark confines of the tent, super-sensitive to the ghosts of wind playing around us, I found myself entering a state of Zen-like calm. During the long-haired phase of my teens, fuelled by a dangerous overconsumption of Carlos Castaneda and Aldous Huxley, I had often tried to meditate my way into an altered state of consciousness. How I had tried!

In a candlelit bedroom, filled with the aromatic smoke of joss-sticks and the trance-inducing pentatonic synthesizer chords of the psychedelic band "Gong," I sat in a half-lotus position and waited to lock on to the astral plane. But no matter how long I spent in the ticket queue, my journey to Ixtlan never began. Perhaps Hemel Hempstead is not the best starting place when you're heading for Nirvana.

Now, zipped into that tiny plastic capsule 8,300 metres above the rest of the world I slipped effortlessly into a state of euphoric trance. The cramped Quasar mountain tent suddenly took on the dimensions of a cathedral, its domed roof becoming a series of soaring arches suspended hundreds of feet in the air. The soothing hiss of the oxygen feeding into my mask took on a musical quality, like pan-pipes, and the wind became a whispering voice murmuring encouraging words for the day to come.

The music faded and was replaced by the thudding beat of blood-rush echoing in the back of my skull. The fantasy changed. I imagined myself diving into the sea and letting my lungs fill with water.

Then I snapped back to consciousness with a horrible gasp, gulping frantically for air. That was why the music had faded: the oxygen cylinder was out of air. Confused and disorientated, I had trouble finding my headtorch and then struggled to unscrew the frozen regulator valve on the dead tank.

The interior of the tent was now encrusted with a thin hoar frost of frozen vapour. With every movement, irritating showers of tiny crystals fell, freezing any exposed skin.

Replacing the valve on to a fresh oxygen bottle, I see the gauge on one litre a minute and slumped exhausted back into the sleeping bag. Now the waking trance was anything but euphoric; the sweet dreams went distinctly sour. I suddenly remembered that not ten metres from our tent the Austrian, Reinhard, was dying, beyond help.

Camp six, which had seemed such a welcome refuge when we'd arrived some hours before, now became a place of overwhelming fear and anxiety. The fact that there was nothing we could do for Reinhard put everything into perspective; the mountain was in control. Altitude, with all its deadly effects, was snuffing the life out of a strong, healthy mountaineer, as if he were a sickly child. In the face of this invisible force, our own enterprise felt fragile and doomed to fail.

For the remaining twenty minutes before midnight I lay in a state of cold fear, praying that the weather would hold, that my body would be capable of meeting the challenge ahead, and most important of all—that I would not make a mistake. My lack of confidence in my own mountaineering abilities had dogged me from the start of the expedition. Now the fear of a trip, of a sudden fall, of fumbling a piece of protection as I'd done with the figure-of-eight on the Col; those were mistakes which I had got away with in the early stages of the climb. On summit day, even the slightest mistake would be a potential killer.

Mallory and Irvine probably died that way . . .

Midnight. Al's digital watch bleeped a feeble alarm and I could hear muffled shouts from the Sherpas' tent. Al roused himself from sleep and we set about the tiresome task of lighting the gas cookers.

The cigarette lighters were now even more reluctant to ignite than at camp five. It took forty or fifty strokes with my thumb to coax a flame out of the frozen gas. By the time I succeeded, blood was flowing freely from the cracked skin.

The gas cooker burned fiercely for a few seconds then spluttered out.

"Bastard!" I was beginning to loathe the cookers.

Al patiently took over with the cigarette lighter and managed to relight it. This had been a regular pattern since camp five. The intense cold and thin air made the propane burners extremely fickle. They frequently flared out for no apparent reason, filling the tent with nauseating gas until they could be relit.

Once warmed up, the gas seemed to flow better, and after ten minutes of frustration, we had both cookers happily burning. Al busied himself cutting up blocks of snow into pieces small enough to fit into the pans while I tried to make some order out of my side of the tent.

Al, canny as ever, had bagged himself the flatter, uphill sleeping platform, leaving me to compete for space with the pile of equipment. Thanks to the precarious angle, leaning sharply down the snowfield, the interior, and my side in particular, had become a jumbled mess.

Used oxygen cylinders, food rations and climbing equipment formed a chaotic heap on the downward slope. The side wall of the tent was sagging alarmingly under the weight of the gear, and I imagined that the slightest tear could split the fabric like the belly of a whale, emptying the contents and me on to the ice slide outside, where a one-way trip down the North Face would rapidly ensue.

I tried to rearrange the heavier objects at the foot of the tent where they would be out of the way. Then I set about extracting the vital pieces of gear which would be needed for the day ahead: the lithium batteries for the video camera, the red wind suit, the outer shells of my plastic boots. Highlighted by the beam of the headtorch I saw the food packets which each of us had prepared with such optimism back at base camp seven weeks before.

Written in blue marker pen were the names of the owners: Tore, Simon, Sundeep, Barney, Brian . . . I ripped open Brian's pack and extracted the precious sachet of muesli. My appetite had become super-selective and this was one of the few foods I could face.

It took over an hour to melt the compacted snow down to boiling water. We shared a pack of pistachio nuts and drank mugs of tea and Bournvita before loading the pans with more snow for another meltdown . . . our drinking supply for the climb.

Gagged by the oxygen masks, we had little urge to talk, but concentrated on the vital task of forcing as much food and liquid down as we could.

Al's long years of Himalayan expeditions had taught him the enviable knack of pissing into a pee bottle whilst lying on his side. Lacking the confidence to risk a sleeping bag full of urine by getting this wrong, I relied on the surer but less energy-efficient technique of crouching on my knees to perform the act.

The minutes ticked by, and with them came another dreaded bodily demand.

"I need a crap."

"Me too." Al was in the same state.

The prospect of putting on the boots and going out into the freezing night wind was extremely depressing. Just the thought was exhausting and demoralizing.

"Better do it," Al advised. "Nothing else for it. No point in taking any excess baggage up. Besides, if you're shitting yourself now, imagine what you'll be like on the second step."

As an avid consumer of Himalayan climbing books, I had always been mystified by the high-altitude mountaineer's obsession with bodily functions. What, I had wondered, was the problem?

It took nearly fifteen minutes to prepare ourselves to exit the tent. Taking our oxygen cylinders with us was not a realistic option. Moving carefully to avoid the cookers, I crawled out of the front of the tent. Doing so, I nudged an empty cylinder which had been propped outside. It fell on to the ice slope and accelerated away quickly. There was a clanking sound as it hit rocks once—twice—and then cartwheeled out of sight down the North Face to land on the glacier some six thousand feet below.

Mistake.

Stumbling across the ice slope, I realized that what I was doing was extremely stupid. I should have crampons and an ice-axe. One slip and I would follow the oxygen cylinder down the Face. With a shudder I remembered that this was exactly how one of the Taiwanese climbers had fallen on the southern side just days before.

I found a narrow ledge and managed to pull down the down suit and thermal underclothes. Calf and thigh muscles protesting, I squatted for what seemed like an eternity, puffing and panting for air. A few metres away, Al was doing the same. There is no such thing as embarrassment at 8,300 metres.

At the Col and above I found myself experiencing acute pain when going to the toilet. This time was by far the worst, bringing tears to my eyes. My whole system was completely dried up, and it felt like I was splitting inside.

"I'm having a baby here, Al."

An answering grunt came in reply.

With the pain came blood—quite a substantial amount. I closed my mind to the implications of this, putting it down to that well-known climbers affliction, piles, even though I was pretty sure I didn't have them.

Collapsing back into the tent I strapped on the oxygen mask and gulped hungrily at the clean-tasting air. In the warmth of the sleeping bags I thrust my hands under my armpits to defrost, another surprising painful process.

Al came in. "You all right?"

"Fine," I replied, not wanting to let on how I really felt. Close to vomiting, with a skull-splitting headache, I now knew why a visit to the toilet above 8,000 metres inspires such dread amongst mountaineers.

Al added some more snow blocks to the pans of water and then curled up in his bag to try and regain some precious warmth. I could just make out his muffled words:

"My feet are frozen."

Outside, I could hear the three Sherpas preparing their equipment. Gyaltsen made his way across the snowfield and shouted into the tent.

"Two o'clock. You ready?"

"We need another brew," Al replied. "Let's leave in half an hour."

The two other Sherpas, Lhakpa and Mingma, came across to join Gyaltsen outside our tent. They began to sort out the oxygen cylinders which were stacked neatly there in a pile.

"There's no way we're leaving with fingers or toes frozen," Al told me "They have to be perfectly warm when we set off or we'll end up losing them."

I took my feet out of their inner boots and massaged them back to life. The smaller toes felt curiously waxy to the touch, as if the skin was thicker than it should be.

By 2:30 A.M., fortified by a last cup of Bournvita and a few lumps of chocolate, we were outside the tent with crampons and neoprene gaiters fitted. Over the "Michelin man" down suits we wore the red Berghaus wind suits with harness fastened over the whole ensemble. Movement was severely restricted by the thickness of this specialist clothing and I had to get Al to tighten my harness buckle up so it fitted snugly around my waist.

We arranged the rucksacks to carry the oxygen cylinders. With this, as with every other tiny part of the high-altitude survival jigsaw, attention to detail is critical. The oxygen bottle must be carried upright. If it falls in the sack the oxygen feed pipe could crimp and cut off the supply. Having tested my system at base camp, I now rolled up my Karrimat and inserted it in the pack. Slid into the roll, the oxygen cylinder was held in place firmly by the foam with the valve clear of obstruction.

There was the added advantage that if we had to bivouac for whatever reason, the Karrimat would be a very valuable asset.

I ran through a mental check-list as we put the final touches to the equipment. Ski goggles ready in the pocket of the wind suit. Spare glacier goggles in another pocket. Headtorch ready with two spare bulbs and spare battery. Two one-litre water bottles filled with "isotonic" high-energy glucose drink. Walkie-talkie checked. Food—chocolate and Christmas pudding—ready. Stills cameras loaded with fresh film. Crampon repair kit. Spare carabiner. Figure-of-eight descendeur. Jumar clamps.

"Where's your drink?" Al asked.

"In the rucksack."

"You're better off putting them inside the down suit next to your skin."

I did as Al said, zipping up one of the plastic nalgene bottles into the suit just above the harness. The Sherpas were clearly ready to go. My mind raced through the mental check-list searching for the one missed component, the one small forgotten item which would bring the summit bid to a grinding halt.

There wasn't one. We were ready.

Without a word, we turned away from the tents and started our climb up into the night. Lhakpa led, with Mingma and Gyalsen behind, then Al and myself at the tail.

After the suspense and tension of the preparation it was a sheer relief to be moving. Those first few steps had, for me, a truly epic quality. I knew we were in an incredibly privileged position—a position thousands of mountaineers would give their eye-teeth (and perhaps a lot more) to share.

We were leaving camp six bang on schedule on as near as the North Face ever gets to a perfect night. We had liquid, food, and adequate supply of oxygen and the assistance of three very strong Sherpas. Our equipment was tried and tested, we were as fit as one can be above 8,000 metres with no major sickness or injury to cope with.

It doesn't get much better than that. The "window" was open. For the first time, I allowed myself the luxury of thinking that we might just make it. If our luck held.

In the precise minutes of our departure from camp six, as we later learned from the Hungarian climber who was with him in the tent, Reinhard died.

The Sherpas set a fast pace up the first of the snowfields lying above the camp. Al kept up easily but I found myself lagging behind. The thin beam of light from the headtorch, seemingly so bright when tested in the tent, now felt inadequate for the task, illuminating a pathetically small patch of snow.

Catching up, I concentrated on watching Al's cramponed feet as they bit into the snow. The conditions were variable with an unpredictable crust. Frequently it gave way, plunging us thigh deep into a hidden hole.

I quickly learned not to trust the headtorch with its tuned vision effect. It confused the eye by casting shadows of unknown depth. Rocks could be bigger than they seemed. Holes in the snow lacked all perspective. Distances became hard to judge. Was Lhakpa's light ten metres in front of me . . . or fifty? I couldn't tell.

We crossed several old tent platforms, abandoned by previous expeditions. Each one was littered with the usual shredded fabric, splintered tent-poles and empty oxygen cylinders. A foil food sachet got spiked by one of my crampon teeth and dragged annoyingly until I could be bothered to remove it.

At each of these wrecked sites, Al, the mountain detective, would pause for a moment to cast his headtorch around the remains. Even now, on our summit bid, his fascination for them was as keen as ever.

The climb continued, step after step, up the snowfield towards the much more demanding terrain of the yellow band. Very conscious of our limited oxygen supply, I tried to concentrate on regulating my breathing; I knew from scuba-diving training how easy it is to waste air.

But the terrain of the North Face is mixed; both in steepness and in composition. Steep ice fields give way to shallower rock slabs. Demanding rock sections end in long traverses. Establishing a breathing pattern is virtually impossible. Mostly I found I was puffing and panting at a very fast rate and there was nothing I could do about it.

After an hour I found I was feeling better. The headache and nausea had faded away with the concentrated physical work of the climb. My feet and hands felt warm, and the weight of the rucksack was not as bad as I had feared.

Reaching the end of the larger of the two snowfields, we encountered the first bare rock. I watched in horror as the three pinprick lights of the Sherpas began to rise up what seemed to be a vertical wall. Surely it was an optical illusion? I had never heard anyone talk about any actual climbing before the Ridge. But, standing at the foot of the rock section, my heart sank. It was steep. Very steep. I was completely inexperienced in night climbing, and fear formed an icy pool in the pit of my stomach.

We were about to tackle the yellow band.

Worse, we would have to climb on rock with our crampons on. This is like trying to climb stairs on stilts. The spiked fangs act like an unwanted platform sole, elevating the foot away from any real contact with the rock. Using crampons on rock greatly increases the risk of a misplaced foothold or a twisted ankle. In a tight spot, where the feet have to move in close proximity, they are even more deadly. A spike can snag in the neoprene gaiter of the other foot, a mistake which invariably leads to a heavy fall.

On other mountains we might have stopped to remove the crampons, but here that was not an option. On the North Face of Everest, removing crampons every time you made a transition from snow to rock would waste hours of precious time and risk almost certain frostbite to the hands

I paused for a brief rest as the others made their way up into the rock band. Turning off my headtorch, I let my eyes adjust to the dark. The sky was mostly still clear of cloud but I could see no sign of the moon. The only illumination came from the stars, which were as dazzling as I have ever seen them. The towering mass of Changtse was now far below us, I could just see the sinuous curves of its fluted ridge.

Further down, thousands of metres further down, the great glaciers were just visible, reflecting the dull metallic grey of the starlight against the darker shadows of their deep valley walls. The whole of Tibet lay beneath us and there was not a single electric light to be seen.

Taking off my Gore-tex overmitts, I reached up to the oxygen mask. Ice was beginning to constrict the intake valve at the front. I carefully broke the chunk away.

Then, my crampons clanking and scraping with a jarring metallic ring against the rock, I began the climb up. The route took a line up a series of ledges, linked by narrow cracks. It was a nasty scramble, involving strenuous leg and arm work to lunge up steps which were often uncomfortably high. More than once I found myself jamming a knee into a crack for support, or squirming up on to a balcony on my stomach.

"This must be the first step," I yelled up at Al. He didn't reply and hours later, when we reached the real first step, I realized how far out I had been.

We came to a platform and took a few minutes' rest before beginning the next section.

The climb was littered with tatty ropes. Some were frayed, some were kinked from unknown causes, others were bleached white from exposure to the intense ultraviolet radiation here above 8,000 metres. Al sorted through them with a professional's eye, muttering under his breath.

Selecting the best of a bad lot, Al attached his jumar clamp and started up, sliding the handgrip of the camming device with each move. I waited for him to gain some height and then followed on. The crampons made every move a nightmare, as they had to be jammed into crevices or rested on protrusions to gain a purchase. Often I found my feet scrabbling frantically for a hold, the metal spikes grinding the flaking rock into granules of grit.

A steady barrage of small stones, and the occasional fist-sized rock, came down from above where the Sherpas were climbing. Normally this is avoidable by all but the clumsiest climber, but here every foothold had the potential to dislodge debris. Our ears rapidly became adept at guessing the size of an approaching missile as it clattered down the rock-face.

"Below!" A flat, briefcase-sized rock slithered down the face and spun off into the dark depths.

After sixty or seventy metres of ascent I made my first mistake. As I pushed down to lift my body weight up on a boulder foothold, my crampon slipped away with no warning, unbalancing me and crashing my knee into a sharp ledge. The down suit cushioned much of the blow but it still took me several minutes to regain my composure as a series of sparkling stars did cartoon laps of honour across my field of vision.

On that fall, as a many other times, my entire body weight was suspended on the rope.

Another twenty metres of ascent brought me to the anchor point of the rope I was climbing on. Shining the headtorch on to the fixing point, I could scarcely believe what I was seeing. My lifeline was attached to the face by a single, rusting metal piton which had been ineptly placed in a crack.

Out of curiosity I tested the solidity of the anchor point with my hand. It moved. With one gentle pull, the piton slid right out. I stared at it dumbly for a few seconds, incredulous that my recent fall had been held by this pathetic piece of protection.

Throughout the expedition the knowledge that fixed ropes existed on the more technical rock had been a reassuring notion. "Get to camp six and then you're on the fixed ropes' was a much repeated mantra, implying that they were somehow safe. In that one heart-stopping moment as the piton slid out of its crack, my faith in the fixed ropes was destroyed. I resolved to rely on them as little as I could.

The incline eased off and I found Al and the three Sherpas waiting for me. As I arrived they continued onwards up a series of steps cut into wind-hardened snow. At the next steep section Lhakpa again led the way up the rocks, climbing strongly and steadily. The light from his headtorch rapidly went out of view.

I had a favour to ask. "Al, can you let me go in front? I'm not happy at the back."

"No problem." Al unclipped his sling from the rope and let me pass. It was a generous gesture which I greatly appreciated.

I started up the next rock section feeling a lot more confident with Al behind me at the tail-end of the rope. This was partly psychological, and partly from the practical help he could give by shining his headtorch on to holds. I found myself moving easier and with more certainty.

As everywhere on Everest, the rock was fragmented and unreliable. Apparently solid handholds came away easily in flakes, boulders trembled under the weight of a leg, and a flow of gravel-sized stones seemed to be perpetually on the move.

Just inches from my hand a stone the size of a telephone directory fell out of the night. Impacting hard, it shattered into hundreds of pieces, showering me with splinters of stone. Mingma's warning cry from above came simultaneously. I saw his headtorch flash down the face.

"You OK?"

"OK." We carried on up.

By now I had no idea of our precise position on the Face. From the Rongbuk glacier the distance from camp six to the North-East Ridge does not look great. In fact, as I was discovering, it is a significant climb. It was now many hours since we had left the camp and my body was already feeling as if it had done a substantial day's work.

There was still not the slightest glimmer of dawn. I began to long for the first rays of light.

Now we started what I guessed was the final section of the yellow band; more steep slogging up an eroded fault in the rock strata. It began with a stretching high step of a metre or more up on to an edge; another occasion when there was no choice but to rely on a fixed rope. Then, with the infernal crampons scraping horribly on the rock, we scrambled up for about thirty minutes, pausing every five minutes or so for breath.

Turning back for a moment, I saw that Al was free-climbing the section. He, like me, had no confidence in the fixed ropes, but, unlike me, had the experience to know he could climb the route without a fall.

As the ground evened off, we began another traverse to the right, across a field of dirty snow. A bright red rope had been laid across it—the newest protection we had seen so far. Clipping on, I wondered who had fixed it: the Indians, or perhaps the Japanese?

The line continued up through a crack and then on to a sloping rock plateau the size of a tennis court. Crossing it, I realized we had finished the first stage of the climb.

The horrors of the night climb ended as we took the final steps on to the North-East Ridge. The crumbling cliffs of the yellow band had been steeper, more complex and much more committing than I had imagined. Climbing them in the dark, with just the glowworm light of the headtorch, had been a nightmare.

Now, with the first rays of dawn to light our route along the Ridge, I reached up and turned the headtorch off. If all went well now, we could be on the summit within the next six hours.

The three Sherpas stood hunched over their ice-axes, alien figures in their goggles and oxygen masks. They had set a blistering pace through the dark hours and now rested as we waited for Al to join us on the Ridge.

One of the Sherpas—Lhakpa—had climbed to the summit before, but I knew the others had never been this high. Each had stalactites of ice clinging to the bottom of his oxygen mask where exhaled vapour had frozen into spikes several inches long. Mingma was having trouble with his mask. I watched him take it off to unblock the frozen pipe and remembered the expedition doctor's warning that we might be unconscious within thirty minutes if our oxygen supply failed.

My oxygen hadn't stopped yet, but the hard frozen shell of the mask was eroding a nagging sore where it rubbed at the bridge of my nose. I eased it away from my face for a moment to relieve the irritation. Then, sucking deep on the oxygen, I prayed it wouldn't let me down.

With the dawn came the wind, our greatest enemy. As Al picked his way carefully up to join us, the first few gusts of the day began to play along the North Face, sending up flurries of ice crystals. While we waited for Al to recover his breath, I moved carefully on to the crest and looked over the knife edge drop down the Kanshung—the Eastern—Face.

There can be few more terrifying sights anywhere on earth. Seen from my vantage point, the Kanshung Face was a sheer 10,000-foot wall of ice falling away beneath me, so steep it seemed almost vertical. Vast fields of ice—hanging glaciers—perch precariously on its walls. It is deeply etched with fragile fissures and crevasses. It wasn't had to imagine the whole Face—all those billions of tons of ice—giving up its fight with gravity and peeling off in one monumental avalanche down into the valleys below.

When Mallory first saw the Kanshung Face during the British reconnaissance expedition of 1924, he pronounced it unclimbable. He would leave it, he decided "to others less wise." Now, looking down the Face, I understood precisely what he meant. The fact that it has subsequently been climbed—and by several different routes—seems to me an incredible achievement.

The Kanshung Face is home to, and creator of, some curious winds. With day breaking, one of those winds was beginning. As I looked down the Face, a billowing cloud of ice crystals was moving vertically up towards me. It was like looking down directly into the gaping mouth of a power station cooling tower. This is the tail of the massive "rotor" that Everest spins out of the constant north-westerly Tibetan gales. As the ice crystals come up to the Ridge, they are blown to the south-east in a deadly plume which can be thirty miles long.

Few people summit when Everest's plume is running.

Lhakpa shouted something to me which broke the spell and I turned back towards the group.

Now our climb along the Ridge itself was about to begin. From where we were standing, it looked incredibly complicated: a dragon's tail of switchbacks, dips and rocky steps. Two of these, the "first step" and the second, are regarded as the most formidable of the obstacles on the North Face route, but it was the sheer length of the Ridge that most worried me.

Back in London, I had met Crag Jones, one of the four British climbers to have summitted via the North Face. We sat in a Soho coffee bar drinking cappuccino while Crag cracked his knuckles and rolled up his sleeves to reveal Popeye muscles and veins the thickness of climbing ropes.

"The first and second steps *are* problems," he told me, "but it's the size of the Ridge you want to think about. When you get on to the Ridge you have to realize there could be another twelve hours of climbing to get back to camp six via the summit. Twelve hours. It's a hell of a long day."

From where I was standing, Crag was right. It was already looking like a hell of a long day and we'd only cracked a tiny proportion of the route. Lhakpa moved towards me and shouted, his voice muffled by the mask:

"We move fast. Move very fast. OK?"

He tapped his wrist to indicate that the clock was ticking away. At 8,600 metres we were the highest human beings on the planet; and we were dying a little more with every hour. In the Death Zone, you have to move fast to keep alive.

Now in full daylight, we set out along the lifeline of tattered ropes which snake along the Ridge, the legacy of previous ascents. With the night hours behind us, I felt a glimmer of optimism creep in. I was feeling strong.

Thirty minutes later we rounded a small cliff and found the first dead Indian climber. We knew that the three Indian bodies would still be there on the Ridge where they had died a few days earlier, but, ridiculously, I had completely forgotten about them.

Now, here was the first body, lying partly in the shelter of an over-hanging rock and ringed by an almost perfect circle of windblown snow.

Al shouted through his mask, "Must be one of the Indians."

We would have to step over his outstretched legs to continue along the ridge.

The Sherpas stood side by side, seemingly rooted to the spot by the sight of the dead man. Their heads were bowed, as if in prayer; perhaps, it occurred to me later, they were praying.

I felt an almost irresistible urge to look at the dead climber's face. What expression would be fixed on it in those final moments of life? Terror? A smile? (They say that those who die of acute mountain sickness have a delusion of well-being in the final stages.)

But his head was thrust far into the overhang, the neck bent so his face rested against the rock. All I could see was the edge of his oxygen mask. From the mask ran that precious, life-giving tube to the oxygen cylinder which was standing upright against a rock. It was an orange cylinder, a Russian one like our own.

I bent down, using my ice-axe for support, to have a closer look at the gauge on the top of the cylinder. It read, of course, zero. Even if he had died before the cylinder ran out, it would have continued to spill its feeble trickle of oxygen into the atmosphere until it emptied.

He was wearing very few clothes, just a lightweight red fleece top, some blue Gore-tex climbing trousers and a pair of yellow plastic Koflach boots similar to our own. His rucksack lay nearby, flat and empty. I wondered about this mystery for a moment. What had happened to his high-altitude gear? His down suit? His Gore-tex mitts? We knew the Indian team had been well-equipped. That left only two possibilities: either he'd ripped them off in the final sages of delirium, or someone had stolen them from the corpse.

In a way I found the first scenario an easier one to imagine.

The tragedy of the Indian team was central to the film I was making. Seduced by Everest's siren call, they had pushed themselves well beyond their own limits of endurance and had failed to reserve enough strength to get down in the worsening conditions which preceded the big storm. Summit fever had killed them.

Yet, even though we had the video cameras with us to record the actuality of our climb, I could not bring myself to film the dead man lying so pathetically at our feet.

I knew that ITN and Channel 4 would want this most graphic illustration of Everest as killer but I couldn't bring myself to do it. Even the victims of war eventually find a grave—even if they are shoved into it by a bulldozer. This Indian climber would remain exactly where he lay now, frozen for eternity. His grave was the bleakest imaginable and to think that his family, his friends, would see the reality of that was too much to contemplate.

As we stepped over the legs of the corpse to continue along the Ridge, we crossed an invisible line in the snow . . . and an invisible line of commitment in our own minds. Altitude is an unseen killer. Human life, any life, does not belong in the Death Zone, and by stepping over the dead body we made the conscious decision to push further into it. The dead body had been the starkest reminder we could have that we were now reliant for our lives on our equipment, our own strength and our luck.

There was the irresistible feeling that it was the Indian who was perfectly in tune with this place, and that we, being alive, were the invaders. All places above 8,000 metres belong to the dead because up there human life cannot be sustained. Wrapped up like spacemen in our huge high-altitude suits, breathing through the mechanical hiss of the oxygen system, I felt for the first time in my life an alien on my own planet.

Our assault on the Ridge continued.

By 7 A.M. we reached the first step. It was both higher, at about twenty metres, and more of a climb, than I had imagined. Overshadowed by the bigger cliff of the second step, it tends to get treated as an insignificant obstacle but, looking up at it with my ski goggles beginning to acquire a frozen internal layer, it looked daunting enough.

It was not possible to remove the crampons to cope with these changing conditions as unfixing and then refixing them would risk fingers to frostbite (it was about-35°F at that point), and also waste too much time.

The three Sherpas went up first and I followed. For three metres or so, the route led up an ice-filled crack on the left side of the cliff. Next came a traverse across to a rocky ledge and then a precarious scramble up between two rounded boulders. I jammed the front metal points of my crampons into a tiny rock crack and pushed up . . . all my weight relying on the insignificant hold.

I paused for some moments to gather breath after the strenuous move, and then tackled the crux.

The move required a delicate balancing act which I could have achieved easily at sea level. Up here in clothes which reduced all sense of being in touch with the rock, and with the added exposure of an 8,000-foot fall directly down the North Face as a penalty for a mistake, it felt epic enough.

I snapped my jumar clamp as high as I could on the best looking of the many ropes which were hanging beguilingly around the crux. It gave a sense of security to protect a fall but that was a psychological advantage rather than a real one. In fact, a fall would leave the unlucky climber swinging helplessly in open space underneath the overhanging section of the cliff. Assuming the rope held.

Moving out into the exposed position, I stuck a leg around the smooth edge of the ridge and planted it on to the foothold which, fortunately, waited on the other side. I had to sense its security rather than see it . . . the leg was out of my field of vision.

My left hand instinctively snaked up to try and find a handhold above. A tentative pull on a possible hold merely made it give way, and I threw the cigarette-packet-sized piece of rock own the North Face beneath me.

Not many people can imagine that Everest is a crumbling wreck of a mountain. It looks as if it should be made of granite, but in fact it is friable limestone . . . the worst of rocks to climb at any altitude.

Locking my fist on to a ledge above my head, I took a deep breath and shifted my entire weight on to the out-of-vision foot. Then I swung over and around the rock, to the safety of the other side.

Lhakpa was waiting there. He put his thumbs up and I replied with the same. Another obstacle over. Another step closer to the summit.

Now the wind was definitely picking up and we were still only halfway along the Ridge. We began to push harder. The plume of ice crystals from the Kanshung Face was now billowing up more strongly on our left, a sign we could not afford to ignore. Whenever we stopped to regain our breath, I looked away to the north, the direction a storm would come from. Plenty of clouds were moving rapidly towards us but nothing so far looked too threatening.

I had been so wrapped up in the climb, I had completely forgotten my stills camera. The tiny Olympus had a brand-new lithium battery and a full roll of transparency film. Squinting through the eyepiece, I took two pictures of the terrain ahead and one shot of Al. Then we pressed on.

At several points, the route took us right on to the very knife-edge crest of the Ridge itself. Then, we would time the dash along the ice to miss the blasts of wind. I had never been able to imagine how climbers could be blown off a ridge. Now, I was acutely aware of that possibility. One of the theoretical ends for Mallory and Irvine had them plummeting off the Ridge and down the Kanshung Face . . . perhaps their bodies, or their ghosts, were close by?

One particularly hair-raising section of the Ridge, only a few metres long, involved stepping down on to what seemed to be a corniced section of crumbling ice cross-sectioned by a crevasse. The Sherpas, lighter and more agile than we were, ran across easily. I took each step with my heart in my mouth, expecting at any moment that the cornice would give way and leave me dangling over the Kanshung Face.

The ice held.

By 8:30 A.M. we reached the second step. This step is another cliff, steeper and more than twice the height of the first. There is no way around it, it has to be tackled head-on.

Back in the 1980s, a Chinese expedition had fixed a lightweight climbing ladder to the most severe part of the cliff. It had been destroyed in a recent storm and the Indian climbers and their Sherpas had fixed another in its place. I had been greatly reassured by the notion of the ladder. Anyone could climb a ladder . . . couldn't they? In my mind it had lessened the severity of the second step.

In fact the ladder, which I had always thought of as a friendly aid, was about to prove a significant problem in its own right.

At the foot of the second step two unexpected thing happened: the first was my discovery that both my litre bottles of juice, boiled from snow so painfully slowly at camp six the previous night, were frozen solid. Even the bottle I had kept next to my skin inside the front of my down suit was a solid mass of ice. At the time It seemed like an inconvenience. Later on during the day I was to realize in the starkest way possible the seriousness of that event.

Al checked his bottles too. They were also frozen solid. Now neither of us would have a single drop of moisture through the whole day. Many experienced high-altitude mountaineers would have turned back at that point.

The other unexpected thing was that Al leaned towards me to speak.

"Open up my pack," he said. "Put the oxygen up to four litres a minute."

He turned his back to me. Taking off my overmitts, and going down to the finger gloves, I undid the clips closing his pack and found the oxygen regulator valve inside. It was a difficult, fiddly job in the close confines of the rucksack. I clicked the regulator round to read four and closed the pack.

Now Al was pumping twice as much oxygen into his system as my rate of two litres a minute. I could understand his desire for more gas to tackle the second step, but even so his request surprised me. We both knew the risks of pumping up the oxygen too high. It runs out twice as fast and, with your body tuned in to operate at a higher level, you comedown with a bigger crash when it ends.

"OK. It's on four," I shouted to him. For a fleeting moment I thought I sensed something more than just tiredness in the way Al was moving. Was he having a harder time than he was revealing?

It was a measure of our increasing disorientation that neither of us thought at that stage of dumping the two litres of frozen liquid. Now we were climbing with two kilogrammes of superfluous weight on our backs up the hardest rock-climbing section of the North Face route.

The first six metres or so were simple enough. A tight squeeze through a chimney filled with ice led on to an easier graded ledge with a snow bank against the cliff. I used the jumar clamp to help my ascent, sliding the device up as high as my arms would stretch, then pulling up where it gripped against the rope. Someone had rigged a virtually new, 9mm rope on this lower part and that helped considerably.

The crampons scratched and bit into the rock steps like the claws of a cat trying, and failing to climb a tree. Then came a big step up. I tensioned my foot against a ripple of protruding rock to my right, and, cursing the crampons to hell, just managed to ease my body up on to the ledge which led to the ladder.

I paused for a long moment to catch my breath. The beat of my heart was sending a pounding rush of blood through my head. I was aware of my pulse-rate being higher than I have ever sensed it before. My breathing was wild and virtually out of control. For one panic-stricken moment I thought my oxygen had failed. Then I realized I could still hear the reassuring hiss of the gas and told myself to calm down.

I was standing more or less exactly in the place where Mallory and Irvine were last seen alive, spotted by telescope from the North Col camp. Their 1924 climb had been the hardest, and perhaps, the greatest, of the pre-war efforts on Everest.

There had been no ladder for them on the second step. If they'd tried it, one of them may well have fallen, taking his partner with him to certain death. The horror of imagining that final moment had always eluded me until now. Now I had no trouble in imagining a fatal fall from this spot. It was the most exposed and dangerous part of the climb.

My friend the ladder was the next obstacle. I put a hand on it and felt it sway and flap against the sheer face it was attached to. I had always imagined it to be solid. I began to climb.

The first problem was caused by the crampons. The metal spikes snagged against the rungs, or grated against the rock and prevented me from getting a proper footing on the ladder. Unable to look down, blinkered by the goggles into a front only view, I had to sense as best I could when my feet were in the right place.

My breathing rate went up again . . . the greater volume of escaping moisture running up through gaps in the mask and freezing inside my goggles. Halfway up the ladder I was almost blinded by this, and I ripped the goggles up on to my head to be able to see. We were all aware of the dangers of snow blindness but I felt I could take the risk for the next few crucial minutes.

The ladder had a distinct, drunken lean to the left. This, coupled with the fact that it was swaying alarmingly on the ragbag selection of pitons and ropes which held it, made it extremely difficult to cling to.

My Gore-tex overmitts were hopelessly clumsy in this situation. I could barely cup them tight enough to cling to the rungs. But, having started with them on, I could hardly remove them now; and any lesser protection would almost certainly result in frostbite from contact with the frozen metal of the ladder.

The "friendly" ladder was anything but. I resolved to move quickly to get off it, and off the second step, as soon as I could.

Reaching the top rung, I assessed the next move. It was a hard one: a tension traverse using only the strength of the arms. The objective was to swing up on to the ledge which marked the end of the second step. To do it, I would have to cling on to a collection of rotting ropes tied to a sling of dubious origin. Then, with no foothold, I would have to tension as many spikes of my crampons as I could push on to the Face, and then in one fluid motion swing chimpanzee-like up to the right.

Down at base camp I had talked about filming this stage of the climb when Brian got there. Six weeks later this now seemed a supreme joke. Firstly, there was never any chance of Brian getting here; secondly, the thought of filming in this most deadly of places was the last thing on my mind. This was a survival exercise pure and simple.

Trying the move, I realized that there was a critical moment of commitment when the body would be neither supported by the ladder, nor safely on the ledge. To complete the climb of the second step, I would be, albeit for a split second, dangling over the North Face by the strength of my arms alone.

I tried it . . . and failed. Clinging to the ladder, I retreated several rungs to get some rest while my breathing rate subsided. Without sufficient oxygen powering the muscle tissue in my arms, they were tiring extremely quickly. Instinctively I felt I would have one or perhaps two more tries in me before I weakened to the point where I would have to retreat.

It was several minutes before my runaway breathing came down to a controllable rate. I tried the move again, and this time succeeded. With both arms fading fast, I pulled up on to the ledge and then stumbled the few metres of rocky slope to the top.

From this new vantage point on the Ridge, the summit pyramid was for the first time fully in view. The four of us waited for Al to come up the second step and then continued.

For the next hour we continued to make good time, climbing up gradually on the mixed ground of snow and rock. I paused several times to take photographs but by the fifth or sixth shot the camera began to behave strangely, winding on erratically and failing to close the automatic lens cover. On the seventh shot the Olympus ground to a halt and gave up completely in the sub-zero temperatures. That left me with no SLR camera as my Nikon F3 had similarly succumbed to the cold down at camp four.

Cursing this piece of bad luck, I unzipped my down suit and put the camera against my thermal layer beneath the fleece in the hope the body warmth might revive it (it never did). Then I took out that eight dollar plastic "fun" camera I had bought in Kathmandu, and realized that this recreational toy was now my only means of taking stills. On the cardboard cover was a picture of a bronzed woman in her bikini playing with a beach-ball. Feeling utterly ridiculous, I stared through the "eyefinder" (Basically just a hole in the plastic) and clicked the first of the twelve shots available.

The camera breakdown brought back the old nightmare; would the video cameras work in the –40 degree winds? The thought of them giving up now was too much to contemplate.

Once or twice I looked back down the ridge we had come up. The figure of Al, bright red in his Berghaus wind suit, was dropping further behind. Somewhere in my oxygen-starved brain a few connections were still working. Al had not asked me to click his regulator back down to two litres.

He was still climbing on four litres a minute . . . and he was dropping further and further behind. On two occasions we waited for Al to catch us up, and then we reached the third step, where we stopped ourselves for a rest.

The third step is nothing like as demanding as the previous two, but it comes higher into the climb. Beyond it is the steep avalanche-prone ice-field of the final summit pyramid, the rock traverse, and then the summit ridge.

Grateful for the rest, I took off my pack and sat down, my heels digging into the ice to prevent a slide. Sensing the pressing need to drink, I pulled out the water bottle from where I had left it inside my down suit, half expecting it to have magically defrosted. Of course it was still frozen; what else could I expect in these temperatures?

Realizing finally, and much too late, how stupid I had been, I took both bottles of ice and put them at the foot of the third step next to some abandoned oxygen cylinders. Two kilogrammes less weight to carry.

Al was resting further down the Ridge where it had flattened out into a broad expanse. I pulled out my camera and took a shot of him lying down on his back. Not far away was the second of the Indian bodies, lying with his face towards us and with no sign of pain or distress on his frozen features. Unlike the first of the bodies, which had shocked me when we came across it, I now felt no sense of surprise at the presence of the corpse—a sure indicator that my mind was occupied with other thoughts.

After a while Al joined us, and we were now contemplating the final stages of the climb. Lhakpa was increasingly agitated about the weather. The wind was now stronger than before, and the spindrift from the summit ridge was filling virtually the whole of our view to the south. The plume was starting to run in earnest, and the sinister howl of a strong wind at high altitude was beginning to fill the air.

I followed the Sherpas up the third step and we gained the steep ice of the summit pyramid. If all went well now we could be on the summit within the next two hours.

After one rope's length on the ice, Lhakpa tugged my arm and yelled above the wind:

"Where's Alan? No Alan."

Looking back down the ice-field, I could see he was right. Al had not appeared at the top of the third step.

Every minute we waited now was putting our summit attempt in jeopardy. The weather was increasingly threatening. The Sherpas were looking to me for a decision. Should we leave Al where he was and hope his oxygen held out? Should we go back down and see if he had fallen and was lying injured at the bottom of the third step?

Of all the scenarios, the trial runs that had run like fast-forward movie previews through my mind, the possibility that Al would have a problem had never occurred to me. I was confused and shocked.

For what seemed like an age, but probably was no more than three or four minutes we looked back down at the windblown lump which marked the top of the third step. The wind played strongly across the snowslope . . . causing the four of us to turn our faces away form the blast.

My brain was struggling to come to terms with the situation and, luckily, a few synapses were still connecting. I ran through the options and realized that it was very unlikely Al had fallen: he was far too good for that. Also, he had the extra oxygen bottle, so there was no danger he would run out of air. Probably he was just resting or sorting out his gear.

That was the logical response, I convinced myself that he would follow us up in his own time. The pause gave my feet a chance to go numb; wriggling them inside the plastic boot, I could sense them freezing up. My hands were also, for the first time, beginning to freeze.

Something inside me made the decision.

"Let's go," I told Lhakpa. The words were whipped away by a sudden gust. He stepped down the slope next to me to hear better. I didn't bother shouting again but just pointed up towards the summit. He nodded and tapped his wrist to indicate we were running out of time.

I tightened the wrist strap of my ice-axe, and followed the three Sherpas up the steepening ice.

Inside me a tiny voice was making a faint protest, posing a few uncomfortable questions: Shouldn't you go back to check? Shouldn't you consider the possibility that here nothing is certain—anything can happen? Some accident might have befallen Al, his oxygen valve might have frozen, he might have broken a crampon, he might have pulled out a rope anchor on the third step.

Pausing for breath, I looked back again at bottom of the snowface. Still no sign of Al. I carried on climbing.

Back came the soothing logic, extinguishing those glowing embers of doubt. Relax. He'll be fine. He's always run his own agenda. He's climbed K2. He's probably stopped for a call of nature. Perhaps he just doesn't want to summit with us . . . preferring to reach the top alone?

Three rope lengths up the ice-field. I looked back again. Nothing. I carried on climbing towards the rock which marked the end of the triangle. And this time I didn't look back.

I had crossed another of those invisible lines in the snow. That same force— the one which had been unlocked from its cage inside me back at the Col—had now taken complete control. I wanted the summit so much that I was turning my back on Al whatever had happened to him.

In that final hour there was really only one single focus in my entire being; the desire to reach the top of the world had become all consuming. It had extinguished my concern for my fellow climber, blocked my capacity for questioning my own actions, and turned me into little more than a robot . . . placing one foot in front of the other like a pre-programmed machine.

Summit fever had me body and soul, and now a new wave of strength seemed to flood power into me. I suddenly felt myself driving upwards almost effortlessly, and only having to stop because the Sherpas in front of me were moving more slowly. Even in my disorientated state it occurred to my mind to wonder where this new surge had come from. I was sure that by now my body should have been running close to the point of exhaustion.

What exactly was it that was propelling me up to the highest point in the world?

Now the Sherpas were tired. Lhakpa's lightning pace had run down like a discharged battery. At the start of the snow pyramid they were resting every five or six steps. At the top of the four-rope-length pitch, they were managing only one or two steps between rests.

8,750 metres. Just under 100 metres of vertical ascent to go.

The snowfield arched up, ever steeper, in a soaring curve towards what I imagined was the summit. But instead of continuing up the ice as I had hoped, Lhakpa led the way back into another of the rock cliffs which flank this final buttress.

My heart sank. More rocks . . . again with the crampons.

In fact, as I saw when I examined the ice route in more detail, the top section was obviously prone to avalanche. Fresh avalanche debris, blocks the size of cars, lay scattered not far away. The way up the rock cliff was the safer of the two, if safe is the right word.

First came a traverse along another tiny ledge, eroded into a fault in the rock. Clipping on to a rope which looked like it had been there for decades, I carefully made my way along, swinging my right foot far out to avoid snagging the left. Midway—about fifteen metres—along the ledge, an outcrop forced a fine balancing maneuver to ease the body around a bulge and back on to the ledge on the other side. At that point, the rope was forced to rest against the rock. The wind had beaten it down to just one single frayed strand, about the width and strength of a piece of knitting wool. And about as much use in stopping a fall.

I found myself laughing as I shifted my cramponed feet into position to make the move.

The drop falling away beneath us here was the most sheer yet. We had made our way across the Face and were now positioned almost exactly below the summit, far to the right of the great couloir. The small stones and flakes of rock which we all unavoidably kicked loose, didn't bounce their way down as they had before . . . they just fell out of sight into the abyss.

My face sliding against the rock to press as much of my weight as possible away from the fall, I inched nervously around the obstacle and then rested, gasping for breath. Only then did I realize that I had held my breath during the move . . . a wave of blackness, a desire to faint, swept over me as I struggled to get oxygen into my body. Regaining my composure, I carried on along the decaying ledge. I had thought I was moving faster than the Sherpas, but they had already rounded the corner and were out of sight.

At the end of the traverse, the route stepped up abruptly in a series of ledges similar to those we had encountered on some of the night stages. I used my arms to pull myself up wherever possible, still stubbornly reluctant to trust my weight to the crampon points.

On one of the steps my safety sling got snagged into an old piece of rope and caught me in mid-move. I had to fall back on to the ledge and regain my balance before clearing the snag and continuing on.

After perhaps twenty minutes of climbing, we emerged on to the upper slopes of the summit pyramid snowfield, having effectively bypassed the more avalanche-prone section and gained about fifty metres of height.

During the detour, the wind had increased again. Now the snow ridge, and the skyline above us were cloaked in snarling clouds of airborne ice. The wind was fickle, blowing with unpredictable violent blasts. The upward view was the most intimidating, with a huge circulating mass of ice particles twisting like a miniature tornado above what I presumed to be the summit, just twenty metres of steep ice above us.

We found some shelter in the lee of a rock outcrop and waited there to gain our breath for the final push. So close to the summit, I found myself barely able to wait. An irrational wave of paranoia swept over me; we were just minutes away . . . what if it was snatched away from us at the final moment?

Lhakpa looked at his watch again and then spoke to Gyaltsen. I couldn't hear their words but, in my paranoid state, I imagined them discussing how dangerous the wind would be on the top . . . agreeing that we should turn back . . .

Then my senses snapped into gear, and I recognized my paranoia for what it was: the insidious beginnings of high altitude sickness where irrational thoughts are often the first stage. Since leaving the tent eight hours before, I had not drunk a single drop of fluid. My body was dehydrating dangerously.

Lhakpa led the way up painfully slowly into the cloud of spindrift, with Gyaltsen and Mingma behind him and myself at the back. There were no ropes here and I took care to dig as many crampon spikes as I could into the ice. Halfway up, I took out the plastic camera and framed it vertically for a shot of the three Sherpas as they rested.

I hadn't thought that it might be a false summit. But it was. Reaching the crest of the snowfield, I was taken completely by surprise by what lay before us. Instead of the short final stage I had imagined, we were now standing at the beginning of the final ridge; with the great bulging cornice of the true summit waiting at the far end. Between our position and the top lay a series of switchback ice waves, blown into shape by the wind, and overhanging the Kangshung Face.

By some trick of perspective, or perhaps another irrational side effect of oxygen starvation, the ridge looked huge, and the summit seemed kilometers away. For another of those bizarre moments of doubt, I thought Lhakpa and the others would pull the plug and decide not to continue. The wind was blowing hard now, and more consistently. The plume was running and we were about to walk right into it.

Then I noticed the clue which revealed the true perspective of the ridge; a string of prayer flags which had been fixed to this summit was not handing sadly down the side. I could clearly make out the individual pennants of coloured silk. That visual reference pulled the ridge back down to scale and I realized it was much smaller than I had at first thought.

The summit was just a few hundred metres away.

Eiger Dreams

JON KRAKAUER

This is the first chapter of Jon Krakauer's book of the same name and details an attempt he and a friend made to scale the North Face of the Eiger, known as the Nordwand. It is a treacherous 6,000 foot wall that was first climbed in 1938, but one that has also claimed the lives of more than 40 climbers. The danger in this harrowing climb might best be symbolized by the body of an Italian climber that hung from a rope for three years, visible to all, but unreachable for rescuers. Krakauer knew all this when he and his friend set out. The story gives some background into the Nordwand, then chronicles their attempt to climb it, which was ultimately unsuccessful, as well as an emotionally draining experience.

Eiger Dreams

In the early moments of *The Eiger Sanction*, CLINT EASTWOOD saunters into the dimly lit headquarters of C-2 to find out who he is supposed to assassinate next. Dragon, the evil albino who runs the CIA-like organization, tells Eastwood that although the agency does not yet have the target's name, they have discovered that "our man will be involved in a climb in the Alps this summer. And we know which mountain he will climb: the Eiger."

Eastwood has no trouble guessing which route—"The North Face, of course"—and allows that he is familiar with that particular alpine wall: "I tried to climb it twice, it tried to kill me twice . . . Look, if the target's trying to climb the Eiger, chances are my work will be done for me."

The problem with climbing the North Face of the Eiger is that in addition to getting up 6,000 vertical feet of crumbling limestone and black ice, one must climb over some formidable mythology. The trickiest moves on any climb are the mental ones, the psychological gymnastics that keep terror in check, and the Eiger's grim aura is intimidating enough to rattle anyone's poise. The epics that have taken place on the Nordwand have been welded into the world's collective unconscious in grisly detail by more than two thousand newspaper and magazine articles. The dust jackets of books with titles such as *Eiger: Wall of Death,* remind us that the Nordwand "has defeated hundreds and killed forty-four . . . those who fell were found—sometimes years later—dessicated and dismembered. The body of one Italian mountaineer hung from its rope, unreachable but visible to the curious below, for three years, alternately sealed into the ice sheath of the wall and swaying in the winds of summer."

The history of the mountain resonates with the struggles of such larger-than-life figures as Buhl, Bonatti, Messner, Rebuffat, Terray, Haston, and Harlin, not to mention Eastwood. The names of the landmarks on the face—the Hinterstoisser Traverse, the Ice Hose, the Death Bivouac, the White Spider—are household words among both active and armchair alpinists from Tokyo to Buenos Aires; the very mention of these places is enough to make any climber's hands turn clammy. The rockfall and avalanches that rain continuously down the Nordwand are legendary. So is the heavy weather: even when the skies over the rest of Europe are cloudless, violent storms brew over the Eiger, like those dark clouds that hover eternally above Transylvanian castles in vampire movies.

Needless to say, all this makes the Eiger North Face one of the most widely coveted climbs in the world.

The Nordwand was first climbed in 1938, and since then it has had more than 150 ascents, among them a solo climb in 1983 that took all of five and a half hours, but don't try to tell Staff Sergeant Carlos J. Ragone, U.S.A.F., that the Eiger has become a scenic cruise. Last fall, Marc Twight and I were sitting outside our tents above Kleine Scheidegg, the cluster of hotels and restaurants at the foot of the Eiger, when Ragone strolled into camp under a bulging pack and announced that he had come to climb the Nordwand. In the discussion that ensued, we learned that he was AWOL from an air base in England. His commanding officer had refused to grant Ragone a leave when the C.O. learned what Ragone intended to do with it, but Ragone had left anyway. "Trying this climb will probably cost me my stripes," he said, "but on the other hand, if I get up the mother they might promote me.

Unfortunately, Ragone didn't get up the mother. September had gone down in the Swiss record books as the wettest since 1864, and the face was in atrocious condition, worse even than usual, plastered with rime and loaded with unstable snow. The weather forecast was for continuing snow and high wind. Two partners who were supposed to rendezvous with Ragone backed out because of the nasty conditions. Ragone, however, was not about to be deterred by the mere lack of company. On October 3 he started up the climb by himself. On the lower reaches of the face, near the top of a buttress known as the First Pillar, he made a misstep. His ice axes and crampons sheared out of the rotten ice, and Ragone found himself airborne. Five hundred vertical feet later he hit the ground.

Incredibly, his landing was cushioned by the accumulation of powder snow at the base of the wall, and Ragone was able to walk away from the fall with no more damage than bruises and a crimp in his back. He hobbled out of the blizzard into the *Bahnhof buffet,* asked for a room, went upstairs, and fell asleep. At some point during his tumble to the bottom of the wall he had lost an ice axe and his wallet, which contained all his identification and money. In the morning, when it was time to settle his room bill, all Ragone could offer for payment was his remaining ice axe. The *Bahnhof* manager was not amused. Before slinking out of Scheidegg, Ragone stopped by our camp to ask if we were interested in buying what was left of his climbing gear. We told him that we'd like to help him out, but we happened to be a little strapped for cash ourselves. In that case, Ragone, seeing as he didn't think he was going to feel like climbing again for a while, said he'd just give the stuff to us. "That mountain is a bastard," he spat glancing up at the Nordwand one last time. With that, he limped off through the snow toward England to face the wrath of his C.O.

Like Ragone, Marc and I had come to Switzerland to climb the Nordwand. Marc, eight years my junior, sports two earrings in his left ear and a purple haircut that would do a punk rocker proud. He is also a red-hot climber. One of the differences between us was that Marc wanted very badly to climb the Eiger, while I wanted very badly only to have climbed the Eiger. Marc, understand, is at that age when the pituitary secretes an overabundance of those hormones that mask the subtler emotions, such as fear. He tends to confuse things like life-or-death climbing with fun. As a friendly gesture, I planned to let Marc lead all the most fun pitches on the Nordwand.

Unlike Ragone, Marc and I were not willing to go up on the wall until conditions improved. Due to the Nordwand's concave architecture, whenever it snows, few places on the wall are not exposed to avalanches. In summer, if things go well, it will typically take a strong party two days, maybe three, to climb the Nordwand. In the fall, with the shorter days and icier conditions, three to four days is the norm. To maximize our chances of getting up and down the Eiger without unpleasant incident, we figured we needed at least four consecutive days of good weather: one day to allow the buildup of new snow to avalanche off, and three to climb the face and descend the mountain's west flank.

Each morning during our stay at Scheidegg we would crawl out of our tents, plow down through the snowdrifts to the *Bahnhof,* and phone Geneva and Zurich to get a four-day weather forecast. Day after day, the word was the same: Continuing unsettled weather, with rain in the valleys and snow in the mountains. We could do nothing but curse and wait, and the waiting was awful. The Eiger's mythic weight bore down especially hard during the idle days, and it was easy to think too much.

One afternoon, for diversion, we took a ride on the train up to the *Jungfraujoch,* a cog railroad that runs from Kleine Scheidegg to a saddle high on the Eiger-Junfrau massif. This turned out to be a mistake. The railway traverses the bowels of the Eiger by way of a tunnel that was blasted through the mountain in 1912. Midway up the tracks there is an intermediate station with a series of huge windows that look out from the vertical expanse of the Nordwand.

The view from these windows is so vertiginous that barf bags—the same kind they put in airplane seat-pockets—had been placed on the windowsills. Clouds swirled just beyond the glass. The black rock of the Nordwand, sheathed in frost feathers and sprouting icicles in the places where it overhung, fell away dizzyingly into the mists below. Small avalanches hissed past. If our route turned out to be anything like what we were seeing, we were going to find ourselves in serious trouble. Climbing in such conditions would be desperate if not impossible.

On the Eiger, constructions of the imagination have a way of blurring with reality, and the Eigerwand station was a little too much like a scene from a recurring dream I've been having for year in which I'm fighting for my life in a storm on some endless climb when I come upon a door set into the mountainside. The doorway leads into a warm room with a fireplace and tables of steaming food and a comfortable bed. Usually, in this dream, the door is locked.

A quarter-mile down the tunnel from the big windows of the midway station there is in fact a small wooden door—always unlocked—that opens out onto the Nordwand. The standard route up the wall passes very near this door, and more than one climber has used it to escape from a storm.

Such an escape, however, poses hazards of its own. In 1981, Mugs Stump, one of America's most accomplished alpinists, popped in through the door after a storm forced him to abort a solo attempt on the wall and started walking toward the tunnel entrance, about a mile away. Before he could reach daylight, he met a train coming up the tracks. The guts of the Eiger are hard black limestone that makes for tough tunneling, and when the tunnel was constructed the builders didn't make it any wider than they had to. It quickly became evident to Stump that the space between the cars and the tunnel walls was maybe a foot, give or take a few inches. The Swiss take great pride in making their trains run on time, and it also became evident that this particular engineer was not about to foul up his schedule simply because some damn climber was on the tracks. All Stump could do was suck in his breath, press up against the rock, and try to make his head thin. He survived the train's passing, but the experience was as harrowing as any of the close scrapes he'd had on the outside of the mountain.

During our third week of waiting for the weather to break, Marc and I rode the train down into Wengen and Lauterbrunnen to find relief from the snow. After a pleasant day of taking in the sights and sipping *rugenbrau,* we managed to miss the last train up to Scheidegg and were faced with a long walk back to the tents. Marc set out at a blistering pace to try to make camp before dark, but I decided I was in no hurry to get back under the shadow of the Eiger and into the snow zone, and that another beer to two would make the hike easier to endure.

It was dark by the time I left Wengen, but the Oberland trails, though steep (the Swiss, it seems, do not believe in switchbacks) are wide, well maintained, and easy to follow. More important, on this path there were none of the electrified gates that Marc and I had encountered on a rainy night the week before (after missing another train) while walking from Grindelwald to Scheidegg. Such gates are installed to curtail bovine trespassers and are impossible to see in the dark after a few beers. They strike a five-foot nine-inch body at an uncommonly sensitive point precisely six inches below the belt, and with one's feet clad in soggy Nikes they deliver a jolt of sufficient voltage to bring forth confessions to crimes not yet committed.

The walk from Wengen went without incident until I neared the treeline, when I began to hear an intermittent roar that sounded like someone goosing the throttle of a Boeing 747. The first gust of wind hit me when I rounded the shoulder of the Lauberhorn and turned toward Wengernalp. A blast came from out of nowhere and knocked me on my butt. It was the *foehn,* blowing down from the Eiger.

The *foehn* winds of the Bernese Oberland—cousin of the Santa Ana winds that periodically set Southern California on fire and the Chinooks that roar down out of the Colorado Rockies—can generate stunning power. They are said to hold a disproportionate number of positive ions, and to make people crazy. "In Switzerland," Joan Didion writes in *Slouching Toward Bethlehem,* "the suicide rates goes up during the *foehn,* and in the courts of some Swiss cantons the wind is considered a mitigating circumstance for crime." The *foehn* figures prominently in Eiger lore. It is a dry, relatively warm wind, and as it melts the snow and ice on the Eiger it brings down terrible avalanches. Typically, immediately following a *foehnsturm* there will be a sharp freeze, glazing the wall with treacherous verglas. Many of the disasters on the Nordwand can be attributed directly to the *foehn;* in *The Eiger Sanction* it is a *foehn* that almost does Eastwood in.

It was all I could do to handle the *foehn* on the trail through the cow pastures. I shuddered to think what it would be like to be hit by one up on the Nordwand. The wind filled my eyes with grit and blew me off my feet over and over again. Several times I simply had to get down on my knees and wait for lulls between gusts. When I finally lurched through the door of the *Bahnhof* at Scheidegg, I found the place packed with railroad workers, cooks, maids, waitresses, and tourists who had become marooned by the storm. The gale raging outside had infected everybody in Scheidegg with some kind of weird, manic energy, and a riotous party was in full swing. In one corner people were dancing to a screaming jukebox, in another they were standing on the tables belting out German drinking songs; everywhere people were calling the waiter for more beer and schnapps.

I was about to join the fun when I spied Marc approaching with a wild look in his eyes. "Jon," he blurted out, "the tents are gone!"

"Hey, I don't really want to deal with it right now," I replied, trying to signal the waiter, "Let's just rent beds upstairs tonight and repitch the tents in the morning."

"No, no, you don't understand. They didn't just get knocked down, they fucking blew away. I found the yellow one about fifty yards away from where it had been, but the brown one is gone, man. I looked but I couldn't find it anywhere. It's probably down in Grindelwald by now."

The tents had been tied down to logs, cement blocks, and an ice screw driven securely into frozen turf. There had been at least two hundred pounds of food and gear inside them. It seemed impossible that they could have been carried away by the wind, but they had. The one that was missing had contained our sleeping bags, clothing, my climbing boots, the stove and pots, some food, God only knew what else. If we didn't find it, the weeks of waiting to climb the

Nordwand were going to be in vain, so I zipped up my jacket and headed back out into the *foehnsturm*.

By sheer chance I found the tent a quarter-mile from where it had been pitched—drifted over, lying in the middle of the train tracks to Grindelwald. It was a tangled mess of shredded nylon and broken, twisted poles. After wrestling it back to the *Bahnhof,* we discovered that the stove had sprayed butane over everything, and a dozen eggs had coated our clothing and sleeping bags with a nasty, sulphurous slime, but it appeared that no important gear had been lost during the tent's tour of Scheidegg. We threw everything in a corner and returned to the party to celebrate.

The winds at Scheidegg that night were clocked at 170 kilometers per hour. In addition to laying waste to our camp, they knocked down the big tele-scope on the gift-shop balcony and blew a ski-lift gondola as big as a truck onto the tracks in front of the *Bahnhof*. At midnight, though, the gale petered out. The temperature plummeted, and by morning a foot of fresh powder had replaced the snowpack melted by the *foehn*. Nevertheless, when we called the weather station in Geneva, we were shocked to hear that an extended period of good weather would be arriving in a couple of days. "Sweet Jesus," I thought. "We're actually going to have to go up on the wall."

The sunshine came on October 8, along with a promise from the meteorolo-gists that there would be no precipitation for at least five days. We gave the Nordwand the morning to slough off the post-*foehn* accumulation of snow, then hiked through crotch-deep drifts over to the base of the route, where we set up a hastily patched-together tent. We were in our sleeping bags early, but I was too scared to even pretend to sleep.

At 3 A.M., the appointed hour to start up the wall, it was raining and some major ice and rockfall was strafing the face. The climb was off. Secretly relieved, I went back to bed and immediately sank into a deep slumber. I awoke at 9 A.M. to the sound of birds chirping. The weather had turned perfect once again. Hurriedly, we threw our packs together. As we started up the Nordwand my stomach felt like a dog had been chewing on it all night.

We had been told by friends who had climbed the Nordwand that the first third of the standard route up the face is "way casual." It isn't, at least not under the conditions we found it. Although there were few moves that were techni-cally difficult, the climbing was continuously insecure. A thin crust of ice lay over deep, unstable powder snow. It was easy to see how Ragone had fallen; it felt as though at any moment the snow underfoot was going to collapse. In places where the wall steepened, the snow cover thinned and our ice axes would ricochet off rock a few inches beneath the crust. It was impossible to find anchors of any kind in or under the rotting snow and ice, so for the first two thousand feet of the climb we simply left the ropes in the packs and "soloed" together.

Our packs were cumbersome and threatened to pull us over backward whenever we would lean back to search out the route above. We had made an effort to pare our loads down to the essentials, but Eiger terror had moved us to throw in extra food, fuel, and clothing in case we got pinned down by a storm, and enough climbing hardware to sink a ship. It had been difficult to decide what to take and what to leave behind. Marc eventually elected to bring along a walkman and his two favorite tapes instead of a sleeping bag, reasoning that when the going got desperate, the peace of mind to be had by listening to the Dead Kennedys and the Angry Samoans would prove more valuable than staying warm at night.

At 4 P.M., when we reached the overhanging slab called the Rote Fluh, we were finally able to place some solid anchors, the first ones of the climb. The overhang offered protection from the unidentified falling objects that occasionally hummed past, so we decided to stop and bivouac even though there was more than an hour of daylight left. By digging out a long, narrow platform where the snow slope met the rock, we could lie in relative comfort, head-to-head, with the stove between us.

The next morning we got up at three and were away from our little ledge an hour before dawn, climbing by headlamp. A rope-length beyond the bivouac, Marc started leading up a pitch that had a difficulty rating of 5.4. Marc is a 5.12 climber, so I was alarmed when he began to mutter and his progress came to a halt. He tried moving left, and then right, but an eggshell-thin layer of crumbly ice over the vertical rock obscured whatever holds there might have been. Agonizingly slowly, he balanced his way upward a few inches at a time by hooking his crampon points and the picks of his axes on unseen limestone nubbins underneath the patina of rime. Five times he slipped, but caught himself each time after falling only a few feet.

Two hours passed while Marc thrashed around above me. The sun came up. I grew impatient. "Marc," I yelled, "if you don't want to lead this one, come on down and I'll take a shot at it." The bluff worked: Marc attacked the pitch with renewed determination and was soon over it. When I joined him at his belay stance, though, I was worried. It had taken us nearly three hours to climb eighty feet. There is more than eight thousand feet of climbing on the Nordwand (when all the traversing is taken into consideration), and much of it was going to be a lot harder than those eighty feet.

The next pitch was the infamous Hinterstoisser Traverse, a 140-foot end run around some unclimbable overhangs, and the key to gaining the upper part of the Nordwand. It was first climbed in 1936 by Andreas Hinterstossier, whose lead across its polished slabs was a brilliant piece of climbing. But above the pitch he and his three companions were caught by a storm and forced to retreat. The storm, however, had glazed the traverse with verglas, and the climbers were unable to reverse its delicate moves. All four men perished. Since that disaster, climbers have always taken pains to leave a rope fixed across the traverse to ensure return passage.

We found the slabs of the Hinterstoisser covered with two inches of ice. Thin though it was, it was solid enough to hold our ice axes if we swung them gently. Additionally, an old, frayed fixed rope emerged intermittently from the glazing. By crabbing gingerly across the ice on our front points and shamelessly grabbing the old rope whenever possible, we got across the traverse without a hitch.

Above the Hinterstoisser, the route went straight up, past landmarks that had been the stuff of my nightmares since I was ten: the Swallow's Nest, the First Icefield, the Ice Hose. The climbing never again got as difficult as the pitch Marc had led just before the Hinterstoisser, but we were seldom able to get in any anchors. A slip by either of us would send us both to the bottom of the wall.

As the day wore on, I could feel my nerves beginning to unravel. At one point, while leading over crusty, crumbly vertical ice on the Ice Hose, I suddenly became overwhelmed by the fact that the only things preventing me from flying off into space were two thin steel picks sunk half an inch into a medium that resembled the inside of my freezer when it needs to be defrosted. I looked down at the ground more than three thousand feet below and felt dizzy, as if I were about to faint. I had to close my eyes and take a dozen deep breaths before I could resume climbing.

One 165-foot pitch past the Ice Hose brought us to the bottom of the Second Ice Field, a point slightly more than halfway up the wall. Above, the first protected place to spend the night would be the Death Bivouac, the ledge where Max Sedlmayer and Karl Mehringer had expired in a storm during the first attempt on the Nordwand in 1935. Despite its grim name, the Death Bivouac is probably the safest and most comfortable bivouac site on the face. To get to it, however, we still had to make an eighteen-hundred-foot rising traverse across the Second Ice Field, and then ascend several hundred devious feet more to the top of a buttress called the Flatiron.

It was 1 P.M. We had climbed only about fourteen hundred feet in the eight

hours since we'd left our bivouac at the Rote Fluh. Even though the Second
Ice Field looked easy, the Flatiron beyond it did not, and I had serious doubts
that we could make the Death Bivouac—more than two thousand feet away—
in the five hours of daylight that remained. If darkness fell before we reached
the Death Bivouac, we would be forced to spend the night without a ledge, in a
place that would be completely exposed to the avalanches and rocks that spilled
down from the most notorious feature on the Nordwand: the ice field called
the White Spider.

"Marc," I said, "we should go down."

"What?!" he replied, shocked. "Why?"

I outlined my reasons: our slow pace, the distance to the Death Bivouac, the
poor condition the wall was in, the increasing avalanche hazard as the day
warmed up. While we talked, small spindrift avalanches showered down over us
from the Spider. After fifteen minutes, Marc reluctantly agreed that I was right,
and we began our descent.

Wherever we could find anchors, we rappelled; where we couldn't we
down-climbed. At sunset below a pitch called the Difficult Crack, Marc found
a cave for us to bivouac in. By then we were already second-guessing the decision to retreat, and we spent the evening saying little to each other.

At dawn, just after resuming the descent, we heard voices coming from the
face below. Two climbers soon appeared, a man and a woman, moving rapidly
up the steps we had kicked two days before. It was obvious from their fluid, easy
movements that they were both very, very good climbers. The man turned out
to be Christophe Profit, a famous French alpinist. He thanked us for kicking all
the steps, then the two of them sped off toward the Difficult Crack at an astonishing clip.

A day after we had wimped-out because the face was "out of condition," it
appeared as though two French climbers were going to cruise up the climb as if
it were a Sunday stroll. I glanced over at Marc and it looked like he was about
to burst into tears. At that point we split up and continued the nerve-wracking
descent by separate routes.

Two hours later I stepped down onto the snow at the foot of the wall. Waves of
relief swept over me. The vise that had been squeezing my temples and gut was
suddenly gone. By God, I had survived! I sat down in the snow and began to
laugh.

Marc was a few hundred yards away, sitting on a rock. When I reached him
I saw that he was crying, and not out of joy. In Marc's estimation, simply sur-
viving the Nordwand did not cut it. "Hey," I heard myself telling him, "if the

Frogs get up the sucker, we can always go into Wengen and buy more food, and then go for it again." Marc perked up immediately at this suggestion, and before I could retract my words he was sprinting off to the tent to monitor the French climbers' progress through binoculars.

At this point, however, my luck with the Nordwand finally took a turn for the better: Christophe Profit and his partner only got as far as the Rote Fluh, the site of our first bivouac, before a large avalanche shot past and scared them into coming down, too. A day later, before my Eiger luck could turn again, I was on a jet home.

Doctor on Everest

KENNETH KAMLER, M.D.

This chapter from Dr. Kenneth Kamler's book is a compelling one which takes place in 1996 during the ill-fated expeditions that resulted in a number of deaths and the one chronicled in *Into Thin Air*. Dr. Kamler writes of the suspense at the lower camps as the people there begin to realize that there is a tragedy taking place higher up on the mountain. The second half of the excerpt deals with the treatment of two severely frostbitten climbers and details how very difficult it is to bring injured climbers down from these huge mountains.

By sunrise we were en route. Though it was cold and windy when I left Camp II, I had intentionally underdressed, knowing that I move a lot faster when I'm a little bit cold. I expected the air to warm after the sun came up, but as I approached the vertical section bridging the crevasse I was just too cold and had to add a layer before starting up. I climbed strongly, by my standards. This part of the route was becoming familiar territory and I didn't waste much energy on anxiety or uncertainty, though not retaining any fear would have required losing touch with reality.

Todd was the first to reach Camp III. By the time I got there, he was busy trying to undercut the narrow platform so the tent would lie flat. I was too tired to help, and with no place to stand, I clipped in to the other end of the tent and sat against the edge with my feet hanging over the two-thousand-foot drop. Steve came up and sat alongside me but didn't clip in right away so I did it for him.

"I'm okay like this," he said as I was reaching over.

"Yeah," I answered, "that was probably what Yu Nan said too."

181

Though crumpled together in a two-man tent, the three of us were having a tough time staying warm. The wind never relaxed and the sun only rarely found its way through the clouds. Heat and light would fill the tent momentarily, only to be repeatedly blown out by the wind.

Todd hung a stove inside the tent entrance, out of the wind, and boiled snow to heat the frozen food packets. Fuel was in short supply so cooking times had to be shortened, a recipe modification I became aware of as I swallowed the ice balls of my partially thawed meal. Lying on one elbow inside my sleeping bag as I ate, I waited for our scheduled radio call to hear the news of the summit attempt going on two thousand feet above us.

It wasn't what we wanted to hear. Rob, his two guides Mike and Andy, and three others had reached the top. There was jubilation and champagne at base camp far below. But five of the group, including Frank and Beck, had turned back early and the others hadn't summited until two-thirty—an hour and a half later than Rob's own cutoff rule. Conditions must be tough up there, I thought, and there wasn't much daylight left. I recalled uneasily that I had treated most of the New Zealand team after their summit attempt last year when they had stayed out too late.

Clouds moved in low over our heads, blocking our view of the South Col. We left the radio on standby, hoping to hear soon that everyone was back safely. Instead there was a long silence as it slowly got dark outside. When the radio did crackle on again, we heard a chilling report: Rob had waited overlong to descend with Doug Hansen, the last one up. Doug was now out of oxygen and too exhausted to descend Hillary Step, a moderately difficult rock face just below the summit. The rest of the New Zealand team was also having trouble getting back. Scott Fischer's team, with the curious exception of Scott, had all summited but none of them had been heard from since. Nor was there any word on the Taiwanese, Makalu. Climbers were still strung out all over the mountain and apparently some hadn't yet descended much below the summit. They would all soon be exhausted and out of oxygen, if they weren't already. Those of use at Camp III could hardly stand the cold and wind, and we were in sleeping bags and tents. The night passed with us in fitful sleep, unable or unwilling to think about what was happening to the exposed climbers several thousand feet above us.

The radio came on at 5:00 A.M. and we awoke to the horror story we didn't want to imagine. Rob had been out all night with Doug, who was now too weak to move. Rob was also long since out of oxygen and could hardly move himself. He didn't say where they were, but climbers had seen a headlight just above Hillary Step. They had made no progress overnight.

The entire Scott Fischer team had still not been heard from, nor had anyone heard from Makalu. On the New Zealand team, Jon Krakauer had summited and gotten back to his tent. He had a radio but didn't much know what
was going on except that it was very cold and there was a whiteout with high
winds and blowing snow. He couldn't see outside his tent. That meant that the
people who were trying to make it back after having been out all night
wouldn't be able to find the camp.

Jon said Andy had been right behind him and also had a radio but as of yet
no one had heard from him. Mike, the other guide, was back at Camp IV but
was hypothermic and frostbitten. Jon hadn't seen Yasuko since shortly after they
all summited, but he had passed Beck on the way down. Beck hadn't summited
but he hadn't returned either. There was no word on Frank, and I remembered
that day in base camp when he had tried to avoid the team photo but had gotten caught in it anyway. I had laughed then about his superstition.

More radio reports came in—most of them conflicting, all of them confusing. Apparently, though, there were about eighteen people who still hadn't
returned to Camp IV. The temperature had plummeted overnight and the wind
was blowing snow into our tents right through the fabric. So loud was the noise
and so violent the flapping of our two tents that it was impossible to talk
between them even by shouting. We had to use our radios to communicate and
formulate a rescue plan.

Despite the wind, Todd in our tent and Pete in the other simultaneously
prepared to make their way up to the South Col. They skipped any discussion
of whether they should go, beginning their radio contact with questions of
how quickly they could get started and what they should bring. As Todd got
ready, I gave him the few medications we had, our extra pairs of gloves, and
some quick advice on treating the medical conditions he and Pete would be
likely to encounter among the survivors. Having worked together with them
for years, I was confident they could take good care of anyone they found alive
but reminded them to be extremely careful before deciding that someone
wasn't.

Just before setting off, they directed their radios down the mountain speaking first to Dave at Camp II and them to base camp. Dave explained where he
had stashed oxygen, fuel, and fresh radio batteries on the Col and them told
them to take whatever they needed. To base camp they read off a list of medical
supplies I had prepared, which I wanted brought up to Camp II as soon as possible. Then they asked, if possible, for a message to be passed up to Rob, I
expected something to the effect of "Help is on the way," but instead what I
heard was, "Tell Rob that the situation is hopeless for both of them if they stay

together. He should abandon Doug and try to get himself down. Better to save one than lose two."

In a swirl of wind and cold, Todd crawled out the tent door and we watched as he and Pete started up the ropes. The air was clear where we were, but the clouds that had rolled in yesterday were still above our heads. Surface snow, stirred up by the wind, mixed with the clouds to form a whiteout completely obscuring the South Col. Todd and Pete climbed up steadily and disappeared into the maelstrom.

We zipped shut the tent door. In the relative calm inside, Jim radioed our Sherpas at Camp II, and asked them to try to come up to the Col to help. The Sherpas refused, saying it was too dangerous to be on the Lhotse Face in that wind. None of us believed them, though. There is no one braver than a Sherpa. We all felt the real reason they were not coming up was that they were spooked by the idea of seeing dead bodies lying all over the Col.

Listening to the wind, we sat in our tents and waited. Hours went by but then the tents became quiet. There was a lull in the wind. Our ears rested until the silence was broken by the buzzing noise of airplanes. They were on the other side of the clouds but no less intrusive because we couldn't see them. As airplanes had no practical reason for being here, it suddenly struck me that this must be a big news story and the planes were trying to take pictures of a life-and-death struggle. Our tight drama was being invaded by the outside world. It made me angry: If you can't help, then don't come to watch.

Todd and Pete made it to the Col and described a scene of torn tents and gear strewn everywhere. On the way up, at the Geneva Spur, just below Camp IV, they had crossed the Scott Fischer team being led down by guide Neal Beidleman. Some were on oxygen, most were frostbitten, and all were exhausted but they were all moving on their own. Painfully missing from the group was Scott himself—whereabouts unknown—and also Anatoli, who refused to leave the Col without Scott.

Todd and Pete also reported that as they entered Camp IV, Sherpas were leaving from the other side, starting up toward the southeast ridge. They assumed they were trying to reach Rob and Doug. Other Sherpas were also out looking for survivors. Huddled in tents were the remnants of the New Zealand expedition, many too weak to boil water or put oxygen masks on their faces.

The members had little information to offer, most of them unaware even of who was in the tent next to them. Stuart Hutchison did report that Yasuko and Beck were dead. He and a Sherpa had gone out in the morning and found them lying in the snow on the Col about a half mile from camp. They had apparently gotten lost in the white-out. Andy Harris was still nowhere to be found. I was relieved to hear that Frank was back safely. I thought I had killed him by forcing him to stay for that team photo.

Based on Todd's and Pete's assessments, we concluded that none of the survivors was hypothermic and no one was in immediate danger of pulmonary or cerebral edema. They were exhausted and dispirited. The danger of having them descend Lhotse in that condition had to be weighed against the risk of further deterioration at twenty-six thousand feet. On balance, it seemed safer to have everyone spend another night there to rest, eat, drink, and mentally refocus. Todd and Pete continued their work of melting snow, serving food, fluids, and oxygen, and generally trying to be the perfect hosts, though Camp IV wasn't exactly a health spa.

Meanwhile those of us at Camp III turned our attention to the string of ragtag climbers who were descending the fixed lines and would soon be upon us. Members of the IMAX team came up from II to bring supplies and help us out. We set up a kind of way station at one of their tents—a place to warm up, hydrate, and take a short rest—but Camp III was no place for them to stay. I had almost no medications here, and anyone who needed to lie down would have to be tied in at the 45-degree angle of Lhotse. So everyone had to continue down the ropes to II.

I watched from my tent as the climbers came by one by one. They were moving slowly but none was uncoordinated or in acute distress. Jim hung out a line below me, acting as official greeter. We dispensed dexamethasone pills to those who looked like they needed it, especially Sandy, who was the most exhausted of the exhausted; then Jim directed each of them to the IMAX tent for food, oxygen, and further encouragement.

Araceli was there, along with some others, smiling as broadly as she could while serving hot tea and soup. As soon as energy and spirits seemed high enough to continue the descent safely, the climbers were sent on their way. No one was allowed to rest too long for fear they would be unable to get going again.

Once our guests were all gone we boiled some water for ourselves and shared a piece of cheese and some chocolate chip cookies. It was pretty meager, so Charles went out to raid the New Zealand tents nearby. He came back with a good haul of food, fuel, and toilet paper. They wouldn't be needing the supplies here anymore and we certainly could use them. Still, it seemed almost ghoulish to be helping ourselves to their supplies while they were in such dire straits.

In quick succession the temperature dropped, it started to snow, and the winds came back—even stronger than before. It had to be much colder and windier higher up and I was beginning to doubt the wisdom of leaving the New Zealand team on the Col another day. Todd reported in to tell us how they were faring.

All the Sherpas had gotten back to Camp IV. Two of them had found Makalu and Scott lying not far from each other. Makalu was still breathing and they dragged him back to camp. Scott was dead.

Anatoli had remained at Camp IV because he didn't want to leave without Scott. Yesterday he had gone out in the blizzard and rescued three climbers. Now with the weather deteriorating rapidly he wanted to go out again to get Scott. It was all Todd and Pete could do to keep him in the camp.

The Sherpas that Todd and Pete had seen leaving camp had tried to go up the southeast ridge. Led by Ang Dorje, Rob's chief climbing Sherpa, they fought their way up but finally were stopped short of the South Summit by the ferocious winds. In the desperate hope that the two stranded climbers could still descend, they left a deposit of oxygen marked with a ski pole at the highest point they had reached. Somewhere, too far above them, were Rob and Doug.

Ang Dorje had just risked his life by climbing a knife-edged ridge buffeted by violent winds to try to save his dying friend, Rob. He cried when he had to turn around. This was the same person who, a week ago at base camp, hadn't shown up to have his tooth pulled because he was too afraid.

We hadn't gotten over that radio call before we received another one. Todd said, "You won't believe this. Beck is alive—but I don't know for how long.

Todd had chanced to look out his tent and saw an apparition in the swirling wind and snow. At first he thought it was one of the climbers from camp trying to go to the bathroom, but as he went out to help he realized what it really was: Beck Weathers, risen from the dead.

"His arm was locked straight out from the shoulder, his forearm dangling from his elbow. He looked like a mummy in a low-budget horror flick. He was staggering toward me, into a freezing sixty-mile-an-hour wind, with his jacket open and no glove on his hand."

Todd brought Beck into a tent and put him inside two sleeping bags. But sleeping bags only retain heat, they don't produce it. A hypothermic person can't generate enough heat to keep himself warm so Todd and Pete placed bottles of hot water inside the bags as fast as they could melt snow. They put him on high-flow oxygen and got him to drink some hot liquids. They were doing all the right things by the time they called me.

Rewarming can be tricky and deadly. We didn't want Beck to survive being frozen only to die from being defrosted. It's got to be done evenly and steadily so that there are no sudden shocks which might cause cold-sensitized heart muscles that normally beat synchronously to start contracting independently. The most effective way to transfer a large amount of heat quickly to Beck would have been to take off all his wet clothes and then have either Todd or Pete strip down and get in the sleeping bag with him. Body heat would provide a constant source of warmth radiating over a large surface. I was about to suggest this when Todd told me Beck was coming around.

Todd said Beck's hands were frozen up to his elbows, but there was nothing we could do about that now. There wasn't enough fuel at Camp IV to make enough hot water to thaw Beck's hands. Plus I wasn't sure just how hypothermic Beck still was. If circulation started up in his hands again, the blood that was trapped in there would flow out like a cold wave. When it reached the heart it might be just the shock he didn't need.

We didn't know if Beck's feet were frozen but we didn't want to find out. Taking his boots off would allow his feet to swell, which they were not doubt ready to do if given the chance. It would then be impossible to get them back in the boots, and Beck's only chance of getting down from Camp IV was on his feet, frozen or not. But first he'd have to survive the night on the Col.

Scott, like Beck, had also been pronounced dead, but he was still out there lying in the snow. Anatoli had barely been talked out of going to look for him earlier but now that Beck had returned from the dead, there was no stopping Anatoli as he headed out into the storm. Hours later he came back, alone, he had found Scott but there was no second miracle.

Rob also was out there but much higher up on the southeast ridge. His terrible ordeal came through the radio when we called our base camp to get any news that had been relayed from his base camp. Rob was still in radio contact but his voice was getting weaker and weaker. He said he was below the Hillary Step now and had crawled into a snow cave for shelter. It was unclear what had happened to Doug but Rob seemed to be by himself. Doug had probably died higher up, rather than Rob abandoning him. Earlier he had gotten the message from Todd and Pete, as well as from several others, to leave Doug and try to save himself. His response was, "We're both listening."

So now, except for his radio, Rob was alone. Climbers at base camp urged him to get up and get going and he said okay, he would try. He shut off his radio to conserve the batteries and everyone waited hopefully through the silence. A few hours later he turned it back on.

"Where are you now, Rob?"

"You know, I haven't even moved."

Todd and Pete radioed to base camp the unhappy message that Ang Dorje and his team had turned around. The bad news was relayed to Rob: The Sherpas were not going to be able to get him. There was no outburst over the radio. Rob just quietly said, "Okay."

Desperate to get Rob going, the New Zealand base camp manager, Helen Wilton, thought maybe Rob's wife could give him some strength. She patched into the satellite telephone system, then held the phone to the radio as Jan, seven months pregnant, at their home in New Zealand, talked directly to Rob, freezing to death near the summit of Mount Everest. I couldn't even dare to imagine the combination of shock, disbelief, horror, helplessness, and hope that made up their last conversation. Jan tried her best to give him courage and then Rob, incredibly, did the same for her. They chose a name for their baby and he told her not to worry. Finally Rob said he was shutting off his radio so he "can rest." It never came on again.

The storm blew through a second night. Wind speed accelerated to a ferocity I had never experienced before, then got stronger. The wind struck from different directions and our tents, caught in the cross fire, jerked wildly up and down, straining at the ropes, trying to break free of the ice screws that held us against the slope. Any second, we thought, the tents would rip apart or pull out their moorings and we would tumble down the Lhotse Face. We stayed fully dressed with our boots on, splayed out over the floor as much as possible to hold the tent down.

In the morning we were still there but we were grimly aware that it was impossible for Rob to have endured the same night much higher up the mountain and fully exposed. Even now, it was bitter cold and the wind was still strong, though it had relented enough to stop torturing our tents. Lying in our sleeping bags, Steve and I called out almost jokingly to Jim and Charles in the other tent: "Hey, you guys still there?"

There was no response, even after a second try. Suddenly there was real fear that they had been blown off the mountain. A third, louder call brought a somewhat muffled answer. A wall of snow had blown into the narrow space between our tents, insulating the sound. It blocked our entrance but we didn't remove it right away since it also provided some insulation against the cold.

Once more the scene at Camp IV entered our tent through the radio. Beck had survived the night. He was conscious and able to take fluids if Todd or Pete held the cup but he couldn't use his hands and was having trouble seeing. Makalu was also still alive, having been cared for mostly by the Sherpas who had found him. His condition was apparently better than Beck's but only slightly. And there was still no sign of Andy. What was left of the New Zealand team had already started down, all of them under their own power. The Sherpas would shortly be trying to take Makalu down, and Todd and Pete were going to try to bring Beck. Andy, Yasuko, Doug, Rob, and Scott would be staying on the mountain.

Our team was holding at III for the moment. The remnants of the New Zealand team would be passing by soon and might need some help. Makalu and Beck were not yet underway, and being the only doctor on the mountain, I wanted to stay high up in case one or both of them collapsed along the route. The supplies which I had asked for yesterday were waiting for me at Camp II. As soon as we were sure the injured climbers could get all the way down, I would descend to set up a medical tent and wait for my patients.

Pete and Todd were preparing Beck and themselves for the descent. I asked Pete to give Beck some dexamethasone now and to keep some more ready in case he needed it on the road. Pete heated two ampules until they melted and warmed. He injected Beck with one and saved the other inside his jacket. Beck could walk but he couldn't hold the ropes and could barely even see them. The three started off down the slope with Pete in the lead as seeing-eye dog. Beck was in the middle so he could lean his arms against Pete's back, while Todd was behind so he could hold Beck's harness to prevent any fall. Bunched in a tight row and trying to move simultaneously, Beck said, "What is this, a conga line?"

That sounded pretty good. Besides being funny, it meant that Beck was lucid and that, thanks to the exhausting efforts of Pete and Todd, they were probably moving well. The New Zealand team had already passed by us, with Jim once more hanging down from his tent on a rope offering hot tea and oxygen. Business was good and I told him he should consider opening a full-service inn. Once I heard that Makalu was also moving better than expected, and in fact was ahead of Beck, I figured it was time for me to leave.

Jim and I started for Camp II at the same time that Dave and Ed from the IMAX team were moving in the other direction to relieve Todd and Pete and bring Beck the rest of the way. We got down in good time. Just in front of the moraine was an isolated tent that hadn't been there before. It was on the ice, apart from the rest of the Taiwanese camp. We all knew what it was but moved past it without comment. At least Yu Nan had a tent. Five others were still lying in the snow.

Skipping by my own camp I burst into the New Zealand mess tent, coming directly from the Lhotse Face and looking it. The survivors had arrived a while ago and the scene was calm until I entered. Between hugs, handshakes, and pats on the shoulder, I started asking questions and hearing about everyone's injuries at once. There was one person whom I didn't recognize and he was looking at me oddly. He turned out to be a Danish doctor, Henrik Hansen, who had come up from base camp to help out. He reassured me the injuries here were minor, everything was under control, and I should have some tea. I hadn't even sat down yet.

The arrival of two critically ill climbers was imminent. They belonged in a modern hospital intensive care unit but soon I would be treating them here, in a mess tent, trying to work out complex medical problems at an altitude where tying your shoes can be confusing. With Henrik's help plus the help of Sherpas and a few climbers who still had some energy left, we cleared the folding tables and chairs out of the room and covered the floor with foam mats and sleeping bags. Climbers went out to their tents to gather together two complete sets of dry clothes. Sherpas were asked to boil up large pots of water and collect all the insulated bottles they could find. I took an inventory of available supplies and was pleased to see that everything on my list had been brought up that morning, including the heavy propane heater. The Sherpa who carried that up the icefall is one of many unsung heroes.

Frostbite, hypothermia, snow blindness, pulmonary and cerebral edema, pneumonia, dehydration, exhaustion . . . I formed a list in my mind of all the problems I might be dealing with in just a few minutes. For each, I visualized in detail the scenario of what had to be done in what order. Then I systematically laid out medications, bandages, and oxygen bottles, presetting the regulators for maximum flow. I verified that my medical instruments hadn't been damaged or frozen on the trip up.

Only the IV bags were frozen. I passed them out to the Sherpas who were boiling water in the kitchen tent. They brought the bags back twice before they felt warm enough when I touched them to my cheek. Two bags were hung from carabiners that had been hooked into the tent frame. Tubing was connected to each IV and the lines were flushed. The loose ends of the tubes were left dangling above the still-empty sleeping bags. Everything seemed to be working. I felt entirely ready.

By radio we were kept advised of my patients' progress. Makalu was already down off the ropes and Beck wasn't far behind. We turned on the propane heater and I instructed the Sherpas to start bringing in the tubs of hot water from the kitchen. Lopsang took advantage of the opportunity to draw off some of the water to serve tea.

In the oddly quiet interlude, we sipped and waited just long enough for my mind to start wandering. Suddenly, there was a commotion outside, the tent door was unzipped and in strode a bulky creature in a hooded down suit with an oxygen mask over his face, escorted by a group of Sherpas. As ready as I was, his appearance took me by surprise and for a split second I said to myself, "What is that?"

It was Makalu of course. We immediately laid him down on a sleeping bag and started taking off his clothes; jacket after jacket, layer after layer. His rescuers had bundled him up in anything they could find. His clothes were all wet, including his underwear. Getting his boots off was difficult since his feet had swelled tightly against them. If they expanded any more, we'd have to find a larger pair of boots to put back on him later. I had to use a scalpel to cut away part of a sock which had frozen to his foot. I left it to the Sherpas to maneuver around me and work a set of dry clothes onto him while I started my examination.

When I removed his oxygen mask, I was shocked. Makalu, the climber who seemed indifferent to his partner's death, was the climber who had kindly shared his water with me when I passed him on the Lhotse ropes—except that now he was missing his nose. Instead, there was a black crust that spread onto his right cheek up to his eye. He probably had some snow blindness but his eyes were puffed closed so tightly that I couldn't tell for sure.

"My eyes, my face, all was ice," he told me. "My hands together—*clink, clink.*"

Makalu had the worst frostbite I had ever seen. All the fingers on both hands were dark gray, plump like sausages. The color extended onto the hands to form a sharply demarcated gray band across the knuckles. There were strong pulses in each wrist, indicating that blood was flowing into the hands, at least up to the gray line. His feet had the same gray color from the toes onto the forefoot, as well as across the heels. I found pulses in his ankles and marked them with a pen so that I could check later to see if they were still there.

The frostbite was probably irreversible, but if we could thaw him out, parts of his hands and feet could be saved. Once thawed, he'd have to be kept warm. When limbs thaw, blood vessels break and surrounding tissue weakens, making it less able to withstand a second onslaught. Any part that refroze would be worse off than if it had never defrosted. His thawed-out feet would be fragile. If he were allowed to bear weight on them, they'd crumble. At twenty-one thousand feet the treatment problem was all in the logistics but with enough help, enough fuel, and more than enough snow to melt, I thought it would be done.

Henrik had started an IV, using a salt solution with glucose to provide fluids and energy. I injected nifedipine to divert blood into the extremities. This would begin to improve circulation in the hands and feet, but the diminished volume in the center of the body could lead to a rapid drop in blood pressure. Having no pressure cuff, the only way to monitor him was by periodically feeling the strength of the carotid artery pulsations in his neck. Any sudden weakening might mean he was going into shock. If that happened, we'd try to counteract by opening wide the IV valve to pump him back up with fluids.

We needed three tubs of warm water—one for each hand and one for the feet. By trial and error we got Makalu positioned so that all his frozen parts could be submerged at the same time. I had a deck of little plastic bubble thermometer cards and dropped one in each tub. Maintaining an ideal defrosting temperature of 104 degrees is a lot of work when the ambient temperature is below zero. The water cools rapidly and has to be canted off so hot water can be added. The Sherpas were eager assistants and quickly got the hang of it, using cups to remove the water and insulated bottles to add more. Most of them had never used a thermometer before, but soon they were reading the temperatures and making their own decisions on when to add water.

Just as we were getting Makalu under control, we got word that Beck was about to arrive. It was time to put dressings on Makalu anyway. The rewarming had no real end point, and getting him waterlogged wouldn't help. My supplies were limited so I had to parcel them out carefully. Beck was reportedly worse off than Makalu but Makalu's condition was plenty bad enough. I decided to divide my supplies in half. After patting dry Makalu's hands and feet, I put on gooey ointment and antibiotic dressings, separating fingers and toes with thin gauze so they wouldn't stick together. Then I wrapped the hands and feet with fluffy cotton dressings which were far too bulky to fit in gloves or socks, so I covered them with down booties to keep them warm. Makalu was tucked into his sleeping bag and pushed to one side to make room for the next customer.

Beck was helped in by Ed and Dave, who had taken the relay from Todd and Pete above Camp III. I was expecting an incoherent, half-blind, semiconscious phantom but, as he was being eased to the floor, he said to me in an easy, conversational tone, "Hi, Ken, where should I sit?"

Ed and Dave and I shook hands and congratulated one another on the great job we were doing. Then they left to let us do our work. Beck was alert and coordinated, showing no signs of hypothermia. Edema, though, had swollen his face to twice its size. I hardly recognized him. His cheeks were black and his nose had burned down to a piece of charcoal. I was afraid if he sneezed, he would blow it away.

Makalu had had the worst frostbite I had ever seen, but that was before I saw Beck. His entire right hand and a third of his forearm, as well as his entire left hand, were deep purple and frozen solid. They radiated cold. There were no blisters, no pulses, no sensation, no pain. They were the hands of a dead man, but bizarrely, he could move his fingers since the live muscles in his forearm, like the strings of a marionette, were able to pull on the dead bones in his hand.

His eyesight was better than I expected, with no evidence of snow blindness. The loss of vision had been due to the aftereffects of eye surgery. He had

had a radial keratotomy to correct his sight, but the operations leaves scars on the corneas. At high altitude his corneas swelled, but the scars made the expansion uneven, causing blurry images. Now with the decrease in altitude, his eyes were curing themselves.

We went through the same routine with Beck as we had for Makalu except that frostbite had only barely touched his toes, so a third tub for soaking his feet wasn't needed. The Sherpas were now masters of rewarming but even with only two tubs to maintain, they were having difficulty keeping up. For all practical purposes, Beck's hands were blocks of ice and they cooled the water too rapidly.

As we worked, Beck talked casually. Anyone hearing the conversation without seeing what was going on would have thought he had just dropped by for tea. He told me his vision had progressively deteriorated on summit day and by the time he reached the southeast ridge he was unable to see well enough to start along that narrow edge. Because Rob didn't want him descending alone, he told him to wait there and he'd pick him up on the way back from the summit. That didn't happen and so Beck finally started down late with another group of climbers. He had just gotten off the triangular face onto the South Col when the storm came up. With the fog and wind-driven snow, visibility quickly went to zero and he became separated from the others. Since the South Col is flat and featureless, he was unable to find his way back to camp. Wandering around in the bitter wind and cold he realized his hands were numb so he decided to take his gloves off to put his hands inside his jacket. He got his right glove off and opened the jacket but the wind blew the glove away and he was never able to get his hand inside. Lost and exhausted, he collapsed in the snow.

He said he was in a timeless, dreamlike state, not unconscious, but unable to move. He became aware of someone bending over him, saying, "He's dead." In fact, he had been lying in the snow overnight and by morning he realized he wasn't dead but if he didn't do something he soon would be. He summoned up all his courage and all his strength, and stood up. He was able to reason that since the wind had been behind him when he started out, he'd have to face into it to get back. He staggered ahead through the whiteout until he became the apparition Todd saw outside his tent.

Beck told me the story quietly and casually but I was struck by the power of what he had done. Out of oxygen, exhausted and hypothermic, he had been able to rally his mind enough to get his body moving and focus his thoughts. He had transcended the laws of medicine. The only way to explain it was that it was a miracle.

It was time to wrap up Beck's hands. As I was preparing the bandages,

Charles came in for the third time. He had been acting as my mother hen, making roundtrips from our camp to bring me food, which I didn't eat, then later to bring me warmer clothes as it got colder. This trip he brought me my sleeping bag and toothbrush, as it had become obvious I wasn't going back to our camp any time soon. He was eager to help, so I had him assist me in applying the dressings. I knew he would be thrilled to participate in the medical treatment. Charles spread the fingers, positioning the hand precisely as I asked, and Beck's hands were soon wrapped like Makalu's. Since all my dressings were now gone, I gave Charles a list of supplies to have sent up from base camp for use the next day, in case we couldn't evacuate these guys.

For most of the New Zealand climbers, fatigue had overcome excitement but a few climbers were still hanging around, including one who had relatively minor frostbite. His hand had been wrapped earlier but he had gone to the bathroom since then and now the bandage was grossly contaminated. Patiently he waited for me to finish, then asked if I could change his dressing. All I could offer him was sympathy. I had nothing left to rewrap him with, nor even any good advice on where he could put his hand.

Frank hadn't left yet either. There was a camera around and he was a professional photographer so, after checking with Makalu and Beck, I asked him to take some pictures. I'm sure the thought occurred to him a lot earlier, but his sense of propriety prevented him from even suggesting it. Once I turned him loose, he set about his work diligently until the camera got stuck, probably from the cold.

Even though Frank looked really tired and wasn't taking pictures anymore, he didn't want to leave yet. I sensed he wanted some attention but he was afraid to ask for it, seeing the severity of the injuries around him. Things were quiet now so I sat down next to him and asked how he was feeling. He was quick to respond, asking if I could just look at his feet to be sure he didn't have frostbite. I took a good, serious look, then reassured him that he didn't. That seemed to be just what he needed. He was in better shape than any of the others because he had been the first to turn around. He said the two best sights were Todd coming into his tent at Camp IV and me coming into his tent at Camp II. I wanted to ask him what happened up there, but this wasn't the time or place.

As I was watching my patients, a pretty Japanese woman knelt beside Makalu and, speaking softly, encouraged him to sip from the bowl of soup she was holding. I was pleased that she was taking it upon herself to feed the patients and make them comfortable, considerations to which doctors often don't give enough importance. As she rearranged the mat Beck was lying on, I realized she was Sumiyo, the IMAX starlet.

Makalu and Beck were stabilized although their conditions were fragile and could worsen suddenly. I was anxious to get them out of here. Base camp had some surprising news for us: A high-performance military helicopter was on alert. If winds were calm in the morning, it would attempt to land at Camp I, avoiding the need to make the treacherous descent through the icefall. At nineteen thousand feet, it would probably be the highest helicopter rescue ever. Pilots had never before been willing to come above base camp. We speculated that this story must be getting big publicity and the Nepalese wanted to try to pull off something spectacular.

Meanwhile, at Camp II, we were in a freezing tent getting colder by the minute. Our only propane heater, aimed directly on Beck and Makalu, did nothing for the rest of us or for the IV bags hanging from the top of the tent. Warm fluids had to keep flowing into our patients. We'd make them hypothermic if the bags got even half as cold as we were. While Henrik and I were discussing the problem, Sumiyo nodded her head and left. A few minutes later she came back and put the solution in our hands—a bunch of chemical hand warmers that we promptly activated and tied around the IV bags.

One by one everyone settled into their sleeping bags except me. Even though I had spent last night holding my tent down, and this morning had made a descent from Lhotse, I was still in overdrive and knew I wouldn't be able to sleep. I out-volunteered Henrik to keep watch, promising to wake him if I got tired. In the cold, silent tent I watched the IV fluids drip and the oxygen tank gauges gradually lose their pressure. I listened to the rhythmic breathing of my patients, periodically took their pulses, and added drops to Makalu's eyes whenever he complained of pain. I could feel the air temperature drop degree by degree as surely as if I had a thermometer to measure it. As much as possible I tried to work from inside my sleeping bag, but my feet were freezing despite putting heavy mitts over my socks and wrapping them in a down jacket. I would have felt guilty turning the propane heater toward myself, so I just stayed cold and had a miserable night.

At about four o'clock Henrik awoke by himself, but I stayed up anyway, by now too cold and too tired to fall asleep. I felt terrible but I didn't dare think about it, knowing what others had been through. Deciding to be optimistic, Henrik and I began to get Beck and Makalu ready for a helicopter ride. It was slow work. I could hardly get myself going, much less them. Progress was minimal until we woke up the Sherpas who took over most of the work and even made us tea.

An hour before dawn we got the discouraging word from base camp that it was too windy. The helicopter wasn't coming. I had to make a hard decision.

We could try to wait out the wind, but it might stay windy for days. At this altitude even a minor cut couldn't heal, and with the injuries they suffered, Beck and Makalu would rapidly deteriorate. Taking them down through the icefall, though, would expose them to further cold and trauma, not to mention the risk to the rescuers who would be transporting them beneath ice walls and through crevasse fields. Climbers are always willing to risk their lives to save others. Knowing that my decision would be carried out without question made the responsibility weigh even heavier, but the needs of my two patients were compelling. I opted for the over-the-ice evacuation.

As the patients were being fed, dressed, and tended to, I discreetly redirected the heater to thaw out my feet. Once I could feel them, I walked over to let Todd know the helicopter wasn't coming and we'd have to do it the hard way. Immediately, Todd began to organize rescue teams and I went back to finish packing up Beck and Makalu. I pulled out their IVs and disconnected them from the oxygen tanks. With the oxygen masks removed, I was able for the first time to treat their frostbitten faces with a burn cream. As I applied the white pasty cream to Beck's nose and cheeks, I remarked that I was putting on makeup so he'd look good at base camp.

The escorts arrived. Since Beck could walk, Todd and Pete led him out and started down the Cwm. Makalu's feet were frostbitten; he had to be carried. The Sherpas, experts and carrying loads, tied him to an aluminum frame and then mounted it to a harness on the back of the first volunteer. They would have to take turns carrying and dragging this unusually heavy load.

The parade stretched out down the Cwm, with Jim and me bringing up the rear. Progress was slow but this was the "easy" part. The difficulties and the dangers would soon increase dramatically as we entered the icefall. I was entirely preoccupied with how the trip would affect Makalu and Beck and how I would manage them at base camp. Methodically following Jim's footsteps, I was barely aware of the surroundings. My enclosed space was disrupted, however, by a noisy green insect coming at us from out of the sky. It startled me back to the present.

The wind had died down and the helicopter was going to try to land. It circled once and came in low, testing the air to see if there was enough of it. The rotor wash, bouncing the air back up off the surface, gave the helicopter some extra lift but the effect was lost when it passed over a deep crevasse. The tail suddenly dropped and swung forward, nearly catching in the ice. The pilot was looking for a landing spot but from the air, hidden crevasses are hard to see. They are hard enough to see even from the ground. Ed picked out a spot that looked safe but had nothing with which to mark it until Araceli tossed him a bottle of red Kool-Aid she was carrying. He used it to mark a big X for a landing pad and then tied a bandanna to a ski pole to make a wind sock. The pilot came straight down but only lightly touched the ice, aware that if the skids got stuck and he couldn't take off, he'd be unable to survive at this altitude.

The pilot held up a single finger—there was only enough lift for one passenger. Beck immediately deferred to Makalu. He knew that because Makalu had to be carried, his trip through the icefall would be the more hazardous one for all involved. He also knew that the pilot might not be able to land a second time.

As the helicopter disappeared, Beck asked Pete if he thought I would be back. Pete replied, "You'll be in time for brunch at the Yak & Yeti Hotel."

The pilot ferried Makalu over the icefall to base camp and then came back for Beck, who boarded with a cry of joy. The helicopter disappeared for the second and final time from the Cwm. In the thicker air at base camp, Makalu was put back on board with Beck. They would both be in Kathmandu before we were out of the icefall. Ahead of use was merely another "routine" descent to base camp. There was a huge sense of relief and pride which we all shared, but I also felt an intense letdown, a sudden sense of disengagement. A challenge far greater than summiting had been removed and the exhilaration that came from rising to it was left hanging in the air behind the helicopter.

Avalanche! (3 Friends Caught in an Avalanche on Mt. Ranier)

MARK STUART GILL

Perhaps the greatest fear of even the most experienced climbers is being caught in an avalanche, one of the most severe examples of nature's fury. Many a veteran climber has succumbed to a sudden and unexpected wall of snow descending on them from above. This story, written by Mark Stuart Gill, tells the story of three California women who decided they wanted to climb a mountain. At first, they thought about Everest, but then settled on Washington's 14,410 foot Mt. Ranier. With limited experience they joined a group that was being guided to the summit. Unfortunately, Ranier can have Everest-like weather conditions and the party was caught in an avalanche. The story describes the terror and fight for survival that followed.

Deborah Lynn was exhilarated. The anesthesiologist and mother of three was part of a group of amateur climbers who had just scaled one of the tallest peaks in the continental U.S.—14,410-foot Mount Rainier, near Seattle.

On the way back down the mountain that day last June, Lynn, forty-five, was about to cross a narrow ledge 11,400 feet up. Known as Disappointment Cleaver, it is regarded as the most treacherous area on Mount Rainier—a place where one mistake can cost a climber her life.

Curt Hewitt, one of the leaders of Lynn's mountain-climbing group and a professional guide, hooked himself and his team onto the 800-foot safety line strung along the length of Disappointment Cleaver and anchored into the mountainside by aluminum spikes.

Halfway across the ledge, Lynn heard what sounded like thunder. A moment later there were shouts of "snow falling!" Then "Run . . . run!!" The entire slope above—literally tons of snow—was sliding toward her in an impossibly large slab. "I thought I was going to die," Lynn says.

A Daring Dream

It had been a logn trip for Lynn and her friends, Nina Redman and Susan Hall, from their homes in Manhattan Beach, California, to the top of Mount Rainier. A year earlier, Lynn and Redman had first come up with the idea of climbing the mountain. Lynn, athletic by nature, felt she was up to the challenge. Redman, thirty-six, a college reference librarian with two children, was excited at the thought of doing something daring. "I needed a goal to inspire me to stay in shape," she admits. Her enthusiasm was shared by Hall, a forty-six-year-old single mother of two and a database administrator, who hadn't taken a vacation in three years.

Lynn and Redman had been captivated by Into Thin Air (Villard, 1997), the best-selling book by Jon Krakauer about a disastrous 1996 Mount Everest climb, in which eight people died. That tragedy, far from dissuading would-be climbers, seemed to increase public fascination with the adventure sport.

Instead of setting their sights on Everest, Lynn, Redman and Hall chose Rainier. Only half the size of Everest, it can be scaled in under twenty-four hours and attracts ten thousand climbers every year.

Yet Rainier presents significant risks. Its potentially massive ice falls and very high winds are so similar to the conditions in the Himalayas that many professional climbers train there before attempting Everest. In June 1981, eleven people were killed in a monstrous avalanche on Mount Rainier. It was the worst climbing accident ever in the U.S.

Despite the potential danger, Lynn, Redman and Hall signed up with Rainier Mountaineering, Inc. (RMI), one of the most renowned schools of its kind in the country, in April 1998. The guided climb, including a three-day course in basic mountaineering skills, cost $765, plus another $150 in equipment rental. The only requirement was that climbers had to be able to haul a fifty-pound pack up four thousand vertical feet. If a group member couldn't hack it once she got to climb school, she would not be allowed to climb Mount Rainier.

To prepare themselves for the physical challenge, Hall, Redman and Lynn began a tough training regimen. Several times a week for two months, the friends met at a local park after work to scale a two-hundred-foot-high sand dune. They increased the intensity of their training gradually by wearing back-packs filled with two-liter bottles of water.

By the time climb school began in early June, the women were in peak physical condition. At the base camp of Mount Rainier—located at an elevation of ten thousand feet—Lynn, Redman and Hall learned dozens of mountaineering techniques from their RMI guides.

They also became friendly with the sixteen other amateur climbers in the group. Patrick Nestler, a twenty-nine-year-old engineer from Rowayton, Connecticut, had been planning the adventure for four years. Forty-two-year-old Gregg Swanson, a California phone-equipment salesman, was using the climb as a way to deal with his grief over the death of his nephew, a former RMI guide, in a helicopter accident in the Canadian Rockies two years earlier.

Once they completed the training course, the group began their trip to the top of the mountain at three A.M. on June 11. The climb "was very difficult," recalls Redman. Because the air has less oxygen at high altitudes, just breathing is hard. "The last one hundred feet [up the mountain] I was asking myself, Is this worth it?"

They reached the summit by noon, and the group broke into a cheer. One of the men began to weep. The climbers marveled at their accomplishment and then spent the next hour gawking at nearby Mount St. Helens, and taking touristy photos of each other.

At one P.M. the group began picking their way back down the mountain in teams of five roped together. But the climbing conditions had deteriorated. Six to ten inches of new snow had covered the eastern slope of Rainier the previous night. All day, the sun had baked the surface and the temperature had risen to about sixty degrees, creating a large mantle of slush on top of hard-packed frozen snow. Under such conditions, an icicle breaking or a loud voice can start an avalanche.

Lynn, Hall and the other three members of their team reached Disappointment Cleaver at two P.M. A few minutes later they heard shouts—then the huge wall of snow bore down on them.

The team members began to run for their lives along the tiny ledge. The snow plummeted down the steep gully between the two glaciers, picking up speed and fanning out in the shape of a deadly inverted V.

Lynn had run just a few yards when the slide broad-sided her off the ledge. "I became airborne," she remembers. "Then I was enveloped in snow." I'm going to be buried alive, she thought. Hall, who eventually blacked out, was submarining face first down the slope.

Fifty feet behind her friend, Nina Redman and the second team were roped together waiting to cross the ridge. Redman watched helplessly as Hall and Lynn tried to run out of the avalanche's path.

Suddenly, the avalanche seemed to expand, enveloping Redman's team. Using what she'd learned in the three-day climbing course, Redman whipped her ice ax over her head and down into the snow as hard as she could to break her fall. But the force of the slide blew the ax out of her hand like a toothpick.

This is it, Redman thought.

"Are We Alive?"

Half a minute later there was nothing but ghostly silence and blinding sunshine. The two teams had tumbled 100 to 350 feet down the steep mountainside. The ten climbers were slung across the eastern face of Rainier, connected by a tangle of ropes like a broken chain of pearls.

Whimpers began to fill the air: "God, don't let me die" . . . "Are we alive?" . . . "Mayday."

When Susan Hall regained consciousness she was lying upside down on a slope. The straps of her pack were pulled so tightly against her throat, she thought she was choking to death. Ten feet below her, beneath the lip of a rocky ledge, Deborah Lynn dangled like a spider from a web. Her boot was stuck on her harness, pinning her foot back against her waist. A stream of 35°F. water—snowmelt from the summer thaw—was pouring over her with the force of a bathroom shower.

Nina Redman had landed fifteen feet below Lynn. She thought of trying to climb to steady ground. But her guide, Ruth Mahre, screamed, "Don't move!" The ropes tying them all together were so twisted that too sudden a movement could take the entire team down.

Worst of all was the plight of Patrick Nestler, the engineer from Connecticut. He was dangling twenty feet below Redman, and like Lynn, he was being drenched by a stream of melting snow. He shouted to Redman, "Tell me what's happening! Will somebody please talk to me!"

"I'm here, Pat. I'm talking to you!" Redman yelled back. But Nestler kept shouting the same desperate phrases over and over.

"The situation was unbelievable," recalls Redman. "It was a perfect day and we had this incredible view. But we were all clinging for our lives."

Below the trapped climbers, Wreatha Carnet, who was climbing Rainier with her husband and another group, had seen the avalanche strike. She immediately called for help on her cell phone.

A rescue effort involving more than eighty people was quickly launched. But climbers hiking up from Rainier's base camp with medical supplies would take hours to reach Disappointment Cleaver. The only aircraft able to conduct upper-elevation missions, a U.S. Army Chinook helicopter, flew to the scene, but was unable to land near the scene of the disaster. It's a grim irony of mountain-climbing that you can survive an avalanche, only to die waiting to be rescued.

A Race Against Time

On Disappointment Cleaver, the situation was getting critical. Susan Hall was still being strangled by her backpack and was gasping for air. Finally she managed to wriggle free—only to notice a throbbing pain in her right hand. When the avalanche had hit, the rope connecting Hall to her teammates had sheared off the fingers of her glove and crushed her pinkie and ring finger.

Meanwhile, Lynn's internal body temperature was dropping. As a doctor, she quickly recognized the first stages of hypothermia.

Fifteen feet above her, Nina Redman saw Lynn shivering. She thought of her young son. The week before, he had asked if she was going to die on the mountain climb. Now all she wanted to do was to get home to him.

"Deborah! Promise me something," yelled Redman. "If I don't make it, tell Steve and the kids how much I loved them. I'll do the same for you."

"I promise," Lynn told Redman.

At that moment dozens of park rangers, staff and RMI guides elsewhere on the mountain were launching a heroic and completely improvised rescue. They climbed to Disappointment Cleaver, where they sank a new safety line into the mountainside, then rappelled gingerly down the rock face to the marooned climbers.

About an hour and a half after the avalanche hit, RMI guide Ned Randolph finally reached Deborah Lynn. Her face was pale and she was hallucinating. "I was in Tahiti, then Hawaii. It was beautiful," she recalls.

"Deborah, you're going to be okay," said Randolph, who would earn an American Red Cross award for his rescue work.

"You're interrupting my dream," she moaned. The rescuers hoisted Lynn up and wrapped her in parkas and sleeping bags.

It took more than six hours to free all the climbers. Then another problem emerged: The closest the helicopter could land was a clearing called Ingraham Flats, hundreds of yards below the avalanche site

At nine P.M., as dusk was falling, the guides and the wounded climbers inched down the unstable crevasse above Ingraham Flats. Fog and high winds would make it too dangerous to fly after dark. If the climbers didn't rendezvous with the helicopter by nine-thirty, they'd have to spend the night on the frigid mountainside, or undertake the treacherous task of climbing down by moonlight.

The group began to move as quickly as they could, reaching the helicopter with just fifteen minutes to spare. Susan Hall and Nina Redman huddled in the helicopter's cargo bay together, worrying about Lynn. The guides slid two bodies wrapped in parkas beside them. One was Lynn. She was alive. But Patrick Nestler hadn't been so lucky. Because of his position on the mountain, the rescuers had not been able to reach him for nearly five hours. By that time, hypothermia had claimed his life.

Moving On

The climbers were flown to a hospital in Tacoma, Washington, where Redman was checked for head injuries and released. Lynn rebounded within hours from hypothermia. But Hall's two crushed fingers needed nine hours of surgery and temporary wires to stabilize the bones.

The Rainier avalanche re-ignited an issue raised after the Mount Everest tragedy in 1996—had inexperienced climbers been encouraged to exceed their abilities? Did guides use bad judgment in descending the mountain so late in the day?

Lou Whittaker, a co-owner of RMI, insisted his guides did nothing wrong. "I would feel as safe climbing in the evening as in the morning," he told The Seattle Times. "The avalanches come all times of the year and all times of the day."

On June 12, 1998, the National Park Service convened a board of inquiry to investigate the incident. But Redman, Lynn and Hall never had any doubts about their guides. "Who's to say if it would have been safer to have come down earlier?" says Lynn. "I know their professionalism and expertise saved us."

The Park Service report found that the avalanche could not have been predicted, and that the guides leading the climbing party had acted appropriately. As it turned out, a climber hundreds of feet above the amateurs admitted that he stepped off the trail while crossing a slope of ice, setting the entire flow in motion.

Some of the members of the RMI climbing group initially suffered post-traumatic stress from the avalanche. But remarkably, none of the three women friends have suffered long-lasting anxiety or trauma. Lynn thinks it's partly because they've talked about it so much with each other. "We came to this conclusion that we had cheated death," she says. "And instead of being paralyzing, it would energize us for the futures we now get to have with our families."

Neither Lynn or Redman currently have plans to do any more glacier mountain-climbing. Susan Hall, however, says she needs to confront the climbing experience again. Perhaps it is because she's left with the most tangible reminder of the avalanche: The limited range of motion in her two fingers still makes it impossible to do even simple tasks, like wringing out a wet swimsuit.

For about a month after the avalanche, Hall was so exhausted, she didn't even want to leave her home. But she says that within the next two years she plans to scale Alaska's Mount McKinley, which rises nearly a mile higher in the sky than Rainier and takes more than three weeks to climb.

"Physically, Rainier got the best of me," she says. "But next time, I'll be stronger."

Blind Corners

GEOFFREY TABIN

An excerpt from Geoffrey Tabin's book of the same name, this is yet another harrowing story from Mt. Everest. It details a 1983 expedition by a team of 13 climbers to make the first ascent of the mountain's difficult Kangshung Face. This is really a story of the camaraderie that is necessary for a long and arduous climb and, if that feeling wasn't there at the beginning, it certainly is at the end. Though the climbers would have to travel through a blizzard on the way down, they had completed their journey. Six climbers reached the summit via a pioneering route that wouldn't be repeated for at least 20 years. At the end, Tabin writes, "More importantly, we did it as a team of brothers who were all leaving the mountain as friends, bonded for life."

Everest 1983—The First Ascent of the Kangshung Face

I returned from Tibet to find that I was out of medical school. I reapplied and was reaccepted with the understanding that I would not leave again. Meanwhile, Dan Reid turned over the permit for the return to the Kangshung Face to Jim Morrissey, who assumed expedition leadership under the condition that Dan remain part of the next team. Dan agreed to just be a base camp doctor and assured Jim that he would not do anything dangerous. Jim was the perfect leader for this type of trip. He had a vast amount of expedition experience, lots of common sense, and strong leadership skills; in addition, because he was primarily a doctor rather than a climber, he did not have a climbing ego that would clash with his team. He was thus able to listen and weigh all options and then make a decision. Tall and powerful, Jim had a commanding personality and a strong sense of self-confidence that persuaded people to follow. Jim selected a team that he felt gave the best chance for success, blending top climbers who would work well together. The common attribute was a shared belief that the Kangshung Face could be climbed.

From the 1981 team he asked Dan Reid, Andy Harvard, Lou Reichardt, Kim Momb, George Lowe, and me to return to Everest with him in 1983. Adding to this nucleus of seven, Jim invited Carlos Buhler, Carl Tobin, David Coombs, Jay Cassell, David Cheesmond, and Chris Kopczynski. The result was not necessarily the best thirteen climbers in America in 1983, but very likely the best team America could have produced. A final addition was John Boyle, a banker, engineer, and yachtsman, to serve as base camp manager. The trip again was well funded, with *National Geographic* magazine as a principal sponsor.

Climbing the last unclimbed face on Everest had become a consuming romantic quest for me. I desperately wanted to go on the trip, but there was no chance of Harvard Medical School giving me leave to go climbing again. Then Michael Wiedman, the professor of eye surgery, approached me and proposed that we do a research project on the physiology of high altitude. In particular, Dr. Wiedman was interested in retinal hemorrhaging at high altitude and whether an ocular exam could be used as a prognosticator of high-altitude cerebral or pulmonary edema. I was thus able to schedule a research elective and did not have to apply for a leave of absence. Beyond learning to perform ophthalmoscopy, I trained for the trip by running the five miles to and from my apartment to school every day, sprinting the steps of the Harvard football stadium, and traversing a rock wall and climbing rock and ice every weekend. I easily completed the Boston Marathon in the spring and ran a complete traverse of the Presidential Mountains in New Hampshire in less than four hours, normally a three-day hike. When I flew to San Francisco in August 1983 I felt prepared and confident.

An optimistic group had gathered in San Francisco. The mood at the airport was one of frantic excitement. Kopczynski distributed stylish Eddie Bauer team jackets; I brought along a double shipment of boots and Gore-Tex running suits from New Balance. Someone supplied a cake covered in mounds of sticky icing, but there were no forks, so we all grabbed a handful. A strip-o-gram, sent by anonymous admirers of Morrissey, waltzed onto the scene and danced through the happy confusion of climbers and their luggage, friends, and family.

We were going to climb the last unclimbed face on Mount Everest—the hardest mountaineering route that had ever been attempted—and we were going to do it with minimal supplemental oxygen and no native support on the mountain. We traveled through China, each day becoming a more and more cohesive team. We spent three days in Beijing where, between visits to the Great Wall and the Forbidden City, we built up endurance by running through the streets in our bright and scanty shorts. Tobin tried to find some rock walls but discovered that the climbing of ornate walls encrusted with the statues of demons long dead is one of the forbidden things in the Forbidden City. As a team, our collective mentality was similar to what I have read about the psychology of people going off to war. A macabre sense of humor prevailed, with lots of "jokes" about climbers who have perished. We all knew that sixty-two lives had already been lost on the slopes of Mount Everest, that no new route had been opened on the mountain without the loss of life, that none had been climbed without native load carriers on the mountain, and that ours was the hardest and most dangerous path. Still, none of us broached the subject of whether an accident could happen to us. Interestingly, there was also a prevalent hypersexuality and much flirtation with flight attendants and other Western sojourners, perhaps our bodies' way of telling us to propagate our genes before embarking on the dangerous mission. I personally adopted an attitude that I had trained well enough and was with such a great team that I would be safe. I had no conscious thoughts of the risk. My mind remained completely immersed in the present, with little talk of the past or future, as we again enjoyed banquets and sight-seeing.

Arriving in Lhasa, I found that Tibet had changed dramatically in two years. The Chinese had eased many of their restrictions. The Potala and Jokang were now crowded with chanting pilgrims, and the streets were bustling with activity. Chinese soldiers were still present, but less obvious. We stayed in a comfortable guest house and ate well. There was little time for tourism, though. We were a team with a mission! We packed our gear on trucks and began the drive to Mount Everest after one day. A monsoon had washed out the main road, so we took an alternate dirt track that was so bumpy you couldn't even pick your nose. The ride was more beautiful than I remembered. We passed alongside rolling hills with layers of brown, yellow, and green banks woven into the sand. The monsoon gave a constant, unpleasant drizzle; still, the swirling clouds made the landscape all the more impressive. We arrived in Xigase late in the evening and left for Xegar early the next morning. Despite the hectic pace we were beginning to get to know each other.

It soon became clear to me that my three-hour-per-day training regimen left me one of the weakest members of our team. Three people stood apart as being in a different physical realm. Kim Momb looked like a shorter version of the Incredible Hulk. He had been high on the West Ridge of Everest the previous spring and trained full-time during the intervening two months. Prior to his becoming a professional climber, Kim was a top-ranked skier, motorcross racer, and black belt kickboxer with an undefeated professional record. He had a ready smile and firm handshake. Carl Tobin's income was derived solely from competing as the mountaineer in a made-for-television event called "Survival of the Fittest." One look at his rippled, muscular physique and it was easy to see why. He had been living in Fairbanks and consistently pushing the limits of what had been considered possible in the mountains of Alaska. Carl was quiet with a piercing sense of humor that left you slightly off balance. For instance, when the group discussed romantic movies, Carl mumbled earnestly, "Yeah, I always get teary at that love scene in *Deliverance*." When Tibetans stared at Carl, he stared back with a look of such profound and—at the same time—simple curiosity that they turned away. Carl would then follow them, continuing his study. The third powerhouse was Dave Cheesmond, a South African living in Canada. Dave had been Carl's partner on many of his hardest climbs and had distinguished himself as one of the most prolific and accomplished moun-taineers in the world during the past two years. "Cheese" was gregarious and helpful and always willing to tip a beer or join in a bawdy song.

A second contingent were the older masters: George Lowe, Lou Reichardt, Andy Harvard, and Chris Kopczynski. George had already established himself as a legendary climber with a will, tenacity, and determination second to none. He had been the driving force on the route in 1981 and exuded a quiet confidence about this trip. Lou, a professor of neurophysiology, had climbed more twenty-six-thousand-foot peaks than any American. He shared George's work ethic. What Lou lacked in technical skills he more than made up for with a physiol-ogy that did not seem to be affected by altitude. Andy had been on a phenom-enal number of expeditions and was a master of logistics. A lawyer by trade, he was thoughtful and articulate. Chris Kopczynski also knew about expeditions. He had reached the top of Everest, via the South Col Route, in 1981 as well as making the first American ascent of the North Face of the Eiger. "Kop" was a building contractor from Spokane, Washington, who had a straightforward western friendliness and a button with a picture of his wife and kids that he wore over his heart throughout the climb.

I thought of myself as being similar in strength to the other three climbers until we went out for a training run in Beijing. Carlos Buhler, Jay Cassell, and Dave Coombs left me in the dust. Buhler, a mountain guide from Bellingham, Washington, was a full-time climber with wider interests than just mountains. Carlos was multilingual with deep thoughts about international and interper-sonal relations. He was warm but intense, and very sensitive to "feelings" on expeditions. I found Coombs to be an upbeat man who was one of the hardest workers I have ever met. His climbing résumé and background were similar to mine. He was a Harvard graduate with an MBA who trained intensively for this trip. Similar in many ways to Coombs was Jay Cassell, an MBA and ex-marine who had the least big-mountain experience on the team. Still, he had finished strongly in the Iron Man Triathlon and Western States 100 endurance run, and was, perhaps, our most aerobically fit member. Jay had a personality that was mentally as solid as a rock; he was a man who would break before he bent.

The final two climbers, Morrissey and Dan Reid, were both busy cardio-thoracic surgeons in California. Neither was able to spend much time training. In fact, Dan had not climbed since his drug-addled solo ascent of the ropes on Everest in 1981. This time he came prepared, though. Dan had THE LITTLE ENGINE THAT COULD embroidered on all of his climbing clothes as well as a formal kilt to wear into base camp. The final member of the team was our "Mister Organization," base camp manager John Boyle. Boyle handled the detail work before the trip and developed a winch system that we hoped would save us considerable time and effort on the mountain. To reach the top of Everest we had a three-part task: We first had to reclimb the sheer initial forty-five-hundred-foot rock and ice buttress. Next, we had to carry enough supplies up the route to support a summit climb. Then we still had to climb a vertical mile and a half up a steep snow ridge to the top of the world. Boyle's plan was to launch a rocket attached to a cord from the top of the buttress. Next, he planned to rig up a continuous nine-thousand-foot loop with high-tech yachting pulleys at the top and bottom. He had a Honda engine to power our loads quickly over the difficult climbing. Most of the team was a bit dubious, but we all hoped it would work.

The trek to base camp again started from Kharta. Our gear was loaded onto yaks for the journey. It was a festive march with the colorfully robed Tibetan yak herders whistling, singing, and chanting mantras as we walked. With us on the trek were a group of seven doctor friends of Morrissey's who had donated to the cause and Jack Alustiza, the owner of a Basque restaurant whom Jim had asked to be the expedition base camp chef, our Chinese liaison officer who was again Wang Fu Chow, and our official interpreter, Mr. Tsao. Boyle, Alustiza, and the scientists were all a bit slower than the climbers, and we adopted a leisurely pace. The views were again stunning with bright red rhododendrons flowering in the monsoon wetness. The mornings were glorious with shimmering peaks dancing above us. By late morning clouds rolled in and covered the sky. Precipitation started before noon every day and lasted until late in the evening. As we gained altitude the rain turned to snow. Dan Reid never wore more than his kilt and stripped naked to bathe in every glacial pond.

It was encouraging to see how close the team grew as our trek in continued. On some evenings the large dome tent we used for cooking and dinner became a climbers' tavern, fraternity house, stage, or minstrel show. On one night bawdy songs replaced more gentle and harmonious melodies as the banquet continued long into the night. Cheesmond led our band of ill-matched voices while Hank played his harmonica. We later switched to limerick song and I improvised, developing a caustic profile for each of my fellow teammates.

> An eccentric doc named Reid
> Follows a bizarre old Scottish creed
> He roams the hills in a dress
> Attempting to impress
> The yaks who still pay him no heed

The last days of the trek passed quickly, with the weather remaining sunny and the rhythm of travel becoming comfortable. We reached base camp at an altitude of seventeen thousand feet at the edge of the Kangshung Glacier on August 26. The area was welcoming. The base camp was large and open, on flat ground with grass and moss and wildflowers and running water nearby. Everyone, including the scientists, pitched in to get things set up. Base camp was a busy place. Between the cutting and coiling of rope, the building of stone walls, and the incessant sorting of food boxes, gear, and equipment, there was always work to be done.

The first task we faced in beginning the climb was to find and mark the route across the Kangshung Glacier so that we could carry gear to the base of the buttress. I, meanwhile, was feeling the effects of altitude. My resting pulse raced at more than one hundred beats per minute, double my normal rate at sea level. With exertion, my pulse pounded in my temples at over two hundred beats per minute. The fourteen-mile-round-trip carry across the glacier to advanced base camp with a heavy pack made for a long, exhausting day. An average of about five hundred pounds a day of food, fuel, tentage, hardware, ropes, personal equipment, and winch gear had to be selected from the two hundred yak loads delivered at base camp and moved across the glacier to advanced base camp by our ten porters and the climbers. Advanced base, in contrast to base camp, was stark and rocky and felt like part of the mountain. It was close enough to the face to feel the blast of avalanches. More so than stocking advanced base, the carries were necessary for acclimatization. The entire team left early in the morning to make the carry, except for Dan Reid. We passed Dan in the afternoon. He was still a long way from the end of the glacier. We suggested that he dump his load and return with us, but he refused. An hour after dark we were organizing a search party to go out onto the heavily crevassed glacier to look for Dan when we heard him yodel. With a big grin Dr. Reid raved about how beautiful it was to be alone on a glacier at night. Jim and Dan had a talk about risk and danger, and Dan agreed to stay in base camp and be good.

On September 1 the actual climb began. Lou, Carl, and I started fixing ropes up the buttress. As the climbing leader from the 1981 trip, Lou had the honor of leading the first pitch of the 1983 effort. The climbing went quickly—we knew exactly where the route should go. We were also helped by several ropes and anchors that were still in place from 1981. We regained seven hundred feet of sheer rock before noon. Dan Reid caught up to us late in the afternoon, carrying more rope. We asked him what he was doing on the route. Reid grinned. "Well, you need more rope, don't you?" Dan soon insinuated himself into the climbing rotation, carrying heavy loads in support of the leaders and helping out everywhere. Once again the crazy doc was a full climbing member of the team.

The lower part of the route climbed up steep rock that had lots of small, sharp, incut holds. We made fast progress, reaching our first campsite on the mountain on the second day. We again called it Snow Camp, as it sat perched on a magnificent snow ridge at the top of the first rock step. The next obstacle was a difficult ridge of enormous snow mushrooms and steep ice. Dave Cheesmond, Kop, and Coombs moved into the front. I joined Dan in the group carrying equipment up to support the leaders. The first ones up climbed the rock and ice that the mountain offered and fixed a permanent rope in place. The rest of the team used the fixed rope to safeguard themselves and climb with heavy loads. As in 1981, we used mechanical ascenders, which slide up the rope but lock when weighted, to move up, and rappelled back down using figure-eight friction rings that slowed our slide down the ropes.

After five days we reached the Bowling Alley, the dangerous ice chute that gives access to the upper face. This gully was still a funnel for debris that melts out of the upper rock headwall and was again one of the scariest sections on the climb. At the top of the Bowling Alley we reestablished Pinsetter Camp beneath the rock headwall that was the technically most difficult section of the route. In 1981 it had taken three weeks to surmount the crumbly, overhanging barrier. Climbing this section required laborious and strenuous aid climbing, where the leader pounds a piton into the rock and uses this aid point to advance. Looking up at the path, we saw a tattered rope swaying in the breeze, a remnant from the 1981 effort. Kim volunteered to "jug" up the weather-beaten cord. He clipped his mechanical ascenders onto the old rope and methodically began climbing like a spider on a thread. We watched with horror as Kim, a couple hundred feet above us, hastily detached first one, then the other ascender, and quickly clipped them back onto the rope a few feet higher. In four hours he regained the entire headwall. When I came up, I saw that where Kim detached his ascenders, the old rope was worn 95 percent of the way through; only one strand of frayed nylon, less than an eighth of an inch in diameter, remained.

I was now supposed to rotate back to advanced base camp for a couple of days of rest while Jay, Andy, Carlos, George, and Cheese moved to the front to push the route up the next section. Above the rock we had to surmount a nine-hundred-foot ice slope angled at seventy degrees that was protected by fifty-foot-high icicles at its top in order to reach the top of the buttress, a place we named the Helmet. Starting down, I met Cheese. He told me that he was not feeling well; he had to turn around and descend to base camp. Carlos and Andy were also ill. We were short of load carriers. I knew that I was very tired, but I decided that the team needed me to stay up and work. I was still insecure about my being on this team of great climbers and believed that this was a chance for me to prove my worth. The next morning I carried a fifty-pound load of ropes and ice screws to the top of the rock. Back in the tent at Pinsetter Camp, I was too tired to help Kim with the laborious tasks of melting snow into water and preparing dinner. I crawled into my sleeping bag and began shivering uncontrollably. Kim gave me tea and helped me throughout the night. In the morning I had not slept a minute and was very lethargic. Kim and George helped me pack up and I headed down.

As I started to rappel down the rock below Snow Camp I heard a roar. Looking up, I saw that a house-sized block of rock had broken off directly above me. It hit and shattered one hundred feet overhead. Car-sized chunks rained down on me. I curled up as small as possible and realized, *I am going to die.* I was calm; my mind was blank as I faced my doom. Three large boulders smashed within five feet of me, but I escaped unscathed. The air was heavy with the acrid, gunpowderlike smell of the rock dust. The sound of the avalanche resonated down the valley. After a moment of calm, my heart began to race. My pulse rose to more than two hundred beats per minute and my whole body shook uncontrollably. It was several minutes before the trembling stopped and I was able to stand and continue my descent.

Jim Morrissey had heard about my shivering and lethargy. He was concerned that I had cerebral edema and insisted that I return to base camp for a rest. High-altitude cerebral edema, a swelling of the brain, can quickly become fatal. Falling rock can end a climber's life in an instant. Walking dejectedly back across the glacier to base camp, I wondered if climbing any route on any mountain is worth dying for. At the same time I thought about my teammates, realizing that I had never been with a group so full of life. There was an intense prevailing appreciation for both the immense beauty surrounding us and the small joys of existence. I came to help this team climb the Kangshung Face and would return to the cause, if I could. I felt awful that I might have hurt our team's chances for reaching the top, not to mention ruined my own summit aspirations, by pushing myself too hard when I knew that I was not feeling well. I vowed to listen to my body from now on.

The rest of the team quickly succeeded in fixing ropes up to the Helmet. The climbing of the buttress has been accomplished in only twelve days. Now we needed to carry our gear up the wall. We all focused on Boyle's winch system. Carlos and Jay carefully uncoiled the polypropylene trail line and aimed the rocket launcher. The first effort dribbled off into an avalanche cone and was lost in the debris. The second firing was also a dud. We only had three rockets. Jim, Lou, and Boyle discussed the options. We could hazard another firing from the top station. If it failed, we would have no winch support. They decided on a second option, which was to fire a rocket from Snow Camp. The route below was sheer to the glacier. They thought the rocket would surely work from there, and it did. We would get some support from the motorized winch.

The second part of the plan was to install a gravity hauling system on the overhanging rock headwall above Pinsetter Camp. Dave Cheesmond and George Lowe engineered a two-thousand-foot continuous line with pulleys at the top and bottom. Haul bags were filled with rock and snow at the top station and clipped onto the rope, while the haul bags filled with our food and equipment were tied on the bottom. The upper haul bags were released and pulled up our gear. Both the gravity system and Boyle's engine-powered winch worked perfectly. We still had to man-carry the loads from Snow Camp up through the Bowling Alley to Pinsetter and from the top of the rock up the steep Helmet ice field. We needed all the manpower we could muster. So after five days of rest at base camp, I returned to the task. I was feeling much better and hoped that I had a virus and not cerebral edema or any other high-altitude illness.

With everyone putting in 110 percent every day, progress moving our gear up the mountain was steady. I again carried as heavy a load as I possibly could, plus ten pounds more every day. The monsoon continued to linger, with wet snow falling every afternoon. Still, every one of us pushed hard, working with no rest days. We all, of course, had our own summit aspirations, and no one wanted to burn himself out. Yet we were in a desperate race against the winter winds and storms. Once the jet stream lowered its one-hundred-mile-per-hour wrath down on the mountain and the winter Himalayan storms unleashed their fury, it would be impossible for anyone to reach the top. So despite having already pushed too hard once on the trip, and feeling exhausted at the end of every day, I continued to work with every ounce of my strength. The rest of the team put in an equal effort, which inspired each of us to do more. Lou, Carl, Carlos, Andy, Dan, Jim, and I were based at Snow Camp, bringing loads up to the gravity winch at Pinsetter Camp, with Lou often making two impossibly heavy carries per day. Jay and Dave Coombs were working the bottom of the gravity winch while George, Cheese, Kim, and Kop dropped down from the Helmet to work the top of the winch and ferry loads back up to the Helmet

Camp. Kim put in a herculean effort—two carries every day for a week. We slowly moved more people up as more loads accumulated at the upper winch station. Finally, on September 29, our entire team of thirteen climbers and all of the necessary gear was on top of the buttress.

After a solid month of work we were only at 21,500 feet. This is the same altitude that yaks can walk to on the north side of Everest and where advanced base camp sits in Nepal. We still had a vertical mile and a half to climb on an unknown route and little time before the weather changed for the winter. Statistically, the jet stream was due to lower during the first two weeks of October. Jim and Lou began to work out a tentative strategy. Everyone had to continue to push as hard and fast as he could. We would establish three higher camps: Camp One at 23,500 feet, Camp Two at 25,500 feet, and Camp Three—High Camp—nearly 27,000 feet. We had a total of thirteen bottles of supplemental oxygen. So each person would carry his own one bottle of gas up to High Camp, sleep without extra oxygen, and use the bottle for the summit climb.

A typical day for us began several hours before sunrise when someone awoke to light the hanging stove suspended inside the tent. We melted pile after pile of snow carried to the stove with a stuff sack. High altitude amplifies the difficulty of melting snow into water. Even at its best, the procedure is like melting cotton candy to get a sugary syrup. A full pot of snow yields less than an eighth of an inch of water. Each morning we fed the pot until we had enough water for tea and soupy oatmeal. After breakfast we geared up and either climbed in a traditional manner—one person is belayed as he climbs upward while his partner plays out the rope for safety—or we carried ropes and equipment to support the upper climb. In addition to working twelve hours per day every day with no rest days, we had to take care of ourselves on the mountain. We had no native cook staff, so after an exhausting day climbing, we collapsed in our tents, still faced with the daunting task of melting snow into water to rehydrate and to prepare our meals.

At 21,500 feet I could feel my pulse beating in my temples, even at rest. Every step upward was a new altitude record for me. On October 1, I wrote in my diary:

> I realize that I am among the weakest of the thirteen of us. I also know the risks involved, even for the strongest. Consciously, I do not think that it makes sense to jeopardize my life to climb a mountain. But I am beginning to understand what Mallory must have meant when he said he was climbing Everest "because it is there." It is not just that the mountain is "there" externally, but it is because it is "there" internally, within me. It has become a personal quest. Yes, the beauty of the high mountains, the camaraderie, the teamwork, and the

joy of movement are all reasons to be climbing here. But in these really high mountains there is a definite element of self-realization, and of learning exactly where my limits are, driving me upward. I do not want to die. But this is my shot at the top of the world, and I'm going for it, savoring every moment of life!

The weather turned perfect, and the massive team effort continued unabated. By October 5 everyone had been to twenty-five thousand feet without supplemental oxygen. Jim decided that the first summit team would be Kop, George, and Cheese. Along with Lou and Kim they headed up to establish High Camp. The group had to break trail through knee-deep snow angled upward at thirty degrees. With their loads they moved at a pace of four breaths per step with many rests. Digging out a tent platform from the steepening ice at over twenty-seven thousand feet was exhausting. They took turns working until they were gasping, then passed the shovel on to the next climber. It required three hours to chop out space for a single two-man tent. All were too exhausted to stay at High Camp. Cheese, who had been the strongest and the hardest worker on the team, developed a wet cough at the end of the day. He worried that he might be developing high-altitude pulmonary edema and elected to drop back all the way down to Helmet Camp. Kop had a bad headache and decided to descend to Camp One. George felt exhausted and realized that he also could not continue without a rest.

Jim hastily reorganized summit plans. He moved Lou, Kim, and Carlos into the first try. George, Jay, Dan, Kop, and Andy were the new second team. Dave Coombs, Carl, Jim, and I would be the third summit team. It sounded great to me. I could use the extra day of rest that being on the third team would afford. Moreover, with two parties ahead of us we wouldn't have to break trail through deep snow, making it much easier for us. Finally, it was exactly the team I wanted. I liked the concept of a Tabin-Tobin summit team. Carl's razor-sharp wit, laid-back personality, and incredible strength made him a joy to climb with. Dave Coombs was as mentally tough as anyone I've ever met and the most safety-conscious member of our team, which is a great asset for an Everest summit partner. Jim was a person I admired greatly and with whom I would be honored to share the big day.

The plan was to rotate the three teams to the top in three days. We had two tents at twenty-five thousand feet and a two-man tent at High Camp. You can descend quickly from the High Camp to Camp Two by sliding on your butt in the snow, braking with an ice ax. The first team would go to High Camp, sleep without supplemental oxygen, and use their bottles to go for the top. They would then descend to the second camp, where the third team would have hot drinks waiting for them. Meanwhile, the second team would have moved to High Camp. The next day, team two would summit and descend to Camp Two, where the first team would take care of them. Meanwhile, the final team would move into position for a summit bid. On the third day my group would climb to the top of Mount Everest and descend as far as possible. An air of excitement engulfed us. In three days we would have either made it or failed.

On October 8 Carlos, Kim, and Lou set out for the summit of Mount Everest at two o'clock in the morning. George, Dan, Andy, Kop, and Jay headed for High Camp. Jim, Carl, Dave Coombs, and I set off for Camp Two. The first big news was that Andy had a sharp pain in his chest and a deep cough. Jim's diagnosis was an inflammation of the lining of the lungs. Andy headed down to base camp. Jim decided that as a doctor he had to stay with Andy and turned around. Next, Carl found that his toes were freezing and he could not warm them. He had developed frostbite in Alaska the previous winter and decided that the summit of Everest was not worth the risk for him, as he would surely lose his toes—and the frozen foot would add to the danger of a fall. Next, Coombs developed a terrible headache and was unable to hold down food. Worried that he was developing cerebral edema, he turned back.

My entire summit team had disintegrated on me. We all returned to Camp One. I was very upset and confused as to what to do. I felt good enough to go for the summit, but was afraid to try it alone. Then Cheese called on the radio to say that he was feeling healthy again and was keen to make a bid. Dave Cheesmond and I thus became the new third team. We planned to move to Camp Two, at twenty-five thousand feet, the next day. Meanwhile the weather remained perfect with a cloudless calm sky. Jay, Dan, and George reached High Camp feeling strong. We all eagerly awaited word from the first summit team. The second team reported that the snow was deep above camp. Trail breaking must have been exhausting for Kim, Carlos, and Lou.

At noon we got an excited radio call from our Chinese interpreter, Mr. Tsao, who was watching the progress from base camp via a high-powered telescope. "I see climbers on ridge! Climbers are on ridge!" he reported. This was at twenty-eight thousand feet where our route merged with the Southeast Ridge. The East Face had been climbed! Now we only needed to follow the ridge to the top. In the background on the radio we heard Tibetans chanting mantras for our success. The next message we heard was bizarre. "Seven climbers, seven climbers going to get them!" We had no idea what Tsao was talking about. We later learned that a Japanese team climbing the South Col route from Nepal met up with our team just below the South Summit at 28,500 feet. The Japanese were climbing without supplemental oxygen and soon fell behind our climbers.

The final climb to the South Summit was steeper and scarier than expected. The angle was more than forty-five degrees with a hard crust over sugar snow. It would have been impossible to self-arrest a fall. To save time and weight they were climbing unroped. Any slip would be fatal. Above the South Summit a heavily corniced knife-edged ridge led to the short vertical obstacle known as the Hillary Step. This thirty-foot wall was passed by strenuously bridging one foot on rock while kicking the other foot's crampon points into the ice. Finally, at two-thirty in the afternoon, twelve hours after starting out from High Camp, Kim's voice crackled on the radio, "We're on top of this fucker!"

Back at Camp One we whooped with joy and hugged all around. Kim, Carlos, and Lou walked the final steps to the top together. Kim was openly weeping on the top of the world. The three spent forty-five minutes in perfect sunshine and air calm enough to light a candle, enjoying the view and taking photographs. All three were out of supplemental oxygen when they cautiously headed down. They encountered the Japanese, still stumbling upward, at the South Summit. None of them had a pack. This meant that they did not have any extra clothing sleeping bags, water, or stoves for a bivouac. It was past four o'clock in the afternoon. Our team suggested that it was too late and that the Japanese should turn around. They shook their noticeably blue faces and continued upward. A Sherpa climbing with the Japanese then fell and started sliding ten feet above them. Lou looked directly into the terrified man's eyes as he tumbled past, missing Lou by only a few inches, before accelerating into a seven-thousand-foot drop into the Western Cwm. A few minutes later one of Lou's footholds gave way and he flipped upside down, suspended by only one foot punched through the hard crust in the snow. He hung unable to right himself, with just a couple of toes keeping him from falling off the mountain. If his foot had let go, he would have torpedoed seven thousand feet, headfirst, following the path of the Sherpa to certain death. Carlos climbed fifteen feet back up to help him. Badly shaken by the near fall and having watched the Sherpa perish, Lou and Carlos faced into the slope and backed slowly down the steep ice.

Kim continued descending alone, unaware of Lou's slip, and reached High Camp at six o'clock. He came down all the way to Camp One, joining me in my tent at 23,500 feet at eight o'clock. I had never seen a human being who looked so exhausted. His eyes were sunk back into his face and he was barely able to whisper. Meanwhile Carlos and Lou still had not returned to High Camp. Our team became progressively more anxious. Kim postulated that they may have opted to descend the easier route down to the South Col in Nepal and stay with the Japanese. We worried that they had fallen. Finally, at nine o'clock, George reported that they had staggered into High Camp. Six people were crammed into the tiny two-person tent; any movement by one person affected everyone else. Lou had terrible nightmares and coughed incessantly. Carlos had full-body muscle cramps and convulsions. No one got any sleep. Dan later said that, physically, the hardest part of his summit day was holding Carlos's arms and legs during the night:

At two o'clock in the morning, on October 9, George started brewing up, melting snow into water. At three-thirty he was set to go. Kopczynski had had a bad headache all night and felt it was getting worse. He was also concerned about Lou and Carlos going down alone. Kop volunteered to help them. Dan and Jay wavered a bit, then decided to go for the summit. Since the track had partially blown in, they decided that George should start out breaking trail; they would catch up. The wind picked up toward morning. After an hour George stopped and looked back. He saw no one behind him. He later wrote in his diary:

> Wind whips snow across my face. Can't even tell if I'm standing up straight. Complete vertigo! So alone! Have never felt such an alien environment, clearly a place where man was not meant to be. Why haven't Jay and Dan started? Storm is increasing—will just continue 'til it seems unreasonable.

Dan and Jay discussed what to do for a long time. When they finally decided to go for it, Dan found that the oxygen fogged his glasses, and they were delayed further as Dan struggled to clear his vision. Meanwhile, down at Camp One, I brewed up for Kim and enjoyed a celebratory breakfast of tinned cake and pudding. Jim Morrissey came over to our tent. He was elated at the teams success and said he now just wanted to see everyone safely off the mountain. Cheese joined us in great spirits, totally optimistic about our summit bid. "The track will be in, so we'll just walk up the steps. We'll have a perfect summit day, Geoff," he said. I was feeling great and very happy to have Dave as my summit partner. We headed up to the next camp carrying our oxygen bottles and personal gear. At Camp Two we had a great reunion with Lou and Carlos coming down. Both were wasted, but healthy. Kop was also feeling better. His headache was gone and he opted to join me and Cheese and go back up. This increased my confidence. Not only was Kop strong and safe, but he'd been to the top before. I only wished that Jim, who had also been powerful and fit, had decided to join us.

The wind increased in intensity as the morning wore on. Clouds began to build down in the valley and move up the mountain. Up high, George was continuing to climb solo and was finding very hard snow and a steeper slope than he expected. He climbed cautiously, because he knew that he could not self-arrest a fall. Then he saw a figure above. In his diary he wrote:

> He moves incredibly slowly, taking a few steps, then collapsing on his ice ax to rest. I am going up and he is coming down. Yet we are covering ground at about the same rate. I ask the Japanese climber if he is okay. He replies, "bivy," and points up. He is very blue and his motions uncoordinated. I have no rope to help him, so just pat him on the shoulder and continue.

Dan and Jay were now struggling up the lower slopes, finding that George's steps had already disappeared with the wind. Cheese, Kop, and I watched the weather carefully. Dave reassured me that the clouds were just down in the valley and conditions should hold for a few more days. I still worried about my own summit chances as I watched the mist slowly creep up the mountain.

The climbing steepened for George. Just below the South Summit he turned up the rate of his oxygen flow. At the South Summit he found a movie camera left by a Japanese climber the day before and wondered how many had had to bivouac. George moved onto the dramatic upper ridge and over the Hillary Step. He continued in his diary:

> Above the Hillary section is a steep bulge of snow. It feels awkward moving over it, especially since I can't see well with the mask and goggles. Immediately above is an ice ax sticking in the snow. Looking down I see scrape marks in the snow until they end at steep rock a few meters below. The realization hits that one of the Japanese died here yesterday. I push on, now just wanting to be finished.

George reached the summit just before ten o'clock in the morning. He spent half an hour surveying the view, turned up his oxygen, and started the descent. He picked up the Japanese ice ax for added security on the steep sections. At noon he met Jay and Dan just below the dangerous part. George told them about the Japanese and urged them to set a turnaround time. He recalled, "Dan says they will turn around by one-thirty. Knowing Dan does not give me any confidence in that prediction."

George stopped briefly at our top tent and left his extra oxygen. He also turned on his headlamp and left it suspended from the top of the tent in case Dan and Jay returned after dark. He then zipped down, stopping for a quick congratulatory hug and a brew at our camp, and reached Helmet Camp by four o'clock in the afternoon. I was very psyched by George's fast ascent. Our team had already achieved great success, and I began to believe that I would reach the top of Everest. Then, over the next two hours, the clouds continued to surge up the mountain and the wind began to whip the tent. I began to worry again about my summit chances.

George's footprints were already invisible outside our tent. Then the realization hit: Dan and Jay were still out there! The storm intensified into a whiteout blizzard as the sun set. "Death-Pact PercoDan" had not been on a mountain in two years. This was Jay's first trip to the Himalayas. Worry gave way to panic, made all the worse because there was nothing we could do. It would be impossible for anyone to survive a night out at this altitude, in this storm. Then, at nine o'clock, Dan and Jay came on the radio to say they had just returned to the High Camp tent.

They, of course, had ignored the turnaround time. Jay and Dan reached the summit at three-fifteen, out of supplemental oxygen. They stayed on top until four o'clock and started to descend, just as the storm hit them. For psychological support they look a small length of rope that Dan had carried and tied themselves together so that if one fell they both would die. Both where totally exhausted and disoriented in the blizzard. It was completely dark. Both were freezing. At eight o'clock they argued about where to go. Dan felt that they must have passed the tent and advocated going back up. Jay was too tired to ascend and insisted they must have lost the ridge and that they should move laterally. Then the storm abated for an instant and they saw a glimmer of a light beneath them. An hour of desperate struggle later they found the High Camp tent and crawled inside. George's headlamp battery had gone dead, but it lasted just long enough to help Jay and Dan survive.

Dawn on October 10 revealed the full fury of the mountain. The blizzard still raged. High winds and two feet of new, windblown snow made it difficult to move, and the avalanche danger was extreme. There was no question. We had to go down. Kop, Cheese, and I waited for Dan and Jay, then began breaking trail down to Helmet Camp. Jay's right hand had fingers black with frostbite, but he never complained. Dan was having trouble seeing because his glasses were becoming covered with snow, but he kept on smiling, even after he wandered off the trail and tumbled twenty feet, stopping only a few inches from a fatal drop. I descended the avalanche chute, tied Dan to a rope, and helped him out. We crawled, wet and miserable, into Helmet Camp after seven hours of hard work. The next day we rappelled down into the swirling tempest, having to dig out icy ropes that had frozen into the buttress. Forty scary times we slid down the slick ropes with freezing hands barely able to work the braking device. We were trying to bring all our gear and garbage off of the mountain with us, and it was difficult to balance the enormous loads. At the top of the

Bowling Alley I slipped, and my pack flipped me upside down. Spindrift avalanches swept over me. I couldn't breathe and couldn't untangle myself. Just as I started to drown, Dr. Dan returned my favor of the previous day and came back up a rope to save my life.

Eight hours later our entire team was reunited at advanced base camp. Everyone was safe. With the exception of Jay, who would lose a couple of fingertips to frostbite, all of us were healthy. Six Americans had reached the top of Mount Everest via the first ascent of the largest, steepest, and most difficult face on the mountain. The route we pioneered remains the most difficult on Mount Everest and has not been repeated in nearly twenty years. Many of the cognoscenti felt our route was too dangerous and too difficult, and that we had no chance for success. Doubts among our peers helped develop the cohesive bonds among us. We did it with a minimum of supplemental oxygen and no native support or porters on the climb. More importantly, we did it as a team of brothers who were all leaving the mountain as friends, bonded for life.

The Kid Who Climbed Everest

BEAR GRYLLS

This chapter from Bear Grylls book is titled *Alone,* and describes the author's final push to the summit, knowing full well the pitfalls that still lay ahead and with the possibility of deadly weather descending upon him. Grylls was a 21-year-old soldier in the British Army who was severely injured in a parachuting accident. Out of the army, he worked hard to rehabilitate his body, then decided to test himself on Everest. In becoming the youngest Briton ever to reach the summit. Grylls describes the difficulty breathing and moving in the Death Zone and begins to more fully understand why people climb. Preparing for his final ascent to the summit, he says, reverently, "I knew I had entered another world."

Alone

I threw the playing cards across the floor of my tent in frustration. It was a stupid game anyway; I hated Patience. Two days ago I decided that if I got all my cards "out," then the weather would give me a chance—if I didn't then the typhoon would move in. I had lost, so made the contest the best of three. Two days later it was 37–38 to me in the lead, but victory still just eluded me. I lay back down and just stared at the roof of the tent. My socks swayed gently as they dried on the string, slung across the poles. I flicked them impatiently.

These past few days had been the longest days I had known. My watch seemed to have slowed down, and the monsoon drew ever closer to the mountain, beckoning in the time when Everest would be buried again under five feet of snow.

My days revolved around the midday radio call from Base Camp, when they would give me the forecast. The call was scheduled daily for 12 noon. Keeping it to certain times saved battery power, and batteries were crucial. I always slept with them down my sleeping bag. It was the warmest place for them and where they would last the longest. I waited anxiously for the forecast today. It was only 9:15 A.M. and already I was fiddling with the radio; checking the squelch just in case.

I desperately longed for news that the typhoon would move away. Yesterday it was reported to be stationary. Today would be vital. I waited anxiously. I knew that we were running out of that precious commodity: time. I checked my watch again.

At 12:02 P.M. the radio came to life.

"Bear at Camp two, it's Neil. All okay?" I heard the voice loud and clear; the reception was good today.

"Yeah, I'm all right," I replied.

"I'm worried you may be going slowly insane up there, am I right?" Neil joked.

"Insane? What do you mean? Mooooo," I grunted in my gorilla voice. Neil chuckled into the radio.

"Daft," he replied. "Now listen, I've got a forecast and an e-mail that has come through for you—from your family. Do you want to hear the good or the bad news first?"

"Go on, let's get the bad news over with," I replied.

"Right, the bad news. Well, the weather's still shit. The typhoon is on the move and heading this way. If it is still on course tomorrow you've got to get down. I'm sorry. We all hate it."

He had said it straight. I paused before replying. I knew he would say something like that. I had prayed so hard, yet it hadn't worked. I shook my head.

". . . and the good news?" I asked dismissively.

"Your Mum has sent a message. Says all the animals are well." Click.

"Well, go on, that can't be it. What else?"

"Well, they think you're still at Base Camp. Probably best that way, you know. Otherwise your mother may just suddenly turn up," Neil chuckled.

"I'll speak to you tomorrow," I replied. "Pray for some change. It will be our last chance, eh?"

"Roger that, Bear . . . oh, and don't start talking to yourself. Out."

"How's Miguel getting along . . . Hello, Neil." He hadn't heard me.

I dismantled the radio and put the batteries down my bag again. I had another twenty-four hours to wait. It was these moments just after the radio call which felt the longest. I lay back down and shuffled the cards once more.

That afternoon I walked for twenty minutes up the glacier to the Singaporean Camp Two. I wanted to see if I could borrow some cough medicine. I had finished all mine but still I was being kept up most of the night heaving and spluttering. I wondered who would be in their camp.

Only a few Singaporeans remained now at Camp Two. The rest had returned to Base Camp some days ago, after their summit bid had failed that fateful night that Mick had fallen. The two who were still here undid their tent flap. One of them was the leader of the team. We sat and chatted for a while. It was good to have company.

"No, Bear, I'm not going any higher, it's my ribs. They're screwed," the leader said. "It's all this coughing. I've managed to actually crack two ribs, I've been coughing so hard. It hurts to breathe. It won't let me go any higher."

I sympathized with him as I coughed hard into my jacket sleeve. My own ribs were taking their own pounding up here. I asked if they had any extra cough medicine.

They produced a vat, the size of about four water bottles. Across the front in felt-tip was written "cough medicine." My eyes lit up. I had been swilling my cough medicine from a tiny pot, the size of a shot-glass. It had made no difference. I filled a big mug full, chatted a bit more then shuffled carefully back down to my own tent. This should cure me, I thought, I mean, just look at the color of it. It reminded me of diesel oil, but it should do. I took a giant swig and smiled as it soothed the inflamed back of my throat.

As I wrestled with life and solitude at 21,200 feet up the mountain, back in England at Mick's parents' home all was very different.

Mick's father had been following the team's progress closely on the internet, from his office. Various other teams were keeping their web sites updated daily, and by the time of the summit attempt a few days earlier they were updating almost hourly. Such was the advance of the Americans' communication that during the confusion everyone had encountered at the South Summit (at 10:00 A.M. on 19 May), Mick's father, Patrick, was receiving live reports on their progress. He knew his son was up there at the same time and shared in the disappointment when he heard they were being forced back, having got so close. Nothing, though, prepared him for what he heard next.

An American report came through saying that a "British climber had fallen," nothing else was known. The words flashed up on Patrick's screen. He stared in horror. It was 8:45 A.M. in the City, the heart of London.

For the next three days he heard nothing more on the incident. Why? What had happened? Couldn't they say? Had someone died? Was it Mick? His mind raced with the possibility, the strong possibility, that the "British climber" reported to have fallen might have been Mick. Our satellite phone was switched off at Base Camp. Everyone there was too busy trying to get Neil and Mick off the mountain safely. Patrick could get no more news.

He dared not tell his wife, Sally. He couldn't. He describes those days and nights as the most "agonizing experience imaginable." He is a man of great strength but even he was shaken. He recounts: "What was so hard was not being able to share it with Sally. I couldn't, as I didn't know for certain. I couldn't work, sitting there, looking at the screen in front of me, the screen that had given me the news originally—it made me feel sick. I dreaded facing the reality. The possibility that our only son was dead."

It was not until Mick eventually returned to Base Camp that he was able to ring his father and tell him he was safe. Mick had had no idea that Patrick knew anything about it. Relief swept across his father's face. A relief that only a father, I guess, can know. Mick assured him all was okay, and announced that he would not return again up the mountain. Ever. He knew only too well how lucky he had been. He took off his Everest crampons for the very last time. He thought of me still up at Camp Two, and looked knowingly up the mountain.

Meanwhile, some 3,700 feet above Base Camp, I waited for that next and final forecast, longing with all my heart for a chance. That chance was now in the hands of the weather.

That night in my tent I could hear the deep rumble of the jet-stream winds above me. The sun had disappeared down beyond the bottom end of the Western Cwm. It left me all alone. I curled tight inside my bag and closed my eyes. I really missed the others.

I crept out of my tent long before dawn. The glacier looked cold and hostile as it swept away to the west. I zipped my down jacket up and stumbled across the ice to have a crap. It was 4:30 A.M. I waited for the sun to rise while sitting in the porch of my tent and wondered what it would bring today.

Thengha and Ang were still asleep in their tent. I wished that I was also.

I couldn't believe that all the work we had done so far, boiled down to today. I prayed for the umpteenth time, for that answer to my prayers. The typhoon had to move or peter out. It had to. My mind wandered to being up there; up there climbing in that deathly land above Camp Three. That land where, as I had read, only the "strong and lucky survive." Please. I dozed off dreaming about it.

By ten o'clock I was ready on the radio. I rechecked the strength of the batteries. They were nice and warm. I looked at my watch again. Come on.

This time they called early. It was 11:58 A.M. I jumped for the set.

"Yep, Base Camp, I've got you," I said anxiously.

"Bear you dog, It's come." The voice was excited. It was Henry speaking.

"The forecast has said that at 11:00 P.M. last night the cyclone began revolving, and has spun off to the east. They think it will clip the Eastern Himalaya tomorrow, but nowhere near here. We've got a break. They say that the jet-stream winds are lifting again in two days. How do you think you feel?"

"We're rocking, yep, good, I mean fine . . . I can't believe it. Alrighty." I punched the air and yelped. Thengba came scurrying across to my tent and peered in inquisitively. I howled again. Thengba grinned and climbed in. I couldn't stop patting him violently on the back. He laughed out loud, showing all his two black teeth. He kind of understood. It had been a long five days.

Neil was already preparing at Base Camp to come back up. Another chance had suddenly opened and he had to take it. It might be his last attempt ever. He had openly said that if he was turned back this year as well, he would never return. Already he had climbed to 28,500 feet and now only a few days later he was preparing to go up again. It was unheard of. People said that his body would not be able to cope. They didn't know, though, what was going on inside him. Just one last attempt. My last one, he thought. And this time something excited him more than ever before.

Mick was staying firmly at Base Camp. He was still in shock. He needed rest. He helped Geoffrey and Neil pack up one final time. If this failed we all knew our attempt was over. The monsoon hovered down in the Nepalese plains, awaiting its grand entrance. In one week's time, we knew it would all be over.

During the course of the day, both the depleted Singapore team and Bernardo had left camp Two towards Camp Three. It meant that they would be a day ahead of us in the attempt. This was good. They would have valuable information on the conditions above the South Col. I prayed that they would be safe. Those of us still on the mountain were a small group now.

By 7:00 P.M. that evening, Camp Two was again full of friends. Neil and Geoffrey were there along with Michael and Graham, both now recovered from their illness. Carla and Allen had also come back up for a second attempt. The weariness of trying again showed dreadfully in Carla. Her body was crying out for relief. She looked understandably gaunt and frail. Allen took two hours longer than everyone else to arrive. The fatigue was showing in him as well.

The Lhotse team were also back. Andy and Ilgvar would try once more. Nasu, alternatively, had decided to leave Base Camp the day before to return to Kathmandu. I wouldn't see him again now. He believed he had actually reached the summit of Lhotse on the first ascent, as he was ahead of the other two. Andy didn't really believe this. He knew that the summit had been still too far away. An air of doubt hung around it all; but no one would ever really know.

I was so relieved to see Neil arrive at Camp Two. He smiled and we hugged. We both knew the chance that was ahead of us—words weren't needed. I had missed him especially.

Darkness came quickly or maybe time just seemed to race by, now that others were here. It was funny how the minutes had crept by so slowly for almost nine weeks in total. Nine weeks I had waited for this chance. And now that it was here, the minutes didn't seem to be able to go slowly enough. Despite the excitement, part of me dreaded what lay before us. In less than ten hours, the struggle would begin. I knew the next four days, God willing, to the summit and back to Camp Two, would be undoubtedly the hardest of my life. But there was a purpose to it. At its end was my dream that I had held on to for so long. The summit of Everest, I felt, was waiting for us.

I shared my tent that had been all mine for so long with Michael, the Canadian. As I had got to know him over the past two months I had come to like him a lot. He had a tenderness under his outdoor rugged image that I couldn't help but warm to. He was as scared as I was. I could tell.

He busied himself nervously in the tent; sorting out his kit, rechecking each item meticulously. Counting glucose tablets, checking the length of straps for water bottles that would hang round our necks (the best place to stop them freezing), checking the simple things which are always the first to go wrong: spare gloves, spare goggles, tape, blister kit, ready-tied prussik knots for emergency rope work, you name it, it all came out and was checked. It took our minds off things.

We shifted around tentatively, trying to give each other some room. I knew Michael needed space to be alone before it all started, we all needed it, but we had to try and cope with what we had. I understood. I tried to quietly rest as he sorted his things out. I lay back on my rucksack and closed my eyes. I felt that mixture of fierce excitement and deep trepidation. I couldn't quite believe what now lay before us.

The words that my grandfather had written to me in one of the letters that Ed had brought when he arrived, rang in my head. They were powerful words to me. At ninety-two years old, he had a wisdom that cut right to my core.

"Keep on in there, your struggles are a triumph for guts and Godliness."

The words guts and Godliness struck me hard. It was all that I aspired to. I knew somehow my grandfather understood me.

That night we tried desperately to sleep. From 5:00 A.M. the next day, the biggest battle of my life would begin. I found it hard to even pray.

Michael and I shuffled nervously all night. I peed at least four times. Michael chuckled as I rolled over with my pee-bottle and filled it again.

At 4:45 A.M. I started to get ready. It was invariably always the worst time; the time when you felt warm and cozy and were trying to shake the heaviness from your eyes. By 5:15 A.M. I crawled out of our tent and breathed deeply in the morning chill. It would allow Michael some space to get ready.

We tried to eat some porridge oats with hot water. I added masses of sugar to try and make it taste a bit better, but still could only manage a few gulps. My mind was elsewhere. I was worried that so long up here would have made me weak, that my body would be drained from living at Camp Two, and would have used up my vital reserves. But I had to be strong enough now; I knew that I would soon find out.

At 5:45 A.M. we all met on the ice and sat in silence as we put our crampons on. I had done this so many times in the last two months, yet this morning it felt like my first time. As we started off, leaving Ang and Thengba watching from their tent, I hoped with all my heart to see them safely again four days later. Much would have happened for better or for worse by then. The glacier ahead of us leading up to the Bergschrund and the Lhotse face seemed eerily still. I felt a mild sickness inside. It was nerves.

My cough was still there but irritated me less now, or maybe I was just used to it; resigned to the discomfort. The angle steepened as we neared the ropes of the ice above us. The Lhotse Face loomed away far above.

In silence we started up towards Camp Three. I hoped it wouldn't take as long as last time. I hoped to be able to reach it in around five hours.

By 10:00 A.M. we were well into the climb. We moved methodically and carefully up the blue ice. It crunched, then splintered beneath our crampons as they gripped firmly with each step we took. I leant back on my harness and reached into my wind suit. I pulled out several glucose tablets. They tasted sweet in my dry mouth. I swigged at the water bottle that hung around my neck and looked around.

Five and a half hours of climbing, and the tents were only 100 feet away. It still took twenty-five minutes to reach them. I climbed with Graham. We were both slow and tired. It showed with him especially. He swore under his breath. It was all taking so long. I tried to keep patient and just keep moving slowly, you would eventually reach your destination. It is just that the process hurt so much.

We collapsed into two tents. Neil, Graham, Michael and I in one, Geoffrey, Carla and Allen in the other. We settled down to the odious task of trying to melt ice. The gas stove had blocked again; frozen solid. I undid it, rubbed it, and put it back together. The flame flickered and then lit.

I thought of my ice axe buried under the ice outside the tent. I had known that it would be impossible to retrieve; Mick had told me so. I had borrowed an axe instead from Pascuale,★ an American climber on the mountain. I had picked up his spare axe the day before from Camp Two, assuring him jokingly over the radio that I would stay alive to return it. He made me promise. He was a friend and knew the risk up there. "Be careful" had been his last words to me.

Up in the tents at Camp Three we tried to get on with things quietly. Living in these close quarters, under pressure, when you are scared, tired and thirsty, is a sensitive business. My time in the Army had helped me in learning how to live with people in confined spaces like this. I had spent enough cold nights in a patrol huddled together waiting for dawn. This was much the same—only a little higher! I needed this training now as we settled down for the night, squeezed in the tent, tucked into the ledge in the ice here at 24,500 feet. The other thing the Army had taught me was about going that extra mile. About pushing yourself that little bit more, and how the finish is always just after the point at which you most want to give up. I reminded myself of this as I lay cramped between all the kit and stinking bodies. I would need that discipline more than ever before now. That extra mile; that little bit further.

Carla, despite our advice to the contrary, had insisted on coming up with us to Camp Three. Henry at Base Camp had refused to allow her up. He knew that she was too tired. She had given her word that she would only go up with us from Camp Three if the winds died down. Henry knew that in anything but perfect conditions she would not survive. Her body was completely drained after her first attempt. The forecast would be given to us at 6:00 P.M. at Camp Three; it would decide Carla's fate. If the winds higher up were above 40 knots, she would have to turn back.

The radio crackled with the voice of Henry from Base Camp.

"The winds are going to be rising, buys. You've still got a window, but the conditions are far, far from ideal. I'm sorry, Carla, but you are going to have to come down. I can't risk you up there. It's too dangerous," Henry announced. There was a long pause.

"No way, no way. I'm going up. I don't care. I'm going up," Carla retorted angrily. "You can't make me come down. Not after I've come so far."

Henry erupted down the radio. "Carla, listen, we had a deal. If the winds were strong you would come down. I didn't even want you up there but you insisted, but now the ride ends. We had a deal and you come down. That's the end of it." He was worried having her loose up there.

She burst into tears, shouting in Spanish at him. I felt for her like never

---

★Pascuale Scaturro successfully reached the summit of Mount Everest late in May 1998.

before. She had given so much for this chance. And now, this close, she was being forced back. I knew what she must be feeling. I would be the same. But Henry was right, she wouldn't make it in the winds up there. It wasn't her fault; she had used her strength on the first attempt. She didn't have that same strength now. It had taken her three hours more than us to reach Camp Three. If she was slow like that higher up, she would die. We all knew this and tried to comfort her in the tent.

It slowly dawned on her that she would go no further. Her dream was ending here and it hurt. She was one of the most determined women I had ever met, and the grief now showed all over her face. She sobbed quietly to herself in front of us. She knew secretly that it was the right decision.

We sat for the best part of an hour in silence. I noticed that my headache had now returned for the first time in ten days. I cursed it and tried to drink some more of the disgusting, lukewarm water in my bottle. I longed for something cool to drink; I swallowed an aspirin.

Geoffrey and I were the first to leave Camp Three. We wanted to leave at different intervals to avoid any delays on the ropes. At 5:45 A.M. the two of us climbed out of the tent and began fixing our oxygen masks. It would be our first time on the mountain breathing supplementary oxygen. We had experimented in breathing the oxygen at Base Camp, but never under extreme exertion and never so high up; I wondered what difference it would make.

We squeezed a large tank into our rucksacks, fitted the regulator and made sure the lead was free and the gauge not caught up in any straps. I hoisted the rucksack onto my back and tried to make it comfortable. It weighed me down and sat awkwardly on my shoulders. It felt four times as heavy as it had when we were testing it at Base Camp; and even then it had been an effort to lift. I shuffled again. It felt a little better.

The balance between the effort needed to carry the heavy tanks and the benefit the oxygen gives, is a constant debate. The conclusion generally is that the benefit of the oxygen outweighs the weight, but not by much. The air above this height now becomes so thin that it is almost impossible to live. Only a very few exceptional and physiologically different people can climb free of supplementary oxygen above here. Even the majority of Sherpas use oxygen high on Everest.

The tanks form what is known as an "open system," where the regulator allows a small trickle of oxygen to flow through the mask. This amount can be adjusted to give between 1 and 4 liters of oxygen a minute. This combines with the normal air you are breathing to marginally boost the level of oxygen inhaled. But not by much. The body needs to breathe about thirty liters of air a minute during extreme exertion; if you used a closed system, of breathing compressed air, the tank would last minutes. It would be impossible to do, as you can only realistically carry one or two tanks at the most. The "open system" therefore is the only real method of using supplementary oxygen up high. A trickle of oxygen mixed with normal air is all this provides.

Generally we would climb on 2.5 liters a minute. This was deemed the most efficient rate. But even this, at these extreme heights, was hardly enough to stay alive, let alone moving at any pace. But as they say, "it is just enough to do the stuff." But there was no scope for mistakes in this. The majority of the bodies we would encounter up above Camp Four had died because of one thing: not enough oxygen. Their bodies had slowly suffocated to death, and the lack of oxygen in their brains made them hardly even aware of what was happening.

I double-checked that the tubes were free and not snagged up. I checked the tubes were soft and that no condensation had frozen inside them. I checked my mask was tight around my face, then carried out the same procedure with Geoffrey. Our eyes caught each other through our goggles and we knew it was time to start across to the first rope that would lead on and up the Lhotse Face, towards Camp Four, somewhere far above us.

Within ten yards though I felt as if I was choking on my mask. I didn't seem to be getting any air from it. It was suffocating me. I ripped it from my face gasping frantically. I hung on my harness from the Face, tubes and connections wrapped round me in a chaotic jumble. This is crazy, I thought. I tried to untangle myself. My mask swung freely beneath me. I found that I had to remove my entire pack to free everything before trying again. I checked the air-bubble gauge that told me that oxygen was flowing. It read positive. I refitted the mask and carried on.

Five minutes later, nothing seemed to have changed. "For fuck's sake," I swore in a muffled cry, as I tried to gulp air through my mask once more. I could hardly breathe with it on. I found myself throwing my head back to get a deeper breath, but still I felt stifled by the mask. I tried to keep going but couldn't. I stopped again and tore it from my face, gulping in the outside air.

It was working; everything said that it was working. I couldn't understand it. It felt as if I was trying to run a marathon uphill, with a pair of rugby socks stuck in my mouth. I was gasping without getting relief. Geoffrey stopped behind me, leaning over his axe. He was also struggling. He didn't even look up. We were both lost in our own worlds; trying desperately to breathe.

I replaced my mask, determined to get used to it. I knew I had to trust it. I had been told over and over to trust it. The only place that I would get life from up here was the Russian fighter pilot's mask that covered my face. I had no choice but to keep it on.

I continued on up, slowly but methodically, I was not going to take my mask off again. I tried to ignore the pain. The rope stretched away above me, straight up the Face.

An hour later Geoffrey was some way behind, but I kept plodding on, three steps at a time. The ice crunched away beneath me.

Eventually the route started to traverse across the Face. Away to my right it soared upwards to the summit of Lhotse far above. To my left the ice fell at an alarming angle straight down to the Western Cwm, 4,000 feet below. It shimmered menacingly as the sun that was now rising glistened on its blue veneer. I couldn't afford a mistake up here now. I tried to stop my eyes looking down, and focused on the ice in front of my feet. Slowly I began to cross the Face towards the rock band that divided the Face in two.

The Yellow Band, as it is known, is a 150-feet high stretch of sedimentary sandstone rock that was once the seabed of the ancient Tethys Sea. As Gondwanaland and Asia had collided, the rock was driven up into the sky. Millions of years later here I was traversing towards it, now only some 4,000 feet beneath the highest point on our planet. It seemed somehow surreal, as the Band loomed closer to my left.

At its foot, I clipped on securely to the rope that the Sherpas had fixed only two weeks earlier. I hoped it was secure; it was all the protection that I had up here now.

I glanced up and could see the sandy, yellow rock rising into the wispy clouds that were now hovering over the Face. I knew that once over this, Camp Four was only a few hours away.

My crampons grated eerily as they met rock for the first time on the climb. They made a screeching noise as they scraped across it. They found it hard to grip, and would only hold when they snagged on a lip in the rock. Leaning back and out from the rock, I rested on my harness. The rock and ice seemed to sweep away below as the Face above steepened.

I turned outwards and tried to sit against the rock, with my crampons jammed into a small crevice beneath me. I leant back, desperately trying to get oxygen into my body, sucking violently into the mask. As my breathing calmed down I looked at where I had crossed. Camp Two was now but a tiny speck in the hazy distance below. I remembered how I had sat there and watched Mick and Neil climbing up where I was now. I checked my karabiner once again on the rope.

As I cleared the steep Yellow Band, the route leveled out into a gentle traverse for 500 meters. At the end of that was the Geneva Spur that would lead up to Camp Four. My body began to feel the excitement again.

The Geneva Spur was named by the Swiss expedition in 1952, the year preceding Hillary and Tenzing's epic first ascent. It is an anvil-shaped black rib of rock that lunges out from the ice. It rises steeply up to the edge of the South Col, the small saddle that sits between the two great peaks of Lhotse and Everest. The Geneva Spur forms the last major hurdle before the Col, the place of our final camp.

There was a stunning simplicity in what I was doing. My mind was entirely focused on every move I made; nothing else clogged my thoughts. It is this straight simplicity that I knew drew men and women to climb. Man is living his utmost, straining everything towards one single purpose. It made me feel alive.

I would aim to reach a point in the ice just in front of me with each bound I took, but invariably I would be forced to stop short; my body needed to rest and get oxygen. I would lean on my axe and stare at the point a few yards in front that had eluded me, then start moving again, determined to reach it in the next bound. In this manner I slowly approached the Geneva Spur.

I passed the point where the Lhotse route led. Up above I could see the tent where Andy and Ilgvar had rested yesterday afternoon, before their summit attempt. Far above that, I could see the tiny specks which were them struggling up for the summit. They still had a long climb ahead of them, I prayed that they would make it, and kept shuffling along.

As I started up the Geneva Spur I could see Geoffrey below and far behind me. He seemed to be moving better now. I wanted to keep in front and pushed on. Behind him I could see the figures of the others below, Neil, Allen and Michael, moving slowly across to the Yellow Band. Carla would be on her descent now. I didn't know whether I envied her or felt sorry for her. I pushed the thought from my mind.

I climbed steadily up the Spur and an hour later found myself resting just beneath the lip. The Col awaited me over the top. I knew this, and longed to see the place I had heard and read so much about. The highest camp in the world at 26,000 feet, deep in the Death Zone.

I hated the term "Death Zone," it conjured up images that I knew were all too real up here. Mountaineers are renowned for playing things down, yet it had been mountaineers who had coined the phrase. I didn't like that.

It would be my first time in the infamous Death Zone. I wouldn't have time now to worry about how my body would cope. For me, this was my chance.

As I pulled the last few steps over the top of the Spur, the gradient fell away to reveal a dark shingly rock plateau. As I swiveled slowly on my crampons, they grated against the slate under them. I swore I could see all of Nepal below. I sat, stunned and alone. Slowly, blanket cloud began moving in beneath me, obscuring the lower faces of the mountain. Above these, a horizon of dark blue sky lay panned out before me. I knew I had entered another world.

Women On High

REBECCA A. BROWN

In *Women on High,* Rebecca A. Brown profiles a group of early women mountaineers, many of whom climbed in anonymity in an earlier time. This chapter profiles London-born Elizabeth Le Blond, who lived from 1861 to 1934, and became a prominent mountain climber in the 1880s. In August of 1883, for example, Le Blond completed a 43-hour epic climb of the Matterhorn with a treacherous descent on the Italian side of the mountain. Brown's profile explores the motivations of these early women climbers who were often criticized for participating in a sport then considered by many as unladylike.

lizabeth Le Blond's early life gave little hint that she'd become an expert climber, a pioneer of winter mountaineering, a respected Alpine photographer, a prolific author of mountaineering literature, and a founder and first president of the Ladies Alpine Club. Because of her accomplishments, her leadership in the field, and her public persona, when people thought about "lady climbers" in the last two decades of the nineteenth century, it's a good bet they thought of her.

Elizabeth was one of those "characters" of the late Victorian age that upper-class British society seemed to breed. Because of her social standing and wealth, she possessed the ability to follow her own path. But she also possessed tremendous self-confidence, curiosity, and a great sense of adventure that aided her not only in climbing mountains, but in other unusual pursuits during her life as well. Her privileged background also belied her ability and willingness to withstand the physical discomforts of mountaineering. As Alpine historian Claire Engel suggested, "She was a typical Victorian lady with a certain amount of eccentricity toned down by beautiful manners and mental poise, which allowed her to do very daring things in such a way that they seemed quite normal."

Le Blond rode a bicycle through France and Italy before most people had ever seen such a contraption. She was also a superb ice skater and the first woman to insist on taking, and then pass, the so-called men's test of expertise by the prestigious St. Moritz Skating Club. She loved what today we'd call adventure travel and made long and arduous journeys all over the world in the years just before and after World War I. Her autobiography starts with the statement, "All my life I have been fortunate in meeting interesting people, visiting interesting places, taking part in interesting events and never knowing what it meant to be bored."

Born into the heart of proper English society in 1861, Elizabeth grew up at a family estate in Ireland with frequent visits to London. She was the only child of a family listing aristocratic lineage all over Europe and was eleven when her soldier father died. In 1878 when she entered London society as a delicate and pretty seventeen-year-old she caught the eye of a distinguished man two decades her senior, a soldier like her father. He was Col. Fred Burnaby, a powerfully built, impressively tall British army officer whom Elizabeth considered a "man of the world." They married, and the following year she gave birth to a son, Arthur St. Vincent Burnaby. Later, her grandmother assumed care of the young child while Elizabeth pursued her peripatetic interests. On January 17, 1885, Elizabeth was widowed for the first time when Colonel Burnaby died in the Egyptian battle of Abu Klea. After this she lived almost entirely in Switzerland and married twice more, first to D. F Main, who died in 1892 and whom she did not mention in her autobiography, and then to Aubrey Le Blond, who outlived her. Le Blond was a porcelain expert who eventually donated his collection to the Victoria and Albert Museum. With him she traveled across Asia on the Tran-Siberian Railway in the years before World War I.

Elizabeth climbed and wrote as Mrs. Burnaby and Mrs. Main, but is most commonly remembered as Mrs. Aubrey Le Blond. While none of her three husbands shared her passion for climbing, the lack of familial companions never deterred her from pursuing her interests. She brushed off the presumption that she needed such "protection," much to the consternation of some of her relatives.

Ironically, Elizabeth's path to mountaineering started with her family's concerns for her health. Like many who suffered from consumption, or tuberculosis, Elizabeth was sent to Switzerland and France for the restorative powers of clean mountain air. She first traveled there around 1880. Until then the closest she had come to mountains was as a young girl listening to her mother read from *Scrambles Amongst the Alps*, by the British climber Edward Whymper. "As for mountaineering," she admitted, "I knew nothing and cared less." Indeed, when she first saw the Jungfrau, it struck her as "nothing more than a far-off vision of glittering snows on which none but the foot of folly could ever wish to tread." Like many others in the aftermath of the Matterhorn disaster and subsequent deaths in the mountains, she condemned the "wickedness" of climbers "who risked their lives 'for nothing.' "

Nonetheless, the Alpine landscape began exercising a profound effect. Elizabeth found walks in the stunning countryside both invigorating and inspiring, and as she grew stronger and climbed higher, the peaks stirred a taste for adventure. Apparently with her son in family care back in England, and her husband off on military maneuvers, in 1881 she and three friends started engaging guides to take them to the ordinary tourist attractions such as the Mer de Glace, the spectacular glacier near Mont Blanc. Then playing to their "youthful vanity and enthusiasm," the guides started urging more ambitious expeditions. Over the next two summers she climbed rocks, crossed glaciers, and otherwise went far beyond ordinary walks. And while young female walking tourists were common enough at that time, those with aspirations for more aggressive climbing finally had a celebrated role model. Years later, Elizabeth acknowledged she owed her start to the example provided by Lucy Walker.

Yet climbing mountains, no matter how propitious for her health, and despite the increasing number of women practicing it, was not met with hearty approval back home. When word of her activity reached relatives, alarm rang through the great halls of the country estates of Elizabeth's extended family. Particularly outrageous was her practice of going off "alone" with her guides and spending nights in Alpine huts and bivouacs. Most offended by this unlady-like behavior was her elderly great aunt, who still possessed the early Victorian belief that a young woman must be chaperoned by a family member, preferably male, at all times. Interestingly, Elizabeth's mother intervened for her.

"I owe a supreme debt of gratitude to the mountains for knocking from me the shackles of conventionality," Elizabeth later wrote, "but I had to struggle hard for my freedom. My mother faced the music on my behalf when my grand-aunt, Lady Bentnick, sent out a frantic S.O.S. 'Stop her climbing mountains! She is scandalizing all London and looks like a Red Indian!'" Elizabeth ignored the aunt's directive. She didn't stop climbing, and unlike women who were horrified at the mere thought of losing their fair complexions (and looking like a "Red Indian!"), she considered her sunburned face a badge of courage and adventure earned as a mountaineer.

But Elizabeth didn't completely leave convention behind, either. She always enjoyed the privileges of her class, and as she started her climbing career she took along its actual accoutrements, such as her personal maid. The story of her initial steps on Mont Blanc reveals both her start in mountaineering as well as her dawning realization that some upper-class habits could be a hindrance.

During the summer of 1882 she and her friends flirted with the idea of going up Mont Blanc, but the mountain's size and reputation intimidated them. Their misgivings seemed justified when they met a young woman just down from the Grand Mulets, the dramatic rock buttresses about halfway up. Enthralled by her bravery, they asked her how she felt after such an adventure. She was happy to have climbed that high, she told them, but she'd "never do it again."

"More than ever impressed, we felt sure that the Grand Mulets was not for the likes of us," Elizabeth acknowledged. But their guides had another plan. They suggested a shorter walk about a quarter of the way up the mountain. The four young women were game, so wearing their usual high-buttoned boots and shady hats, they set out, following a rocky path past the treeline and leading between the mountain's great glaciers. They lunched at a little restaurant looking out over the valley. Then, alpenstocks in hand, they trudged up a steep and winding path right to the edge of the glacier.

As they approached the ice, they met climbers coming down with ice axes and rope—and "other thrilling accessories of an expedition to the summit of Mont Blanc," Elizabeth noticed. The guides for this other group asked if the four women were on their way to the Grand Mulets. Their query thrilled Elizabeth with its inference that her group was actually a climbing party. "We hadn't supposed anything of the kind, but at that same moment at least two of us began to suppose very hard indeed," she recalled. Conveniently, their guides "happened" to have ropes, she noted happily, and agreed to lead them "up there." For Elizabeth, at least, any lingering feelings of intimidation vanished in a rush of adrenaline. "By this time 'up there' was the one place in the world we were determined to go," she recalled. Not sharing her determination, however, two others in her group turned back. She and her remaining friend tied in to the rope and were soon clambering up and down among the séracs and crawling over ladders bridging the biggest crevasses. When they reached the hut at the Grand Mulets they assessed their condition. "Our boots were pulp, our stockings wet sponges, our skirts sodden," Elizabeth reported.

But the guides had brought along dry clothes, including enormous felt slippers. Wearing these, the two young women climbed to the top of a rock pinnacle and enjoyed a dramatic sunset. Coming down from their perch flush with the day's accomplishments, they begged their guides to take them the rest of the way to the summit the following day. The guides refused, pointing out the necessity of proper footwear and clothing. The next morning when she reached for her boots, Elizabeth appreciated the wisdom of their advice. She could tell from their shriveled condition the boots would never survive a climb up the rest of the mountain. She also experienced a minor epiphany. For the first time in her life she faced putting on her own boots; she wasn't even sure which shoe went on which foot. Her maid had always seen to such mundane tasks.

Although it probably occurred to Elizabeth that if she was serious about mountain climbing she'd have to go without some of the conveniences of home, for several years afterward she insisted that her maid accompany her on mountain trips. These young women didn't have an easy time following in their mistress's footsteps. On a late-autumn expedition in the Italian Alps, for instance, her maid fainted and suffered frostbitten hands. Like a piece of luggage, she was carried down the mountain on a guide's back. Eventually Elizabeth realized she could do things for herself and dispensed with the maid. She considered this step a form of "independence" and part of breaking the "shackles of conventionality." Besides, she viewed her maids as providing as much frustration as assistance. "One of the species had incessant hysteria whenever I returned late from an expedition," she wrote. Another eloped with a courier.

After returning from her first foray up Mont Blanc, Elizabeth outfitted herself with proper mountaineering apparel and began climbing in earnest. By summer's end she twice reached the summit of Mont Blanc. She also climbed the rugged Grandes Jorasses, the second highest peak in the Mont Blanc massif.

The Grandes Jorasses excursion showed Elizabeth the importance of being prepared for all contingencies in the mountains, for a planned one-day climb lengthened into an overnight ordeal. And the story of this climb demonstrates that even early in her climbing career, she possessed a great deal of physical and mental toughness. After a long and difficult day reaching the summit, she and her two guides were still high on the Grandes Jorasses when darkness fell. They hadn't brought lanterns or extra food, but the guides deemed continuing in the dark too risky. Without any other type of shelter they dug into the snow and spent the night huddled together in their impromptu bivouac, Elizabeth wrapped only in a red Indian shawl.

What must have been an uncomfortable and even nerve-racking experience didn't deter her from her growing passion for climbing mountains. Indeed, several weeks later, after she'd left Chamonix to spend fall and winter in Montreux on Lake Geneva, the mountains kept calling her back. "Six weeks of damp . . . proved too much for me," she wrote, explaining her return to Chamonix, "in spite of kindly warnings against ten feet of snow, starvation, isolation, dullness and many other evils." With a lack of other interesting diversions, she started winter expeditions.

In more than two decades of mountaineering Elizabeth compiled an impressive list of more than one hundred ascents. Her first important contribution, and her true place as a mountaineering pioneer, is in winter mountaineering. In her initial season she racked up several first ascents. One of her failures, in the sense of not making the summit, was her attempt on the Monte Rosa in March 1883. But the venture illustrated both her matter-of-fact approach to the risks of winter mountaineering and her solid reputation. It is reasonable to imagine that Italian mountaineer Vittorio Sella, who'd already established his credentials with his winter ascent of the Matterhorn, would not have consented to share the risks nor the potential rewards of the summit with just anyone.

Elizabeth chronicled her early winter experiences in *The High Alps in Winter; or, Mountaineering in Search of Health*. This was the first book by any author devoted entirely to winter climbing. Her expeditions caught the attention of the climbing establishment and she was "electrified," she recalled, when the *Alpine Journal* stated, "This unparalleled series of ascents executed by a lady will form one of the most brilliant chapters in the history of winter mountaineering." Years later, at the very end of her climbing career, she contributed another chapter in climbing history by making what is regarded as the first "manless" climb. Without men or guides in their party, in 1900 she and her friend Lady Evelyn McDonnell completed a winter traverse of the beautiful, snow- and ice-capped Piz Palü, a 12,800-foot peak on the Swiss-Italian border. This feat, the great twentieth-century British climber Dorothy Pilley later wrote, was "hushed up and regarded as somewhat improper." At that time, two women "alone," facing and beating the odds on a tough winter ascent, seemed a bit more than the still-male-dominated climbing establishment could handle.

Elizabeth made notable ascents in summer as well—one being her Matterhorn traverse of August 1883, an epic lasting forty-three hours. Led by guide Alexander Burgener, she and a porter left Zermatt at 11:00 P.M. and reached the summit the next morning. A glaze of ice—called *verglas*—made the descent on the Italian side extremely treacherous and painstakingly slow. The three climbers spent the day negotiating icy rocks, dodging falling stones, and avoiding avalanches. Nightfall found them still on the mountain, feeling their way down by moonlight. After the moon set, the men slept the few hours until dawn, but Elizabeth stayed awake and moving the entire time in an attempt to stay warm. The next morning they finally reached the Italian village of Breuil and by mules and then on foot made it back to Zermatt that night. Interestingly, this climb with Le Blond was not the first time Alexander Burgener had seen a woman on the Matterhorn. Years earlier he'd encountered Meta Brevoort there. Perhaps as a result of his familiarity with the abilities of both Le Blond and Brevoort, he later encouraged other women with the opinion that females "really can climb."

Evidence of Elizabeth's expertise and reputation as a climber emerged again the following summer. She joined one of the preeminent guides of the time, Joseph Imboden, in climbing what they christened the Beishorn (and now called the Bishorn). Imboden considered the 13,625-foot mountain north of Zermatt one of the only great 4,000-meter Alpine peaks left unclimbed. It was his ambition to lead one of his clients to the top, and he chose Elizabeth to share his wish. The guidebooks, she noted, considered the ridge leading to the Beishorn impossible to climb, but she was thrilled at the chance for a first ascent. Despite Imboden losing his ice ax, the pair found their way up the knife-edge ridge to the summit. It was one of the few times Elizabeth had the pleasure of helping build the "stone man," or large cairn used to mark a summit, and leave her name first in the bottle tucked within. This ascent was just one of many climbs during her fifteen-year, mutually rewarding relationship with Imboden. In addition to climbing many more Alpine peaks together, he later joined her on a trip to Norway, where they made a series of first ascents above the Arctic Circle.

In another illustration of how she led her sport, Elizabeth bucked convention by occasionally going without guides. In the 1880s guideless climbing by men was just gaining acceptance in summer; it was still extremely rare in winter. It would be another forty years before women habitually climbed without guides—or men. An incident one winter in the mid-1880s reveals Elizabeth's relationship with male climbers, as well as her careful judgment in the face of potentially hazardous conditions. Good judgment is always important in mountaineering, but in winter it is doubly so, for the consequences of miscalculation are vastly heightened by the short days, the tricky snow conditions, and the cold.

She'd agreed to guide two friends up the Diavolezza Pass near St. Moritz, an area she knew from summer excursions. She didn't consider the pass particularly challenging but realized that winter snows could conceal treacherous crevasses. While the surface might appear solid, a climber could fall through the brittle snow and into a crevasse. Her companions, a German whom she identified as "Mr. H." and an Englishman, "Mr. S.," both had some mountaineering experience, and she figured they knew to look out for such conditions.

Mr. S. found the morning's climb unusually tiring, and it was midafternoon by the time they reached the top of the pass. Elizabeth advised returning the way they'd come. Fortified with a swallow of brandy, however, Mr. S. insisted they climb down the other side. They roped up and started their descent through a snowfield littered with crevasses, some so deep they couldn't see the bottom. But at least they could see them.

When the snowfield broadened into a smooth, unbroken slope they unroped, leaned on their axes, and glissaded down, making much better time. Still, dusk had robbed the terrain of details by the time they reached the séracs guarding the glacier's lower reaches. Elizabeth considered maneuvering around these ice pinnacles easy enough in summer. But with snow hiding the crevasses between them, and no lantern for illuminating the way, she grew concerned. Both she and the men knew the correct path bordered a deep and treacherous whirlpool in the ice called the Grand Moulin. If in the dark one of them accidentally tumbled into this steep, smooth-sided chasm, getting out would be extremely difficult. But knowing they were on the right track meant finding the Moulin. They roped together again.

When Mr. S. claimed he knew the area well and offered to take the lead, Elizabeth gladly relinquished. Cautiously he led them forward, and within a few minutes they found the gaping Moulin. Relieved, they paused and listened to water gurgling from deep within. But an hour later they were still zigzagging around séracs, not making much downward progress. Mr. S.'s energy was flagging, and conditions were not improving. They inched along until they found another gaping crevasse. In the dark they could hardly discern the other side, but retracing their steps seemed just as precarious as going forward. Grimly, Elizabeth wrapped the rope around her ice ax and dug in as far as she could to hold Mr. S. in case he jumped short. He made it. She got up, took a deep breath leaped, and scrambled to keep her footing on the other side. She held her breath again as Mr. H. joined them with an acrobatic tumble.

Finally, they thought, the rest of the way was clear. But before long Elizabeth realized they'd veered far off course. Anxiously she asked Mr. S. if he was sure of his bearings. He replied he was not and in fact felt "quite stupid." He was apparently suffering from what today would be recognized as hypothermia. Another swallow of brandy revived him a bit, and Elizabeth resumed the lead. But before long, the Englishman felt faint and had to stop. Brandy alone wasn't enough to power him over the remaining miles. Elizabeth reviewed their choices. She could continue on for help and leave the German with Mr. S. But even if she were fortunate enough not to fall into a crevasse on the way, it would still be at least six hours before a rescue party could get back. By that time Mr. S. might be frozen. The only choice was to lead him down.

Propping Mr. S. between them, she and Mr. H. slowly and carefully edged their way down, prodding the snow with their axes at every step to test for hidden crevasses. They proceeded this way for two exhausting hours. It was after 11:00 P.M. when they finally left the glacier and started on the path toward the village. They cheered when a search party met them in a horse-drawn wagon. At the hotel, while celebrating with their would-be rescuers, Elizabeth was astonished to hear Mr. H., whom she had trusted as understanding the risk of their nighttime descent, remark, "There was no danger, all the crevasses were covered with snow!"

Elizabeth's prolific and sometimes acid pen gives us a flavor of the Alpine social scene in the 1880s and 1890s. By this time tourism had become big business, and all sorts of people flocked to the mountain resorts and hotels. Her stories reveal the pleasure she derived from tweaking others' expectations and playing the role of the iconoclast. While no one escaped her wry eye, she especially enjoyed needling Americans. Among their irritating traits, she pointed out, was the habit of asking endless and detailed questions in butchered French. She also found them annoyingly self-confident and at the same time endlessly gullible.

One afternoon she was enjoying a hotel lunch when it became apparent that a tableful of American tourists were examining her. One of the women approached, and with a shaky voice inquired whether Elizabeth's reddened face was the result of *glacier* travel. "Because, if our faces are likely to get so blistered and burnt, I guess we won't go!" the questioner exclaimed. Elizabeth confirmed the cause of her condition, but helpfully suggested the woman and her friends might avoid sun damage if they each wore three gauze veils at one time. She figured "the temporary disfigurement" of all three veils (as well as the snickers they'd certainly elicit) would be "nothing when compared to the horror of having to appear at *table d'hôte* with a skin like mine." She then noted that many Americans fell victim to salesmen with "broken English and insinuating manners" who convinced them that wearing wool socks over their shoes would keep them from slipping on the ice and falling down precipitous glaciers. She described these tourists sitting all in a row pulling wool socks over their fancy, high-heeled boots and shoes, and then returning from their destination, the useless socks "hanging in draggled fringes" around their ankles.

But most tourists, Americans included, usually ventured no farther than the Mer de Glace. She thought it notable, then, when she encountered a group of three young American men intent on climbing Mont Blanc. Despite no previous climbing experience or even hard training walks, they were quite confident in their success, and had already instructed their hotel to fire the customary cannons upon their triumphant return. Even this practice of cannon firing got the Le Blond treatment. Each hotel, she informs us, "has two or three very diminutive cannons, which are fired by the respective porters, who give a prod with a long stick, and then turn and run, while a majestic puff, about the size of an egg, is seen to emerge from the mouth of these warlike machines, followed by a report resembling that of a pistol."

As it turned out, Elizabeth had her own ascent planned the following day. When she reached the Grand Mulets, the hutmistress told her three young men anxiously awaited her. They were the Americans. She found them lying prostrate on their mattresses, unable to move. One of them explained what happened. They'd left the hut that morning bound for the summit but had floundered up to their waists in soft snow. They struggled on for ten hours before finally deciding to turn back. Elizabeth related the conversation: " 'Madam,' he continued, feebly thumping the mattress with his fist; 'Madam, no woman can go up *Mount Blank* in all this fresh snow, or no man either, as far as that goes!' "

She commiserated with them while inwardly marveling at these youngsters' confidence in their own success as well as others' failure. The next day she completed her climb, and "to avoid any well-meant salutations from the cannon," snuck back into Chamonix after dark.

Elizabeth also offered an interesting assessment of other "lady climbers," who were becoming much more numerous by the turn of the century. One class of these women ordinarily makes the summits and enjoys favorable weather, she tells us. But there is another "species against whom all the winds of heaven are arranged . . . who encounters a gale impossible to withstand, on one part of [a] ridge while another party is basking in hot sun and still air a little higher up." These ladies are forever "having their tents blown away, and [are] very critical as to the achievements of other lady climbers, by reason of the fact that they have failed to imitate them." Unsurprisingly, these ladies also have a hard time engaging the best guides. Whether she considered their "vinegary temperament" the cause or the effect of these climbers' experiences she didn't say.

All the while she was building her skills as a climber, Elizabeth also worked on her techniques as a photographer and writer. After *High Alps in Winter* she published a succession of other mountaineering titles, including a novel, and illustrated them with her own photos. The Alpine Club applauded her photographs as important contributions to the records of mountaineering, and her books earned her public acknowledgment as "an Alpinist of world-renowned fame."

By the late 1890s Elizabeth gradually slowed the pace of her climbing, and by 1902 she retired completely. She was then forty-three, and other interests demanded her attention. She loved traveling, and for her journeys through Spain around this time wrote a small guidebook. A few years later, with her third husband, Aubrey Le Blond, she traveled through China, Russia, Korea, Turkey, and Japan, returning to England at the brink of World War I. During the war, when the British Red Cross deemed her too old to volunteer (she was fifty-three), she worked instead in a French army hospital. Later, she considered efforts to improve relations between postwar England and France her life's most important work, and her greatest honor the French Legion of Honor, awarded for her work restoring the Reims Cathedral.

But part of her heart was always in the Alps and with climbers. In 1907 she helped found the Ladies Alpine Club in London, the world's first climbing organization for women. During her term as its first president and for years afterward, she was known for encouraging younger and inexperienced climbers. In a move to honor her long career and contributions to the club, its members reelected her president in 1932, when she was seventy-one years old. She died of a heart attack two years later.

The Ladies Alpine Club devoted many pages in its *Yearbook* to memorializing her in 1934. "She was one of a small group of adventurous spirits . . . who did so much to pave the way for women climbers of a later day, by bearing the brunt of, and calmly ignoring, the criticisms heaped upon them for indulging in so 'unwomanly' a sport," the editor wrote. Men, too, recognized her achievements and contributed to the memoriam. Wrote Col. E. L. Strutt of the men's Alpine Club, "She was a highly skilful climber and, in her best days, was certainly rivalled in performance and form by Miss [Katherine] Richardson alone. Her chief characteristic was her extraordinary judgment. In this writer's opinion, as one who knew her well and made many ascents—both in summer and winter—in her company, this judgment has never been surpassed in any mountaineer, professional or amateur, of the so-called stronger sex."

Elizabeth Le Blond dedicated her life to "meeting interesting people," and she certainly led a fascinating life herself. From starting out as a frail and sickly woman who couldn't tie her own shoes to becoming one of the champions of winter mountaineering, hers was the kind of life that few people witness, let alone experience. Her ascents, her writing and photography, and her work bringing the cause of female climbers to the forefront established her as one of the sport's great early ambassadors, as well as the first real leader in women's mountaineering.

Does a Woman Have to Be One of the Boys to Excel in Climbing?

ABBY WATKINS

One of the finest woman climbers at the outset of the 21st century, Abby Watkins feels that more women should take up the sport. Here she writes about all the positives she has found in climbing and discusses what she feels are some of the advantages women have in climbing, advantages that make them well suited to the sport.

Gasping, I belly flop onto the glazed, sun-drenched ledge at Camp 5 on the Nose of El Capitan. Evening light softens the stark lines of Yosemite Valley, which makes the meadow below seem even further away. I'm bone tired. Since 5 A.M. (was it only this morning that we were on the ground?), Vera and I have been tackling the sheer, unforgiving lines of this magical monolith.

"Your lead," Vera says as she hands me the rack. She's just led the last five pitches and now it's my turn to do the same. I look at the upper dihedrals towering above us: still so far to go.

"Thanks." My weary reply reveals the fatigue engulfing my body and mind. "How's your water supply?"

"Gone." Monosyllabic responses are easier to muster and are all our partnership requires after climbing acres of rock together in many countries over the past few years.

We're out of water and food. This is when we must dig deep. Somehow I drag myself to my feet and start climbing. The first move is sheer will, but slowly my body takes over where my mind is too tired. My body understands the intricacies of granite climbing and moves instinctually across its smoothness. Soon I am 100 percent engaged, and the rock slowly passes beneath me. Four hours later I am crawling onto the summit under a full moon. The Nose in a Day: A dream come true.

One Pitch at a Time

Ascending the Nose in a day was a big turning point in my conception of what was possible in my climbing. Moving over that much rock in such a short time opened the door of possibility as to what I could do in the mountains. Yet when I first conceived of the climb, it seemed like an impossible dream. In my mind, such ascents were the realm of supermen with grim, set jaws and strength as rugged as the mountains—and with these men I did not identify.

The media did nothing to quell my insecurities. On the page opposite the hard, scruffy, satisfied men portrayed in the popular climbing magazines were airbrushed beauties hanging delicately onto sunset-drenched rock. Though there are signs of change, it seems that the mainstream climbing media is not ready to showcase female climbers based on their merits rather than their appearances. I know that when I am three days into a big wall or two weeks into an expedition, I do not look anything close to a poster girl. I did not identify with the gorgeous, young faces staring blankly at me from the glossy magazine pages any more than I did with the mighty men of the mountain.

Luckily, however, I was born with stubborn confidence and an inclination toward athletics. Whether competing in gymnastics, playing tennis, or climbing, I have always felt strong and competent. This mind-set, combined with seeing real women going for it—tired, grimy, and happy after a full day of testing their limits—pushed me to pursue lofty goals. Meeting the perfect partner vaulted me to new heights.

A Different Dynamic

I first met Vera Wong in a climbing gym in Melbourne, Australia. We began climbing together, and after a while I knew I'd met a woman with strengths and aspirations similar to my own. Unlike my climbing partnerships with men, ours was truly equal—and not because my male climbing partners were stronger than Vera or me. (Vera's one of the most accomplished and determined climbers of either gender.) The dynamic was just different. My male partners tended to expect to take more of the leads, or at least the crux, no matter if they were stronger or not. Vera and I shared the leads, the planning, the cruxes; we used our individual strengths to create a whole greater than the individual parts.

I have noticed a difference in the way women and men approach climbing and other physically and mentally demanding sports. Men tend to hurl themselves at the obstacle, regardless of whether they are ready for it or not. I have seen this on El Capitan, when two young men dragged themselves onto the top after eight epic days on a route. They just went for it, ready or not, and probably gained a healthy respect for the Captain along the way. Women tend to stay off a route until they feel ready to complete it in a comfortable way in good time.

Women are often intimidated to try something new in the presence of men, because men have a tendency to take over, often with genuine intentions of helping out. This trait leads to a fear of failure when women climb in mixed groups. If a woman waivers when she is climbing with a man, his tendency is often to take the lead—"Okay, I'll do it"—rather than offer the encouragement she needs at that moment—"Come on, I know you're capable of this. Dig deep!" This automatic assumption of incompetence, whether from onlookers or the woman herself, manifests itself like a self-fulfilling prophecy; she will probably fail without a base of confidence from which to reach. Somehow, this dynamic changes in the presence of women. A woman loses her fear of failure because she will only fail in front of other women, who do not have the preconceived notion that she is incapable.

Built for Climbing

My female partners are my greatest role models, and I enjoy taking that role for other women when I can. When I am teaching climbing, I perceive the impact I have on the women in my classes. When women see a man do something, they think, "Oh, he can do that." When they see me do the same exact thing, I can see them thinking, "Perhaps I can do that." It gives me great pleasure to unlock people's belief in themselves.

When I teach technique, I base the class on fundamentals of the body and gravity. When I show women how to put their bodies in a position where they are taking advantage of gravity, I see the lightbulb go on above their heads. They realize that climbing is a sport for which they are perfectly built.

Climbing with and teaching climbing skills have helped me realize many of the advantages that women have in climbing. Their center of gravity is low, which gives them great balance on the vertical. Women can quite comfortably stand on micro-edges in complete balance, and thus can take much of the weight off of their arms. Their strength-to-weight ratio is usually very good, because they are smaller and lighter, in general, than men. Women have good hip flexibility, which again allows them to use their low center of gravity to greater advantage. And they are mentally tough and persistent. I have found that most women won't give up until they succeed.

Of course, these are generalizations. Climbing relies on kinesthesia and physics just like any other activity we engage in. Everyone's body is different, and the differences are sometimes more pronounced within the sexes than between them. I look at the multitude of body types in climbing today—all are successful. I believe that the important thing is to learn to use what you have. Any body can be the perfect body for climbing.

Ascending Women

This February, I taught two women's ice climbing clinics in the Canadian Rockies. World Cup competitor Kim Csizmasia and I came up with the idea over coffee a few months back. We were discussing the state of women in the sport of ice climbing and lamenting the fact that there weren't enough women out there.

Kim and I have the luxury of being confident enough to excel in the sport of ice climbing. We know women are capable of climbing to any level they wish—we have proven that for ourselves. Why, then, are the frozen waterfalls not crawling with other women climbing well and independently? Our conclusion was that opportunities and role models were still lacking within the sport. Thus, we founded a new company, Ascending Women, so that we could provide events for women. We hardly had the word out when the women's ice clinics filled up. We created something that speaks to women. It's not that they do not want to ice climb—they just want to learn from and with women.

The two weekends brought together amazing women from all walks of life to experience ice climbing in the heart of the Rockies. We had all levels of climber, from raw beginners to women who were quite advanced and accomplished. Thus, goals varied from just making it to the top of a climb to learning the subtleties of weight shift and balance in order to lead more efficiently. My most vivid memories from the weekends are seeing the group get behind whoever was pushing herself to accomplish a certain climb, whether it was the grade-3 flow or the M7 testpiece.

Ice climbing is empowering to women. I watched as each person dropped her persona from her everyday life and hurled her axe into the ice. It makes me smile to think of each of these women back at their jobs, whether marketing executive or teacher, travel agent or designer, with the feeling of firing her way up a frozen waterfall still fresh in her mind.

Because of the response we received to these women's ice clinics, I am excited to create more events: summer rock and alpine clinics, women-only climbs of remote peaks, slide shows, and women-only climbing gatherings. The interest is out there.

Going Forward and Going for It

Today I can clearly see the gifts that climbing has brought me: learning, partnership, perseverance, and success at a high price (if it were easy, I'd quickly move on to something else). There's also the pure kinesthetic joy, fitness, problem solving . . . I could go on. For many others, however, climbing seems to remain the domain of men.

This is backed up by the numbers of men at the crags and by the appearance of women in climbing rags. I counted only two pictures of women really "going for it" in a *Rock and Ice* magazine on the shelves at the time of Ascending Women's ice clinic. It was nice to see that they were both pushing boundaries. (One was Lisa Rand bouldering V10. The other was Nancy Feagin climbing a rad-looking mixed alpine route.)

Women are coming into their own within the sport. Documentation of their evolution within the larger community provides motivation for aspiring women. My female guiding colleagues continue to impress me with their competence and knowledge. More and more, I see male clients taking for granted that the mountain guide to whom they have trusted their lives is a woman. Yet I think there is still room for improvement, especially in the arena of women's expeditions. Until a women's team in the mountains is seen as equal to a team of men, it is important to give credit to women's accomplishments.

I am delighted to see women climbing hard, climbing for themselves, climbing for the love of it. I have seen women—my partners—out there really going for it, attacking pitches with tenacity and skill. I've seen them overcome startling fear. I've watched my peers grit their teeth to pull off hard leads. I hope that it is just a matter of time before I can hear their stories from the climbing media directly, rather than extrapolating the real story from a softly lit picture.

The Mutant and the Boy Scout
Battle at 20,000 Feet

BRUCE BARCOTT

Bruce Barcott penned this profile of climber Alex Lowe, considered by many the best of his generation, a complex man and great athlete who was well aware that he was in a life-and-death sport. The story chronicles some of Lowe's major achievements, his absolute love of climbing, and his continuing desire to climb the unclimbed, and take up new challenges. It was while he was combining two sports in October of 1999, that Lowe was killed by an avalanche. He was part of a six-man team attempting to climb and then make the first ski descent of 26,291 foot Mt. Shishapangma in China. This portrait shows the human side of a very great climber who loved every aspect of his sport.

On a stone buttress high above Montana's Gallatin River, Alex Lowe picks his way up a wall of layered gneiss warmed by the sun. Flakes of his climbing chalk drift down and speckle an old pine snag at my feet. A raven drifts by and crawks. Lowe's friend Jack Tackle, belaying at the foot of the wall, adjusts his sunglasses and suppresses a yawn. I catch the virus and yawn too.

Lowe rises along his single-pitch 5.11 route up the Skyline Buttress as smoothly as a man on an escalator. To say that Lowe climbs quickly, however, might imply that he projects a sense of urgency. In fact, photographer Gordon Wiltsie, who frequently climbs with Lowe, told me that the problem with shooting the man who is arguably the best climber on the planet is that his progress appears so effortless that it's nearly impossible to capture moments of graphic drama or tension. Sure enough, when Lowe reaches the wall's crux—the trickiest section—he overcomes it with a slight traverse and then a long stretch to a thin dime of a handhold. "What a day!" he yells after topping out. "God, I love this!" He rappels down the cliff and rejoins us. "I'm a little out of practice," Lowe announces as he clips out of the rope. Tackle snorts and rolls his eyes.

The two climbers trade places, but Tackle doesn't get six feet off the ground before the mendacity of Lowe's performance becomes apparent. Steps that seemed to be carved into the rock for Alex vanish as soon as Jack touches the wall. Cracks have closed, ledges have thinned, traverses have widened. Tackle is a superb climber, a local legend and one of Lowe's heroes, but he's simply not in the same league.

"Falling!" Tackle misses at the crux. Lowe crimps the rope and arrests the dangling climber.

"You hand-traverse left along the break, Jack," Lowe calls up. "Couple of thin edges for your feet, but good handholds."

After Tackle's climb, Lowe chooses a more difficult passage up the wall, and this time I see him with different eyes. For weeks I'd been asking his partners what sets Lowe above other elite climbers. Their answers often focused on his physiology—specifically, the arm strength that lets him hoist 200-pound haul bags up granite spires and hang from his ice tools for hours. But powerful guns are only part of it; he also possesses a cerebral delight in technical challenges. As a teenager growing up in Missoula, Lowe developed a passion for mathematics at the same time that he was falling in love with climbing, and neither enthusiasm has gone cold. On long expeditions, he'll pull out a copy of *Differential and Integral Calculus* and amuse himself by working the equations by headlamp. Watching him spider up the cliff, I can see now that the buttress isn't an objective he intends to conquer, but rather a problem he wants to enjoy. "Alex is constantly being entertained by the rock," explains Steve Swenson, who has accompanied Lowe on expeditions to Everest and Gasherbrum IV.

Late in the afternoon, a wintry breeze sneaks upcanyon and nips our fingers. Packing up for the drive back to Bozeman, Lowe and Tackle exchange climbing gossip and small talk, and soon another realm of knotty equations and exquisitely difficult balancing maneuvers enters the conversation: Lowe talks about how great it is to be home with his wife, Jenni, and the kids, and somewhat sheepishly admits that he just cleared a climbing trip with his wife before buying the ticket.

"I thought I'd do the chivalrous thing and offer not to go," he says.

Tackle tries not to smile. "It's called common sense, Alex."

Although the exchange is as casual and relaxed as Lowe's climbing seems to be, it reflects a persistent identity crisis, a 20-year tug-of-war between competing tendencies. It's as if two separate entities have battled for tenancy in his body. There is the Mutant, as Lowe's climbing partners have nicknamed him, in tribute to his otherworldly talent and his astonishing drive. And there is the Boy Scout, the diligent partner in a dual-career marriage and the stalwart father who holds tight to his humility and old-fashioned values in a climbing world populated with macho egotists and vagabond stoners.

This longstanding tension has produced an oddly patterned life. Lowe rode a prestigious scholarship to college but dropped out to climb in Yosemite and beyond. When his first son was born a decade ago, he buckled down and yoked himself to a family-man job as an oil-industry engineer. The nine-to-five life lasted until the day a chance to climb Everest suddenly materialized. The pattern, then, is that the Boy Scout holds a good job for a few months or years, and then the Mutant starts climbing the walls, erupts, and heads off for first-ascent nectar. Licking this contradiction may become his greatest maneuver yet. The two halves of Alex Lowe may never live in perfect harmony, but lately he has edged ever closer to the balance that has eluded him: composing outbursts of Mozartian climbing while tending a soul devoted to hearth and home. In short, he's figuring out how to set the Mutant free to bankroll the Boy Scout's cozy life.

Stewart Alexander Lowe is a terminally optimistic man of 40 years whose dark hair and geometric jaw give him a slight resemblance to Prince Valiant. Off the mountain, most of his friends have never seen him in anything more formal than a T-shirt, tennis shoes, and twill sports pants. He lives in Bozeman, Montana, with Jennifer Leigh Lowe, a painter, and their three sons (10-year-old Max, 6-year-old Sam, and 2-year-old Isaac) in a 1920s Craftsman-style house that Norman Rockwell would dismiss as a greeting-card cliché. He often employs the word "gosh" without irony, and his only vice is strong coffee—preferably lattes. With his lank, muscular physique and chronically sunny disposition, he walks and talks like a poster boy for climbing, which in fact he is. After rising from humble beginnings as an early-80s big-wall rat, Lowe has become the unofficial captain of The North Face's so-called "dream team" of top climbers, which the outdoor company has put under full Nike-style contract. When climbing veterans like George Lowe (no relation) or fellow dream team member Conrad Anker hear of some young hotshot, their first reaction is: How does he stack up to Alex? "We're all at this one level of competition," says Anker, "and then there's Alex."

His résumé, though impressive, does not tell the complete story. He has climbed Everest twice. During K2's notoriously deadly season of 1986, he came within a thousand feet of the summit before being beaten back by the storm that claimed five lives. After posting the first winter ascent of the north face of the Grand Teton with Jack Tackle in 1984, he returned a few years later and did it again, solo, in a single day. He has put new routes up some of the toughest mountains in the world: the Himalayan 20,000-footers Kwangde Nup and Kusum Kanguru, the Peruvian peaks Taulliraju and Huandoy Este. He and Lynn Hill, also a member of The North Face's team, free-climbed (roped, but without mechanical aid) the Bastion, an immense 4,000-foot wall in a remote corner of Kyrgyzstan. Two years ago he teamed up with Anker to record the highly publicized first ascent of Rakekniven, a deadly-smooth granite knife that juts 2,000 feet straight out of the Antarctic ice cap. Last spring, with team member Greg Child, he paced Mark Synnott and Jared Ogden, a pair of young turks 10 years his junior, up Great Sail Peak, a 3,750-foot virgin wall on the coast of Canada's remote Baffin Island.

Those are fine, but not world-beating, accomplishments. Among American climbers, Carlos Buhler has a more impressive Himalayan record, and Ed Viesturs boasts more experience at high altitude. But sheer loftiness and Seven Summits-style peak-bagging bore Lowe. "Alex could be much more famous if he'd spend more time climbing Everest or K2," says one of his partners, "but he'd rather spend his time climbing this unbelievable stuff out there."

It's the difficulty of that "unbelievable stuff" that drops his colleagues' jaws. At the tender age of 22 he cramponed his way up Hot Doggies, a radical new line of rock and ice in Rocky Mountain National Park—a feat that inspired climber Jeff Lowe (another example of the weird plenitude of mountaineering Lowes; also no relation to Alex) to introduce a new "M" (for mixed) difficulty rating. He laid the first spikes up Vail's fearsome Fang; recorded the first one-day ascent of Andromeda Strain, a perverse mixed rock-and-ice route on Mount Andromeda, in Canada's Columbia Icefields; and posted solos of Root Canal (at the time, the toughest ice climb in the Tetons), and Mont Blanc du Tocul's Supercouloir. He has pioneered so many mixed-climbing ascents that he no longer keeps track. "The thing about Alex is, when he gets to these places, he doesn't look at the regular routes," says Synnott, who watched Lowe "do a bunch of sick stuff" in Synnott's Vermont stomping grounds before they shared the rope on Baffin Island in 1998. "He looks in between the routes and asks, 'Has anyone done that?'"

Inside the Lowes' downtown Bozeman home, Jenni's western folk paintings hang on the walls of the living room, which is otherwise rife with signs of three boys underfoot. There are no tools of the climbing trade in sight; the only hints of Lowe's profession are the Tibetan prayer flags fading in a backyard tree and a dog named Anna (short for Annapurna). Essentially, upstairs is all Jenni and the boys; downstairs, in a basement apartment the Lowes used to rent out in leaner times, is an office-warehouse littered with haul bags, harnesses, ropes, and hardware—the Mutant's lair.

On the day I arrived, Lowe had just returned from a long road trip, and he was busy reacquainting himself with his family. It was Max's 10th birthday. When Lowe and I walked into the kitchen, Jenni was cooking seafood stew (Max's favorite), and Isaac, the toddler, began tugging at my arm, wanting to introduce me to his rocking horse, while six-year-old Sam beckoned me to a chair draped suspiciously with a towel. "Why don't you sit down right here?" he said.

After admiring Isaac's horse, I played the stooge, sat, and deflated the hidden whoopee cushion.

"BAH-ha-ha-ha-ha!" Sam exulted. "You had beans for dinner!"

"And what relative can we thank for bringing this treasure into our lives?" asked Alex, shaking his head and laughing.

"The boys talked me into buying it at Safeway the other day," Jenni said.

"How long was I gone?" Alex ventured quietly. "21 days?"

"I think it was more like a month," Jenni said.

"Wow. Long time."

"Too long," Jenni replied, gently, firmly.

Clearly, the reentry process has not yet been rendered seamless. In the previous weeks, Lowe had been fulfilling a commitment to visit The North Face shops around the country, show the new fall line, and give employees a chance to crag with the master. But the traveling poster boy had been restive. "I'm not spending enough time with Jenni and the kids," he kept telling his climbing mates.

The tug-of-war can become intense. If a climb isn't going to work, Lowe starts weighing days spent in a foul, damp tent against hours spent with his family. "Every cell down to the molecular level starts to twitch to get back to Bozeman," says Anker.

Less easy to know are the ways that the Mutant begins to make his demands after a long spell at home. In any case, Lowe was on his best behavior during Max's birthday dinner. Trying to instill some of his love of numbers in his eldest son, Alex coaxed Max into calculating how many children are born in the United States every day.

"So if a child is born every 10 seconds, how many are born every minute?" Alex asked.

"Uh . . . six."

"And how many in an hour?"

"360?"

"Gosh, that's great work, Max. How many in a day, do you think?"

This took some guessing, but eventually Alex guided him to 8,640.

After dinner Sam appeared with a violin and squelched out "Happy Birthday to You" for his older brother. Not to be outdone, Max put the fiddle to his chin and honored us with a tear-jerking rendition of "I'll Fly Away." Alex took it all in from the couch, sitting there smiling with his long legs splayed, his fingers knitted in back of his head.

"Maybe you should open your gifts now, Max," Jenni suggested.

Max ripped into the ribbons and wrapping and unveiled a graphite fly rod and reel, followed by scale models of the USS Constitution and Christopher Columbus's Santa Maria, and finally a copy of the *Macmillan Dictionary for Children*.

"Wow, that's pretty neat, Max!" Alex exclaimed when he saw the book.

"That one's from you, dear," Jenni said.

"Oh! Happy birthday, Max," he said sheepishly. "Boy. Guess I have been gone a while."

Sitting amid wrinkled and torn paper on his living room floor, the Alex Lowe who wants to be home and wants to be away examined the rigging of the Santa Maria. "Look at this, Max," he said, holding up both models. "Look at the difference in size."

Lowe seemed to be calculating the 1492 odds: open ocean, unknown destination, only 128 feet of Spanish hardwood between the crew and oblivion. "Wow. They didn't even know what was out there." His tone was oddly intimate, as if he were admiring the new route a colleague had put up on Cerro Torre. "Pretty bold. Pretty audacious."

More than his new routes, first ascents, and pioneering mixed climbs, it's the way he climbs that has made Alex Lowe's legend.

"Alex's Grand Traverse is one of those stories that's taken on a life of its own in the Tetons," reports Doug Chabot, a guide with Exum Mountain Guides, where Lowe worked off and on for 10 years. Most mountaineers hope to do the Grand Traverse once in their lives; many of the strongest climbers require at least 24 hours to complete it. Lowe squeezed it in between breakfast and dinner. "He came in one morning at Exum," Chabot recalls, "and when he found there wasn't any work that day, he took off in his tennis shoes and did the whole traverse by himself, climbing 10 peaks. He was back by four that afternoon."

There are stories about ice climbs Lowe put up in Montana and Wyoming that nobody has ever repeated. There are tales of his showing up at walls all around the world and on-sighting routes the locals have been trying to solve for years. (A climber "on-sights" a route by climbing it with no prior knowledge.) There's the old yarn—confirmed—about the time he blew out the toe in his rock shoe halfway up Yosemite's El Capitan and completed the climb wearing it backward.

Part of his mystique derives from the perception that he has tapped into some inexhaustible life force. Climbers trade intelligence about his pull-up obsession—he gets itchy if he can't do 400 a day—as if they want to be assured it's nothing but hype. (It isn't.) On an expedition in Queen Maud Land, a stir-crazy Lowe dove into an Antarctic whiteout equipped with only a shovel and a pair of skis. An hour later his companions stumbled out to find Lowe down in a freshly-dug, eight-foot-deep pit, chinning himself on the skis. "Hey guys!" he said. "How about a pull-up contest?"

When Lowe tells some of his own favorite stories, he tends to use the word "epic" a lot. To a climber, the word means something like "near total disaster." An epic is usually bad (as opposed to a "sufferfest," which refers to an expedition during which inhuman conditions were happily endured). Perhaps the granddaddy epic of them all was Lowe's June 1995 expedition to Mount McKinley, which gave the Mutant full license to express himself.

Lowe and Conrad Anker had planned an excursion up the Cassin Ridge, one of McKinley's most difficult routes. Lowe flew in to base camp on the Kahiltna Glacier a couple of days before Anker, and trekked up to the 14,000 foot camp to acclimatize. That night, for fun, he ran up to the summit with veteran American climbers Marc Twight and Scott Backes and McKinley's high-altitude doctor, Colin Grissom. Along the way, they passed three Spanish climbers bivouacked on the ice. "They'd sort of quit moving," Lowe recalls, "but they were still trying to climb up." The next day, with their tent shredded by the wind, the Spaniards radioed for help. "They were talking to somebody out in the Gulf of Alaska," says Lowe's friend Andrew McLean, who happened to be on McKinley at the same time. "All they could say was 'Rescue, rescue.'" Somebody got word to the Park Service, which called in an Army Chinook helicopter and asked Lowe, Twight, and Backes if they'd help out. Although a storm had struck the mountain, they agreed to try, and the helicopter pilot control-crashed the climbers onto McKinley's 19,500-foot-high "football field," the highest landing ever in a Chinook. "It was really scary," the not-easily-scared Lowe admits.

"They told us we had two hours to climb down the West Rib and get these guys back up," Lowe continues. The West Rib is a technical climb down a 50-degree slope of ice and rock. "By the time we got to them, one of the Spaniards had already fallen to his death. The other two weren't wearing gloves or hats. They were in the last stages of hypothermia—they were delirious—and their hands were frozen way up past the wrist." Twight and Backes went back up with the first climber, who could still walk, with the idea they'd return to help Lowe carry up the second man, who was in much worse shape. Lowe decided there wasn't time to wait.

"I stood him up, leaned him against me, and started up, but he just passed out, so I cut a chunk of rope, tied him directly into my harness—he was 20 feet below me—and just started climbing up this thing, dragging the guy. It was fully epic. When I reached the fixed ropes, I couldn't keep dragging him, but he wouldn't get up. So I finally picked him up, piggyback, and staggered uphill to 19,500 feet and carried him on to the football field. It was one of those things you do because you have to do it, one of those Herculean things where you get a lot of adrenaline going and you just do it." They all flew off to Talkeetna in the Chinook.

With the Spaniards safely thawing, Lowe returned to McKinley. Anker arrived at base camp the next day and was making purposefully slow progress to 14,000 feet, in order to acclimatize before their Cassin Ridge attempt. Lowe, who already had his high-altitude lungs, was antsy to get after something, anything. What to do, what to do? He decided to see if he could climb McKinley in a day.

"So I took off at midnight, got all the way up to the football field, about 500 feet below the summit, but the weather got really bad and I couldn't see anything, so I didn't quite make the summit." On his way down, Lowe passed a party of nine Taiwanese climbers at 17,000 feet. Soon afterward, despite white-out conditions, the Taiwanese group tried to summit and became separated. Only six made it back to their camp. "The Park Service was like, 'Deja vu,'" says Lowe. Once again, he was drafted, and he and Anker found one climber dead and towed two other half-frozen survivors down to safety. Apparently refreshed by their exertions, but without enough time left for their Cassin Ridge climb, Lowe and Anker attempted a single-day dash up nearby Mount Hunter, getting most of the way up its north buttress before running out of daylight. "That was kind of it," Lowe says, winding up the story with a shrug.

Sometimes the stories aren't so much epic as bizarrely comic. As Lowe climbed that summer on McKinley, his forehead bore the scar of a near-fatal fall the previous winter. The problem was an icicle in Hyalite Canyon, a few miles outside of Bozeman. Lowe, Tackle, and two others attacked it with ice tools, crampons, and screws. One pitch up (a pitch is half the length of a standard climbing rope, or about 100 feet), with Lowe swinging the lead and Tackle belaying, Lowe's entire section of ice broke free. With Tackle looking on, Lowe rode the ice 40 feet before crashing onto a ledge. Upon impact, Lowe's forehead whiplashed into the adze of his ice ax. He stood up, ecstatic at having survived, and shouted, "Fuck, man, I'm OK!" In fact, Lowe looked like a mangled victim in a Wes Craven movie; his companions could see that a broad section of his scalp was draped over one eye, exposing a section of skull. "Oh, man, you're not OK!" Tackle yelled back. "You're fucked up. Sit down!"

"We rappelled off and kinda taped the scalp back into place, and put a hat on, and taped around the hat, and started skiing out," Lowe recalls. "Kinda knew it was time to go to the ER. But we also knew it was going to be a long evening there, so we stopped down at the coffee shop and got lattes. It was great. My clothes were saturated with blood. We parked in the handicap spot in front of the coffee shop, marched right in, and then headed for the hospital."

"Alex was one of those little kids who never felt tame," says his mother, Dottie, a retired schoolteacher. She and her husband, Jim, raised Alex and his two brothers, Andy (older) and Ted (younger) in Missoula. "He always had trouble sitting still, was always the first one down the trail, always climbed the highest."

Jim, an associate professor of entomology at the University of Montana, often took the boys scrambling in Kootenai Canyon, and by the time Alex was in the fifth grade he started going off on his own. Several years later, Lowe hooked up with a U of M student named Marvin McDonald who, desperate for a partner to belay him on the walls of Blodgett Canyon, taught the 16-year-old the rudiments of climbing, using a sink-or-swim pedagogical technique. Soon Lowe was doing advanced multipitch routes with McDonald and starting to climb on his own with friends, using a ridiculously unsafe nylon rope he bought at a hardware store. He finished high school in 1976 with only one clear idea of the future: "All I knew was that I wanted to climb some more."

A chemical engineering scholarship took him to Montana State University in Bozeman, but Lowe's college career was geographically doomed from the start. Too many mountains beckoned through the classroom window. At the end of his sophomore year he dropped out, gathered his rack, and headed for the Sierra Nevada. Before he left, Dottie—who would spend the next 20 years praying for the safety of her son—anointed his VW bug with holy oil.

For Lowe, Yosemite in 1979 was "a place of dreams." The free-climbing revolution, in which young climbers eschewed the traditional hammered-in pitons for a purer, hands-and-feet-only esthetic, was taking place daily on El Capitan. Camp Four buzzed with climbing-mad kids like Lowe pitching their grubby tents alongside free-climbing masters like Ron Kauk, Jim Bridwell, and Dale Bard. He was the quintessential dirtbag. When his money ran out, Lowe engaged in the hallowed Camp Four tradition of scarfing: hanging out in the tourist cafeteria waiting for someone to leave a half-eaten stack of pancakes or sandwich behind.

He was "wandering aimlessly forward," as he recalls it, following a path that blossomed into a five-year climber's pilgrimage. When he had money he used it to get to Yosemite, the Canadian Rockies, New York's Shawangunks, Wales, the sea cliffs of Penzance, the Mediterranean Coast, and the French Alps. When he didn't have money—usually after a long spring, summer, and fall of climbing— he earned it roughnecking in the subfreezing Wyoming oil fields. In the winter of 1981–82, he and Jenni, whom he'd met a year earlier through a climbing buddy, hired on with a seismic exploration crew. "It was the perfect job for a climber," Lowe recalls. "Every day they'd fly us into high mountain areas in Colorado, Montana, Utah, and drop us off with cable, dynamite, and recording equipment. We were the flunkies there to roll the cable ahead of the geophysicist. We did that for about three months, saved another wad of cash, and bought plane tickets to London."

A Montana native and avid climber, Jenni was as hooked on vagabonding as Alex. Together they practiced the art of living cheap in mountain towns in England and France. "I really didn't think it would last," she says today, sounding bemused that she fell for this "kid"—Lowe is three years younger—who eventually won her heart with his "pretty boundless energy" and "unstoppable spirit."

For a while at least, the two climbers enjoyed an existence as carefree as anything Rimbaud or Kerouac tasted. "It's amazing how vivid those memories are," says Lowe. "Climbing was so vibrant and new, plus I was falling in love with Jennifer. I remember climbing all day on the granite sea cliffs near Penzance. The wild appeal: surf crashing at the base of the cliffs, seagulls crying around you. Jenni and I climbed a whole bunch of routes in the Alps. Most of these places have their climbers' haunts, and Chamonix had this foul place called Snell's Field. You could live in Chamonix and it didn't cost you anything. And most of the time you were out climbing—the North Face of Les Courtes, the Aiguille du Midi, classic alpine rock climbs."

When it was over, Alex and Jenni returned to the States so broke they had to hitchhike across North Dakota in a December blizzard to get home. The next spring they married, reality kicked in, and the new husband set about trying to find a steady career. He went back to Montana State University, finished his degree in applied mathematics, and in 1988 entered a graduate program in mechanical engineering. Meanwhile Jenni, who wanted to have kids and start a career as an artist, had given up climbing. Instead of finishing graduate school, Alex took a well-paying engineering job with Schlumberger Oilfield Services, the first solid career move of his life. "We thought our ship had come in," recalls Jenni, and none too soon. By this time their first son, Max, had arrived.

Lowe gave it his best shot, but he lasted barely a year. "It was just work all the time, which was cool," he says, "but then I realized I only got two weeks' vacation a year. That wasn't going to work." In the fall of 1990, when Hooman Aprin, a climbing buddy from Exum, offered him a slot on what turned out to be one of the first guided trips on Everest, Lowe bolted to Nepal and helped lead three of five clients to the summit. He celebrated Max's second birthday, jobless, on top of the world.

Lowe's subsequent stabs at a nonclimbing career followed a similar pattern: He'd stick with it for a year or two, then quit to climb or try something else. Quality-control engineer for Black Diamond, the climbing gear manufacturer. Snow avalanche forecaster. Exum mountain guide. In the early 1990s, after Sam arrived, Lowe was spending most of the year working as a private guide, and dashing overseas to tackle ambitious expeditions and climbs when the opportunity would arise. He was seeing less and less of his family, and spending more time guiding than climbing. Neither the Mutant nor the Boy Scout was getting what he needed.

Still, his reputation kept building, and Lowe capped off this period with a virtuoso display of sheer mountain steel. In 1993 he and Anker became the first westerners to compete in the Khan Tengri International Speed Climbing Competition, an annual race held on Kyrgyzstan's 22,950-foot Khan Tengri. The idea is simple, if suicidal. Thirty climbers start at the 13,000-foot base camp. Each is given a numbered padlock, which the racers lock onto a tripod at the summit to make sure nobody pulls a Rosie Ruiz. The fastest climber back to base wins. The only way to win is to go all out. "It's totally sketchy—I mean, people die doing this thing," Lowe says.

Lowe took the lead early and never looked back. Though unacclimatized and unfamiliar with the route, he smoked the field with a time of 10 hours and eight minutes. In a competition in which climbers are usually separated by minutes, Lowe destroyed the previous Khan Tengri record by more than four hours.

The speed climb confirmed his stature among climbers but earned him little more than a plane ticket and all the vodka his Russian hosts could manage to pour down his throat. The big problem remained: Only a fool becomes a mountain climber to make money, at least in this country. Homebodies with mortgages, children, and fantasies of middle-class security are not often found among the rarefied upper echelons of the climbing profession.

Four years ago this picture changed for a lucky handful of marquee climbers. In 1995 William Simon, then president of The North Face, decided it was time for his company to back climbers the way other companies back baseball and basketball stars. Lowe, Anker, Greg Child, and Lynn Hill all became employees with travel budgets and full benefits. Lowe is expected to put in a certain number of days with sales reps and the R&D department, but the rest of the year he is free to climb.

After leeching off the Boy Scout for all those years, the Mutant finally got a job.

I meet him one morning in his basement office. It's 6 A.M. Jenni and the boys are still asleep upstairs, but he's been up working for three hours, which is standard operating procedure. When he's home in Bozeman he tries to devote the daylight hours to the boys, so he'll often rise at 3 A.M. for a "dawn patrol" run or ski up nearby Bridger Bowl, and be back at the house in time for breakfast. "It's hard to fit this many lives into one lifetime," he says.

I take the only chair in a spartan and tidy bachelor pad, furnished with a bookshelf, a Macintosh, a poster of Pakistan's Trango Towers, and a file cabinet stuffed with dossiers on mountains yet to be climbed. "Alex always has 15 things planned for the future," Jenni told me a few days earlier, so I thought I'd see if I could pry Lowe's to-do list out of him. After all, climbing's true icons— the names that resonate beyond the climbing shop—all have a single crowning achievement attached to their names. Heinrich Harrer had the Eiger. Hermann Buhl had Nanga Parbat. Tenzing Norgay and Sir Edmund Hillary had Everest. Reinhold Messner had his 14 8,000-meter peaks. Alex Lowe has a hundred mind-blowing ascents, but no One Big Thing that sticks in the public's mind.

If Lowe is plotting some paramount accomplishment to lift his reputation to that higher level, however, he's not saying. The Boy Scout keeps the file cabinet locked. He's just out to have a good time in the mountains, he insists. Anyone who climbs to make his name is climbing for the wrong reasons—and won't continue for long. "There are people who can't bear to fail," he says. "Those people are on the short track, as far as their careers go. You have to push hard, do hard things. But you also have to be able to say, 'OK, today's not the day.'"

Lowe is stimulated by danger, but he knows how to factor in fear as an element of the equation. "What I value is the soul-searching head game of getting a little out there," he says. The serious consequences integral to climbing only deepen his tie to the mountain and intensify the bond with his rope partner. "You go into a multipitch natural route, get a little scared, and the name sears itself into your mind." Given the high cost of a mistake, he says, a mountain apprenticeship should be long and slow, and it demands as much humility as strength and will. And acceptance, too: Together with the warmth and abundant affection in their marriage, Alex and Jenni share a kind of detachment—an understanding that his livelihood derives from calculated risk-taking—and a philosophical equanimity in the face of what could happen. She has spoken forthrightly of her ability to carry on alone if necessary. Meanwhile, Lowe sticks to the principle that has taken him this far: Let the Mutant race up the mountain, but make your crux decisions in light of the long view. Hard-core ambition is something you deal with down on the flats.

"I've definitely got lists of things I'd love to accomplish as a climber," he acknowledges, after I prod him further. "But let's face it: The world's full of climbers, and the realm of unexplored, unclimbed peaks is shrinking rapidly." In other words, he who blurts out his dream ascent is only inviting the world to spoil the party. It's no secret, however, that Lowe's attention for the past two years has been drawn to the Antarctic. The trip to Queen Maud Land in the winter of 1996–97 opened his eyes to the possibilities: an entire continent of mostly unclimbed—even unseen and unmapped—mountains. The main focus of his obsession is the Transantarctic Range, a spine of mountains as long as the Rockies that runs up the opposite side of the continent—a forbidding and insanely cold setting for the last big collection of first ascents on the planet. "The place is totally unexplored," he says excitedly, and he pulls out an article that includes the notes of a geologist-climber who was one of the first to set eyes on these mountains: "During the austral summer, the sun never sets, and mountaineering is limited only by your endurance and need for sleep."

And by a third factor: cash. Only one outfit, Adventure Network International, can get you there, and a round-trip ticket in their C-130 Hercules will set you back $30,000. The North Face and the National Geographic Society ponied up for the Queen Maud Land trip, but further expeditions may require Lowe to tolerate some odd collaborations. This winter he was planning to climb in the Transantarctics with Conrad Anker and the president of Adventure Network, Mike McDowell, a raffish Australian entrepreneur who made headlines last year by offering deep-sea tours of the *Titanic*. McDowell was waiving the price of the ticket so he could climb with Lowe. "He's kind of like your dad," Lowe told me. "He's got the keys to the car."

It's easy to see how irresistible Antarctica must be to Lowe. The challenge of the "great game" of climbing, he'll tell you, is pushing right up to the line where boldness and wisdom part ways, but "the ultimate attraction is the unknown. I want to climb routes that are remote and technically difficult. Climbing for me is all about solving the magnitude of the problem. The best projects are the ones with big question marks hanging over them."

He calls back in early December and leaves a message. "The rumors are true," Lowe says. He's just undergone reconstructive knee surgery. "I tore my

ACL an hour before I left for the airport to head to South America. Had to bag the Transantarctic climb and come home." Irony ahoy: He tore it playing soccer with the boys.

He'd mentioned his knee problems before, but this time he confessed, "Actually, I first tore it six years ago jumping off some cliffs at Alta." His doctor had recommended immediate surgery, but Lowe had plans to climb Gasherbrum IV. He flew to Pakistan with his knee in a brace. Over the next six years his knee popped out a half-dozen times, and he'd coped. After the soccer incident, it didn't heal. He made it only partway to Antarctica before a Chilean doctor ordered him back home to the hospital.

Add a footnote to the library of Alex Lowe stories: He has done all this stuff—Rakekniven, Khan Tengri race, the dawn patrols—absent his left anterior cruciate ligament.

For now at least, the never-ending problem has been solved. The torn ACL has given him six months of quality rehab time with Jenni and the boys, with no nagging exploration itch. But when the knee heals, the Mutant plans to run wild. Lowe's 1999 datebook includes an expedition to the Great Trango Tower and a run up Tibet's Shishapangma, the 13th-highest mountain in the world. He and Andrew McLean plan to ski off the summit, making them the first Americans to schuss off an 8,000-meter peak. After that, it's back to Antarctica to enjoy his own personal sufferfest on some remote wall thousands of feet above the ice cap.

"It's really a blessing in disguise," he says. "Last time I did Trango, I had to walk up the Baltoro Glacier with a brace. I'll be able to dance up it this time."

Queen of All She Surveys

MAUREEN O'NEILL

No climber can deny the tremendous toll the mountains take in terms of human life. Every single climb has inherent dangers built in and life can end in a swift second. In this essay, climber Maureen O'Neill discusses and remembers friends lost to the mountains, how fellow climbers react, and why they continue to seek the positive things that climbing brings them, including a tremendous sense of camaraderie. As O'Neill puts it, "In the mountains, climbers are bound by absolute necessity. We depend on our partners and routinely, through the use of a rope, trust them with our lives."

My mother calls, and in her voice I can hear her wonder if she is the first to reach me: "Have you heard? One of your climbing friends, Eve, died on Mt. Index this weekend. They think it was an avalanche. Her partner died, too; they fell roped together. Your sister just heard it on the six o'clock report and said to call. She said you climbed with her." I tell her I know already, and she is relieved, then asks quietly, "Do you think she suffered much?" My mother is from the East, and these Northwest mountains are foreign to her. I doubt she can even imagine the landscape against which a woman's body fell and shattered.

I can imagine it only too well. How many times have I scrutinized an ice-lined corridor such as the one Eve died in to see if it might *go*—lead magically, without dead ends, to the summit. I can feel the angle of snow so steep it seems to push her outward, her calves straining to support her body on only the front points of her crampons, forearms trembling as the urgency to move quickly is telegraphed from mind to muscle: hurry, this gully feels unsafe, the warmth unseasonable. Why this stillness in the air? This heaviness?

Did she sense the avalanche? The pulse of kinetic energy about to snap? I cannot stop myself from imagining the moment she fell, delivered into the wide hands of that warm, blue air. I know she screamed in terrible frustration—she always screamed, at even the most minor defeat. This day it was not simply a move she could not make and a fall of a few feet, but her life wrenched from her hands as quickly as she was torn from the ice. Two days later, her body, broken in many places, was discovered half-buried in avalanche debris.

Other climbers have said that she pushed beyond the limits of even her brilliance, that she was somewhere she shouldn't have been, but few climbers can claim never to have found themselves in the wrong place at the wrong time. "Pushing" is only the natural impulse to grow, to improve. I answer with less than complete assurance: "I don't think she suffered. She was probably unconscious or dead when she hit the ground." Maybe it helps my mother to know that some die quickly, although it seems little comfort, given the fact that both her daughters climb and that climbing is a sport in which risks, however carefully considered, are an essential element.

When the mountains claim another life, a single aspect of climbing—the possibility of death—invade and eclipses all other meanings. For we survivors, the significance of her death pales against the fullness of a life anchored in the mountains.

The Olympics, Rainier, the Cascades: whether you climb them or not, the mountains of the Pacific Northwest are impossible to ignore. From the beginning of my life, I heard them praised. Whenever we plowed down a certain hill in the old Rambler, my Dad would say, "Look at those Cascades!"

Inevitably, on even a vaguely clear day, people will ask, "Have you seen the mountains?" If the reference is singular—the mountain—they are referring to Rainier, who so dominates her territory that on a sunny day thousands of city workers step outside on their lunchbreaks and turn their heads to the southeast, to the star-white glaciated peak transcending, or is it levitating, above the clouds.

Such a climate of appreciation for the environment produces people who seek immersion in the wilderness. I began climbing my last year in college for the most common reason in the world—because my best friend climbed. She took a course through our college, and it sounded like fun. Because she had shown the potential to become passionately involved in the sport, I knew I'd never see her unless I signed up, too.

It seemed easy then. Beg or borrow the gear, grab someone, set your sights on a place very far or very high—say that humpback peak or the one with a shark-fin ridge or the glacier-frosted cupcake that was Mt. St. Helens—and then do it, by placing one foot in front of the other, over and over and over.

My friend and I and another friend completed that college mountaineering course and did our first climb together. In our desire to make the summit, we made a typical beginner's mistake and neglected to turn back early enough. Benighted, we were forced to descend an entire glacier, honeycombed with crevasses, without headlamps. At eleven P.M., after what seemed an eternity of tenuous footwork, we reached the moraine. With a heavy sigh, Vaughn sat all six long feet of himself down on a rock, looked up at the moon, and cried, "I want my mother."

Those early climbs were endurance tests, and we always found ourselves equal to them. What a feeling! We ran up trails just to see how fast we could go, wondering if our legs would accordion under us, if we would ever reach the limit—but we didn't. We discovered we did what we had to do. The climbs were simple, often long snow slogs with a bit of scrambling on rock and more than a bit of tortuous bush-whacking if you lost your way. Climbing The Brothers, a peak in the Olympic range, we got lost on the descent and spent the night first lowering ourselves down a series of small cliffs by swinging on slide alder and, when that was done, swimming through a sea of neck-high foliage, wild spring growth coated with sap that shellacked the hair and tasted sweet when licked off a bare forearm. My companion navigated by the stars, aiming to bisect a foot-wide path, and to my great surprise, the plan worked. On the trail out, I learned to sleep while walking, since we had taken twenty-three hours instead of the usual eight to complete the climb.

I progressed to more technical climbing with a group of women as ignorant as myself. We banded together from a lack of money for instruction, a determination to climb and a desire to learn with other women. Our motivations were as varied as the individuals involved, but we all wanted to take complete responsibility in all aspects of climbing, including leading, and felt that being in a group of women best served that purpose. One spring weekend we packed up and drove across the Cascades to a cluster of sandstone formations set like prehistoric monoliths behind an apple orchard. The area resembled an outdoor jungle gym with a wide range of climbs to choose from. After consulting the guidebook, we chose peacefully named climbs located on gently angling slabs and avoided route such as Vertigo, Bomb Shelter, Testicle Fortitude, Slender Thread, and Cro-Magnon.

Eventually we felt brave enough to try an imposing hunk called Orchard

Rock, scary because of its verticality. I went second on the rope and had an easy time of the first thirty feet, which led to a secure resting place—a ledge with enough room for two feet at once. The crux move lay just beyond this ledge and involved climbing around a corner out onto an exposed face. I made one brave attempt, slipped, and retreated to the ledge. Clearly, it was impossible. How had I gotten into this fix? Because I was being belayed from above, any fall would have been minimal, but that seemed irrelevant. My tongue sealed to the roof of my mouth, and although I was perfectly still, I began to sweat. In short, I was gripped. Ten fingertips made pathetic forays across the rock searching for a decent hold (that is, a big one) but my body would not follow. I was rapidly becoming living sculpture.

Below me, third on the rope, Laura waited patiently. Dusk shadowed her face as her brown eyes gazed with maddening serenity over the orchards and dusty-green fields stitched together with roads and fences. Above me, birds chimed on a sunlit ridge and the air had the feeling of an embrace. "This really is for the birds," I muttered. "That's OK. Take as long as you want," she responded. I took forty-five minutes. How the hell could she be so calm while I agonized before the fact that this rock wasn't going to move for me. *I* had to move. With the bloodless precision of a slowly developing photograph, those forty-five minutes of deliberation revealed nearly everything I know about fear. Since then there have only been exquisite refinements.

To the climber, fear serves several purposes. It can make you attentive to possible danger, can warn you, infuse you with energy, serves as a gauge of your mental condition, and prevents you from taking risks beyond your ability. Fear deserves recognition but not one iota more of your attention, though it is usually eager to consume all of it. The natural flow of fear must be channeled or paralysis can result. And paralysis is serious. For me, fear manifests through resistance and hesitation, both of which cause unnecessary energy loss.

Those first few years taught me the simple things: eat before you're hungry and drink even if you don't want water because often the body reacts to stress and cold by erasing the desire for food and water at exactly those time when it is most needed. If you wait until your hands are cold before putting on gloves, they take an immense amount of heat to rewarm, creating an unnecessary energy drain. If you forget even the smallest thing—a spare mitten, an extra bulb for a headlamp—the consequences can be disastrous. If you upper body is so strong that you can haul yourself up a rock with just your arms, instead of using your legs, which are much better suited to hold your weight, you are a wastrel. In the words of Yvon Choinard, climbing depends on conservation of energy, which translates into economy of movement coupled with reasonable speed.

Those years also taught me the range of movement involved in climbing—from the clumsy ferrying of loads to the base of the "climb" to the delicate moves or sequences of moves that were the cream and usually took only a fraction of the total time spent out. Yet what I grew to love above all was the pure luxury of spending two uninterrupted days with someone. As a teenager I spent a summer at a hiking camp; I remember being startled and disturbed at how naked people appeared outside the city: no makeup, no fancy clothes or houses, no supporting actors (parents). All the girls were tiny figures, cut and pasted against a background of sea and trees. As an adult I began to appreciate this nakedness. I was no longer disturbed by it and grew less afraid of the emotional exposure climbing creates.

This intimacy, this insight into the wilderness that is another person, is a gift. Not to mention a true test of friendship. Let me count the ways: withstanding the smell of your partner at night, stripped down to her fragrant long underwear and equally fragrant wet socks; the shove she gives you in her sleep, pushing you toward the wall of the tent dripping with condensation; the rude way she steps on you in the middle of the night as she heads out for relief; the hours spent reading to you by candlelight; the bites of chocolate fed to you at each bend of the trail to inspire you onward.

Seven years later I still climb with the woman who couldn't stop laughing at the sight of me splashing in a creek in midwinter like some huge wooly beetle trying to right herself with a pack on her back. From the other side, she offered only these words of consolation: "I told you not to cross with your snowshoes on."

Certain climbs are described as "committed." Put simply, a committed climb means there is no easy escape: once begun, both ascending and descending are difficult. These climbs require a firm intention to finish, simply because the alternatives are unappealing. Ptarmigan Ridge on Mt. Rainier falls into this category. My partner Kathy, her friend Karl, and I planned to do Ptarmigan Ridge one Memorial Day weekend. It was to be an apprentice climb for me; Kathy and Karl were to share the leading, and I was to go along as a third, knowing it would technically approach my limits. I read the route description with growing apprehension: ". . . steep snow/ice slope . . . snow/ice apron . . . rock buttress . . . steep ice chute . . . crevasse/serac pattern . . . sustained rockfall . . . gentle slope above . . ." Fortunately, preparation left little time for worry.

The day of the climb finally arrived, and we left the parking lot at 7:00 A.M. After a lengthy approach we at last reached our high camp, a breezy rock perch with just enough space, if we squeezed, for our three bivy sacks. Sleep came easily, and the next morning we were wakened at 3:00 A.M. by the steady pulse of an electronic alarm. The day promised to be windless and clear—ideal conditions. Karl, propped up on one elbow and still enjoying the warmth of his bag, was kind enough to boil water for coffee. After eating, we packed quickly and set off, arriving at the base of the climb before light. We had agreed to rope up at the start, and happy to shear weight off my load, I took out the Mammut and laid its brilliant, diamond-back coils loosely on the snow. Kathy glanced at our faces, barely defined in the twilight. "Ready?" she asked. I nodded, palm resting on my ice axe, and waited for the rope to stretch out between us. Cold seconds passed as the steel of the adze bit clear through my woolen mittens to the skin. With agonizing slowness, energy dammed up in my legs and lungs. I wanted desperately to move, to step out of that moment of extreme tension that marks a beginning, and start climbing the mountain.

We all commented on the perfect snow conditions: cramponing was effortless. My primary responsibility was to follow and keep myself on my feet at all times, always a challenge. It seemed my two partners must have tremendous faith in me: if I fell, and I was the most likely candidate, we would all fall. I thought about that a good deal and paid the closest attention to each step, no small task when ascending a thousand feet of snow.

After perhaps an hour, Kathy stopped to rest on a bit of rock. As I drew near her, I detected a difference in texture in the ground ahead, a smooth pond of light in the wind-scored snow. I stood still for a moment, "testing the water" with a delicately placed front point. ICE. "Oh, that bit's easy," said Kathy, between hearty bites of her sandwich, "And it's just a taste of what's up ahead." As I was afraid, she was completely right.

We continued to inch upward, in a race between three snails and the sun, which upon reaching its zenith, would begin to warm and dangerously soften our route. At the apex of the slope, we began our traverse of the "apron." Each footstep punched in the rotten, icy snow seemed likely to give way with the weight of the next person, but somehow never did.

Just under the rock buttress we stopped for lunch. Removing my gloves, I laid three fingers against the pulse in my throat. "Hey, it's 120 per minute," I said. Kathy and Karl were unimpressed, already surveying the next fifty feet—a sheet of ice rounding a hump of rock with a nice, clear view several thousand feet down. Lunch was rather short and strained since we were all anxious to move.

Karl took the lead and danced over the ice with typical, angular ease. Kathy went next. Then he and Kathy waited quietly for me to cross. Too quietly. They seemed to be holding their breath, as though afraid any small draft might prove fatal. Using two tools, I began my crablike traverse and suddenly understood why Gwen Moffat, the famous British climber, titled her book *Space Below My Feet*. Midway through, I panicked and briefly hesitated, but standing still was much more terrifying than moving. I kept on, if only to evade the nasty fall line, making small explosive noises as I tried to place all four points with decision. The hip belt of my pack came unbuckled, and my hat (tied on the belt) began a direct descent. From the corner of my eye, I noticed Kathy wishing it a silent bon voyage.

Breathing deeply, I reached the other side, but there was no time to reflect, as Karl was nearly up the next lead, a narrow icy chute that was actually easier climbing but complicated by a cascade of spindrift, dreamily blowing down. From the top I heard Karl shouting at me to hurry, afraid heavier snow would follow and knock me off. His voice sounded remote, and his directions impossible to follow. I was overcome by the altitude and the odd sensation of moving against the flow. Under a misty white veil, I climbed steadily upward, groping for contact with ice and fighting to maintain my balance, constantly threatened by the swaying of my pack.

The chute led to the crevasse/serac pattern, a section of slopes tiered like a giant, white layer-cake and riddled with crevasses. Probing carefully, Kathy led out and immediately fell into one up to her hips. She climbed out and promptly fell into another. Turning back, she grinned and said, "Think light." Somehow we managed to weave our way out to what appeared to be the final tier leading to the fabled "gentle slope" and to the ridge for which the climb was named. As Kathy made a few tricky moves over the chest-high ice shoulder and onto the slope, Karl and I felt the entire crust shift and drop below our feet. Fired by wildly beating hearts we nearly jumped over the shoulder in our eagerness to reach solid ground.

At last Ptarmigan Ridge resembled a ridge, with that exhilarating combination of firm ground underfoot and airiness on all sides. The worst was over, and I began to relax, although we were at least two hours from the summit with the descent yet to come. As we ascended, clouds blew in and we were forced to use compass bearings for direction. Soon we all needed a rest from the effects of fog and altitude, especially Karl who, exhausted from the lower part of the climb, stumbled and lurched like a drunken man. In the shelter of an overhanging crevasse, we nestled together sharing an ensolite pad and gingersnaps. "Look at where we are," I said, "this is heaven." "Now if we could only be sure of that." Kathy joked.

Suddenly the air cleared and *voilá,* the sun. Kathy and Karl leapt up and scurried off in different directions to see if they could sight any landmarks. Serious business, obviously. Their quick, neat movements temporarily distracted me, but finding myself out of cookies, I began rooting in Kathy's private stash. She'll never know, I reasoned, absorbed in the luxurious ebb and flow of the clouds, teased by views through windows with drifting and torn edges. My reverie was cut short by a shout from Kathy. She had recognized Sunset Amphitheater, an unmistakable western slope of Rainier, scooped out as though to form a gargantuan rock echo chamber.

Greatly encouraged, we slogged forward until the clouds descended again. This time, however, we were certain of our direction and felt our way with the Braille of steps kicked by Kathy, seventy-five feet ahead. By early evening we came upon the false summit, Liberty Cap, and were able to inform several other climbers, who had converged through the whiteout from different routes, of their location. Since we had neither time nor energy to build a snow cave, we scraped out a hollow in a small bank, which protected the lower half of our bodies. Kathy and I shared a bivy sack for warmth. She crawled in right away, uncharacteristically leaving her gear strewn about. As I was relatively refreshed, I put everything away in her pack, then lay awake most of the night, amazed at how warm we were at 14,000 feet with only three thin layers between us and the snow. Kathy slept the twitching, jerking sleep of the exhausted. Since it was impossible to keep the top of the bivy sack closed, downy flakes of snow caught in her red hair and melted slowly. She seemed infinitely vulnerable, protected only by skin that tears so easily. I gently pulled her hat over her head, marveling again at my warmth and the brightness of a night that never seemed to fall.

Climbing, like any exacting activity, draws one deeper and deeper into its own territory, a territory often as narrow as the ice-blue thread of a couloir. In return for this extraordinary sacrifice of energy, the climber receives visions of earth. In the moment before a difficult move, she may turn her head away from what is directly before her and the beauty—or is it the fear—lays her open. Her eyes are the eyes of God, the land flows in and through and from her like a river. As night falls she may gaze across an oceanic glacier rinsed with aqua to yet another sea of black peaks, wreathed by coral clouds. She has a view of earth where everything seems unmasked, naked. Forces corresponding to her own emotions are at work, visible in the sudden rapid devastation of avalanche, in the moraine foaming up and around the tip of a glacier as that tongue of ice furrows through earth, century after century. Something inside says yes, yes, I recognize this. I want to see the earth above all with nothing hidden. The same laws that govern this world govern the life of my body and soul and it is a relief, finally, to see violence and beauty erupt, both parts of the whole.

Venturing into the wilderness the climber inhabits two worlds. Place them side by side, and the contrast makes each distinct. What does it mean to survive in the mountains? What does survival in the city mean? What defines courage in the mountains; when is one courageous in the city? What is the nature of commitment in the mountains? In the city? None of these questions are easily answered. I am a slow learner and understand best through my body. The lessons I learn in the wilderness work into my urban life. When I have moved through fear and taken a risk, such as crossing a stretch of ice unroped at 12,000 feet, other risks, especially emotional ones, become easier.

My survival in the city has not meant physical survival (although there is always the threat of violence against women). I have not gone hungry or been without shelter. Usually I must contend with less tangible forces, such as the volatile energy created by many lives denied expression and many voices silenced. The physical stress of climbing can actually be a reprieve after, for example, the mental stress of searching for work. Both are difficult. One simply gives me the strength to face the other. I need to see success measured in physical terms: climbing a mountain, or weathering storms and changing conditions.

We all know intuitively that our survival depends on each other, but in the city, recognition of our interdependence is often reduced to providing and paying for services. In the mountains, climbers are bound by absolute necessity. We depend on our partners and routinely, through the use of a rope, trust them with our lives.

The climber is vulnerable to her companions the way she is rarely vulnerable in the city. Observing the way in which a woman climbs can be an intimate experience without the exchange of a single word or touch. You may learn more than her mother knows about how she approaches problems and whether she can persevere. You are allowed to witness your friend struggle and eventually reach the top, or fail and learn to accept that failure. You will perfect the art of encouragement: when to speak and when not to, what to say when your partner is frightened, and how to praise her when she succeeds. On occasion, you will be graced by the sight of a woman when everything in her being says yes: when intelligence and skill are transformed into strong, sure movement upon any medium—snow, rock or ice.

I have been asked how I can justify taking risks with my life. I often respond that driving to work scares me more than climbing a pitch of ice. Some days, when asked that question, I remember a thunderous crack that split open a sunny August morning as three women, strung together like pearls, scanned the rocky cliffs for the source of the sound. I remember how I stood perfectly still, keeping mute vigil as, seconds after the crack, a gully directly above my sister and my friend came alive, showering them first with a pressurized spray of snow and rocks and then, after a pause the length of three breaths, with carsized blocks of ice. During that pause I remember the sense of terror radiating form Nancy's body as she realized she was trapped, and how she moved as though the ice itself burned her. And my sister's face, tilting upward, with an expression I cannot describe. Later she told me, "I though I was going to die."

Why are the three of us alive today? The only answer is grace. We were roped, parallel a yawning crevasse twenty feet below us. If not crushed by rocks and ice, we could easily have been swept into the crevasse. Why did we do it to begin with? For me, that question alone is easy to answer. I climb from a deep love for the wilderness, for my partners, and for my own body and its amazing strength. I don't climb *because* of the risk, although that element must be reckoned with.

Eve Dearborn took a risk, and she lost. But I remember her alive: she climbed hard, she pushed, she had not yet accepted any limits. Many women in the climbing community were influenced and inspired by her. Eve was one strong woman. Clearly, her spirit was a gift to us, and her spirit lives.

Even now, the promise of future climbs and expeditions shapes my days. I try to soak up the Arizona sun and store it like bear fat against the coming sub-zero temperatures. During my daily run I compare road grades to the slopes I will ascend on unknown mountains. I want to sweat out all the poison and worries clinging to my skin. I want to be so tired that my only desire is to put my back against the earth. A ritual of purification? Yes. And I wouldn't trade anything for a bird's wing embossed on the snow or the morning I woke above the clouds to find the spiraling tracks of mountain goats beside my tent. I long to visit again that land between earth and sky, the middle kingdom, to see the red hair of my partner flame in the sun, casting a jeweled fight on the white hand of the mountain.

Nine years have passed since I wrote the first part of this essay. Last year, on January 28, 1991, Kathy Phibbs and her partner Hope Barnes died in a climbing accident in the Cascades. Six months later, another member of our community, Nancy Czech, also died in a climbing accident. Hope and Kathy had been friends and climbing partners; Nancy and Kathy had been friends, climbing partners, and lovers. The deaths of these three well-loved women sent waves of shock and grief through Women Climbers Northwest; many of us will feel the reverberations for years to come.

As Eve's death was the occasion for writing the first half of this essay, Kathy's is the occasion for the second. I remember that one of my initial responses to Eve's death was to worry about how my mother would feel if anything should ever happen to me. Recently, I found an eerie echo of that feeling in a letter written by Kathy, days after Eve's death. After describing the accident and the viewing of Eve's body at a funeral home, she gives an account of the memorial service, where she met Mrs. Dearborn for the first time. Talking with Eve's mother, she said, gave her faith for her own mother's strength in a similar situation.

I remember writing the first half of this essay with a kind of desperation, hoping to shift my mother's gaze away from the accident; climbing was about living to me, not death, and I wanted her to understand that. For some, risk is the primary element in climbing's alchemy; for me, it's friendship. Women, adventure, a whole shining world: that's what I wanted to talk about. Then, as now, climbing was surrounded by concentric rings of questions. On the outside, I heard the world asking, "Why climb?" or "How can you justify risking your life?" Inside that, I heard myself asking, What does it mean to climb with women? And last, the inner circle, the cauldron: What is the nature of my friendship with this woman? With Kathy? Still, I am most interested in the last questions.

When the first half of this essay was published, I was ready to move in a brand new direction, satisfied that I'd put risk in its place, or at least explained myself to my mother.

It took years, but late last January, I had slogged forward to what I hoped was the end of another essay on climbing. I knew it needed more work, but I was excited because I'd made a start in the direction I'd long since mapped out. I couldn't wait to hear what Kathy thought. The day I finished it, Hope and Kathy fell from Dragontail. Three days later, when the search party went into the mountains, I heard about the accident, and I put the essay away.

Now, shortly after the first anniversary of her death, I find myself completing this, a good-bye to Kathy, and discover that something has changed in the nine intervening years.

In the face of her death, the old questions are raised, and though I still love climbing, I find I don't want to talk about it at all: not to defend it, or explain it, or glorify it. I feel tired when the subject is brought up, because I am more absorbed with her loss than the vehicle of her loss. And this perspective, finally, feels right: climbing was both the means of her death and a wonderful expression of our friendship when she was alive.

When a climber dies, you hear a lot of people say, "At least she died doing what she loved." That was never much comfort to me, but I was happy that Kathy spent so much of her life climbing—as Eve did, as Hope did, as Nancy did, as many of us still do.

Now, instead of dreams winging into the future, I have only memories of our friendship and a deepening, pervasive sense of mystery. My last image of Kathy belongs to a cold, wet day in January when I went to Leavenworth, Washington, with several of Kathy's friends to view her body in a funeral home. I had been away on a writing break in Arizona when Kathy died and had flown home immediately when I received the news. A public viewing had not been scheduled, but Mr. Phibbs was kind enough to arrange a private one at my request.

I drove to Leavenworth with Saskia, a woman with whom Kathy had recently begun a relationship. Both Saskia and Hope's companion had joined the rescue party that carried the bodies out of mountains. Through Monroe, Sultan, Startup, Goldbar, Index, the drive we could have done blind, I listened to Saskia describe the accident and how Kathy looked when she found her frozen in the snow beside Colchuck Lake. Seconds ticked by; I scanned the passing sky, the pastures heavy with standing water, the road—all were colored a dull gray-green that worried my eyes with its sameness. Again and again, I came up against the familiar fringe of dark firs corralling the dumb land. On the east side of Stevens Pass, I looked out at the winter forest and wanted something from it—we were so close now to where they had died—but I was met again with silence.

When we arrived at the funeral home, the owner tried to discourage us from seeing Kathy, saying she hadn't been prepared. Nancy spoke to him, politely, but made it clear that she would brook no interference. He gave in reluctantly, adding that he was sorry but because of the short notice, he didn't have a room for her—the hallway was the best he could offer.

We filed in one by one. Nancy and Saskia first. They gasped as they walked through the door, then reached out to each other and stepped back, leaning against the wall. Kathy was lying on a hospital gurney in a maroon corduroy body bag zipped up to the neck, a white silk scarf covering her throat. Her head was tilted back slightly, and an agonized expression drew all her features tight. Her face was cut and bruised, and her mouth was open, as if she were still breathing hard and in pain.

Looking down at my friend, I knew I had found what I came for—the story of Kathy's death was written on her face. I could see the anger, the loneliness, and her fear of her last moment. She had fought hard before leaving this world.

The long habit of touching her moved my hands hesitantly toward her, to the cold that had overcome her body, hardening her skin and draining the light from her hair. I was filled with an immense desire to continue loving her even through death.

Yes, she was gone. But this home of flesh and bones was where we had known her, and the only place we could come to say good-bye. Our hands laid gently on her beautiful, strong body, our tears, the words whispered alone to her, were our good-yes, and the first step toward loosening the knot of grief that bound us to her.

We stood in a circle around her, and then each of us spent a few minutes alone with her. While we were all in the room together, Mr. Phibbs called and asked Nancy to say good-bye for him and to tell Kathy he was proud of her.

On the drive home, Nancy said it looked as if her death had been as hard as her life, the past year; Donna said she would have liked to stay beside her longer, she would go again to see her if she could; Bill said he'd kept looking up to the corners of the room, thinking he might catch a glimpse of her—he wondered if she was with us.

We'd planned to climb in Alaska in the spring. Instead, I returned to the Southwest, this time to the high desert of Northern New Mexico. I think of her constantly, during days so hot that thousands of creamy pods from the elms near my house fall to the ground fluttering and swooning in dizzy descending circles.

Her death feels like a retort that left me silent. The jokes I had saved to tell her, the new essay I'd written that needed her point of view. Always in these months, I look up to the night sky for signs of her, as if a galaxy might suddenly reshape itself in her image, or a string of stars form the profile I loved—even an ice axe would be welcome. Couldn't you at least do that, I ask.

The cottonwoods, so tall the tips of their branches brush the sky, are closer to her than I am. She is at once everywhere and nowhere, and the words I want to say to her work themselves inside, becoming hard seeds in the muscle of my heart.

Then she finds me, through the memory of a climb. It's almost as if she re-enters the day so that she can leave this life and our friendship on her own terms, as if in death, time has softened between her hands.

The memory is of the day we climbed Sahale. We didn't set out to climb it, we'd planned to do the North Face of Forbidden. It was summer and we slept out on the moraine in just our bags. A small wandering pack of deer woke us before daybreak, happy to find salt in patches of bare dirt near camp, our boots, and our pack straps. Shapely hooves and big, casual licks. Only half-awake, Kathy muttered something about the deer lacking manners, and how it was entirely possible we'd be trampled in our sleep.

It was time to get up anyway; so we rose, ate, and packed. I realized my sore throat had developed into something more serious, but I couldn't bring myself to say anything. We started off and she immediately gained fifty yards on me. Realizing I was too weak to do the climb, I sat down on a rock and cried with shame and disappointment. Her back slowly disappeared into the twilight, then she turned and came back into focus. We decided to go back to bed and get up at a decent hour to climb Sahale. Kathy dispensed a few Sudafeds, her cure-all, and we slept soundly until the sun warmed our bags.

We woke the second time to a blue sky, which grew brighter by leaps. Sahale looked friendly, and Kathy was the best of company with her gift of taking great pleasure in the smallest things—in this case, a bit of tiptoeing between two crevasses, a chance to use an axe like an ice tool, a single move causing a few quick beats of the heart. All ease she was and so pleased with herself she treated me to a running commentary on my style and the "route." The fact that we had full packs was not to be forgotten or discounted. Indeed, and neither was the proximity of the only two crevasses on the glacier, just inches away, nor the flexibility I demonstrated with my cramponing technique, nor the presence of the ferocious North Cascades, kept at bay for at least one glorious day.

Then we gained the summit, and Kathy, with her ready box of gingersnaps and red crown of hair, seemed queen of all she surveyed. She talked about routes, first stabbing the air with her finger, then rubbing her hands together in excitement and wiping the sweat off against her legs. So northern, she said, of the rich greens, browns, and grays, and I remembered that unlike me, she knew and loved other ranges.

But the best was yet to come—the walk down Sahale Arm. The day grew bigger and bigger and finally burst into night, shedding the light softly, for a quiet dusk. We descended the sandy, winding path, arm of the giant, through heather where tiny white blooms shone like footlights. All around us rose the night mountains, sisters of the day mountains, but black and splendid and jagged and twice as fierce, baring gleaming slopes of snow and ice.

But we were happy and safe, enjoying the evening's warmth. I will never forget how she walked, the discipline of years showing in her steady stride, always a sense of purpose about her. I didn't ever want the trail to end. I would have followed it with her forever, watching the falling light melt into the snow, happy to carry one more successful climb home.

Once she paused, and when I reached her, she took my hand without words. We continued walking, and everything fell into place—our bodies on the path through meadows among mountains on an earth spinning in an ocean of stars.

Finally we reached Cascade Pass, and this is where the memories diverge. Instead of descending the endless switchbacks as we did on that summer evening, she pauses at the pass, and I notice how the darkness clusters around her, dense and purple. Then she waves, a single wave that doesn't ask for a response, and I understand she is leaving now—this is the moment she's chosen.

She gives me the smile I know so well, the one she saved for summits and hard leads, and I can't help but smile back. Not so much leaving me, she seems to say, but going home, home from this last evening walk in the mountains.

She turns and begins moving away from me, back into her Beloveds, whose sleeping profiles are now barely visible. Her body vanishes, sinking like a torn leaf into the smooth vast darkness.

The Fight

The Fight is climber/photographer Ed Webster's story of a 1988 ascent and descent of the difficult Kangshung Face of Mt. Everest. As with so many climbs on the world's highest mountains the descent became an absolute fight for survival. This was a climb that became legendary. It was at once called "the best ascent of Everest in terms and style of pure adventure," and also described as "among the most remarkable examples of survival in the history of Himalayan mountaineering." As Webster himself says at the beginning of the story, "My choice was to live."

I t has often been said that descending a mountain is harder and more dangerous than climbing one. Perhaps nowhere is this truth more sharply evident, and statistically proven, than on Mount Everest. Now that the three of us were reunited, standing together outside the Japanese tent at 27,000 feet, it became imperative that we descend to the South Col. We needed to reach our own tents, sleeping bags, and stoves to rewarm and rehydrate our tired, parched bodies. As of yet, I hadn't begun to consider how difficult it would be to retrace our route down the Kangshung Face. Roping up somewhat symbolically on our 7-millimeter rope, we left the Japanese tent and headed back down to the Col. Robert went first, guiding Stephen, who was very wobbly legged and weak, while I came last, wondering if I could belay the rope if someone slipped. Luckily the terrain quickly eased, and soon we were back on the flat, frozen, windswept desert of the South Col.

As we stumbled back to our two tents at camp 3, the full realization of how extended we were began to sink in. At this extreme altitude there was absolutely no chance of rescue, or help, really, of any kind. Helicopters don't fly much above the 20,000 foot level, and while several expeditions were currently climbing up the mountain's Nepalese side, none were close enough to lend assistance—nor did they even know we were here. We were three people very much alone, utterly exhausted, with virtually no possibility of any outside assistance. It was also now that we most felt the lack of the usual Sherpa companions to make hot tea and soup, care for us, carry our packs, and otherwise speed our safe return. Back down at Advanced Base Camp (a full 8,000 vertical feet lower than our present altitude), Mimi, Joe, Pasang, Kasang—and Paul, too, we hoped—would be searching for us through the binoculars.

When Stephen and Robert paused to rest, I hiked on ahead across the Col toward our two tents. Then, still unaware of the extent of my frost bite injuries, I took off my gloves and pulled out my Nikon to photograph my partners walking toward me. I took two portraits of my half-frozen companions. In the first image, Stephen leans in fatigue against Robert, but in the second, Stephen stands alone, his ice ax raised in well-earned victory. It was a particularly proud moment.

I do not remember very much about the rest of that day. Oxygen deprivation, our overwhelming fatigue, and the lack of food, water, and sleep combined to make us incredibly lethargic. Our lives began to be acted out in super slow motion. I know that we lay down and rested in the tents, that we took our high-altitude climbing suits off and crawled willingly into the luscious warmth of our sleeping bags, and that we then made a brew of tea, only because somehow I took pictures of these things too.

I dimly recall taking off my overmitts and liner gloves to inspect my fingers. Gray in color, cold, numb, and woody feeling, the fingertips of my left hand, I noted, appeared considerably worse than those of the right. Fretting over what to do, I finally decided to rewarm them in our tiny pot of hot tea water. Stephen did the same with his frozen left toes. Then of course we drank the tea. While we knew that rewarming frozen tissue should only be done when all chance of refreezing the injured tissue had passed, we were positive we'd have little trouble descending the Kangshung Face. What could possibly be worse than the nightmare that we had just survived? Our previous hour-and-a-half-long descent from camp 2 to camp 1 made us assume that in two days time at the most, we'd be safely in Doctor Mimi's loving care at Advanced Base

Finally we collapsed, dead tired and oblivious to the world, and slept. If we knew that we should have tried to descend to camp 2 that day, we never discussed it. Careful, rational observations were no longer terribly important, or even possible. Subconsciously we knew that spending this third day above

26,000 feet was dangerous, perhaps even deadly, but our bodies craved only sleep and rest. The summit push had exhausted us almost beyond human limits. At last we were ready to go home; the question was, Could we still get there?

Time crept by. I blinked awake from the depths of sleep and peered at my watch's luminous dial. It was 2:30—but in the morning or the night? I no longer knew. My mind could not function. And what day was it? And where were we? Oh, right. We're on the South Col . . . on Mount Everest. After my long agonizing night huddled next to Robert in the Japanese tent, it felt so deliciously warm to be burrowed deeply inside my sleeping bag. Couldn't we just lie here a bit longer, I thought to myself. But wait. Who was I even asking permission of . . . ? I didn't know. I just didn't want to have to move a single inch, so I fell back asleep, never waking once, for the rest of that day and the entire night.

With no food left, the next morning we realized that our physical and mental condition had gone from bad to worse, as had our hopes for an easy, rapid descent. This was our fourth day above the 8,000-meter level without bottled oxygen. Our bodies would not respond to signals from the brain, movement was barely possible, and every effort, no matter how large or small, became a superhuman effort. Stephen's and my last gas canisters had run out the day before, but luckily Roberts's stove was still going. Unable to make a single effort to prepare to descend, Stephen and I lay inert inside our bags and waited hours for Robert to deliver us a single, half-filled pot of hot water: our breakfast. We were a pathetic sight—unmotivated, listless, and uninterested in doing anything to save ourselves from the certainty of what would happen should we not act. I began to realize the terrible truth, that slowly and inexorably, we were dying.

Standing up required an effort we could only marginally begin to grasp; to carry the weight of our two tents, or any of our additional heavier equipment back down the mountain was virtually impossible. We decided to leave the tents here on the Col, and we would risk bivouacking out in the open in our sleeping bags at camp 2, where we had left behind a few extra gas canisters—but no food. At camp 1, we had two tents and a large food cache. Trying to cut even more weight, I also left behind my wonderfully warm down-insulated bibs. Last, reasoning that my wool mittens (though by now fairly worn out) would be easier to rappel down our fixed ropes with, I discarded my thick overmitts, which saved only ounces, and in retrospect was yet another costly error.

I crawled outside the tent, alternately lying and sitting in the snow until the final, most awkward task of fastening crampons to boots was accomplished. But could I stand? I glanced over at Robert, flat on his back in his tent, boots protruding out the entrance like a dead man's. Yet every so often he would come to life, sit up, fiddle with his crampons, and collapse again. Stephen was also preparing to go, and lay on the ground, corpse-like, in front of our tent. I pulled out my autocamera to take a picture of him, and he waved at me halfheartedly to prove that he was still alive.

Yes, I could stand up, with difficulty. Shuffling to the east side of the Col, I carefully stepped down the initial steep slope and plunged into waist-deep fresh powder snow—which was good for skiing, but not very easy to walk through! Afternoon snowstorms over the past two days were the culprits. Snow had also been blown over the Col onto the leeward side by the powerful winds. The avalanche danger in the upper part of the bowl was extremely high.

Earlier in the expedition we had discussed the possibility of our descending into Nepal, into the Western Cwm, if conditions or circumstances high on the mountain warranted such an extreme change of plan in our descent. And while that escape down Everest's normal South Col route was probably now fully justified given that the snow conditions on the Kangshung Face were so atrociously dangerous, in my debilitated condition I realized that several steps down Everest's East Face were several steps too many to reverse. As soon as we stepped off the South Col, we were irrevocably committed to fully descending our route. So, with no going back, I continued stumble-stepping down the slope, plunging each boot deep into the powder, my ears straining for the slightest sound of the snow cracking or settling. To make matters worse, thick moisture-laden monsoon clouds smothered my view.

I could only listen and wait for disaster.

"What's it like down there?" A voice yelled from above. It was Robert. I could see him standing in silhouette on the rim of the South Col, 500 feet above.

"Dangerous! Whatever you do, don't glissade," I shouted back. "Don't slide down the slope. Follow in my tracks!"

Minutes later, I shook my head in disbelief. Far to my left, Robert was now almost level with me! A small and lonely figure, he stood in the very center of the vast snowfield. How did he get there so fast?

"What are you doing!?" I yelled, with not a little consternation.

"I glissaded. It looked fine," Robert replied. "I guess I got going kind of fast . . . and uh, I dropped both of my ice axes, too. Could I borrow your extra ski pole?" His voice revealed increasing alarm as he discovered the dire consequences of his slide. His two ice axes were nowhere to be seen; they were lost.

"I wanted to get down as fast as possible. So I jumped off the edge of the South Col," Robert later explained to me, using some high-altitude-riddled logic. "And everything was fine for the first few seconds. 'This is great,' I thought until I hit some rocks, tumbled forward, and the slope avalanched. Which sent me cartwheeling down the hill, but then fortunately, I stopped."

Stephen left camp 3 ten minutes after Robert, so he did not see Robert fall. When Stephen reached the Col's edge, he saw only Robert's initial toboggan-slide dent in the snow. Now far below the Col, Robert and I had already been swallowed by the clouds. Stephen also decided—just as unwisely—to glissade off the edge of the South Col and slide down the slope. And he also lost control and took a dangerous fall.

"It was the only time on the entire expedition that I heard Stephen's British reserve crack," Robert related. "I think he was truly frightened. He stopped above me, then he yelled down that his ice ax had been ripped off his wrist, nearly taking his Rolex with it. At least he kept his priorities straight."

Within twenty minutes of leaving our camp on the South Col, both Robert and Stephen had lost their ice axes. As a result, during the remainder of our descent of the Kangshung Face, I held in my hands our only ice ax—our one ice ax. I left my spare ski pole for Robert, and after his fall, Stephen now had nothing to use for safety or support, neither ice ax nor ski pole.

I continued down the snow slope. Peering through the enshrouding mists, I searched for a landmark to tell me that I was on route, hoping and praying that somehow I could still find the way to camp 2—which, after my teammates' falls, felt increasingly distant and perhaps unreachable. I made each plunging, plowing, downhill step through the fluffy powder with the greatest of effort, lifting legs and boots and crampons, moving always forward, but finding no food to eat except for my singular desire to live, my strength flowing from a hitherto-untapped reservoir, from a life stream flowing deep within me, and of course I was thankful this new supply of energy existed, but how long would it last?

Suddenly, I heard a dull muffled roar break loose from the mountainside high above me. I turned uphill; every muscle in my body tensed to iron. Hidden by the gray curtain of cloud, sounds of chaos and destruction multiplied wave upon wave as tons of unseen snow began to race downhill. An avalanche! Quickly I ascertained that it was not heading directly for me but had originated above and to my left. Then, to my horror, I realized that the avalanche had started from the direction of the huge, unstable snow slope where I'd last seen Robert standing alone and helplessly vulnerable. My stomach tightened into a fierce sick knot.

The clouds were so dense that I could not actually see the avalanche. I could only hear the crashing sound of the falling debris, emanating now well to my left, now below me, as multiple thousands of tons of snow and ice—carrying one human body—erupted over the edge of the immense Lhotse ice cliffs.

A sharp, crippling wave of anguish overcame me as I imagined Robert being swept along with the debris. I could picture the terrible sequence of events in detail: Robert standing in the center of the snowfield one moment, hopeful of survival, then his sudden panic as the billowing white tidal wave overwhelmed him, sweeping him down, down, down, before tumbling him over that horrifying edge to his final, excruciating plunge into the abyss. Robert had just died—after everything that we had been through. The finality of such a death shocked me profoundly, even through my exhaustion, even as I grappled with disbelief.

Turning back downhill, breathing hoarsely, I resumed my descent. There was nothing else to do. I imaged the two of us, Stephen and myself, walking into Advanced Base Camp without Robert. What would we tell the others? How could we explain something so inherently unfair, that after all we had survived together, Robert had died in an avalanche on the descent? I didn't know. Robert's death was an impossibility; I wanted to cry out in anguish, to rage against Everest, to blaspheme God, to curse fate itself, but I fought back my tears and bit my lower lip to hold back my vile and desperate words. My body quivered with emotion; each breath came in a creaking, throat-tightened spasm.

My determination to reach the mountain's base became furious and indignant. Stephen and I had to survive; we could not give in and let ourselves die.

After a few minutes, I glanced back uphill. Only a single dot, a small black figure standing in the white snow, was following in my footsteps. Even as I tried to cling to the chance that Robert was not dead, I saw my worst fears confirmed. There was just one dot, not two. I was certain now that Robert had been killed. I crumpled into the snow, struggling once again to keep from breaking down. In the ultimate conviction of the truly desperate, I found myself proclaiming: "We are as alone as any humans can be. This is a fight to the end." There seemed nothing melodramatic in such a thought—in fact, I found that it clarified things wonderfully. "I am going to live," I insisted to myself. *"I am going to live!"*

Adrenaline carried me downhill once again. Stopping momentarily to rest, I turned around to check on Stephen. I saw two small dots in the distance! I counted them twice, and then even a third time, just to make sure that my eyes weren't deceiving me. I had been so sure it had been otherwise! I shook my head in disbelief, then felt a surge of gratefulness and joy as I watched the dots continue down the snowfield. As quickly as disaster had seemed to descend upon our group, it had passed away again, leaving me in stunned amazement.

I still thought that we could reach the Flying Wing and the snow platform at camp 2 before nightfall. Carefully, I stepped across a partially hidden bergschrund, trying to remember at what level we had diagonaled across the lower portion of the treacherous snow basin below the South Col. After descending vertically several hundred more feet, I slowly began angling to my left, facing downhill. We'd made a long traverse upward to the left from the right-hand end of the Flying Wing; I now had to reverse this section. Unfortunately, the snow conditions had completely changed since our ascent. Far from the easy hard-packed snow we'd savored on our climb up, I now waded forward through thigh-deep, unconsolidated powder ripe for an avalanche of massive proportion.

As I began to traverse across the snowfield, I was cognizant that it was heavily laden with freshly fallen and windblown snow. The surface could fracture at any second, and without warning. Traversing almost horizontally to get across it, I also knew that I was breaking a cardinal rule of mountaineering—traversing straight across an avalanche slope and creating, in effect, a man-made fracture line—but here there was absolutely no alternative. Somehow, somehow, we had to cross to the opposite side.

We were trapped; this was sheer and utter madness! And if the snow did avalanche, as I had every belief that it would, the tumultuous deafening roar of untold tons of falling snow would send me hurtling into one of many deep and waiting crevasses, or tumbling into eternity, into the Witches' Cauldron at the base of Lhotse, 7,000 vertical feet below. There would be no escaping death if the snowfield gave way, but maybe the others would survive. Maybe the snow would fracture below them, and only I would be swept away. Perhaps they would be spared. I continued forward, making each footstep as softly and gently as possible, my heavy boots sinking nonetheless into the snow's downy cushion. We were rolling the dice to win our own lives. If I heard or felt a crack or a settling of the snow, I was prepared to run for my life—in a last futile effort.

I endured these soft sinking velvet footsteps one by one, knee-deep, waiting for death, expecting to die, experiencing the embrace of eternity known only by the condemned and the dying. Thirty minutes later, when I at last reached the slope's far side above the Flying Wing's right-hand end, I hunched over with relief. The snow should have avalanched, but miraculously, unbelievably, it had not. Slowly I recovered from this torment and prepared myself for the next one.

Days earlier, on our ascent, we had crossed the deep crevasse formed by the detached uphill side of the Flying Wing snow block. This lethal gap was somewhere just below me. We'd crossed it via a fragile snow bridge, but where?

As I stumbled downhill toward this crevasse, an alarming thought found its way into my brain. Why weren't we now roped together for safety? In fact, where was our climbing rope? I didn't have it. And neither, I thought, did Robert or Stephen. Before we left the South Col, we hadn't discussed if we should rope up—tie into the rope—or not, presumably because during the summit climb we'd each become accustomed to climbing solo and unroped. No doubt we just assumed that we wouldn't need to bother roping up below the Col either. Only months later, while looking at a picture I'd taken, did I discover the missing rope lying coiled in the snow in front of Stephen's and my tent on the South Col—right where we had left it.

Confused by the thick clouds and the almost total white-out, I could see only about fifty feet, far enough to discern the Flying Wing's jagged and icy upper lip extending far to the right. I squinted my eyes and scanned the slope. An apparition materialized out of the clouds. Were my eyes tricking me? No: it was a tiny orange flag, the highest of our bamboo wands, which I had placed four days earlier to mark our route over the impasse. I hurried forward through the snow and grabbed the wand. It was real! Carefully I tiptoed downhill toward the snow-bridged crevasse. I couldn't tell if the snow was solid enough to support my weight, so I jumped across the span's midsection instead.

All I heard was a "Whoompf!" behind me when I landed on the far side—the sound of snow collapsing and falling into the mountain's unknown depths. Five feet from where I now stood, a round black hole clearly identified the part of the snow bridge that had given way. There the crevasse was much wider. I decided that the others would see the black hole and know to be careful.

Camp 2 was almost in sight. I descended the next easy-angled slope, circled around the overhanging ice cliff at the right end of the Flying Wing, and waded over to our old tent platforms. At dusk, I cleared away the loose snow from where we'd tented on the way up. Then I found four or five extra fuel canisters hanging in a stuff sack suspended from ice screws pounded into the Wing.

Robert straggled in. We got into our sleeping bags and lit the stove for a brew. Stephen appeared just as darkness fell. Robert produced some tubes of Japanese instant coffee and milk he'd found two days earlier, which we drank. Unfortunately, we hadn't cached any sugar, extra tea bags, or soup here. Later the weather cleared, and Makalu and Chomolönzo thrust into view above the dissipating valley clouds, and the cold black sky, in its turn, froze around us. At Stephen's suggestion that we should try to signal Mimi, Joe, and Paul at Advanced Base Camp—to let them know that we were alive and descending—I stood up and shone my headlamp for some minutes in the direction of our friends at the mountain's base. Several more cups each of hot water quelled our thirst before we each passed out, snug inside our warm feathery wombs.

On the morning of May 15, we could not move from our sleeping bags for several hours. Merely sitting up, let along the astoundingly difficult feat of standing completely upright, demanded impossible physical endurance. Instead, we talked sluggishly between naps, or passed out collectively. Twice Stephen tried to melt snow for drinking water, but each time the hot stove melted into the snow—and when we fell asleep, it tipped over, spilling the hard-won liquid. Well, it didn't much matter, did it? Did anything really matter? As the daytime temperature grew hotter, in our collective numbed stupor we were lulled into a passive denial of the truth—the stark, undeniable reality that if we did not leave the Flying Wing, it would soon become our grave.

Although nearly incapacitated by lethargy and inertia, I was becoming increasingly angry at the apparent hopelessness of our situation and the nearness of my own death. Stephen and Robert lay asleep in their sleeping bags, but for some reason I was slightly more alert. I didn't know why. As I fiddled awkwardly with the stove canister with my frostbitten fingers, turning the on-off key and fumbling with the lighter to ignite the burner, surges of anger and rage welled up inside me. I turned and shouted at Robert and Stephen. We had to keep going, we had to move, we had to act. We couldn't just lie here and die.

I suppose at this point I recognized that maybe I'd assumed the temporary role of leader, but it was leadership by default. I did not want this duty. I was much more comfortable with a shared democratic leadership, but I also knew that personally I couldn't hold out much longer. Another day without food, two at the most, and I thought I might be finished. If it was my turn to lead us through the fray, then so be it. If through my anger and outrage at my own impending death I could rouse Stephen and Robert, then so much the better.

All three of us had been frostbitten on summit day and during our forced bivouacs during that night of May 12, but Stephen and Robert's injuries didn't appear as severe as mine. Amazingly, Stephen's hands and fingers hadn't been injured at all during his 28,600-foot bivouac. (Back on the South Col, Stephen had related to Robert and me that the miraculous preservation of his digits during his summit bivy was thanks to the warmth of a yak herder's fire, and because of some solicitous care of his health given by the spirit—or presence—of Eric Shipton, the British Everest pioneer of the 1930s.) Stephen's nose, however, had been exposed to the wind that night, and the end had now turned a mottled ashen gray. The condition of our toes we could only guess at. Because of the extra insulating layer of the supergaiters that Stephen and I each wore over our plastic mountaineering boots, neither of us had as yet inspected our toes. And the toes of his left foot, Stephen mentioned, were numb. Nine of Robert's fingertips, like mine, were covered with the sickening bulges of black frostbite blisters, and Robert added that the toes of his left foot also felt cold.

It was with a growing mutual concern that we discussed our dwindling chances of survival. Our ascent of Everest's Kangshung Face had been the best climb of our lives. It had been so enjoyable, so thrilling, so tremendous. And Stephen had summited. As a team, with Paul, by our collective efforts, we had triumphed. Furthermore, we'd become the best of friends. We'd laughed, cried, and shared a great adventure. To be killed now did not seem at all fair.

As the morning waned, the weather turned cloudy and held off the midday heat as we tried to prepare ourselves to descend. Let's leave by eleven o'clock, we agreed—before our departure time slipped to twelve noon, one, two, and then three o'clock. Try as we might, we could not pack our belongings, or clip on our crampons, or stand up, that most demanding challenge of all. Every exertion had to be willed by a tremendous effort commanded from our oxygen- and energy-deprived brains. As Robert later phrased it, "we possessed the collective energy of a mouse." We talked very little. Had Joe and Mimi and Paul seen us descending? Or had they seen our headlamps last night? If not, then surely they would be looking through the binoculars from Advanced Base for signs of us.

Hours slipped away, fading seamlessly into mere seconds of consciousness. A third attempt at brewing hot water succeeded. Then Stephen discovered a packet of potato flakes, plus some freeze-dried shrimp and clam chowder. He suggested that we eat it, but the mention of food nauseated me. I declined, but he and Robert ate some mashed potato.

As the afternoon ticked away, a single thought kept circling through my mind. "I must get to Advanced Base so Mimi can take care of me." My fingertips looked increasingly ghastly; my frostbite blisters were growing bigger. After first propping myself up on one elbow, I succeeded in sitting up with a great effort. Two hours later, after repeatedly collapsing onto my platform, I had stuffed my sleeping bag. I continued to urge Robert and Stephen to descend. When I left camp at 3:45 P.M., they were still fastening their crampons. I would be dark at six. The fight for our lives was on.

Almost as soon as I departed, the sky congealed into a bleak gray sheet. Snow-laden monsoon clouds thickened around and above me, blending evenly with Everest's undulating snow slopes and ice cliffs. At least the clouds masked the sun's heat, but soon it was snowing again. Visibility diminished to forty feet. But the waist-deep snow was enveloping, somehow comforting.

To sit down for a long rest would be the easiest thing in the world.

Unconscious of any danger, I slid unexpectedly down a thirty-foot-tall ice slab that had been concealed by a two-foot layer of snow. Landing on a powdery bed, I brushed myself off and began angling to my right down a snow ramp leading into a maze of crevasses that we'd threaded through on our ascent. Nervously, I surveyed my surroundings. Near the ramp's base, I knew that I needed to turn sharply left above one of the largest crevasses. The turn was unmarked; we'd been conserving our remaining bamboo marker wands.

My fatigue was growing, Continuing downhill, I tripped over a short icy step and fell forward. My next thought was the unpleasant realization that I was sliding down the mountain head first, on my back. Instinctively, I clutched at my ice ax, jabbed the metal pick into the snow, swung my legs around, pivoted my body uphill, jabbed my boots and crampon points into the snow—and stopped myself—all in several seconds. Trembling with fear and surges of adrenaline, I kicked my crampon points viciously into the hard ice buried beneath the top snow layer and managed to reestablish myself on the mountain. Then I looked down.

One hundred feet lower, a gaping crevasse leered its icy grin upward, its fathomless blue void wanting to swallow me whole. By the narrowest of margins, I had escaped death again. I looked uphill. Stephen and Robert were descending slowly toward me; I could see their ghostly figures shuffling through the mist and lightly falling snow. Insanity! It would be dark in an hour; what did we think we were doing, descending so late in the day? I realized then that it would be better to return to camp 2, use our remaining fuel to brew hot water, get some sleep, and descend early the next morning. We had wasted the entire day.

"This is crazy!" I shouted up to Robert. "I just missed falling into a huge crevasse!" Robert soon arrived beside me and promptly slumped in an exhausted heap. A minute later, Stephen joined us. I pointed to the crevasse just below us, recounted my near-death experience all over again for Stephen's benefit, then launched into a high-strung exhortation on the foolishness of continuing our descent. "If we don't climb back up to camp 2, we'll be sleeping out in a snowdrift!" I knew that I was sounding unduly melodramatic, but I was adamant. To continue descending in such poor visibility, unroped, surrounded by hidden crevasses, risking a forced bivouac in the open, could easily have fatal consequences. In fact, to do so I thought would be suicidal.

Stephen eventually agreed with me that we had no option but to retrace our steps back up to the Flying Wing; Robert was too tired to care. Accepting our fate, we willed ourselves uphill toward camp 2. What had taken one hour for us to descend required three killing hours to reverse.

Just below camp, we were stopped by the thirty-foot, sixty-degree ice slab we'd slid over on the way down. With only one ice ax between the three of us, I was wondering how we would negotiate this section. Somewhat comically, Stephen and I balanced up on our front points, climbing side by side, while each holding on to the ice ax. Then, while Stephen clung on tightly to my jacket, I swung the ax until the pick lodged. After repeating this procedure several times, we reached easier angled snow.

Robert watched questioningly from below. "Don't forget to leave that ax!"

"Okay, I'll leave it here, partway up." I replied, then climbed down a move and slammed the pick firmly into the ice. The only problem was that the ax was still two full body lengths above him.

"How am I supposed to climb up to it?" he demanded. I wasn't quite sure, but Robert was inventive. He'd figure something out. He would have to!

Stephen and I continued to camp. It was pitch dark by the time all three of us were resettled under the Flying Wing's ice canopy. We collapsed, having eaten virtually nothing in two days. I made a brew of hot water, and we shared several meager grit-filled mouthfuls. We absolutely had to get an early start in the morning. My strength was dwindling, and I knew that our chances for escape had almost run out.

The sun rose gold over Tibet. Feeling the sun's warmth penetrate into my sleeping bag, I peeked outside to see towering Makalu resplendent in the dawn light. Inside my sleeping bag, I was deliciously warm. I could have stayed there forever. That was the problem. I struggled to prepare to leave, made two brews of hot water, and invariably knocked over the stove once or twice. Every action was made with a fragile economy of effort and in the slowest possible motion. Stephen and Robert were awake too, but they had hardly stirred.

I hounded them. "Stephen," I half-joked, "you're not going to be famous unless you get down alive."

We also talked about the mountaineers who'd perished on K2, the world's second-highest mountain, two years earlier. Trapped in a storm at 25,900 feet on the Abruzzi Spur, they ran out of food and fuel and died in their sleeping bags, or soon thereafter, making a last-ditch effort to descend the mountain

Among those killed were two of Britain's best mountaineers, Alan Rouse and Julie Tullis. It was a tragedy we did not want to repeat.

I remembered what an ordeal it had been to stuff my sleeping bag, so I decided to abandon both my sleeping bag and my parka. By carrying an absolute minimum of weight, I hoped to increase my chances for living. But by abandoning my survival gear, I was irrevocably committing myself to descending to Advanced Base camp in a single day—or I'd be stranded this evening without a sleeping bag or any warm clothing. I dressed in my Capilene expedition-weight underwear, my one-piece pile suit, a pile jacket, hat, and wool mittens. In my pack I carried half a quart of water, my two cameras, and the rolls of film that I had taken at the South Col and above, on summit day.

Again, I left first, departing from the Flying Wing at about 10:00 A.M.

Robert and Stephen said they were coming, but glancing over my shoulder occasionally, I didn't see them for a couple of hours. Our Everest climb had become a battle. We could encourage each other, we could lend moral support, but physically, we could not carry each other back down Chomolungma. Ultimately, the determination to survive was an individual commodity. Robert later told me that when he'd left camp 2 that morning, he did try to get Stephen moving, but Stephen hadn't budged from his sleeping bag. Would he lie there and die? Robert couldn't tell, but finally Stephen did muster himself to stand up and follow us.

I waded through the softly enveloping snow like an automaton. More snow was falling from the heavens. My leaden limbs moved as if by magic, by rote muscle memory, driven by the primal instinct to live. I wasn't going to give in without a fight. My almost seething anger at our shared frostbite and our possibly impending deaths remained, but I sternly reminded myself not to do anything rash. I had to think my way out of this nightmare. I had to create my own destiny if later I wanted to live it. There had to be a way to escape from this crevasse-riddled, snow-walled prison. I realized, too, that my will to live had also spawned a deep hatred for Everest. Chomolungma, mountain of my dreams, how could you kill me? Our brief views of heaven had come at an enormous cost.

Soon I reached the ice step where I'd stumbled and self-arrested the previous afternoon. Sitting down in the soft snow, resting, I decided I'd gone too far right before. I gambled instead on traversing left around a steep snow rib to look for a big crevasse I remembered vividly from our ascent six days ago. But how much the mountain had changed! It was nearly impossible to recognize landmarks because of the tremendous amount of new snow and the smothering clouds. There remained only the slender hope that I could somehow choose a safe path and not be swallowed alive by a lurking crevasse.

But if I did fall into a crevasse, well, what then? I held our only remaining ice ax in my left hand. We no longer had a climbing rope. Even if I fell into a relatively shallow crevasse, I still might not be able to escape. Death would come quickly, I rationalized, and Stephen and Robert would see which trail not to take. It was better to make the effort, to reach out for life no matter what the consequences, than to sit down in the snow and passively die.

Using every route-finding skill that I'd learned in twenty years of climbing, I began breaking trail through the crevasses in an increasing blizzard. I excavated a trench to my left through a deep snowbank, climbed down a steep fifteen-foot incline, and saw several crevasses directly in front of me. None of them looked familiar. Cautiously, I waded toward them, holding my ice ax at the ready in case I fell in. A snow bridge spanned the first crevasse; gingerly I trod out onto it and pooled enough energy to jump over the weak-looking midsection. Breathing easier once I reached the far side, I then jumped a second crevasse and plowed straight ahead, thinking now that maybe I knew the correct direction of our route to camp 1. Not altogether positive of the way, though, I moved ahead slowly and cautiously and prayed that some higher power would guide me.

Then, through the cloud, I caught another glimpse of orange. I'd found the next bamboo wand! We were on our route! The marker wand also gave me a tangibly solid connection with my not-so-distant past. I stopped in my tracks. Paul, Mimi, Joe, Pasang, and Kasang; they were all waiting for us below. We were not completely alone. Finding that slender stem of a once-growing plant shook me from my dream world and gave me new incentive to return to earth.

There was still no sign of either Stephen or Robert, but I was convinced that my partners were alive and would soon be coming. Though they'd been far from energetic looking when I left camp, I never once imagined that they were dead or in trouble. We had survived so much already through our collective will and by sticking together that I began to assume that probably we would all live. Death was a possibility, yet it no longer seemed as certain as it had the day before. But we still had over 5,000 vertical feet to descend.

I repositioned myself in my mind's eye at where I thought I was along our route, then set off downhill toward the next landmarks, Stephen's Ice Pitch and the next big crevasse. Halfway down the slope, I located another wand, fallen over and half buried by the new snow. "Keep going," I changed under my breath, my optimism growing. "Keep going, keep going, keep going, keep going."

I felt as if the clouds surrounding me, thick as ocean fog, could have been sliced like a loaf of bread. Downhill through this misty uncertainty was the only direction that my legs would carry me. As I plunge-stepped down the smooth snow slope, my sixth sense prickled with awareness. An avalanche trap! The gently curving slope was smothered in three feet of new-fallen snow. Had the powder had time to bond with the old layers beneath it? I kicked at the snow with my boots. The adhesion seemed vaguely secure, I continued. What choice did I have? The lambs were being fed to the wolves for breakfast. I vowed with every stumbling forward and downhill step toward safety that if I did live through this climb I would never, ever do another route that was this dangerous.

What I would have given to be transported virtually anywhere else from the hell of this frozen, frostbitten world? I fantasized warm, white sandy beaches, or a sunny Colorado, or the normal everyday things in life—going for a walk, eating dinner with friends. Or events that perhaps too often I'd taken for granted. As soon as I escaped from this hated mountain, I would revel in the mundane.

My strength faltered. My arms began to feel light and buoyant. My legs were lead bars. I breathed from the hollow pit of my empty stomach. My breath gave me back energy to move, but my motions became jerky and slow, one foot placed marginally in front of the other as I pushed through the snow like a human plow, moving closer to salvation and a release from this wretched cage. I couldn't recognize any landmarks, but I knew I must be getting near the steep incline of Stephen's Ice Pitch.

My mind began to falter. Just keep moving, I told myself. Don't dare stop or you'll never start up again. Pace yourself, don't hurry. You don't have the strength to hurry! Don't even bother to think, just let your legs move. Walk. Walk slowly. Breathe. Breathe slowly. Slowly, breathe, slowly.

I heard a shout. Robert was a hundred yards above me.

My companions were alive! In my heart, I'd known all along that they were okay. Once more, I began my halting, awkward movements downhill. The next crevasse was 150 feet lower. It was wide—and unfathomably deep. One slip and I'd disappear without a trace.

Tilted straight into the crevasse, the snow slope I was standing on was church-roof steep. I began to traverse left across it, toward the snow bridge we'd used to cross this impasse on our ascent. The snow was bottomless. Each foot-step collapsed into the one below it. I realized that I'd descended too far. I would have to climb back up and make a higher diagonal traverse. I began retracing my steps, and yelled up to Robert to head left earlier than I had.

"Left?" he responded weakly. I nodded, too exhausted to speak. I'd eaten nothing in over two days and had consumed only a few cups of tea and a bowl of noodle soup in over four days. I thought the climb back up those hundred feet would finish me off. Moving against gravity at that altitude, in our condition, was an incomprehensible trial.

"I'm not feeling very good, you know that?" my brain said.

"Neither am I," answered my body.

"Well, don't let me down now," said my brain.

"What do you mean?" my body replied. "You always told me you liked a challenge. You're getting one now, aren't you?"

My eyelids grew heavy; my head began to swim.

"Well, you always said you wanted to experience the ultimate challenge, to feel what life was like on the edge," yelled my body to my brain. "And guess what, you idiot—I have news for you. *This is what you wanted, and this is what it's like!* How much longer do you think you can hold on?"

I managed to take another uphill step. Through the mist and the clouds I saw a second stumbling figure appear. I was Stephen! "So you're alive, too," I thought. Good for you.

We had reached Stephen's Ice Pitch, now buried beneath several feet of powder snow. Angling left, we carefully plowed a trench down the slope. After passing Robert, Stephen and I tiptoed along a ledge underneath a vertical ice wall, across the snow bridge spanning the crevasse, and began the final slog toward the top of our fixed ropes, still a thousand feet below.

Again, I went in front, breaking trail. The snow bridge and ice wall were solid landmarks I remembered from our ascent. We were definitely on route, and I felt a new burst of energy. However, we'd placed far too few wands to mark this section, and I followed my instincts down the short ridges and small snowfields that characterized this portion of the route, relieved that the worst of the avalanche and crevasse danger was at last behind us.

Eyes shifted nervously from side to side, searching for the correct route. Here? There? Maybe that way. Legs faltered, stopped, then started. Energy, what was energy? Air was food. My muscles had degenerated into near uselessness, but with each downhill step I began to gain nourishment from an invisible ally: the increasing percentage of oxygen in the atmosphere.

Move legs, move! You've got to keep moving! I remembered Fritz Wiessner's words, and began to chant them over and over again in a solemn incantation:

"Sometimes you've got to fight it."

"You've just got to fight it." Rest. Breathe.

"Sometimes you've got to fight it."

"You've got to fight it." A few more staggering steps.

"You've got to fight it."

"You've just got to fight it."

My breath became labored. Stay in control! Left foot, right foot, another few steps. Good!

"You've got to fight it."

"Fight it!"

I found another bamboo wand at the start of a snowy prow. I walked to the end of the plank; the ridge was corniced and overhung on both sides. We must have climbed up one side. I returned to the wand. Stephen and I walked to the drop-off for a second look.

"I think we went this way," he said with surprising conviction, and began to descend a steep snow trough. Suddenly there was a loud crack, then a whoosh, and Stephen was caught in a small avalanche. Riding atop the wave of falling snow, he flew down a fifty-foot drop and landed in a huge mound of soft snow on the flat terrace below. Springing up out of the drift like a hippo jumping out of a mud hole, Stephen shouted cheerfully: "Yes, that's definitely the right way!"

Shaking my head in disbelief, I returned to the wand. A shorter trough led down to the left. Several steps later, I was also avalanched and fell twenty feet. I brushed myself off. We continued. Stephen broke trail. We could no longer see Robert, but Stephen assured me he had seen him coming.

Then I noticed Stephen had stopped. I joined him.

"Don't you think we should try over there?" I suggested, motioning to our right down the next snow slope.

"What?" Stephen said, seemingly perplexed.

"Well, it looks better that way to me," I replied.

"Ed! We're at the fixed ropes!" He blurted out, pointing to a short piece of orange 8-millimeter rope emerging from the snow.

My gaze settled fondly on the colored length of rope. I couldn't believe it. We were going to live! I reached over, embraced Stephen in a bear hug, and shook him in celebration. All we had to do was rappel three thousand feet to the glacier. Maybe we could still get to Advanced Base Camp tonight. Before starting down the ropes, we glimpsed Robert some distance above us.

"You okay?" I shouted up to him.

"See you at camp 1!" he yelled, adding that he was fine, just slow.

"No—not at camp 1. We're going to Advanced Base no matter what!" I shouted in reply. Robert waved back, and Stephen and I once again began to descend. We dug our harnesses and descenders out from under three feet of new snow (we'd cached them here to save carrying their extra weight any higher), and I strapped on my harness and immediately began racing down the ropes, hurrying from one anchor to the next across the Jumble. I'd been so concerned with staying alive that, until I stated rappelling, I hadn't given my stiff, wooden fingers much attention. It took a while to get used to holding the rope, and for the first time I began to realize that my fingers, especially those of my left hand, were very, very cold. I now began to worry. My fingers were not mending as I had hoped. In fact, they felt much worse.

Laboriously, I ripped the fixed ropes out from under their snow mantle. I felt a surge of relief seeing that the Jaws of Doom crevasse had not widened or collapsed. But the seracs had definitely moved downhill, because the ropes spanning the Tyrolean Traverse were stretched tighter than ever! I crossed Jaws and continued down to the Webster Wall. There the rope disappeared into the snow, so I unclipped from my rappel and walked without a belay to the edge of the 75-foot overhanging ice cliff. The pink 11-millimeter rope down the Webster Wall was buried deeply, but by stamping out a platform and carefully peering over the edge, I just caught a glimpse of it hanging free.

I dug the rope out of the snow and rappelled to camp 1. It was 5:30 P.M. when Stephen joined me. We had a short discussion about whether we should continue down or remain here for the night. What little body warmth I still possessed I was rapidly losing through my frostbitten fingers. Since I no longer had a sleeping bag or parka, I told him that at all costs I must keep moving to generate heat and to stay warm.

When we'd left camp 1 almost nine days before, we'd collapsed our two tents to protect them from damage. They were now buried under several feet of snow. I hardly recognized the campsite. Stephen pointed out a large trough created by an icefall of recent vintage, directly over where our tents had been pitched. It would have taken us an hour of hard work to excavate them, and since the descent from camp 1 to Advanced Base took two hours in good conditions, I lobbied strongly to continue. Reluctantly, Stephen agreed.

I started down the snow slope below camp. The fixed rope here was also completely buried. All of our 9-and 11-millimeter static fixed ropes were white in color (we'd gotten a good discount on the price), which made them virtually impossible to detect (hence the cheap cost!) against a white snow slope. Now where was that darned rope? Unroped, I gingerly climbed as far down as I dared and began digging with my ice ax. Below me was a two-thousand-foot drop straight into Big Al. As I continued to chop at the snow, suddenly I heard a pronounced crack—and the slope avalanched just above me. Two feet of silky snow cascaded through my legs and into the fearsome abyss. I gripped my ice ax with a burst of adrenaline—and didn't fall.

"Oh, there's the rope," I said matter-of-factly, spotting it at the base of the avalanche fracture. Stephen volunteered to go first, and we rappelled to the bottom of Paul's Ice Pitch, with Stephen digging out each rope length from under the snow. It was a peaceful evening, the bad weather was clearing, and I remember even being nostalgic rappelling past the Greyhound Bus—the first Cauliflower Tower—thinking fondly that I'd never see it so close up again.

Once more, we were about to be caught out in the dark on the mountain. I became increasingly worried and told myself to stay calm and in control. We'd soon be down, Paul, Mimi, and Joe would take care of us. It was getting dark, no stopping it, and we had no choice but to deal with the situation like we'd dealt with the rest of this hellish descent. Which was as best as we could.

As darkness closed upon Everest, we discovered that neither of our headlamps worked. Then Stephen fumbled and dropped his spare headlamp bulb.

When Stephen couldn't pull up the next section of fixed rope, I rappelled down and joined him at the bottom of Paul's Ice Pitch. Taking my ice ax with him, Stephen headed down and chopped the rope free, inch by inch, from beneath a two-inch-thick layer of ice that had frozen over it during the previous week. It was painstaking work—and one poorly aimed blow could cut through the rope. I hadn't thought our situation could worsen. It just had. I was shivering so hard my limbs trembled. For the next several hours, all I could hear was Stephen's chopping, then his much anticipated signal of "Right!" or "Off!" which meant that he'd reached the next anchor and it was my turn to descend.

But something wasn't right. I looked down. The toe bail of my right crampon had come unclipped. Held by its ankle strap, the crampon dangled uselessly below my boot. With frostbitten fingers, I couldn't fix it. Rappelling down the ropes at night with no headlamp, frozen fingers, and only one crampon became and endless nightmare. Multiple sections of rope were so well frozen into the mountain's icy coating that it was impossible to pull up enough slack to clip our figure-of-eight descenders in for a proper rappel. The painful alternative was a wrist rappel. This meant clipping the rope into a short safety sling and a locking carabiner attached to our harness, then wrapping the ice-encrusted rope around our wrists and forearms for friction. Gripping the rope as tightly as I could with my useless fingers, I would begin to slide down the rope. Several times I lost my grip, and proceeded to fall, slide, and bounce down the slope until my safety sling stopped me at the next anchor attaching the rope to the mountain. I prayed that a stupid mistake wouldn't kill me when I was now so close to safety.

Stephen led the entire descent down the buttress. We were more dead than alive when we reached the Kangshung Glacier at about 1:00 A.M. Using our short length of 11-millimeter rope stashed at the resting rock, we roped up. The recent warm weather and monsoon clouds hadn't allowed the glacier surface to freeze at night, and the crust was now in about the worst possible condition. Instead of well-frozen snow which would have supported our weight, a thin, breakable snow skin masked over a mush of unstable depth hoar—loosely packed snow resembling large Styrofoam pellets. When the crust broke, as it did about every thirty feet, it was like plunging feet first into a jar of marbles. Extricating oneself was extremely difficult, especially in our weakened state.

We attempted to keep our sense of humor about the situation. This too became impossible. Hopefulness and grim determination gave way to anger and sudden outbursts. I slipped back into my old habit, getting pissed off at Venables for moving too quickly, for pulling the rope tight and yanking me off my feet, while Stephen became increasingly angry with me for not moving faster to get back to camp.

About halfway to Advanced Base, Stephen began a ceaseless tirade for a hot cup of tea. "Paul! Mimi! Joe! *Tea!*" he shouted at the top of his lungs about every five minutes. I was craving a hot orange drink, and Stephen wanted his bloody cup of tea. That wasn't too much to ask for, was it? We stumbled across the glacier, got lost, finally found our way through the crevasses, and inched progressively closer to camp—to safety, to warmth, to our friends.

"Paul! Mimi! Joe! *Tea!*"

Suddenly I fell into another pit of unstable snow. We were roped together about fifty or sixty feet apart to safeguard each other from hidden crevasses. Stephen's patience grew thinner and thinner as I struggled to escape from this new bear trap. But my right leg—and the loose crampon dangling uselessly beneath my boot—remained firmly rooted in the oatmeal-thick concrete.

"Ed, can't you do something?" Stephen protested after watching me struggle in vain for fifteen minutes. I could tell his patience was at an end.

"You look like a bloody floundering bird!" he bellowed.

We were in the middle of a now-starry Everest night, barely alive, and it seemed we were never going to reach camp, even though safety was probably only minutes away. Stephen was angry, my leg was firmly stuck, and all he wanted was a hot cup of tea. I didn't know what to do. I couldn't budge my leg or my boot, and I was completely exhausted. I leaned back against the snow to catch my breath. We were so close to camp, but I couldn't escape from this damn hole! Then I glanced back up toward Stephen—but Stephen had gone.

After untying from his end of the climbing rope without a word, Stephen headed toward camp. I watched his ghostlike figure disappear into the darkness. Moments later, from the crest of the moraine ridge off to my left came a sudden and animated commotion. Other voices rang out, friends' voices, Paul's and Mimi's voices, shouting and exclaiming, and I knew we were safe. I struggled again to free my boot from its slushy prison, but I couldn't. Slumping backward, I simply waited and looked up at the stars.

Then, momentarily, a wavy beam of light ran along the moraine beside me and a familiar soothing voice shouted out my name. It was Paul Teare. I had never been so happy to hear a friend's voice, a voice which a day or two earlier I was not sure I would ever hear again. I shouted his name back, and Paul bounded across the snow toward me, falling in and leaping back out like a gazelle, springing forward until he reached me and threw his arms around my neck.

"Why didn't you let us know you were alive?" Paul demanded. My attempt to signal from camp 2 with my headlamp had obviously been unsuccessful. Paul asked if I was all right, and I had to admit that . . . well, actually, I wasn't. I told him that my hands were frostbitten, but that my feet, I thought were all right. In his exuberance over our survival—that we were, amazingly enough, still alive—our frostbite was fairly inconsequential.

"I'm so glad you guys are okay!" he exclaimed. Then Paul asked after

Robert, about his condition, and where he was. I replied that Robert was fine, just a bit slower, and that he would be following us down soon.

With Paul shouldering me, I pried my right boot out of the snow, and we retraced his tracks back to the moraine where the walking was easier. Minutes later, back in camp, I was greeted with a joyous welcome home hug from Mimi. Joe was in Base Camp, sending word to the Chinese for a helicopter to come look for us, and Paul and Mimi had been so distressed, thinking we had all died, that they could only sleep by taking sleeping pills.

It was 4:00 A.M. on May 17.

I collapsed beside Stephen inside my dome tent, grateful, so very grateful, for sleep and rest and warmth, just to lie down flat and rest and be warm, and to drink a hot drink, even if it was grapefruit juice, to feel it trickle past my parched lips and down my scratchy sandpaper throat before consciousness failed me. I do not really remember what happened during the next two days. I can recall only a string of hazy dreams: Paul putting me on warm, hissing oxygen, the clear plastic mask slipping over my face, while Mimi tenderly soaked Stephen's and my fingers and toes in sterile warm water baths and fed us soup and crackers, and later, Kasang stared blankly at us, not understanding and very worried, and Ang Chu's brother, Sonam, was crouched beside Kasang, and Sonam's body was trembling, he was so frightened and concerned for us, but then Pasang's fatherly face looked down at me, gave me his comforting smile, and his calm hand reached out to gently hold my shoulder and reassure me that everything would be all right, before Robert, after spending the night sitting alone in the mountain snows one last time, finally returned safely to camp with Joe, who'd hiked out to help him, and Robert stood in the sunshine outside our tent before he bent over, peered quizzically at Stephen and me lying inside, looking like death—and Robert said to us, grinning that Robert grin: "So, boys, how are we feeling today?"

What I remember most is the sweet delicious sensation of being alive, of lying in my warm sleeping bag on the soft foam pad inside the yellow tent, and of savoring that simple radiant joy, that great gift, of having survived.

And drinking the hot grapefruit juice.